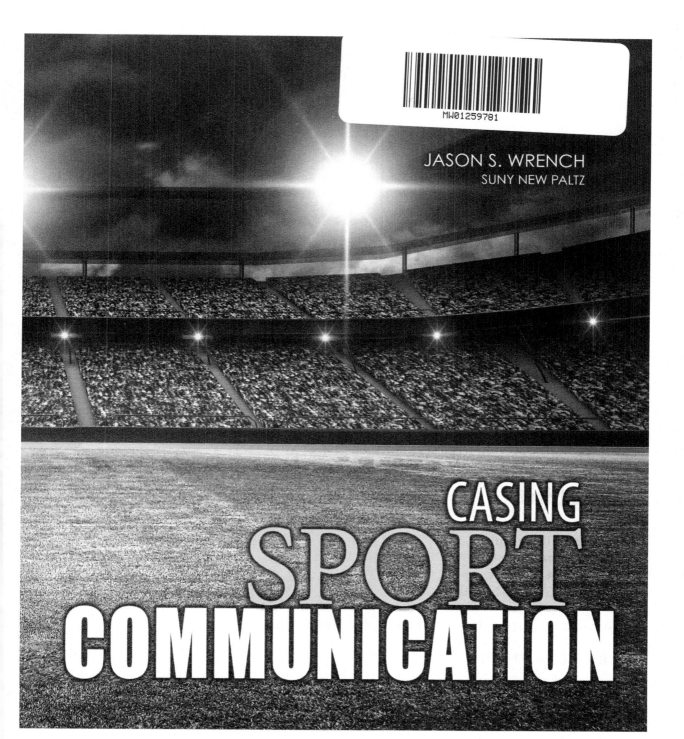

JASON S. WRENCH
SUNY NEW PALTZ

MW01259781

CASING
SPORT
COMMUNICATION

Kendall Hunt
publishing company

Kendall Hunt
publishing company

www.kendallhunt.com
Send all inquiries to:
4050 Westmark Drive
Dubuque, IA 52004-1840

CONTENTS

Part 2: Team Communication and Sport   91

WHY CASES?

Casing Sport Communication is a book written with fictional scenarios dealing with real issues developed in the cases. The cases represent a variety of scenarios, scenarios facing all levels of decision makers in pressing matters in the sport industry.

The book is edited to include cases that are written for undergraduate and entry-level graduate courses in sport communication—whether those courses are taught in the liberal arts, business, or education. Because of the enormity and diversity of the work currently being done by those in the broad and global field of sport, whether they are coming from the perspective of corporate, consumer, professional athletic organizations, nonprofit, business-to-business, or individual and family dynamics concerning sport, this book and these cases can be used in many ways within the classroom or online instructional settings.

For each case presented here, there are defining moments in the situations that create defining problems for the main characters under discussion. Cases are written and created by diverse scholars and practitioners from across North America, yet all follow a similar style and structure of writing so that students reading the cases are able to distill the defining questions or problems into several sentences, no matter the background of the author or authors. There are never more than five problems in any one case. This limited scope of problems and style of writing, from diverse authors, is crafted intentionally because in real-world sport communication situations, practitioners and the average person involved in sport might need to distill a handful of key problems at any given moment. This is also done so that readers do not become confused and unable to focus on the important problems the writer intended to address.

A case study with more than five problems is difficult to discuss in a practical amount of time (a class period, for example,) and is apt to require many hours of rambling discussion. There are often multiple approaches to solving problems and several answers to a single case. Case writers do not indicate potential solutions or best solutions, enabling a class to apply the concepts of a sport communication course to the case itself and come up with a decision on their own. It is in the case analyses that students will decide upon the best solution, and most importantly learn the reasoning process that leads to good decision making in the fast-paced sport communication world.

Each case is written to end with a protagonist needing to make some decision that relates to a major sport communication issue, or issues, at hand. This open-ended approach allows professor and students to grapple with the scenario presented, with an intentional approach, and come to conclusions, rather than having the author come to the conclusions and do the thinking for everyone else. Students engaged in case analysis learn to think, analyze, react, and evaluate so that they develop transferable critical, analytical, problem-focused skills that they can transfer to other situations in workplace settings and in life in general.

This book allows students to take apart the scenarios, imagine themselves in those scenarios (but at the safe distance of students rather than as entry-level managers and employees whose divisions, jobs, reputations, and causes are on the line). This approach to teaching and learning was most notably developed in the legendary Harvard Law School over a century ago, and later adopted by *Harvard Business Review.*

Within each case, a situation is displayed and explored, using dialogue, setting, and internal thoughts of the protagonist, to create dilemmas that give readers a clear delineation of the problems and point the way to a discussion about possible solutions. Because the most effective way to depict a problem is to write situations or scenes that have conflict in them, many of the scenes have characters represent opposite points of view, enter into disagreements, and offer different solutions.

In the literary world, we call this drama. In the work world, we call this the safe distance Case Method of study, so that decisions made in the work world are not based upon drama, but upon reasoning through the drama for information and ideas that bring the best decision-making abilities of the team and its members to the fore.

This book is made up of good cases, and what is meant by a "good case" is that it first and foremost is a good story written in narrative fashion. As such, each situation or scene in every case study carries the narrative forward, relates directly to one of the major problems in the case, or provides insight into the personality and motives of one or more of the characters. In addition, you should easily be able to identify one or more communicative behaviors and sport communication concepts you have been learning about in your class. The authors of the cases outline ideal situations that the writer knows will elicit conflicting opinions about potential solutions.

The authors of all of the cases are scholars of sport studies (whether in management, communication, education, etc.), and while the backgrounds of the authors and writing styles are diverse, all authors have written the cases for students and discussants who may not be familiar with the background, details, and terminology of the situations in the different types of scenarios under discussion. Jargon is kept to a minimum and information is kept in laypersons' terms.

Each and every author, or group of authors, uses short story writing techniques with flesh and blood characters, characters who are intriguing throughout the case. This style of writing helps to maximize retention, and is used in the cases for that purpose. Contextual memory is often overlooked in academic study, but it is the way human beings are naturally gifted in great memory recall, and it is the way we remember in everyday life.

Each story element moves the narrative forward and authors do not "tell" the reader what happened but rather "show" the reader within the story itself, with the words, thoughts, and actions of the characters within the cases. While some exposition is at times necessary, the authors have kept in mind that this is a short story and the writing is void of academic jargon, references, and digressions into too much detail.

In each case, the authors grab the attention of readers with a character facing his or her biggest problem related to sport communication. Whether the problem has to do with family communication issues revolving around sport or public relations crises the scene is set for the confrontations, frustrations, concerns, ethical and economic dilemmas, conflict, and deliberation to allow the readers to analyze the situation from multiple perspectives, but to come to their own conclusions.

Authors present situations and scenes without any attempt at analysis: Scenes follow a logical order and illustrate a point, concept, or issue that relates to the problems to be analyzed. Readers should know that no signals are intended so that no one solution is implicitly preferred. The solutions and conclusions are left up to the students who read, discuss, and analyze the cases.

Our authors provide relevant details after presenting an opening that sets up the situation, details related to goals, strategies, dilemmas, issues, conflicts, roadblocks, appropriate research, relevant financial information, people, and relationships. Authors are intentionally stingy with numbers in these cases, using them only to help to solve the problems. This is done to avoid confusing readers or sending them off on unproductive analytical tangents. After analyzing these cases, students will know how to reason through arguments and ideas, come to a decision, and then implement a plan of action.

Each case uses as much dialogue as possible to bring the characters and the stories to life and to show the readers what is happening, rather than tell them what is happening. Thoughts of characters are also used at times, appearing in italics. So in these dialogues, external and internal, students can reason, feel, and react alongside each character.

Diana L. Tucker (Ph.D., Southern Illinois University Carbondale) is an academic coordinator in the College of Undergraduate Studies at Walden University. She coordinates the communication courses in the general education program and also teaches some of those courses. In addition, she acts as the coordinator for the Walden study abroad, internship, and public service courses in undergraduate education. Dr. Tucker's specialty in teaching is public relations and organizational communication courses, although she has taught a wide variety of courses from basic interpersonal communication and public speaking to journalism. Her previous publications include cases in two earlier texts in Jason S. Wrench's *Casing* series. In addition, she has published articles in an international sport journal, *Football Studies,* and has chapters in two edited books. Most of Dr. Tucker's publications involve looking at the rhetoric of sport, specifically from the point of view of football coaches' wives. She has presented over 50 papers and panels at regional and national conferences and serves as the vice chair elect for the Public Relations Division of the Central States Communication Association (CSCA). She has served CSCA as Chair of the Great Ideas For Teaching (GIFT) Division as well from 2010 to 2012. Dr. Tucker also serves as the vice president of publicity for the Women's Club of Powell, Ohio.

Jason S. Wrench (Ed.D., West Virginia University) is an associate professor and chair of the Communication Department at the State University of New York at New Paltz. Dr. Wrench has published numerous books on a variety of communication topics: *Intercultural Communication: Power in Context, Communication, Affect, and Learning in the Classroom* (2000, Tapestry Press), *Principles of Public Speaking* (2003, The College Network), *Human Communication in Everyday Life: Explanations and Applications* (2008, Allyn & Bacon), *Quantitative Research Methods for Communication: A Hands-On Approach* (2008 & 2013, Oxford University Press), *The Directory of Communication Related Mental Measures* (Summer 2010, National Communication Association), *Stand Up, Speak Out: The Practice and Ethics of Public Speaking* (2011, Flat World Knowledge), *Communication Apprehension, Avoidance, and Effectiveness* (2013, Allyn & Bacon), *Training and Development: The Intersection of Communication and Talent Development in the Modern Workplace* (2014, Kendall Hunt), and *Organizational Communication: Theory, Research, and Practice* (2015, Flat World Knowledge). Dr. Wrench has also edited a number of books: *Casing Organizational Communication* (2011, Kendall Hunt), *Workplace Communication for the 21st Century: Tools and Strategies that Impact the Bottom*

Line: Vol. 1. Internal Workplace Communication, Vol. 2. External Workplace Communication (2013, both with Praeger), and *Casing Public Relations* (2014, Kendall Hunt). Dr. Wrench was the editor of the *Ohio Communication Journal* from 2005 to 2007, served as an associate editor for *Communication Research Reports* from 2007 to 2010, and has been on the editorial board of numerous academic journals. Furthermore, Dr. Wrench has published over 30 research articles that have appeared in various journals: *Communication Quarterly, Communication Research Reports, Education, Human Communication, Journal of Homosexuality, Journal of Intercultural Communication, Southern Communication Journal, The Source: A Journal of Education,* and *The NACADA Journal* (National Academic Advising Association).

CHAPTER 1: A REVIEW OF SPORT COMMUNICATION

Whether you love sports or hate them, you most likely encounter something sport related every day of your life. Statistics show that the sport industry and interest in it is only growing. One report states that a low estimate of the sport market value is between $440 and $470 billion every year.[1] This includes everything from tickets, merchandise, equipment, sport related video games, and membership sales to advertising and media rights.

If you are not a lover of sport, you still can't escape how pervasive it is in our society. You may see articles in the newspaper or catch the sport report as you watch the evening news. Or sometimes an event in the sport world makes the national news. Perhaps your friends post about their favorite teams or about their children playing sports on their Facebook, Instagram, or Twitter accounts. You might drive by a children's soccer game on the way home from school, or notice flyers listing your school's sports teams' schedules hung around campus. Even if you don't happen to encounter something specifically sport related, you will likely find sports metaphors that abound in your and others' word choices. Have you ever told someone "the ball's in your court," or described obtaining something as a "score"? These are just a couple of examples of how sport metaphors crop up in everyday life.

Of course, if you are a fan of a sport, or many sports, you may purposely surround yourself with some of the numerous sport outlets or paraphernalia available to you. The Internet certainly makes it easy to check scores, get the latest news, buy tickets to a game, or purchase clothes to promote your love of a certain team. Social media allows us to communicate our thoughts about any sport-related item. We can debate friends and foes about draft picks or calls by referees through Facebook and Twitter while watching games from opposite sides of the country. And fantasy sport leagues give us the chance to get further involved by requiring that we follow more games, check statistics more often, and even engage in drafts of our own.

There are also people who might not consider themselves to be interested in sport, but their favorite activity is considered sport related by those who work in and study the sport industry. Boating, RVing, fishing, hiking, and even simply walking are all recreations that are included in the sport industry. This is why, in many colleges, the studies of sport sciences, sport management, recreation, and leisure are sometimes located all together in one department or college within a university. These majors may be located in business, sometimes education, and often a department or college all its own. However, rarely is the study of sport communication located within these other departments.

WHAT IS SPORT COMMUNICATION?

Although the study of sport communication does not have as many departments or majors of study as sport management or other sport sciences may have around the country (and world), the development and growth of sport communication as an area of study within a communication department increases every year. At the writing of this textbook, there were at least 34 schools with a major, minor, certificate, or concentration of sport communication offered by the communication studies department.[2] The same report by the John Curley Center for Sports Journalism at Penn State states that 215 schools offer at least one course in the sport communication field.

The discipline of communication and sport is one accepted and promoted by the International Communication Association (ICA) and the National Communication Association (NCA). In 2014, the ICA welcomed a sport communication interest group to its prominent list of groups. NCA's interest group was developed the following year. The September 2014 *Spectra*, the monthly magazine of NCA, published a special issue about communication and sport. In this special issue, there was an article from a university president on the promotion of her university's athleticprograms, an interview with an openly gay athlete, a piece analyzing the "mascoting" of Native Americans, as well as one concerning the use of social media in sport communication.

Sport communication is differentiated from sport management, recreation, and leisure studies because of the communication component. Communication scholars look at communication in a variety of human endeavors. That might include studying communication in romantic relationships or how a business communicates its mission to consumers. Both the study of sport and the study of communication have numerous contexts that scholars can study. Scholars of sport communication often like to emphasize the communication aspect of their studies and will refer to the discipline as the study of communication and sport.

The authors of the first comprehensive textbook in communication and sport, Billings, Butterworth, and Turman, explain that it is important to "explore how and why sport can be understood and studied specifically from the perspective of communication, a field with a far-ranging set of interests and applications."[3] Using the phrase "communication AND sport" instead of "communication IN sport" allows communication scholars to incorporate more of their interests concerning the sport industry in their studies and still consider it sport related. Were we to use the phrase "communication IN sport," we might only include studies of communication that occurred within the boundaries of a certain sport and those who are playing, coaching, or somehow involved in the day-to-day work of the sport.

Communication AND sport allows us to look at all sorts of communicative aspects surrounding the sport industry. Besides looking at how coaches and players communicate, we might look at how fans talk about a favorite sport on social media. We could examine how the media covers certain events and how sportscasters talk about the sport itself. Maybe we would study how a certain team's PR campaign involving a nonprofit organization created a frenzy of donations for the charity. We might even go more abstract and look at the use of sport metaphor in language used to talk about violence against women. As long as the study links an aspect of communication with one of sport, the sky is the limit. Thus, the study of communication and sport often has a wider boundary than that of sport management, recreation, and leisure studies.

After a discussion of calling the field "communication and sport," you might wonder why we have chosen to refer to studies involving communication and sport as "sport communication" in this textbook. As the study of communication and sport rose in prominence as a significant area in the communication discipline, one that could stand on its own and not be considered a type of "mass communication," or type of "organizational communication," scholars started to use the term "sport communication" (or sometimes sports communication). We presume that because so many other areas of communication study have an adjective before "communication" to designate it (such as "mass communication," or "interpersonal communication") as a certain type of communication study, the term "sport communication" sounded natural among them. Most communication scholars of any area would agree that their study is about communication AND their particular interest (i.e., communication AND mass media). So, when we use the term "sport communication" in this textbook, it is not to say that the "sport" aspect of the study is more important than the "communication" aspect. It is just a conventional way to refer to this area of study.

Scholars acknowledge that defining the term "sport communication" is difficult.[4] However, Pedersen, Laucella, Miloch, and Fielding provide a clear definition in the *International Journal of Sport Management & Marketing*, a "process by which people in sport, in a sport setting, or through a sport endeavor share symbols as they create meaning through interaction."[5] This definition highlights the important components of any definition of communication: Process, sharing, symbols, creating meaning, through interaction. It also allows for a wide interpretation of connection to the sport world. It does not say that the people have to be involved in a sport themselves, but that the communication process may occur in a sport setting, or through interest in a sport endeavor.

Because communication and sport occurs in journalism, advertising, management of sport-related organizations, on the field/court/pitch/pool/slope/greens/ring/rink/etc., in the stands, through social media, in video games, and so on, the word "endeavor" is a relatively small one to encompass all the possibilities. For the purposes of this text, "endeavor" will do. As you read cases in this text, remember that, while the issues discussed in the cases here may not always fit your traditional idea of a sport "endeavor," the authors of this textbook and many other scholars of communication and sport would certainly include the issues and settings of the cases in this book in the field of sport communication.

SPORT COMMUNICATION SCHOLARSHIP

Before we get into how to work with cases and the cases themselves, this chapter will briefly explore a little more of the background of the field of sport communication and then describe the organization of this textbook.

Before the present century, most of those who studied communication and sport were often marginalized for their work in the field. Their colleagues would not even acknowledge the study of sport as a "field."[6] The acceptance of scholarship in sport communication first came in journalism, as a smattering of articles between 1934 and 1986 can be found in journals dedicated to journalism studies.[7] Most communication scholars outside of journalism link the first study of communication and sport back to 1975 when Michael Real had his article, "Super Bowl: Mythic Spectacle" published in the *Journal of Communication*.[8] Real's thesis was that "the Super Bowl (i) combines electronic media and spectator sports in a ritualized mass activity, (ii) reveals specific cultural values proper to American institutions and ideology, and (iii) is best explained as a contemporary form of mythic spectacle."[9]

In the 1990s, interest in the field of sport communication grew and more and more articles were published in communication journals that had a sport focus. More schools began to offer courses in sport communication and a few even began to offer majors in sport communication. But it was not until the early 2000s that the field really began to take hold and gain recognition with the publication of a few foundational pieces and the beginning of an organized association dedicated to the study of communication and sport.

In 2003, Robert Brown and Daniel O'Rourke of Ashland University co-edited the first collection of sport communication studies in *Case Studies in Sport Communication*. Their case studies were not like the fictional ones you will find in this book, yet each chapter was a type of case study. The cases in Brown and O'Rourke's text were mostly rhetorical analyses of real-world sport events and phenomena. For instance, Andrew Billings examined how announcers for the 1999 US Open Tennis Tournament demonstrated a gender bias. Then Todd McDorman wrote about how Pete Rose's resurgence in 1999 demonstrated clear apologia tactics. You will learn more in Chapter Two about how the cases we include in this textbook are different from those articles in *Case Studies in Sport Communication*. The authors of the ten articles in *Case Studies in Sport Communication* have become known as some of the foremost scholars of the sport communication field today.

According to the International Association for Communication and Sport's (IACS) history page, in 2002, eight scholars who were interested in studying how sport and communication intersected met at the first ever Communication and Sport Summit. These scholars worked together to come up with ways to promote the study of sport within the communication discipline.[10] From 2006 to 20012, the IACS held a summit bi-annually, but today the IACS has enough interest and support to hold a summit every year.

The initial group of eight collaborated on a piece for the 2004 *Communication Yearbook* and planned future summits. The *Communication Yearbook* article is another influential piece in the growth of the field. The authors made a compelling case for why the process of engaging in sport (whether as a participant or a consumer) is a communicative activity. "Communication is the vehicle by which community members participate in the enactment, (re)production, consumption, and organizing of sport."[11] The authors also built the case for why sport communication is a significant avenue for study. Because the community of sport is bound by certain demographics, is complex and multi-layered, and is influential in other areas of society, it is a unique area for study.[12] Having this article in such an esteemed publication helped to build momentum for accepting the study of communication and sport in the communication discipline.

In 2008, members of the IACS proposed a special issue on sport communication for the *Western Journal of Communication*. This was "the first time a disciplinary journal devoted an entire issue to communication and sport research."[13] There was a breadth of scholarship within the five manuscripts that comprised the special issue. Articles examined performance of masculinity in wheelchair rugby, negotiation of identity in professional women's soccer, the link between baseball and the American political scene, the effect coaches' behavior on team cohesion, and the impact of blogging on local sports television. The authors also employed a wide variety of methodologies in conducting their studies. As Bob Krizek, the editor of this special issue, explained, "This is a diverse community with often disparate interests that compel us to employ a wide variety of research practices and theoretical frameworks."[14]

March 2013 marked an exceptionally important notch in the growth of the IACS and sport communication as a field because the inaugural issue of *Communication & Sport* was published.

> *Communication & Sport* publishes research and critical analysis from diverse disciplinary and theoretical perspectives to advance understanding of communication phenomena in the varied contexts through which sport touches individuals, society, and culture.[15]

One might say a field of study has "arrived" when there is a journal that publishes articles focused solely on that field. Having an organizing body and journal dedicated to the study of communication and sport means that the field has roots, a solid foundation, and a bright future.

With textbooks such as Pedersen et al.'s *Strategic Sport Communication*, Stoldt et al.'s *Sport Public Relations*, and Billings et al.'s *Communication and Sport: Surveying the Field*, courses, concentrations, and majors in sport communication have more sure footholds in their departments. This textbook hopes to complement these foundational works by providing fictional case studies for students to use as they study theories and concepts in these other textbooks.

WHAT'S TO COME

The first part of this *Casing Sport Communication* book consists of three chapters. This first chapter has given you a background on sport communication and provided readers with an idea of how this current textbook is situated within the discipline's scholarship. The second chapter gives a history of the case study as developed in Harvard Law School by an extraordinarily gifted professor over a century ago. The third chapter gives students and discussants the tools to use to prepare for case-based class writing, discussion, and participation. Chapter Three includes a mini case to analyze regarding crisis communication, social media, and viral videos. Finally, Chapter Three provides specific instructions on how to write a case analysis. This intentionally simple instruction saves instructors time, so that class assignments and discussions can focus on the case at hand, rather than on "how to analyze the case" since that is covered in Chapter Three. Chapters Two and Three are revised versions of similar chapters found in Jason Wrench's *Casing Organizational Communication* revised for the sport communication context.[16]

In all, there are five parts to this textbook. In each of the following sections, you will find an opening that reviews some of the real-world cases that one might fit into that particular area of sport communication. Part One has cases that focus on relational communication and sport. Some of these cases involve communication between two people, such as between a parent and child involved in sport or communication between a coach and athlete. For instance, Taylor Wilson and John Spinda explore the issue of parents as coaches in "Parents Make the Best and Worst Coaches." Then other cases involve more than two people, such as when Deleasa Randall-Griffiths investigates how sport affects family interaction when one person is obsessed with always being able to "watch the game" in "Every Day is Game Day."

The cases in Part Two target theories and concepts that concern team communication. This could concern communication within an athletic team or in any other group setting, such as a family. For instance, Corey Jay Liberman looks at the phenomenon of loyalty and dissent in team communication in his case, "Victory Isn't Everything." And Angela Jacobs provides a look at how religious devotion might affect a team's interaction and success in "Sports vs. Church: The Dilemma of Choosing Sides."

Part Three includes cases that concern public relations in sport organizations. In this part of the book, you will find cases such as Dariela Rodriguez's and Gwendolyn Nisbett's narrative of how momentum is built for a match through public relations tactics in the mixed martial arts (MMA). Then Margaret Stewart and Jeffrey Eisenberg share a story of how social media can distract athletes and how a social media policy might help.

Part Four's cases revolve around internal organizational communication and sport. These cases have more business-related content than those in the team communication section, but are focused on matters within the business, not those that are oriented toward external publics as the public relations and advertising cases do. In this section, samples of cases you will find include an ethical dilemma in "To Gain or Not to Gain, That is the Question" by Michael W. Kramer. In this case, he investigates the choices players might be asked to make by their organization concerning their health. John Borland looks at the issue of race and hiring practices in a college golf program in the Deep South in "History or Hubris: A College Golf Program Reaches a Crossroads."

Finally, Part Five opens the doors a bit wider and delves into the rhetoric of sport culture. This section includes cases from a cultural point of view. These cases involve gender and racial issues, the subject of fandom, and controversies surrounding matters such as the Bowl Championship Series. Carlee Tressel Alson opens this section with a case that looks at gender and sexual violence issues in "Tiger Trouble." Then Gust A. Yep and Nicholas T. Chivers provide us with a case that looks at issues of hegemonic masculinity and a transgender rugby player in "Fetuao's Dilemma: Negotiating Gender and Sexuality in the Hypermasculine World of Rugby."

Each section also contains a separate installation called "Voice of a Pro." These short pieces include words of wisdom from professionals working in the field of sport communication. The Voice of a Pro series includes a former pro athlete, a vice president from a sport marketing agency, a sideline sport reporter, a college sports information director, and a longtime coach. All give advice about getting into their respective fields and share their knowledge about engaging with others in the sport community.

REFERENCES

[1] Plunkett Research, Ltd. (2014). *Plunkett's Sports Industry Trends & Statistics 2014: A Summary Version of Plunkett's Sports Industry Almanac 2014.* Retrieved from: http://www.plunkettresearch.com/sports-recreation-leisure-market-research/industry-trends.

[2] John Curley Center for Sports Journalism at Penn State (23 January, 2012). Schools across country increase focus on sports communication. Retrieved from http://news.psu.edu/story/152329/2012/01/23/schools-across-country-increase-focus-sports-communication.

[3] Billings, A.C., M.L. Butterworth, & Turman, P.D. (2012). *Communication and sport: Surveying the field.* Thousand Oaks, CA: Sage.

[4] Ibid.

[5] Pedersen, P.M., Laucella, P.C., Miloch, K.S., & Fielding, L.W. (2007). The juxtaposition of sport and communication: Defining the field of sport communication. *International Journal of Sport Management & Marketing* 2(3), 193–207. Quote on page 195.

[6] Trujillo, N. (2003). Introduction. In R.S. Brown & D.J. O'Rourke (Eds). *Case studies in sport communication.* Westport, CT: Praeger.

[7] Ibid.

[8] Trujillo (2003) and Billings et al. refer to Michael Real's article in this manner.

[9] Real, M. (1975). Super Bowl: Mythic spectacle. *Journal of Communication,* 25, 31–43.

[10] International Association for Communication and Sport. (n.d.) Summit history. Retrieved from http://www.communicationandsport.com/#!history/c9bc

[11] Kassing, J. W., Billings, A. C., Brown, R. S., Halone, K. K., Harrison, K., Krizek, B. Meân, L. J. & Turman, P.D. (2004). Communication in the community of sport: The process of enacting, (re)producing, consuming and organizing sport. In P. J. Kalbfleisch (Ed). *Communication Yearbook,* 28, 373–409. Quote on page 374.

[12] Ibid.

[13] International Association for Communication and Sport. (n.d.) Summit history. Retrieved from http://www.communicationandsport.com/#!history/c9bc

[14] Krizek, B. (2008). Introduction: Communication and the community of sport. *Western Journal of Communication,* 72(2), 103–106. Quote on page 105.

[15] International Association for Communication and Sport. (n.d.) Summit history. Retrieved from http://www.communicationandsport.com/#!history/c9bc

[16] Wrench, J. S. (Ed.). (2012). *Casing organizational communication.* Dubuque, IA: Kendall-Hunt.

CHAPTER 2: WHY CASES FOR SPORT COMMUNICATION?

*C*asing Sport Communication is a book written with fictional scenarios dealing with real issues developed in the cases. The cases represent a variety of scenarios, scenarios facing all levels of decision makers in pressing matters in sport communication.

The book is edited to include cases that are written for undergraduate and entry-level graduate courses in communication and sport, whether those courses are taught in communication departments, business departments, or sport management departments. Because of the enormity and diversity of work done by those in the broad and global field of sport communication, these cases can be used in many ways within the classroom or online instructional settings.

For each case presented here, there are defining moments in the situations that create defining problems for the main character or project team under discussion. Cases are written and created by diverse scholars and practitioners from across North America, yet all follow a similar style and structure of writing so that students reading the cases are able to distill the defining questions or problems into several sentences, no matter the background of the author or authors. There are never more than five problems in any one case. This limited scope of problems and style of writing, from diverse authors, is crafted intentionally because in real-world sport communication situations, members of teams must be able to distill a handful of key problems to tackle at any given moment. This is also done so that readers do not become confused and unable to focus on the important problems the writer intended to address.

A case study with more than five problems is difficult to discuss in a practical amount of time (a class period, for example) and apt to require many hours of rambling discussion. There are often multiple approaches to solving problems and several answers to a single case. Case writers do not indicate potential solutions or best solutions, enabling a class to apply the concepts from the sport communication course to the case itself and come up with a decision on their own. It is in the case analyses that students will decide upon the best solution, and most importantly learn the reasoning process that leads to good decision making in the fast-paced world of sport communication.

Each case is written to end with a protagonist needing to make some decision that relates to a major issue, or issues, in sport communication. This open-ended approach allows students to grapple with the scenario presented, with an intentional approach, and come to conclusions, rather than having the author come to the conclusions and do the thinking for everyone else. Students engaged in case analysis learn to think, analyze, react, and evaluate so that they develop transferable critical, analytical, problem-focused skills that they can transfer to other situations in workplace settings and in life in general.

This is a book that allows students to take apart the scenarios, imagine themselves in those scenarios (but at the safe distance of students rather than as entry-level managers, coaches, and other sport field employees whose divisions, jobs, reputations, and causes are on the line). This approach to teaching and learning was most notably developed in the legendary Harvard Law School over a century ago, and later adopted by *Harvard Business Review.* This approach is called the Case Method.

The Case Method is a fun and active way to learn about a wide range of different topics, but is a method of teaching that definitely takes preparation on the part of both the instructor and the student. In the next few pages, we are going to introduce you to the Case Method, including its history, types of cases, and benefits. In the next chapter, we will walk you through a process we recommend for analyzing a case that is based on a wealth of research written by a range of business-related scholars from accounting, industrial psychology, management, organizational behavior, organizational communication, and so on.

HISTORY OF THE CASE METHOD

In 1870 Christopher Columbus Langdell was asked to take over as the dean of the Harvard Law School.[1] Prior to his taking the helm at Harvard Law School, the primary method for teaching law students was a practice called the Dwight method, which required students to memorize information about the current status of law and regurgitate this information in front of their peers. Langdell believed that this method was not the best possible method for teaching students, so he set out to develop a method based on his own personal learning experience. As a law student, Langdell read every legal precedent that was handed down by the various state and federal courts. These legal precedents, known as case law, generally included the facts of the case and a judge's decision and application of law to the specific case. Instead of having students memorize and regurgitate facts, Langdell believed that it was important for students not only to know the basic concepts of law, but also to be able to apply those concepts in a meaningful manner. Langdell put together a set of diverse legal cases into a single volume, which students would read and analyze prior to coming to class. During class, Langdell would pose questions related to a case and then randomly choose a student to answer the question, which ultimately became known as the Socratic method.

In 1908 the Harvard Business School was founded, and the original dean, Edwin F. Gay, tried to implement a similar method to that of the Harvard Law School, which he deemed the problem method. Unfortunately, the problem method wasn't really developed, so faculty ended up spending more time lecturing than actually discussing problems. In 1919 a former lawyer who had gone to Harvard Law School and had been teaching corporate finance at Harvard, Wallace P. Donham, was appointed the dean of the Harvard Business School. As a former student of the Socratic method, Donham saw the immediate benefit in learning by legal cases. However, businesses provided a fundamental difference from law as there are not business precedents written in the form of case law for students to digest. To help fill this gap, Donham created the Bureau for Business Research and encouraged faculty to spend time creating case studies about specific businesses and business leaders as a form of scholarly research.[2] These early cases were transcriptions of interactions between the professors and business leaders related to a specific decision or a set of decisions the individual had made. Ultimately, this form of teaching practice became known as the Case Method, and quickly became one of the primary tools for teaching business students at all major business schools.

Today, the Case Method is taught around the world in a variety of different educational contexts. Every field from graphic design to surgery has employed some version of the Case Method crystallized by the Harvard Business School. However, the Case Method is still most widely used in those fields related to various aspects of organizations: business, industrial psychology, management, organizational communication, organizational sociology, public relations, and so on. Because sport has links to all these fields, this also makes sport and sport communication another perfect discipline for the Case Method.

TYPES OF CASES

Before we can delve into the various types of cases that exist, we really need to examine what we mean by the word "case" in the sport communication context. Obviously, we do not have case law as lawyers have in the legal profession. As such, our use of the word "case" in the organizational context refers to a "description of an actual [or fictional] situation, commonly involving a decision, a challenge, an opportunity, or a problem or an issue faced by a person (or persons) in an organization. A case allows you to step figuratively into the position of a particular decision-maker."[3] In essence, a case is a story about a real situation and how people could theoretically act and communicate within that situation. Most often, these cases are used in the business world, but we will also use cases to look at issues of interpersonal communication and cultural questions in sport.

Most importantly, cases do not arrive at a specific decision for the reader. As Wallace Donham wrote when he first popularized the Case Method, a business case "contains no statement of the decision reached by the businessman [or business woman] . . . and generally business cases admit of more than one solution . . . [business cases] include both relevant and irrelevant material, in order that the student may obtain practice in selecting the facts that apply."[4]

Ultimately, cases have three basic characteristics: Significance, sufficient information, and no conclusions.[5] First, a case must contain some kind of significant issue or a series of significant issues in the business world. For our purposes, a good case must take on some facet of sport communication that is relevant in the modern world. While examining how an organization uses the telegraph would not be significant in today's world, seeing the trials and tribulations of how a sport organization is communicating with people via Twitter would be significant. Second, a case needs to provide the reader with sufficient information to draw possible outcomes. While all cases will provide sufficient information, not all possible relevant information is presented in every case. As often happens in the real world, people must make decisions based on limited information. Lastly, cases will not clearly spell out what the most appropriate decisions should be for a specific case.

One of the goals of the Case Method is to enable readers to examine the facts, in light of their own knowledge and research, and arrive at a possible decision. Could your decision be wrong? Yes. Could your decision be right? Maybe. Obviously, the Case Method is ultimately dealing in the world of hypotheticals, so you will not know the ultimate ramifications of making the decision. The results, while important to consider, are secondary to the Case Method. The goal of the method is the learning experience and the application of course content to the case. One of the more fascinating parts of using the Case Method as a teacher is how different groups of students can arrive at radically different decisions for equally valid reasons.

There are often many possible decisions that could be arrived at when analyzing a case, so some students often become frustrated because they want to know the "best" way to solve the case. If you ask 100 different scholars for an answer to a case, you're likely to get 100 different answers. While not every possible outcome is equally valid, every outcome can be examined and discussed (We'll discuss more on this in the next chapter). Ultimately, there are two types of cases that you may encounter in academia: profile cases and fictional cases.

What we refer to as "profile cases" are cases that profile actual phenomena and show how various real people handled those situations in real life. These cases tend to be lengthy because they must provide a great deal of detail about real-world occurrences. For example, let's say we were going to write a case about the strategies Native Americans took to try to convince the Washington Redskins owner, Dan Snyder, to change the name of the team to something less derogatory toward Native Americans. In such a case, you'd have a few pages about the history of the name and the overall protest, including important names and dates. Then you'd explain in detail the various strategies that different groups have used to protest the name. You would need to describe how the Redskins responded to the various protests. Then you would have a section on independent experts and the use of social media, and then you would have a detailed retelling of the various communication strategies utilized by both sides and by social media activists and independent experts. As you can well imagine, covering all of this information could result in a book if you really get into the detail. Yet students need information and scenarios that they can read, digest, and analyze each week in class. The non-fiction cases require an enormous amount of background knowledge, and each case could be an entire semester. Such non-fiction case approaches most resemble the original form of the case created by Harvard Business School in the 1920s.

Fictional cases, on the other hand, are shorter cases that are based in actual communication problems but have been fictionalized in an effort to make the case more succinct. This method of case writing was popularized in the *Harvard Business Review,* which concludes each issue with a short fictional case and then asks a handful of notable experts to weigh in on the case itself. For the book you have in your hand, we have chosen to utilize fictional cases because they are great for undergraduates or lower-level graduate student engagement. Furthermore, because these cases are more focused on a specific communication issue within the sport world, readers can more easily apply sport communication content, skills, and theories to the cases when determining possible courses of action.

BENEFITS OF THE CASE METHOD

By this point, you may be wondering why anyone would want to use the Case Method. And you'd be remiss if you didn't question the utility of this teaching technique. Besides the fact that the Case Method has been shown to be a highly flexible and meaningful learning experience for both undergraduate and graduate students, there are five basic reasons that the Case Method is beneficial.[6, 7]

Cases Lend Reality to Indirect Experience

While the best form of learning is to learn something directly yourself, there is definitely reason to learn from the insights, strategies, and mistakes of others. As such, we can learn from others and the experiences they have had in the real world, which will ultimately make us all more prepared for handling situations. In terms of case studies, the case is an easy way to see what types of situations others have found themselves in, and then think through how we would behave in that same situation.

Cases Focus on Concrete Problems

One of the biggest obstacles that many undergraduates face when learning business-related concepts is that they have no frame of reference. What we mean by "no frame of reference" is that your average undergraduates (and many graduate students) have limited or no corporate experience. As such, when we talk about theoretical ideas or how some corporate offices function, the only frame of reference many have is what they've seen through their parents or on television. These viewpoints may be slightly skewed, if not completely inaccurate. By delving into a specific case, you have the opportunity to engage a story based on real occurrences that happen in modern organizations. While the cases have been fictionalized in this book, the cases are based on a range of real-world problems that sport organizations have faced. Fictionalizing the cases helps the authors make them more concrete and easily understood.

Cases Develop Skill in Decision Making

Decision making is one of the most useful skills you will learn in the Case Method. In the next chapter, we will walk you through a highly formalized way of analyzing a sport communication case. The tips and strategies we employ for analyzing a case can be applied to any type of decision-making enterprise, so this skill will be very useful in all parts of your life.

Cases Broaden Student Insight

The fourth reason that the Case Method is useful for students is that it helps you broaden your own insight into a complex decision. While the decision you arrive at on your own may seem very logical, when you start to examine the decision in great detail you start to see that there are a wide range of possibilities inherent within a decision. For example, when you think about a simple decision like purchasing a hamburger from one restaurant over another, you may think that you're just purchasing a hamburger. The Case Method asks you to go further than just your taste buds and really delve into the ramifications of your decision. How does purchasing a hamburger from one fast-food restaurant over another one impact the world around you? If one restaurant uses Styrofoam to place its burger in and the other uses paper, the second burger joint is actually going to have a smaller negative impact on the environment. Often when we make decisions, we fail to take into account all of the possible risks and long-term outcomes associated with them. The Case Method is designed to help you more thoroughly think through how decisions are made and evaluated.

Cases Help Students See Varying Points-of-View

When you read a case study, you'll undoubtedly come to some kind of decision that you believe is the best one. One of the fascinating parts of the Case Method is the interaction that occurs during a class that uses the Case Method. When you have the opportunity to discuss a case with your peers, you'll quickly see a broader range of possible decisions that you didn't even think about while reading the case. Furthermore, you'll be asked to defend your own perspective and find the flaws in others' perspectives as well. While the Case Method is not a formalized debate, there are definitely parts of the Case Method that rely on an individual to think logically and systematically when arguing for a specific decision alternative. One of the goals of the Case Method is to help you see a wide variety of points-of-view. However, do not just assume that because your ideas and someone else's differ that the other person is always right. Instead, think logically and really analyze both your argument(s) and the other person's argument(s). While examining all sides of a case can help you see and understand varying points-of-view, the process can also help you sharpen your own argumentative skills.

Within each case, a situation is displayed and explored, using dialogue, setting, and internal thoughts of the protagonist, to create dilemmas that give readers a clear delineation of the problems and point the way to a discussion about possible solutions. Because the most effective way to depict a problem is to write situations or scenes that have conflict in them, many of the scenes have characters who represent opposite points of view, enter into disagreements, and offer different solutions.

In the literary world, we call this drama. In the work world we call this the safe distance Case Method of study, so that decisions made in the work world are not based upon drama, but upon reasoning through the drama for information and ideas that bring the best decision-making abilities of the team and its members to the fore. This book is made up of good cases, and what is meant by a "good case" is that it first and foremost is a good story written in narrative fashion. As such, each situation or scene in every case study carries the narrative forward, relates directly to one of the major problems in the case, or provides insight into the personality, motives, and/or communicative behaviors and strategies of one or more of the characters. The authors of the cases outline ideal situations that the writer knows will elicit conflicting opinions about potential solutions.

The authors of all of the cases are scholars of sport communication or practitioners in the field, and while the backgrounds of the authors and writing styles are diverse, all authors have written the cases for students and discussants who may not be familiar with the background, details, and terminology of the different types of businesses, organizations, or situations under discussion. Jargon is kept to a minimum and information is kept in laypersons' terms. An actual sport communication practitioner would, in actual situations, be expected to understand the business and its goals, policies, practices, and expectations.

Each and every author, or group of authors, uses short story writing techniques with flesh and blood characters, characters who are intriguing throughout the case. This style of writing helps to maximize retention, and is used in the cases for that purpose. Contextual memory is often overlooked in academic study, but it is the way human beings are naturally gifted in great memory recall, and it is the way we remember in everyday life. Each story element moves the narrative forward and authors do not "tell" the reader what happened but rather "show" the reader within the story itself, with the words, thoughts, and actions of the characters within the cases. While some exposition is at times necessary, the authors have kept in mind that this is a short story and the writing is void of academic jargon, references, and digressions into too much detail.

In each case, the authors grab the attention of readers with a character facing his or her biggest sport communication problem ever. Whether the problem has to do with interpersonal communication, organizational communication, public relations, traditional media, or social media in the sport world, the scene is set for the confrontations, frustrations, concerns, ethical and economic dilemmas, conflict, and deliberation to allow the readers to analyze the situation from multiple perspectives and come to their own conclusions.

Authors present situations and scenes without any attempt at analysis: Scenes follow a logical order and illustrate a point, concept, or issue that relates to the problems to be analyzed. Readers should know that no signals are intended so that no one solution is implicitly preferred. The solutions and conclusions are left up to the students who read, discuss, and analyze the cases.

Our authors provide relevant details after presenting an opening that sets up the situation, details related to goals, strategies, dilemmas, issues, conflicts, roadblocks, appropriate research, relevant financial information, people, and relationships. Authors are intentionally stingy with numbers in these cases, using them only to help solve the problems. This is done to avoid confusing readers or sending them off on unproductive analytical tangents. After analyzing these cases, students will know how to reason through arguments and ideas, come to a decision, and then implement a plan of action.

Each case uses as much dialogue as possible to bring the characters and the stories to life and to show the readers what is happening, rather than tell them what is happening. Thoughts of characters are also used at times, appearing in italics. So in these dialogues, external and internal, students can reason, feel, and react alongside each character.

The process enables students to apply theories and concepts that they are learning in an immediately applicable fashion. This maximizes retention. Currently there are no case study books like this on the market for sport communication. However, because many courses within the sport communication discipline take theories from courses in organizational communication and public relations, both disciplines that have multiple case study books to choose from on the market, we believe that the sport communication discipline is due for such a book. We go a step further and include cases concerning interpersonal and group communication as well as cases concerned with cultural communication issues. This *Casing Sport Communication* collection mirrors the content currently being published in the major textbooks in the history and field of sport communication. As such, *Casing Sport Communication* is not a sport communication textbook, but rather could be used as a supplement to traditional texts and utilized across sport communication courses.

Most popular case books in the public relations and organizational communication disciplines do not teach students how to utilize and prepare for case studies and real-world scenarios with multiple elements to weigh; instead they examine non-fictional case studies of "what went wrong" or "what went right" in high profile cases. Those cases provide useful historical knowledge, but do not tend to develop critically engaged students who can think through new situations.

REFERENCES

[1] Garvin, D. A. (2003). Making the case: Professional education for the world of practice. *Harvard Magazine, 106*(1), 56–107.

[2] Donham, W. B. (1922). Business teaching by the case system. *The American Economic Review, 12*(1), 53–65.

[3] Mauffette-Leenders, L. A., Erskine, J. A., & Leenders, M. R. (2007). *Learning with cases* (4th ed.). London, Ontario: Richard Ivey School of Business.

[4] Donham, 1922, pp. 61–62.

[5] Ellet, W. (2007). *The case study handbook: How to read, discuss, and write persuasively about cases.* Cambridge, *MA:* Harvard Business School Press.

[6] Graham, P. T., & Cline, P. C. (1980). The case method: A basic teaching approach. *Theory Into Practice, 19*, 112–116.

[7] Ford, L. (1969). *Using the case study in teaching and training.* Nashville, TN: Broadman Press.

CHAPTER 3:
ANALYZING CASE STUDIES

The types of cases you are going to be presented with in this book are what we call decision-based cases, or cases that require the reader to come to some kind of decision. Every case is essentially laid out in a very similar pattern. First, you will be introduced to the main character of the case. Second, you will be introduced to other individuals involved within the case. Third, you will be introduced to the main communication problem or a number of communication problems that either the main character or her or his organization currently face. Lastly, you will be left with a character who is not sure in which direction he or she should proceed. In essence, you, as the reader, will need to come up with the decision the main character should make.

DECISION MAKING AND CASE STUDIES

To help you work your way through the decision-making process, we have created a worksheet (Appendix A) that will help guide you through the decision-making process. Please understand that this is a formalized decision-making process based on the work of communication scholars Dennis Gouran and Randy Hirokawa.[1] The functional approach created by Gouran and Hirokawa involves five basic steps.

Step One – Understand the Problem

First, and foremost, someone making a decision needs to make sure that he or she completely understands the issue at hand. If you look at the worksheet provided in Appendix A, you'll notice that the first few questions all involve making sure you understand the decision that needs to be made. First, you're asked who the important characters are within the case. In some cases you'll only have two or three characters that are important, but in other cases you could have ten different characters that you need to know their importance to the case. Second, you'll be asked about the main communication problem within the case. One of the hardest parts of making a decision is understanding what needs to be solved. As such, clearly articulating the communication problem very early in your analysis is essential. Lastly, you'll be asked to look for any causes that you see within the case that have led to the communication problem. No communication problem exists within a vacuum; so clearly articulating what the problems are will help you ultimately select decisions that are useful within the confines of the specific case.

In addition to the basic understandings of the problems and causes of the case, we also think it's important to start thinking about how relevant sport communication literature applies to the case at this point. One mistake that we can make is to come up with a decision and then try to find relevant research to support the decision we've already made. However, when we look at research in retrospect, we often miss out on more logical choices.

Step Two – Select Criteria

The word **criterion** refers to a standard by which we can judge something (FYI – criterion is singular and criteria is plural). Of course, in the case of a decision, we are searching for standards by which we can judge our decisions. Previous research in the area of case study analysis has identified both quantitative and qualitative criteria that may help individuals and organizations judge their decisions.[2] **Quantitative criteria** are called such because they can be easily numerically measured and computed as having an impact on business functioning. **Qualitative criteria**, on the other hand, are criteria that are not easily numerically measured or computed. Table 1 shows a list of both quantitative and qualitative criteria for sport communication

Table 1 Decision Criteria

QUANTITATIVE	QUALITATIVE
Profit	Customer Satisfaction
Cost	Competitive Advantage
Return on Investment	Corporate Image
Cash Flow	Goodwill
Inventory Turn	Cultural Sensitivity
Productivity	Employee Motivation
Efficiency	Job Satisfaction
Capacity	Employee Health
Delivery Time	Safety
Quality	Synergy
Quantity	Ethics - Business - Communication
Errors	Innovation
Growth Rate	Obsolescence
Market Share	Flexibility
Risk	Pragmatism
Staff Turnover	Ease of Implementation

cases. Please understand that these criteria are not exhaustive, so other criteria could definitely be added to the list. Furthermore, there are some instances where quantitative criteria are qualitatively applied and vice-versa, so this list is intended as a general list of possible criteria to be applied in a case study. While some of these criteria may be familiar to you, others may not, so let's briefly explain what each of the criteria are.

Quantitative Criteria

Profit. **Profit** is the money a business makes after accounting for all the expenses. At the end of the day, all organizations must be profitable or they will disappear. As such, whether an organization is a for-profit or a nonprofit organization, the organization must be concerned with profit. This is true for sport organizations as well.

Cost. If profit is the right hand of an organization, then cost is the left hand of the organization. **Cost** can be defined as the price paid or required for acquiring, producing, or maintaining a product or service. All organizations have costs. The obvious goal is to ensure that the costs of your organization are less than the profits. However, the old adage that sometimes you have to spend money to make money is also true, but the goal is to ensure that your profits outweigh your costs.

Return on Investment. One concept that isn't overly discussed in many communication textbooks is an organization's return on investment or ROI. According to Patricia and Jack Phillips, an **ROI** is the "ultimate measure of accountability that answers the question: Is there a financial return for investing in a program, process, initiative, or performance improvement solution."[3] The return on investment focuses on the benefits and costs gained from a specific endeavor. While the idea of conducting a cost-benefit analysis dates back to an article written by a French engineer named Jules Dupuit in 1848, the process of conducting a cost-benefit analysis was practically developed by the United States Army Corps of Engineers during the 1930s. A basic cost-benefit analysis is simple to calculate:

$$\text{Benefit-Cost Ratio} = \frac{\text{Benefits}}{\text{Costs}}$$

The return on investment is an extension of the cost-benefit analysis that was developed in the 1970s and 80s and really became a hallmark of business measurement in the 1990s. Where a simple cost-benefit ratio examines whether the costs outweigh the benefits, the ROI wants to know how beneficial something was once the costs are balanced out of the equation. For example, putting time, money, and energy into coaching an athlete would be a cost. Then winning a championship would be a benefit. That win would likely help improve ticket and memorabilia sales; thus, this endeavor is a positive return on an investment in the sporting world. In terms of actual money, imagine you invest $1 in a lemonade stand. At the end of the day, the lemonade entrepreneur hands you back $2. Because your initial investment was $1, we automatically subtract that from our returned benefit, which leaves us with a net benefit of $1. Here is how we would calculate the ROI:

ROI (%) = (Net Benefits / Costs) * 100
ROI (%) = (1 / 1) * 100
ROI (%) = (1) * 100
ROI (%) = 100

What this analysis says is that, for every $1 we invested in the lemonade stand, we got back $1 after the costs were covered. Obviously, in the business world, the goal is to have much higher returns on investments than an ROI of 100%.

Cash Flow. Another important concept related to the amount of money an organization is taking in and spending is cash flow. **Cash flow** is the amount of cash a company generates and uses during a period. **Cash inflow** is money an organization has entering an organization from profits or investments. **Cash outflow** then is money that an organization has to spend because of expenses or investments. An organization must have enough inflow to balance its outflow. Having enough cash on hand ensures that an organization can meet its basic obligations in terms of expenses. If an organization's money is tied up in various investments and the organization does not have cash on hand, then the organization may become insolvent because the organization cannot meet its basic financial obligations.

Inventory Turn. **Inventory turn** is very important for organizations that produce any kind of product. Inventory turn can be defined as the number of times inventory is sold or used in a time period (e.g., a month, six months, one year, etc.). Obviously, if inventory is sitting on your shelves, then you're not making money off of that inventory. As such, the goal of any production-oriented organization is to turn their inventory as often as possible.

Productivity. **Productivity** is a concept closely related to capacity, but it examines the relationship between the amount of input into a system and the resulting output. Let's say you run a personal training service and you know that if you hire three trainers (input into the system), then you can cover twelve clients a day (resulting output).

Efficiency. From a business perspective, **efficiency** examines the relationship between means and ends and is closely related to productivity. If a business process is efficient, then the right amount of means are in place to achieve a desired end. If an organization is inefficient, then the organization could either A) use less means to produce the same end result, or B) the current means should produce a greater end result. The goal of efficiency is to streamline a process without reaching the point of diminished returns, when the new means level is no longer able to reach the desired end.

Capacity. **Capacity** refers to the maximum amount or number that can be received or contained. Imagine you own a sport team and your sport venue holds 70,000 maximum in its seats. At some point, your stadium will reach a point where you can no longer physically put any more fans in the venue; this is capacity.

Delivery Time. Organizations that deal with products or services must be concerned with their **delivery time**, or the length of time it takes to deliver a product or service once a customer has ordered the product or service. If you're building a sport venue, then your delivery time may be seen in years, but if you're delivering a baseball glove ordered on the Internet, your delivery time should be in days. Different products and services will require different delivery times. One way to make your organization stand out is to ensure that you deliver a quality product or service as quickly as possible.

Quality. **Quality** refers to producing or providing products or services that meet the expressed and/or implied requirements of an organization's customers. While all organizations should strive for a specified level of quality, perfection may not be a realistic ultimate goal.

Quantity. Quantity is one of the easiest criteria to understand because it's a base count of some product or service. More formally, **quantity** is defined as the extent, size, or sum of countable or measurable discrete events, objects, or phenomena, expressed as a numerical value.

Errors. Whether we like them or not, eventually errors happen. In this sense, any product or service may lead to a mistake or a deviation from the intended output. The public often doesn't complain about some errors but becomes enraged at other errors when they occur. Obviously, errors that lead to harm are considerably more important than a basic product defect. There is a strong negative relationship between delivery time and quality. Depending on the product or service, you may side on either delivery time or quality. The faster you try to produce a product or deliver a service, the more likely you will have errors. If, on the other hand, you desire a high quality product or service, then delivery time will be slower as quality inspection is built into the system to prevent errors. There is also a negative relationship that often occurs between quality and quantity. The higher the quantity, the more likely you will have errors along the way. The higher your desire for quality, the fewer you'll make, and the less likely you'll have errors.

Growth Rate. In an ideal economic environment, an organization will continue to increase its ability to provide products and services at a desired pace. As such, **growth rate** is the increase in the demand for a particular product or service over time. For growth rate to be effective, the organization needs to be able to balance the requirements for new raw materials, employees, etc. into the organization (input), and the processing of those inputs in the creation of products and services (throughput), with your customer needs and desires (output). If an organization has too many new inputs and no outputs, the organization will become insolvent over time. If an organization doesn't have enough inputs or the throughput process is too slow, then the organization will not meet its obligations to its customers, which could lead to insolvency as well. Ultimately, an organization wants to ensure that they are able to increase the amounts of input and increase the throughput process in direct relationship to the demand from customers.

Market Share. Market share refers to the percentage of total industry sales that are made up by a particular company's individual sales. If you're in a very niche industry (e.g., fan face stickers or knitted team logo beverage cozies), you may have 100% of the market share. On the other hand, if you're an athletic wear company specializing in team logo T-shirts, then you may be competing with a large number of other organizations for the same market share.

Risk. For our purpose, **risk** can be defined as the chance that something negative will occur. We can break risk down into two categories: physical risk and organizational risk.

Physical risk. **Physical risk** is the likelihood that an individual will suffer loss of life or be injured in some fashion. As mandated by federal law, all organizations must be somewhat aware of the types of physical risks to which their employees are exposed. Some sport organizations innately have more physical risks associated with the organization (e.g., pro football, mountain climbing, etc.), and so considering the importance of risk becomes very important when making all kinds of decisions.

Organizational risk. Organizational risk, on the other hand, examines an organization's return on investment. Whether the investment is in a new employee, product, service, or financial investment, all organizations take risks when they invest. Often these investments do not turn out in favor of the organization. While having some risk will definitely help an organization grow, too much risk can end up sinking an organization if all of the returns on investment are lower than originally anticipated.

Staff Turnover. The final quantitative criterion is **staff turnover**, or the rate at which an employer gains and loses employees (includes both voluntary and involuntary turnover). **Voluntary turnover** occurs when an employee quits her or his job; whereas, **involuntary turnover** is when an employer must ask an employee to quit (either in a firing situation or a downsizing situation). If you have too much staff turnover, the costs of training new employees may go through the roof. If you don't have any staff turnover, you may end up with a stagnant employee base that doesn't innovate. Most organizations attempt to hire and cultivate a working environment that keeps employees satisfied and engaged in their work to avoid voluntary turnover.

Qualitative Criteria. The word "qualitative" refers to the relating to or the measurement of or by the quality of something rather than its quantity. In this respect, the word **quality** then is an examination of a degree or standard of excellence related to something. As such, when we discuss qualitative criteria we are examining how organizations can excel within a specific category, but these categories are innately more arbitrary and not immediately numerically measurable. For example, the first criterion we'll examine is customer satisfaction. While most people can intrinsically understand what is meant by "customer satisfaction," there is no clear quantity immediately associated with the idea of customer satisfaction. While there are metrics that have been designed to attempt to measure all of the qualitative criteria discussed below, their basic ideas are innately non-numerical. Let's look at all of the qualitative criteria discussed in Table 1.

Customer Satisfaction Most organizations understand that making sure you have customers who are satisfied with the product or service is extremely important for ensuring that current customers become repeat customers. As a criterion, one must always question whether a decision being made is likely to increase customer satisfaction, maintain current satisfaction levels, or possibly decrease customer satisfaction.

Competitive Advantage. **Competitive advantage** is the superiority gained by an organization when the organization compares its products and services to those of other organizations within its target market. There are two ways an organization can make itself competitive. First, the organization can provide the same value as its competitors but at a lower price. In this case, the organization is figuring out how to manufacture a product or deliver a service in a fashion that is cheaper than its competitors. Another way an organization can set itself apart competitively is to set itself up as a luxury option and then charge more for the base product but sell less of the actual product. In essence, you're creating the myth that your product is a luxury product to be desired. While you may not sell as many products or services, the increased price off-sets any value you lose and makes you competitive within your target market.

Corporate Image. **Corporate image** refers to the representation an organization creates about itself for various stakeholders (employees, stockholders, customers, fans, etc.). While an organization's ultimate image is based on the perceptions of various stakeholders, organizations can help foster a specific image through both internal communication and external communication. Common thematic areas involved in corporate image include the prestige of the organization, quality of its products and services, reputation of organizational leadership, perception of the organization in terms of its relationship to the environment, etc. . .

Goodwill. Goodwill as an organizational criterion relates to an accounting concept that has been around for many years. In this respect, **goodwill** is seen as the intangible value of the organization that goes beyond the physical and non-physical assets of the organization (e.g., people, property, finances, etc.) and is generally based on customer perceptions of the firm's reputation. From a communication perspective, goodwill refers to an individual's perception of another's perceived caring.[4] In this case, do you, as a consumer, believe that an organization cares about you as an individual both as a customer and as a person? Ultimately, the accounting and communication perspectives on goodwill are not mutually exclusive. While the accounting perspective tries to determine how organizations can quantify goodwill and make it an asset that can have clear value, the communication perspective lends itself to understanding how an organization actually develops goodwill. Organizations can build perceptions of goodwill, but these perceptions are built over a lengthy period of time. Ultimately goodwill is built through four basic functions: 1) expenditures on public relations and marketing; 2) products and services that meet and exceed customer expectations; 3) investment in the creation of long-lasting customer-provider relationships; and 4) organizational leadership that is perceived as ethical. Once an organization has built goodwill, generally the only way to negate that goodwill is through some kind of indiscretion by organizational leadership.

Cultural Sensitivity. Cultural sensitivity is the degree to which an organization is aware of the differences and similarities of different cultures and how culture impacts individual attitudes, values, beliefs, and behaviors. In the United States, there are many different cultures represented and organizations should be sensitive to their employees' needs and their customers' needs with respect to those cultures. Often organizations must balance various cultural needs that conflict, so organizational decision makers should tread thoughtfully when making decisions that relate to cultural issues.

Employee Motivation. **Motivation**, generally speaking, is the force that drives an individual to achieve her or his goals.[5] For organizational purposes, employee motivation then is the forces that drive individual employees to achieve both the employee's goals at work and the organization's goals. Generally speaking, we break employee motivations into two basic categories: internal and external. **Internal motivators** are those forces that exist within an individual and drive her or him to achieve a goal. An example of an internal motivator could be a work ethic. If someone believes in a strong work ethic, he or she may be more motivated to help achieve an organization's goals. If another person has a weak work ethic, he or she may be unmotivated to achieve an organization's goals. The second category of motivators are **external**, or factors outside an individual that can influence the individual to strive toward achieving a goal. One of the most common external motivators is monetary reward. If you're told that you'll receive a bonus if a product is produced on time, you'll be more motivated to achieve the organization's goal because you see a direct personal benefit.

Job Satisfaction. Job satisfaction, like employee motivation, are concepts that are very intangible and ambiguous. **Job satisfaction** is the emotional reaction an individual has about her or his job. If people have a positive emotional reaction to their jobs, they will be satisfied and content; whereas individuals who have a negative emotional reaction will be unsatisfied. Ultimately, an individual's job satisfaction will impact her or his attitudes, values, beliefs, and behaviors on the job.

Employee Health. **Employee health** looks at the totality of an individual employee's physical, psychological, and spiritual well-being. In an ideal world, people would be able to disassociate their work lives from other parts of their lives, but that is highly unrealistic. As such, there has been an increased focus on considering employee health.

Physical Health. **Physical** refers to the physical well-being of an individual. When individuals are sick and unhealthy, they miss more work and are not as productive as when they are healthy. As such, many organizations are now investing a great deal of money to ensure that employees maintain their physical health because it is actually a very good return on investment.[6] Of course, one might argue that in the NFL, the health issues often do not crop up until later in life, after a player has retired, and thus investing in players' health for the long term was not something the NFL saw as a good return on an investment. As more and more cases of player head trauma leading to worsening health issues crop up, the NFL may decide that the loss of goodwill means that more investment in player brain health will be a good return on their investment.

Psychological Health. **Psychological health** is the extent to which an individual is cognitively and emotionally well. Not only can a decrease in someone's psychological health be problematic for the individual, her or his work performance can be greatly negatively impacted as well. While there are some characteristics that can negatively impact an individual's psychological health that are outside the organization's control (e.g., divorce, ailing parent, mental disorder, etc.), there are others that are clearly based within the organization and can be curtailed by a vigilant organization (e.g., excessive stress, bullying, charlatanism, incivility, etc.).

Spiritual health. The notion of spiritual health is a fairly recent one for many organizational academics. As such, many organizational communication textbooks do not really broach the subject. **Spiritual health** can be defined as the "the enhancement of spiritual oneness with whatever a person considers to be more than oneself as an individual with reason, experience, and intuition; the ongoing development of an adherence to a responsible ethical system."[7] As with both physical and psychological health, when individuals do not feel spiritually healthy, their work performance can be negatively impacted to the organization's detriment.

Safety. One of the basic needs anyone has in a modern workplace is the feeling of safety. Whether this is safety from being exposed to an organizational hazard (e.g., chemicals, heavy machinery, etc.) or safety from being exposed to workplace aggression and violence, people have an inherent need to be safe. You will never get people to work at their optimum levels within an organization if they don't feel safe.

Synergy. The notion of synergy stems out of systems theory and basically states that the sum of the whole is greater than the sum of its parts. Practically speaking, **synergy** is the idea that individual actors, dynamics, materials, objects, processes, or systems will not help an organization as much as all of those parts working harmoniously with one another can. For organizational optimization, all parts within an organization need to be working together to produce an optimal organizational outcome.

Ethics. Ethics, at its most basic level, is the discussion of whether a set of means justifies the desired ends. **Ethics** can be further explained as a "critical analysis of cultural values to determine the validity of their vigorous rightness or wrongness in terms of two major criteria: truth and justice. Ethics is examining the relation of an individual to society, to the nature, and/or to God. How do people make ethical decisions? They are influenced by how they perceive themselves in relation to goodness and/or excellence."[8] For our purposes, we divide ethics into two basic categories: business and communication.

Business ethics. **Business ethics** is defined as the determination of various business practices, processes, and outcomes as right or wrong. Owen and David Cherrington[9] discuss twelve common ethical lapses that happen in modern organizations:

- Taking things that do not belong to you (stealing),
- Saying things that you know are not true (lying),
- False impressions (fraud and deceit),
- Conflict of interest and influence buying (bribes, payoffs, and kickbacks),
- Hiding versus divulging information,
- Unfair advantage (cheating),
- Personal decadence,
- Interpersonal abuse (physical violence, sexual harassment, emotional abuse, abuse of one's position, racism, heterosexism, ageism, and sexism),
- Organizational abuse (inequity in compensation, performance appraisals that destroy self-esteem, transfers or time pressures that destroy family life, terminating people through no fault of their own, encouraging loyalty and not rewarding it, and creating

the myth that the organization will benevolently protect or direct an employee's career are all examples of how organizations abuse employees),
* Rule violations,
* Accessory to unethical acts,
* and moral balance (ethical dilemmas).

Communication ethics. Communication ethics is defined as the determination of various organizational communication practices, processes, and outcomes as right or wrong. W. Charles Redding[10] created a typology of six different types of ethical problems commonly seen in organizational communication:

* **Coercive** (intolerance of dissent, restrictions of freedom of speech, refusal to listen, resorting to formal rules and regulations to stifle discussion or to squash complaints, etc).
* **Destructive** (insults, put-downs, back-stabbing, character-assassination, using the untruth as a weapon, and not providing expected feedback)
* **Deceptive** (evasive or deliberately misleading messages, bureaucratic-style euphemisms designed to cover up problems, and "prettifying" unpleasant facts)
* **Intrusive** (hidden cameras, the tapping of telephones, and the application of computer technologies to the monitoring of employee behavior, etc.)
* **Secretive** (hoarding information and sweeping information under the rug)
* **Manipulative-Exploitative** (hiding one's true intentions and demagoguery)

Innovation. **Innovation** is the creating of something new. In the organizational realm, innovation can come in two distinct forms. First, innovation can be viewed as the extent to which an organization creates new and improved products and services. Second, innovation can also be an organization's ability to strategically streamline processes, increase its market share, increase its competitive advantage, etc. . . Organizations that value innovation will be able to adapt more quickly to changing environments than organizations that do not value innovation.

Obsolescence. Obsolescence is what every organization should fear and is often the result of a lack of innovation. **Obsolescence** occurs when there is a significant decline in customer desire for an organization's products or services. Obsolescence often occurs for a variety of different reasons: availability of alternatives that perform better or have new features; availability of alternatives that are of equal quality and cheaper; the product or service is no longer viewed as necessary in the current market; and changes in customer preferences or requirements. In the sport world, obsolescence can occur when a team does not win for years on end and has very little likelihood of offering the excitement of a championship run. Over the years many organizations die out because they sank all of their capital into creating one product or service that eventually became unnecessary or passé. Two classic examples (you may never heard of) are Generra Sportswear Company's Hypercolor clothing line (popular in the early 1990s, bankrupt in 1992) and the World POG Federation (popularity hit peak in 1993, bankrupt in 1995). While both of these organizations had numerous problems, one of the largest problems was that their income was based on a fad that quickly became obsolete.

Flexibility. The next qualitative criterion is **flexibility**, which refers to whether an organization, process, or decision can modify or adapt within a certain range and given timeframe. In environments that are highly chaotic, you need considerably more flexibility to adapt to changes than in environments that are highly stable. As such, if you're in an organization where flexibility is very important, then a decision being made should be equally flexible.

Pragmatism. One of the hardest questions for some to answer is whether or not a given decision is actually **pragmatic**. Is the decision that is being advocated realistic or practical given the business or the environment? When discussing some larger issues like innovation, sometimes decisions that are arrived at that may be very lofty but are not overly pragmatic. For example, if you're a small business, running a million dollar advertisement campaign may be a great way to raise your market share, but it clearly wouldn't be pragmatic for most small businesses.

Ease of Implementation. The last qualitative criterion is **ease of implementation**, which refers to the speed and the simplicity of a decision alternative. If an organization is making a decision in a highly chaotic environment, then having a decision that can be easily and quickly implemented becomes very important. If, however, your organization can take the time to implement a decision, then ease of implementation may not be a criterion that your organization is overly concerned with at all.

Figure 3.1

Sample Case Coach-Athlete Conflict
Lanceville High Lady Lions
Mary Collins and John Spinda

ABSTRACT

The establishment and continued growth of the coach-athlete relationship depends on cooperative and positive interpersonal communication and decision-making skill. While these relationships can be very positive and rewarding for both coach and athlete, conflict is inevitable. Sometimes an athlete may feel betrayed or even bullied by the coach's decision making, because he or she has his or her own goals that he or she is attempting to achieve regardless of the goals set as a team. The coach often faces the dilemma of upholding his or her values and policy and deciding what will be best for the goals of the individual and, more importantly, the team as a whole. The case of the Lanceville High Lady Lions softball team is one that displays the relationship between a well-respected head coach and a senior second baseman who wants to have a successful final season. When a tense moment arises, the coach may have a big decision to make while taking the player's goals and the coach-player relationship into consideration.

***

Figure 3.1 (*continued*)

BACKGROUND

"Wow, what a season that was," said Lanceville High Lady Lions Baseball Head Coach Allen Smith. His face could barely contain a beaming, prideful grin as stood gazing at the photograph of the 2011 State Champion Lady Lions softball team hanging above his desk at his alma mater, Lanceville High. It also happened to be the same season that marked his 20th year as a coach.

Coach Smith turned to look at the twelve 2012 Lady Lions softball players who stood before him waiting to begin the day's practice. "Softball had always been a sport than many Lanceville supporters put on the backburner until that 2011 season when we won the state championship. So far, the 2012 season is proving to be just as successful, but we have to take advantage of the momentum we have left," Coach Smith preached.

"The last game before the playoff is quickly approaching, and today is our last chance to practice," Coach said as a concerned yet stern look appeared on his face.

"As you all know, we will be facing the Hawks this Friday. I need full team focus and leadership to come out with a strong win." The Huntington High Hawks were infamous as the Lions' long-time rivals and it always proved to be a tension-filled, yet exciting match up.

"Alright ladies, let's go start warm ups," exclaimed Sarah, the senior team captain.

As the girls rushed out of the office, Ray Link, the athletic director, came strolling in. "Time to give the Hawks another loss, coach," said Link. There was obvious tension surrounding the match up, even though the Hawks hadn't beaten the Lions in the past five seasons.

"Yeah, well take a look at this," Coach Smith slammed a crumpled page of the day's newspaper on his desk directly in front of Link. The front page of the sports section read "Lady Hawks Ready to Compete" complete with quotes from rival coaches and players. Link snatched the paper and proceeded to fling it into the trash bin.

"I truly believe it's our year, Coach, the girls are ready." Coach Smith gave Link a confident nod, then headed out the door to practice.

GAME DAY

Lady Lion supporters filed in as the sun began to set over the Lanceville softball field. There was a sea of blue and white and a tingling excitement in the atmosphere. While Mr. Link assisted with seating and various game day operations for the visiting Hawks, Coach Smith gathered his team for one last pep talk before the first pitch.

"Take all of this in, the support from your families and community and the excitement, and remember teamwork, dedication, and hard work have gotten you here and will take you further if you put forth the effort," Coach Smith spoke softly and seriously.

Figure 3.1 (*continued*)

"Lions on three," Sarah shouted, "Let's go!"

As the game progressed, there were a few instances of tension when a few pitch calls were not received well by the Lions, or when the Hawks stole a base that was perceived to be an undeserved "bad call." Each inning brought new excitement and challenge for Coach Smith and the Lions.

OUT OF ORDER? A TURNING POINT

"Take a look at the scoreboard," Coach Smith demanded as he slung his sweaty hat off of his head. It was the start of the seventh inning and the Lions' last chance to bat and attempt to score a run to tie up the score. The metal bleachers were beginning to clear as the supporters in blue and white gathered closer to the rusted metal fence surrounding the field. With a runner on third, another Lady Lion came up to bat with two outs. The first pitch was thrown and called a strike.

"Time out ump," shouted Coach Turner of the Hawks as she emerged from the dugout and stomped onto the field to confront the official. Coach Smith entered the field as well, dust kicking up under his heavy footsteps.

"You batted out of order, number 9 is not listed as the next batter in the lineup," Coach Turner argued as she pointed to number 9 for the Lions. The player was Sarah, the team captain.

Coach Smith was shocked as the skin between his eyebrows began to tense up. "That's impossible, the girls know when to hit," Coach Smith denied. *I trust that my players are aware of the order and that it is followed*, he thought to himself. Sarah dropped her bat and removed her helmet in an attempt to rebuttal. After double-checking the batting order, Coach Smith found that the Hawks coach was correct. Sarah did bat out of order and neither Coach Smith nor the assistant coach recognized the error before it happened.

Coach Smith, with beads of sweat rolling down his face, frantically apologized. "Our honest mistake ump, this is rare for us," said Smith.

"Sorry, Coach, I'm gonna have to count that as an out," the umpire replied.

That settled it, one more inning had to be played. Sarah began to trudge back to the dugout in disgust.

"Hustle on back, Sarah, there's still game left to play," Coach Smith encouraged her.

"No way coach, you know that call was unfair, why didn't you fight back? Batting order doesn't matter!" Sarah screamed.

Coach Smith halted in his tracks, calmly turned to Sarah and said, "Sportsmanship is all about playing fair and following the rules of the game. You are a senior and you know this. What is a win if you don't earn it?"

Figure 3.1 (*continued*)

Sarah, visibly upset at the coach's response, proceeded to sling her bat at the dugout fence and raged "Why can't you ever trust us, you aren't fair! You are failing us as a coach!"

Coach Smith glanced at the scoreboard, knowing that the final inning was about to commence. *I have to handle her inappropriate behavior, whether it is her last game as a senior or not.* Considering his values and coaching policy, Coach Smith quickly addressed Sarah, saying, "That's it, take the bench for the remainder of the game."

Sarah stormed off of the field and immediately approached her parents. Coach Smith glanced through the fence and began to shake his head as Sarah and her parents left the ballpark. The remainder of the game seemed to pass within seconds as the Lions held the Hawks and scored the single run they needed to take the win. Coach Smith gazed at the team in their celebratory huddle as parents and supporters flooded the field. Coach Smith began to exit the field as thoughts flooded his mind. *We may be advancing to the playoffs, but I know another challenge is waiting.*

THE NEXT DAY: A CONTINUED CONFLICT

As the Monday morning school day began, Coach Smith sat down at his desk and picked up the newspaper, hopeful that he would see a well-written story about Friday's game. Just as he peeled open the sports section, the harsh ring of his office phone broke the silence. He quickly answered. "Good Morning. Coach Smith."

"Could you please stop by my office when you get a chance?" said Athletic Director Ray Link.

Without wasting any time, Coach Smith rose up from his office chair and made his way to Link's office. *I know what this is about.* As he turned the corner into the athletic office, he locked eyes with Sarah. After a moment to register the situation, he noticed that Sarah's mother was sitting next to her.

"Come on and sit," Link suggested to Smith.

"Let's get right to it, then! Can someone please tell me why my daughter was not allowed to finish what could've possibly been the last game in her career?" Sarah's mother demanded.

"Please understand that policies are set for a reason and are put in place for the benefit of the team. Disrespectful behavior is absolutely not tolerated, especially on the field," Coach Smith explained.

"Sarah has always been a great player and an asset to your team," her mother argued. "What about the first playoff game? I suppose you plan to put her at a disadvantage again?"

"I value Sarah as a member of the team just as I do each person on the team. However, I cannot make exceptions, even for a senior. If you look in the team rules, it states that if a player is removed in the middle of a game, they must sit out for the full time of the following game," Coach Smith stressed.

Figure 3.1 (*continued*)

Link, feeling the tension, spoke up, saying, "Each athletic team is given their rule manual before they even step on the field for their first practice. It is important that each player fully understands these policies and their permanence." Silence filled the office. Link stepped in once more. "There is still a week before the game, so I trust Coach Smith will come to a decision in a timely manner and I will consult with him. In the meantime, we will conclude this meeting. I appreciate you and your mother coming in, Sarah."

As Sarah and her mother left the office, Link gave Coach Smith a concerned look. "You have your hands full with this one. I know it is rough, especially when a parent is involved. However, I trust your judgment and will support whichever action you decide to take."

Coach Smith gave a nod of agreement and got up from his seat. With a long walk back to his office, Coach Smith was again flooded with thoughts. All of his current and former players have described him as a great mentor who is always fair and leads by example. *I know Ray is counting on me to make this a quick decision. What about the other girls? I can't be unfair to them.* He also thought about his relationship with Sarah. There had always been a level of trust and respect. *She is only one player, and I am confident in my values and team policies. I can't let this get in the way of the upcoming game.*

Finally, Coach Smith reached his office and plopped down into his desk chair. Again, he picked up the sports section of the Lanceville news and began reading. He felt a feeling of confidence that he would make the right decision today.

Using Criteria. In the previous sections we've discussed the quantitative and qualitative criteria that can be used for making organizational decisions. Remember, criteria are tools that we use, as decision makers, to help us evaluate or judge potential decisions. As such, the selections of the criteria we view as the most important, given a specific decision, are very important. Figure 3.1 contains a short sport communication case; before proceeding with this section please read the case.

In any business-related decision, the types of criteria can vary. In some decision cases, all of the criteria could be theoretically applicable. For this reason, we recommend limiting the number of criteria you select to three (total – not three from quantitative and three from qualitative). Depending on the criteria that you select, you may end up with radically different types of decisions.

In our sample case (Figure 3.1), Coach Smith needs to make a decision about how best to deal with his player, Sarah. He could keep his punishment in place and not let her play the next game. He could let her play the next game, or he could devise a new punishment. In cases that are more focused on relational issues, it is likely that more qualitative criteria should be chosen. In contrast, in cases involving an organization's internal and external communication, you will be able to use more quantitative criteria. It seems that Coach Smith might have several different options, but let's first evaluate each of these options through a few different criteria.

The first criterion you could select could be goodwill. Coach Smith would be generating goodwill with Sarah. Likely there would not be much goodwill lost with any other party involved in the case. So, when it comes to the goodwill criterion, choosing to repeal Sarah's punishment and let her play the game might be the best decision.

Another possible criterion you could select could be customer satisfaction. In the current case, the Lady Lions' fans would be considered customers. Those customers might expect to see a good game and have the Lady Lions win. Without Sarah, that might be impossible. So, letting Sarah play might lead to customer satisfaction, but finding an alternative punishment where Sarah gets to play, but "does her time" in another way could also lead to customer satisfaction.

Lastly, let's examine the case using a third criterion, ethics. One of Owen and David Cherringtons' common ethical lapses involves rule violations. Under this classification, we can argue that two wrongs don't make a right. Sarah violated a rule by batting out of order; if the coach violates the team rule (that if a player is taken out of a game midway, she has to sit out the whole next game), then he would also be violating a rule. While it might benefit the team in the playoff game, it does not benefit teaching lessons in ethics to the team.

Hopefully, you can see how, depending on which criteria you select, you can end up with very different conclusions. Ultimately, the criteria that you select for evaluating possible decision alternatives will guide your decision-making process.

Once you've selected your three decision criteria, you also need to think about your criteria in terms of how you will measure these criteria. One of the goals of any decision criterion is to help guide the decision making, but you need to have the ability to think through how these criteria will be achieved through the decision. For example, if one of your criteria is customer satisfaction, you need to ask yourself how a decision alternative will improve customer satisfaction. But you need to take this a step further and think about how you will know when customer satisfaction has been increased because of your decision alternative. In other words, how are you going to measure customer satisfaction?

Obviously, the quantitative criteria have a pre-built-in measurement tool, that's why they are quantitative criteria. Qualitative criteria, on the other hand, still must be measured, but you, as the decision maker, need to really think through how you will measure the specific criteria. In the case discussed in Figure 3.1, how would you measure whether or not a specific decision is communicatively ethical? While using Redding's six criteria for ethical organizational communication is one tool you could use to measure the ethicality of a decision, it's not the only way of evaluating communication ethics.

Overall, when it comes to selecting and using decision criteria, you need to really think through the selection, use, and measurement of the criteria you select. The last part of the worksheet discussed in Appendix A asks you to then rank the three criteria you've selected. We ask you to do this because often we have to make a determination of which criterion is the most important. If we had selected the criteria image, flexibility, and ethics as our three criteria for the case in Figure 3.1, we clearly need to know which criterion is more important to our decision making process. If we value image more, then we would select the decision that leads to a likely win for the Lady Lions. If we value flexibility we might change Sarah's punishment. But then, if we choose the ethics criterion, then we would choose to leave Sarah's punishment as it is.

Step Three – Identify Solutions

The third of Gouran and Hirokawa's[11] five basic steps of decision making is identifying possible solutions. Some decision cases will come with pre-determined decision alternatives, but most cases will require you, the reader, to come up with possible decision alternatives. For the purposes of the Case Method, most case scholars generally agree that you should develop at least three well-articulate decision alternatives. Nils Randrup[12] recommends four possible tools for determining possible solutions: visualization, experience, knowledge of other solutions, and academic discipline/theory/models.

Visualization. The first way to come to a possible decision is to really put yourself in the position of the main decision-making character within the case. Really try to see the different issues and possible decisions from the main character's position within the story. Often when we put ourselves into the shoes of the main character, decisions will become very apparent.

Experience. A second way of generating possible alternatives comes from our own experiences in life. Maybe you've faced a similar dilemma either in playing a sport yourself, or working in the field. If so, how did you proceed? Maybe you made a good decision or maybe you made a horrible decision. Either way, using your own experience can help you think of possible decision alternatives.

Knowledge of Other Solutions. We often hear about how sport organizations or athletes handle various situations through the modern press. Maybe you heard about a specific decision on the nightly news or read about a decision in a sport magazine like *Sports Illustrated*. In either case, we can use the decisions we hear or read about and apply them to the cases in this book.

Academic Discipline/Theory/Models. The last way you can arrive at various decisions is through the application of academic content. Whatever textbook your professor uses in your sport communication course is filled with all kinds of theories and history that can lead to actual decision alternatives. One of the great things about the Case Method is the ability for students to take the course content they are learning and clearly apply that content to the decision-making process. We would recommend trying to find at least one decision alternative that clearly stems from your course readings. However, your professor may have other guidelines, so make sure you always follow your professor's guidelines.

Once you've created a list of possible alternatives, you really need to weed them down into a list of practical and realistic guidelines based on the context of the case. Here are some tips to consider when creating your final list of three decision alternatives.

Here are some helpful hints when creating and selecting decision alternatives:

- **Be Realistic!** First, and foremost, the decisions that you arrive at should be realistic given the context of a given case. While it may be fun to ship all of the annoying characters to the moon, there are no cases where that would be a realistic alternative. Instead, really think through what types of decisions you think the main character could make in a given case.
- **Avoid Overlap!** One problem that many new case analysts have is a problem with overlap. In other words, their decisions tend to overlap one another, making each decision fairly

indistinguishable from the next. The goal of writing three different possible alternatives is to have three different alternatives. So try to make sure that all of your alternatives are mutually exclusive.

• **Decisions Mandatory!** One copout that some people will try to use is just not to make a decision. Not making a decision is not allowable in a case-based class. You need to make a stand and really make a decision. While there are definitely some decisions that are better than others, not making a decision is generally going to get you nowhere in life.

• **Status Quo!** While not making a decision is not a viable decision-making tool, keeping the status quo can be a viable decision-making tool. There are some cases where not changing one's behavior or course of action can be appropriate. While we recommend you use this method of decision making sparingly, you can definitely argue that the status quo is better than other possible decision alternatives.

• **Don't Sandwich!** When we use the word "sandwich" here, we're talking about taking two really weak decisions and buffering the one decision you think is good with those two weak decisions. All three of the decision alternatives that you create for a given case should be strong and viable. While different decision alternatives may prove problematic when you evaluate them using your criteria, all of the decisions you create should be practical given the context of the case.

• **Think Implementation!** At some point the actors within a case will have to implement the decision you have selected. Think through any possible risks or obstacles that could interfere with selected decisions. If a decision is ultimately not pragmatic given the confines of the case, then it's probably not a viable decision.

While these six strategies will help you think through the alternatives you come up with, there is no single best way to arrive at your three decision alternatives.

Step Four – Review Decision Alternatives

Once you have created your list of decision alternatives, it's time to start evaluating those decision alternatives. First and foremost, we evaluate all of our decision alternatives using the decision criteria we selected prior to creating the decision alternatives. One reason why it is important to select your criteria first is because it prevents you from selecting criteria that specifically lead to one decision alternative. Think logically as you apply your criteria and really think through how each possible criterion either supports or doesn't support a given decision alternative. If you examine the Case Study Worksheet provided in Appendix A, you'll see that the various parts of analyzing the decision alternatives is broken down to help you take each criterion and see how it either supports or doesn't support each decision alternative.

Step Five – Select the Best Decision Alternative

Ultimately, you will select the decision alternative that you believe best supports the context of the case and is most supported by the decision criteria that you have selected. Once you've selected the criteria, then you need to start thinking about how the decision will actually play out as it is implemented. For our purposes, we broke down this section into two basic areas: goals and action steps.

Goals. The first step in the post decision selection process is to think through the ultimate goals of the decision. What are the basic goals or outcomes that you hope to achieve by implementing your decision alternative? Additionally, based on how you decided to measure your criteria, think about how you will determine if your goal is being met. In our sample case (Figure 3.1), if your goal is to ensure that you have customer satisfaction, how will you determine if the decision you make results in happier fans?

Action Steps. Most decisions do not happen in a vacuum and often require a series of short-term and long-term action steps to implement the decision fully. Ask yourself, "What short-term and long-term steps do you feel are necessary to implement completely your chosen decision alternative?" In the case example we've been evaluating in this chapter, a short-term step may be the actual decision on what to do with Sarah. A long-term step may be putting together a group to review and perhaps revise the current rules. Most decisions involve some level of long-term monitoring to ensure the overall effectiveness of the decision made.

CONCLUSION

In this chapter we have introduced you to the basic steps of implementing the Case Method. At first, the Case Method may seem a little clunky and hard to manage as you start evaluating cases and discussing the cases in your sport communication course. As with any new skill, learning how to evaluate and discuss cases takes time and effort. If you really work through the Case Method before, during, and after class, you will quickly see how important a formalized decision-making process is for all areas of the sport world and in your own life.

REFERENCES

[1] Gouran, D. S., & Hirokawa, R. Y. (1983). The role of communication in decision-making groups: A functional perspective. In M. S. Mander (Ed.), *Communication in transition: Issues and debate in current research* (pp. 168–185). New York: Praeger.

Gouran, D. S., & Hirokawa, R. Y. (1996). Functional theory and communication in decision-making and problem solving groups: An expanded view. In R. Y. Hirokawa & M. S. Poole (Eds.), *Communication and group decision making* (2nd ed., pp. 55–80). Thousand Oaks, CA: Sage.

[2] Mauffette-Leenders, L. A., Erskine, J. A., & Leenders, M. R. (2007). *Learning with cases* (4th ed.). London, Ontario, Canada: Richard Ivey School of Business.

[3] Phillips, P. P., & Phillips, J. (2005). Return on investment (ROI) basics. Alexandria, VA: ASTD Press, p. 1.

[4] McCroskey, J. C., & Teven, J. J. (1999). Goodwill: A reexamination of the construct and its measurement. *Communication Monographs*, 66(1), 90–103.

[5] Latham, G. P. (2007). *Work motivation: History, theory, research, and practice.* Thousand Oaks, CA: Sage.

[6] Berry, L. L., Mirabito, A. M., & Baun, W. B. (2010). What's the hard return on employee wellness programs? *Harvard Business Review, 88*(12), 104–112.

[7] Giacalone, R. A., & Jurkiewicz, C. L. (2003). Toward a science of workplace spirituality. In R. A. Giacalone & C. L. Jurkiewicz (Eds.), *Handbook of workplace spirituality and organizational performance* (pp. 3–28). Armonk, New York: M.E. Sharpe. (p. 8).

[8] Parhizgar, K. D., & Parhizgar, R. (2006). *Multicultural business ethics and global managerial moral reasoning.* Lanham, MD: University Press of America. (p. 77)

[9] Cherrington, J. O., & Cherrington, D. J. (1992). A menu of moral issues: One week in the life of the *Wall Street Journal. Journal of Business Ethics, 11*, 255–265.

[10] Redding, W. C. (1996). Ethics and the study of organizational communication: When will we wake up? In J. A. Jaksa & M. S. Pritchard (Eds.), *Responsible communication: Ethical issues in business, industry, and the professions* (pp. 17–40). Cresskill, NJ: Hampton Press.

[11] Gouran & Hirokawa (1983, 1996)

[12] Randrup, N. (2007). *The case method: Roadmap for how best to study, analyze and present cases.* Rodovre: Denmark: International Management Press.

PART I

RELATIONAL COMMUNICATION AND SPORT

INTRODUCTION

There are all kinds of relationships in sport. We might immediately think about coach-athlete relationships or athlete-to-athlete relationships, but there are so many more to consider. The cases in Part One revolve mostly around parent-child relationships when it comes to sport, but also include family communication in sport as well as athlete-to-athlete communication for those not on the same team. In Part Two, we will focus on team communication where cases involving coach-athlete communication and communication within a team abound.

There are many concerns when it comes to children engaged in sport. Injury certainly is one, but pressure and proper support of the child have become paramount in recent years. The "helicopter" parent is one that many coaches find themselves dealing with. This phenomenon is when the parent of a child is overly involved in the child's life. In the sport world, this means that the parent will often be complaining to a coach about their child's amount of play time and they might critique the coach's methods constantly. Another issue might be that the parent IS the coach of their child's team and thus is bombarded with other parents' wants for their children. Then, that coach might be accused of favoring his or her own child.

The blog *Changing the Game Project* explains that helicopter parents might be a reason why kids quit sports. In fact, 70% of children are dropping out of organized sports by the age of thirteen.[1] The number one reason why kids quit is because the sport is no longer fun. In her 2014 study, Amanda Visek says that children define "fun" as trying their best; being treated respectfully by coaches, parents, and teammates; and getting playing time.[2] The second highest reason why children quit a sport is because adults (either parents and/or coaches) are taking too much ownership of the experience by scrutinizing too much; focusing too much on winning; or not being encouraging, supportive, and respectful.[3] Thus, children become afraid to make mistakes, which leads to the game not being fun for them. The authors of the *Changing the Game Project* developed the blog and project to help keep youth sports fun and safe for kids. The authors of the blog argue that treating the kids with respect and supporting them for just making the effort to play the sport will go a long way in keeping children interested in the sport.[4] Various issues of parental support are addressed in the first three cases in this part of the book.

Another issue in relationships where a sport can interfere with relationships is when a member of a family becomes very engrossed in the sport as a fan and lets the watching of the sport dictate his or her life. Case Three illustrates this issue. Of course, violence is also an aspect of sport that can interfere with a relationship. There is a popular belief that violence toward women on Super Bowl Sunday increases every year by 40%.[5] In actuality, there is no solid evidence that Super Bowl Sunday does have higher reported incidences of domestic abuse.[6]

This is not to say that there are not acts of domestic violence involving the world of sport. There have been numerous recent incidents of famous athletes caught abusing their significant others. For instance, there is the case of Ray Rice, who was caught on video abusing his then fiancée, and now wife Janay Palmer, in an elevator in 2014. But not until recently has the leadership of any of the major leagues set up strict guidelines for how their league will address such cases. Before 2014, the sanctions were paltry at best. For instance, from 2000 to 2013, of the 84 NFL player arrests due to domestic violence, no player received more than a one-game suspension.[7] The NBA's labor contract states that a player convicted of a violent felony (such as domestic abuse) "is subject to a minimum of a 10-game suspension (which in an 82-game season is equivalent to a two-game ban in a 16-game NFL season).[8] The fact that such leniency is afforded to athletes no doubt contributes to the view of domestic violence as just "part of the game." Some players whose teammates were guilty of domestic abuse even state that the best thing they can do for the team is to "put it behind us. It's something that's not talked about."[9] Not talking about such issues can lead to complacency and acceptance of such violence. Case Seven gives you the chance to discuss issues of violence and sport and decide how this issue should be dealt with by those in the position to make changes.

Other issues concerning relationships in sport are those between two athletes. In Part Two, we will address issues surrounding communication on a sport team, but in this part, we have a case involving sportsmanship and communication with an opponent. Certainly sportsmanship is a topic that crops up in every sport endeavor. For instance, in 2014 a video made its way around the Internet of a boy who showed class after losing the final match in the Minnesota State High School Championships. Malik Stewart, a Blaine High School sophomore, knew that the opponent who just beat him had a father who was battling terminal cancer and was given only months to live. Instead of stalking off or leaving the mat showing signs of being upset that he lost, Stewart strode over to the opponent's father, shook his hand, congratulated him on his son's win and told him to "stay strong."[10]

Of course there are also stories of the opposite happening when an athlete or team does not show class and sportsmanship during an athletic event. Perhaps one of the more notorious incidents is when boxer Mike Tyson bit a chunk out of his opponent's (Evander Holyfield) ear in the third round of the 1997 heavy weight rematch when Tyson felt he was losing.[11] Certainly, most unsportsmanlike communication does not take place in this kind of profound nonverbal way. But many a sporting match is rife with foul language and often bouts of more physical violence. In some sports, such as hockey, the violence is almost expected and many fans consider a game without fights as less of a game. Sports broadcasters will even begin to call the shots as play erupts into a fight. Case Five deals with a lighter side of sportsmanship, looking at the ethics of calling fouls on the tennis court, but any time ethics and properly following rules of the game is involved, a game can slide into unsportsmanlike conduct by any participant (whether athlete, coach, or spectator).

As you read and analyze the cases in Part One, remember to continually consider the interpersonal communication and other relational communication issues that crop up. Sport can have a profound effect on relationships. Sometimes it is what brings people together; other times it can tear people apart. Many people think of sport as "just a game;" to others it is part of their livelihood or a very important part of their life in general and to consider it "just a game" with no real importance is demeaning to those whose lives revolve around it. Then again, for those who do not have much or any involvement in sport, to put so much emphasis on athletics may seem demeaning to life in general. These are topics that you will be able to discuss as you work with the cases in Part One.

Other relational communication concepts, theories, and models to consider as you review these cases include:

- Family socialization model,
- Parental control,
- Sports rage,
- Verbal and nonverbal communication behaviors,
- Self-disclosure and closeness,
- Empathy,
- and cohesion

REFERENCES

[1] Changing the Game Project, (n.d.). Why kids quit sports. Retrieved from http://changingthe gameproject.com/why-kids-quit-sports/

[2] Visek, A.J., Achrati, S.M., Mannix, H., McDonnell, K., Harris, B.S., DiPietro, L. (2015) The fun integration theory: Toward sustaining children and adolescents sport participation. Journal of Physical Activity & Health, 12(3), 424–33.

[3] Changing the Game Project, (n.d.).

[4] Ibid.

[5] Gorov, Lynda. (29 January 1993). Activists: Abused women at risk on Super Sunday. *The Boston Globe.* (Metro; p. 13).

[6] Gantz, W. et al. (2006). Televised NFL games, the family, and domestic violence. In Raney, A. A. (Ed). *Handbook of sports and media.* Mahwah, NJ: Lawrence Erlbaum Associates, pp. 365–381.

[7] Jones, L. H. (29 November 2013). One year later, Belcher tragedy still shakes NFL. *USA Today.* Retrieved from http://www.usatoday.com/story/sports/nfl/2013/11/29/nfl-chiefs-jovan-belcher-kasandra-perkins-tragedy-anniversary-troy-vincent/3785307/

[8] Associated Press, (19 September 2014). MLB, union meet to establish new domestic violence guidelines. *Fox Sports.* Retrieved from http://www.foxsports.com/nfl/story/mlb-addressing-domestic-violence-issues-after-nfl-problems-091914.

[9] Jones, L. H. (29 November 2013). One year later, Belcher tragedy still shakes NFL. *USA Today.* Retrieved from http://www.usatoday.com/story/sports/nfl/2013/11/29/nfl-chiefs-jovan-belcher-kasandra-perkins-tragedy-anniversary-troy-vincent/3785307/

[10] Seavert, L. (7 March 2014). Wrestler loses match but moves crowd with kind act. NBC affiliate KARE 11. Retrieved from http://www.kare11.com/story/news/local/2014/03/06/mitchell-mckee-father-cancer-malik-steward-wrestling-state-championship/6145249/

[11] History.com (n.d.) This day in history. Retrieved from http://www.history.com/this-day-in-history/mike-tyson-bites-ear

VOICE OF A PRO

Kevin Hartman
Color Analyst for Orlando City Soccer Club and Retired Major League Soccer Goalkeeper

Photo courtesy of Kevin Hartman

Being a good teammate is very similar to being a good friend except that you have the convenience of time to make things work. Over a season, you go through successes and failures together and will share quite a few experiences. Those are important building blocks within relationships. As I grew as a professional, I realized that the closer that I was with my teammates, the more willing they were to help me achieve the work that I knew needed to get done. I had learned quite a few valuable lessons that, if properly relayed, could help the entire group become more successful.

Sometimes the information that I communicated to teammates involved running more, putting someone's body in front of the ball, or defending an oversized opponent. The tasks weren't easy and if my teammates didn't trust me like a close friend they wouldn't do it. However, when they trusted me and found success, it reinforced an incredible bond. Some quick suggestions for being a good teammate would be going out of your way for others, open yourself up, be honest, genuinely care about others, and be patient while the relationship grows.

Many of the athletes who play at the collegiate level or higher have a very unique perspective on things, and they certainly may not have the same point of view as you do. It's important that you consider that if you hope to be effective. As a professional, I remember getting extremely irate about an 18-year-old Colombian that the team had just spent a massive amount of money on. He was always late and was never very apologetic. Here's a guy that I'll need to go to battle with on Saturday night in front of 60,000 angry fans and I can't even count on him to show up to training. It turns out that he had grown up very poor in a South American country and was living alone for the first time in his life. He had no idea what an alarm clock was and certainly had no idea how to use one. It turns out that at 6:30 PM every night his alarm clock was going off instead of 6:30 AM. As soon as someone cared enough to go to his house to sort out the problem, he was fine. He's become an excellent player within the league and will probably go on to make millions of dollars in a European league.

With that said, many athletes kept their grades up through high school and are extremely good with time management. They would hate to be lumped into the same group as the struggling pro from Colombia. If you are a player, coach, or involved with players in some way, take each interaction on its own and remember these athletes often have had totally different life experiences than the rest of the population.

Now, dealing with reporters is another story. I've been extremely lucky from the time that I was in college to be able to engage with some excellent reporters. I always knew what the good "nuggets" were and would share them with the reporters whom I respected the most. The interviews varied as the relationships did. If I was infuriated, I'd vent to reporters whom I trusted, and even told them to make sure that I didn't come off as over the top. They usually did. They would make sure that the point got across, but they might edit things that I would have to answer to management about. I didn't rely on their better judgment and was actually prepared to stand behind the words that came out of my mouth; however, it was nice having some close acquaintances in the press.

For those students who want to be sport reporters, I'd suggest devoting enough time to learning about the game or the person with whom you're doing the interview to be able to come off as sincere. As the playoffs drew to a close and games got bigger, the interviews became more and more awkward as it became obvious that some reporters had no clue what soccer was or how it was played.

I always had a unique perspective when it came to playing sports. I loved playing the game, but it was extremely personal and very stressful. Luckily, my parents and my family were extremely supportive and at times I, unfortunately, was way too dismissive of them. I was a self-evaluator and a perfectionist. They would tell me that I had a great game but I would pick the game apart describing minute details about what had gone wrong and what could have been better. Now that I'm a parent, I worry about the stress that my daughters might play under. I tell them how much that I love watching them play and how proud I am to see them battling. I talk to them about goal setting, perseverance, and the fact that the best things in life aren't easily achieved. Finally, I tell them to enjoy it and that I'll always believe in them.

Kevin Hartman is one of the most decorated players in Major League Soccer history and is the only player in MLS history to play and start over 400 regular season matches. He's also the holder of the all-time record for shutouts with 112.

Drafted by the LA Galaxy in the third round in 1997, the former UCLA standout appeared in eight games for the MLS club in his rookie season, recording three shutouts.

From 1997-06 Hartman played 243 games for the Galaxy winning two US Open Cups and two MLS Cups. He joined Kansas City in 2007, moving to Dallas in 2010. He retired as a member of the New York Red Bulls in 2013. He left the MLS with the record for most victories at 179.

Overall, the 14-time MLS Cup Playoffs participant amassed a 180-143-89 regular-season record and a 1.21 goals against average. Hartman earned five caps for the US national team.

In retirement he has been in the broadcast booth for FC Dallas and now for the Orlando City SC. In addition, he is the Technical Director/Director of Goalkeeping at the IMG Academy, an elite youth sport training school in Florida.

CASE 1: PARENTS MAKE THE BEST AND WORST COACHES

Taylor Wilson
Clemson University

John Spinda
Clemson University

ABSTRACT

Some parents think they are coaches, and then some parents are coaches. This case study examines a specific instance of a parent coaching his own child and presents the problems that accompany that situation. As the head coach of the Ellerton Trojans football team, Mike Rollins coached his son, Brent, and, during their time on the team together, Mike not only acted as Brent's coach, but his parent as well, blurring the lines between the two roles. The dilemma arises when one asks, is it fair? Should a parent be allowed to coach his or her own child? This type of situation could be banned, but when parents account for a large percentage of coaches, what would that mean for sports? It would definitely change things, but many wonder if it would be worth it.

***

BACKGROUND

Parental involvement on the sidelines of youth, collegiate, even professional sporting events has been posing problems for years, but what if the parent is also the coach? This kind of situation is often evident in youth sports where parents often serve in leadership roles. However, this sort of situation can occur at the higher levels of sports, and in this specific case, at the high school level. The problems that may present themselves when a coach is a parent of a team member are many. The most common is special treatment of the child, which may include harsher treatment of the child or more favorable treatment. Other problems may include bias toward a child's friends or foes, conflicts with other parents, or even volatility in the home life of the parent coach and child athlete. How can one go about fixing these problems without prohibiting parents from being coaches of teams where their children are members?

WHAT IS OR IS NOT FAIR?

As the sun beat down on a hot, muggy summer afternoon in Northern Louisiana, Coach Rollins wiped the sweat from his brow and barked in his trademark gruff tone: "Who wants to be the next Ellerton legend? Who wants to play in an All-America Bowl game and go play for a top-10 team in college? This is where it happens gentlemen! Right here, right now!" The high school boys, gassed from two-a-day workouts in the intense summer swelter, ceased their mutters and quiet complaints and quickly regained their laser-sharp focus on practicing to be the one who resoundingly answered their coach's questions. They knew Coach Mike Rollins was right. After all, he was a successful wide receiver at Georgia in his playing days and had been leading high school teams for 25 years, including the Ellerton Trojans for past 12 years. These players all believed they would be the ones who added their legacies to the massive glass case at the front of the school. The case that housed the four state championships in seven tries, as well as photos of the numerous successful college players from Alabama, Georgia, and other big time programs that were once Ellerton Trojans just like them, grinding through the rigorous summer days: Five days a week, practice from 7:00 AM to noon, then again from 1:00 to 6:00, followed a team dinner and film study to cap off the night.

Although Coach Rollins's harsh regimens had forged Ellerton into one of the best football programs in the nation, it had also created an air of concern and ridicule among many parents. Joan Gardner, mother of starting quarterback Chase Gardner, had been especially worried. "I feel like I don't even know my boy anymore" Joan told a close friend as her lip trembled, trying to hold back tears of frustration. "We can't even go on a vacation…and he'll be going to college soon." Joan's best efforts were futile, as she burst into tears. After composing herself, she continued: "Thank you for hearing me out. I can't tell my husband or people at the high school about my worries. They just tell me how 'lucky' I am that Chase is the Trojans' starting QB and that he'll have his choice of college scholarships or about the seven state title appearances Coach Rollins has. But they just don't know how tough it is for us, especially when he gets in his face and berates him over every little mistake. I can only imagine what life is like for poor Brent."

Brent Rollins was one of Mike and Katherine (Lindburg) Rollins's children. A 17-year-old senior, Brent was neither especially outspoken nor quiet. He told Chad Meeks, a close friend on the team, "I just don't want people to think I am a starter or trying to lead because I am the 'coach's son.' I just want to be another guy on the team; it's really tough." He was the starting wide receiver, just like his father was many years earlier, and was known as an above-average player. Chad responded, "Nah man, no one thinks that at all! You are pretty awesome at WR! I know your dad gives you a hard time, but he does that to all of us. Just look at his track record, we all leave here as really strong students and players. I know he can be like a junkyard dog, but he just wants to prepare us all for the future."

All throughout Brent's previous years on the team and as a current senior, there had been speculation about unfair treatment of Brent by Coach Mike. However, most dismissed the perception of special treatment simply because of the dynamic of their relationship, and mostly because no one had a problem with the record of the team. Yet, the speculation had come to a head during Brent's senior season.

It was not uncommon for players at different positions to be given specific film to watch and analyze, so when Coach Rollins gave Brent extra footage to review, there was no problem. As the season started, Brent was recognized as one of the top players on the team when compared to the previous years. While Brent had always been a good player, in past years he was not known to be one of the breakout stars and team leaders. However, when this year's season started, the team named Brent as a captain. "What!" exclaimed starting QB Chase Gardner to his group of friends after the captains were named before the season opener. "I know Brent is a decent player, but as the QB, I am supposed to be the team leader! Why in the hell else did I give up my life the past three years? This sucks!"

Once the season got underway, practices became more hostile and players noticed a dynamic change between coach and son. During practices, Coach Rollins began screaming at Brent, more than usual, and was even seen pushing or shoving Brent by his facemask and shoulder pads on occasion. Brent's good friend Chad said that during practice a few weeks ago, he heard Coach Rollins yell at Brent saying, "What are you doing? Don't you remember what we practiced?" This seemed a bit puzzling, *because the team practices together right*, thought Chad. He decided to talk to Brent after practice and make sure everything was all right. "I am cool man, thanks for asking," said Brent. "You know my old man, such a drill sergeant," looking at the floor stoically. "You know he's been having me do extra drills at home too, that's nuts, isn't it?" Although it's common for players at Ellerton to develop their own skills away from practice it was then realized that technically Brent was receiving extra practice time and one-on-one opportunities with the coach that other players weren't. While this may not seem like a big deal, *is it truly fair*? This was the question that some teammates began to ask themselves once word spread through the grapevine about what was going on behind the scenes with Coach Rollins and Brent.

As the clock expired on a cold, soggy November night, the towels over the players' heads and dejected faces said it all; the Trojans' valiant effort had fallen short and they had lost in the state finals. Despite losing, Brent Rollins was named game MVP for his four touchdown receptions. The Ellerton High School football awards banquet was slated to take place soon, and parents of other team members had become increasingly frustrated with the reports of Coach Rollins's treatment of his son during the year, both regarding the aggressive physical contact and also the additional film study. A father of another wide receiver shook his head and quipped, "maybe if coach cared as much about my boy, he would have had four touchdowns last week." Despite these frustrations, most were still considering this season a great success, and the sting of the championship loss appeared to dwindle with each day as the team, school, and the parents realized what was accomplished on the field of play.

The night of the team banquet had a celebratory feel. "Finally, Chase and his teammates get to...you know, be high school kids again," remarked Joan Gardner to another parent, forcing a smile. Another parent at the table said, "I really don't want to jinx it, but with the stats and the season Chase had, there is no way he isn't the team's most valuable player" (MVP). After dessert, the result of the MVP award seemed anticlimactic as the Emcee went to the podium. "Now, for our final award of the night, the 2006 Ellerton Trojans' MVP award goes to… Brent Rollins!" The reaction was a mix of polite applause and stunned faces, with the most perplexed faces being those in the Gardner family. "Let's get out of here," said Chase to his parents, as the seething, bright red anger began to show in his face.

At Ellerton, each of the end-of-the-year awards is selected by a combination of team members and coaches; the coaches' decision having more pull than the team's. Another important note is that the quarterback almost always receives the MVP award since other special awards are geared more toward other positions. Chase had an exceptional season, ranking in the top three quarterbacks in the state, and signed a letter of intent to play quarterback at the University of Alabama. It was known that almost the entire team had voted for Chase to win, even if simply for the fact the quarterback usually won the award. That is when the award seemed obvious evidence of Mike's favoritism toward his son. However, when questioned about the recipient, most coaches explained that Brent won fair and square after their votes were counted as well.

As mentioned before, when parents are coaches, they may display both harsher and better treatment of their child athlete. Mike was said to have done both and even showed some bias toward Brent's closer friends. Many accounts of what unfolded in that final year came from fellow teammates and their parents. The dilemma stems from the fact that, although Mike may have done the accused behaviors, his credentials as a coach kept him sitting comfortable in his head coaching position. Another factor is that there are no school district rules regarding parents as coaches, and, at the time of his hiring, Mike Rollins was the best fit for the program. The other coaches did not know that Brent would eventually come up through the football program under his father, and it is likely that it would not have changed their decision if they had known. It is difficult to separate what is appropriate for a father and son and what is appropriate for an athlete and coach when they are one and the same.

CONCLUSION

Although there may be many solutions to the problem, there are none that will fully correct the problem without posing other obstacles. For example, the team could prohibit parents from coaching their own children, but either Mike or Brent would have been unable to coach or play. With Mike's credentials it is illogical not to let him coach simply because his son is on the team. If there were rules about parents coaching their own children, almost all youth teams and even some high school and collegiate teams would not have their current coaches. Coach Rollins could have also been asked not to give outside help to Brent at home, but then Brent would be at a disadvantage, because other teammates would have still been allowed to practice with their parents even though they were not coaches. Another solution could be to allow all football players the opportunity for one-on-ones with the coach, but time-wise, that would not be logical and perhaps not even possible. So what should be done? Do you tell a father not to coach his son or to treat him like he would treat an athlete whom he did not know?

Because instances like the one examined in this case are so common in sports, it is hard to know what the right choice is. Given the facts, it may sound like something you have heard of before. If parents are banned from coaching their own children, youth sports could become a completely different game, pun intended. Although some parents may think they are coaches, sometimes they might actually be the coach, and the relationship between parent and child may blur the lines of what should or should not be done.

DISCUSSION QUESTIONS

1. If you were a parent of an athlete on this team, what communication strategies would you use in a face-to-face situation with Coach Rollins?
2. What role should Brent have in solving this difficult situation? Should he have accepted the MVP award if he believed Chase was more deserving?
3. What kind of disclaimers should coaches have to make regarding their children in sport? Is it discriminatory not to hire a coach based simply on him or her having an eligible child in the future?

KEY TERMS

Coaching-athlete relationships, Parent-athlete relationships, Face-saving

CASE 2: THE "HELICOPTER" PARENT AND COLLEGE ATHLETIC DISAPPOINTMENT

Chuka Onwumechili
Howard University

Joanna Jenkins
Howard University

ABSTRACT

This case focuses on relational communication in sport and involves a "helicopter" parent, Alicia, who hovers over her son and pressures him to be a successful basketball player from high school to college at State University. In college, Alicia's son, Esteban, struggles to adjust to the "Old School coach," Mr. Foothead, who reduces Esteban's minutes on the court. Eventually, Esteban walks off the team after not playing in an important game against State University's rival, Premier College. Now, both Esteban and Alicia must decide what is next.

***

"I can't stand this anymore," Esteban says sharply to Cedric.

"I work my behind off in practice, I do all Coach has asked and yet he won't play me. . . . I am done with this," he adds.

Cedric responds, "Es, you need to calm down, bro"

"Why do I have to do that? I practiced so hard and I waited for today and yet all I get is this . . . Man, it hurts baaad" Esteban goes on.

Esteban walks off abruptly, leaving Cedric behind. *Coach Foothead is really crazy. He knew I wanted to play. This was the biggest game, against my friends at Premier College and yet he sat me all game. Enough is enough. I will text my mother and let her know what happened.*

***

Though Esteban now feels that his time at State University is over, he thinks about why he is at State in the first place. His mind wanders to his famous half-court shot against a rival school with four seconds remaining in regulation. After that, Esteban became one of the most sought-after recruits from high school. During those days, it was clear that the years of hard

49

work and dedication paid off. Esteban started playing basketball in the fifth grade and was always one of the biggest and strongest males among his peers. It was no surprise that Esteban earned a basketball scholarship to State University near his hometown, Sharptown.

State University, nicknamed "The Cyclone," is a perennial basketball power with top athletes from both in and out of state. The School is just 20 miles from Esteban's home. Esteban does not find State University's recruitment particularly appealing. He is aware of the university's basketball legacy. He considers some of the facilities outdated and the gym is not as large as some others that he saw during recruiting visits to other universities. Importantly, Coach Foothead never bothered to visit his home, unlike other coaches. Coach Foothead also appeared less enamored with Esteban's high school basketball achievements.

Though Esteban agreed to attend State University, he prefers Premier College where three of his friends attend. One of them, Chris Smalls, has been a friend since eighth grade and both played for the same high school. The others – Isaiah and Jewel – are friends from travel teams. Esteban wishes that they all were on a college team together – preferably the Premier College "Eagles." *That really would be exciting,* he thinks. He recalls a recent conversation with Chris:

> "We can make the Eagles one of the best teams in the country and become No. 1 in the rankings," Esteban told Chris.

> "Yes, that will be cool," Chris replied.

> Alicia, however, thought otherwise.

Esteban was widely recruited by several schools but he, at the behest of his mother, chose State University because of the school's top basketball program. At State University, Esteban joined several top athletes who all are determined to gain the visibility that will lead them to professional basketball, just as Alicia wishes for her son.

Esteban's journey to the basketball elite is partly due to his talent, but there is no question that it is also because of the involvement of his mother, Alicia. While Esteban is reserved and taciturn, Alicia is different. She is upfront with her communication style and believes that confrontation brings fulfilling results. Esteban's choice of interaction is nonconfrontational and he expects his sport performance to be easily recognized. Alicia, a single parent, is always particular about Esteban's athletic development. Often, it appears that Alicia wants to represent all that Esteban's father never did for him. Alicia gave birth to Esteban while a senior at the Davidson College in Sharptown. She was only 22 years old then and Esteban's father, Alfonso, was 24 and a college dropout whose parents migrated from Mexico. Alfonso left Alicia right after Esteban's birth and he never turned back.

Alicia, with the help of her mother Gabriella, raised Esteban. They had little means and lived in a studio in the low-income neighborhood of the town. Alicia works very hard to raise Esteban. Alicia acts the role of mother and father to Esteban. She is determined to fill a void that should have been filled by Alfonso. She put Esteban in the best schools and ensured that he played in the top travel teams in their hometown, Sharptown.

Sharptown is a growing city next to two smaller towns of Lovetville and Lamston. It has one major college and two community colleges. But these institutions are not known for top sports performances. They focus on meeting local learning needs.

Alicia wants more for her son in Sharptown. Beyond the classroom, Esteban's mother, Alicia, was coach of Esteban's recreational team at the town's Boys' and Girls' clubs. That provided Esteban extra work and preparation both at home on the driveway hoop and then attention on the practice court. She was not bashful in giving him the most minutes on the team. After all, no other parent complained. Esteban was, even then, the biggest boy on the team and used his strength and height to overpower other kids and win most games for his recreational team. But, at times, Esteban resented his mother's bearish behavior as his coach. In one of the games, her behavior particularly irked Esteban:

"Son, get stuck in! You are the biggest kid out there, prove it and stop whining!" Alicia screamed.

"I am trying my best," Esteban responded.

"Nah, you have to do more," Alicia retorted.

"Okay, Okay!" Esteban quietly responded while thinking, *She would never understand. I feel that I should respond to her and let out exactly how I feel.* But he decided against it. Instead, he held it in but let her know with his nonverbal reactions, which included not looking her way and simply ignoring her even when she continued to call out at him to listen.

He was on travel teams while in high school and grew to about 6 feet 8 inches tall with a developed upper body, which enabled him to dominate underneath the basket. Esteban also demonstrated a variety of skilled moves, as he could dribble the ball like a point guard and could shoot it from distance. Most of those skills he learned from playing on several travel teams under former professional basketball players. The coaches easily noticed Esteban as he was taller than most of the other players who trained under the coaches and he was quick and skilled. Importantly, Esteban followed directives from the coaches. One of his travel-team coaches, Daniel Southern, once said about Esteban, "He is a good kid. You do not have to worry about him. Many of his friends would often play to the crowds and to their friends on the stands, but Esteban is different . . . he follows the game plan and we can always rely on him." Another coach, Robert Fields, complimented Esteban often and told others, "That kid (Esteban) will go places . . . boy, he is a quick learner. You only have to tell him once and he gets it. I wish I had a team full of kids like him, instead of some of the knuckleheads that come through here." Esteban became a coach's dream and was usually presented as an example for others on the court. However, the unwritten rule at the recreational and travel-team levels is to give each player time on the court. Thus, coaches would prefer to allocate playing minutes to each player on their roster, but the pressure from Esteban's mother always meant that Esteban was on the court for longer than the coaches would like.

"You know, I have to give other kids a chance to play. I have other parents breathing down my neck about playing time after they have paid club fees," Mr. Fields once informed Alicia.

"You and I know that everyone wants to win. I am only asking that you have Esteban on the court as he presents our team with the best chance to win and nothing else," Alicia said.

"It is not that I do not want to win but there is some balance required," said Mr. Fields. Though Mr. Fields knew in his mind that *Alicia was right*.

"Well, these same parents will complain if we lose. It is your choice," she reminded Mr. Fields.

"Okay, I heard you," Mr. Fields said as he walked away from further conversation. Mr. Fields and Esteban's other coaches knew they benefitted because Esteban's presence on the court often ensured victories. But they did not particularly like Alicia reminding them of Esteban's value.

USING SOCIAL MEDIA

During Esteban's high school years, Alicia used social media to publicize her son's athletic performance. She created Facebook and YouTube accounts for this purpose. The Facebook page focused on Esteban's basketball achievements with video highlights of his best plays. Periodically, Esteban posted updates on his Facebook page to show his volunteering activities and his social participation in school. In high school, social activities are numerous and he was a popular student involved in several of those activities. He made brief videos and took still photographs of most of his activities and subsequently posted them on Facebook. He also volunteered at the town library, retirement home, and his local church. He also, briefly, reported those activities with pictures on his Facebook page. In addition, his mother posted videos on YouTube and periodically texted the top college coaches extoling Esteban's qualities. These activities attracted the attention of several college coaches. Importantly, they were coaches from some of the top basketball colleges in the country.

The decision to include Esteban's non-basketball activities on Facebook proved important as several recruiters cited it and spoke to Esteban about those activities. It made Esteban appear special, an athlete with some social and community commitment. Esteban, though not particularly voluble, was charming during recruitment interviews. He was not stuck up about his talent and appeared genuinely concerned about academics and other college activities. One of the schools that recruited Esteban was Alpha University, which was more than 250 miles away from Sharptown. The head coach was a very enthusiastic and humorous man, Esteban noticed. The coach talked about his plans for Alpha, a rising program. Esteban's visit to the university was memorable. He liked various entertainment events he attended in company of Alpha University recruitment guides and he loved the housing for sports teams and the expansive gym in the athletic center. However, Alicia pointed out to Esteban that "Alpha is just too far out" and she would not be able to attend most of his games. There were other schools that Esteban also liked. It seemed that he could choose to attend any of the colleges that recruited him. He had the grades and the colleges loved him for both his talent and other qualities.

But, Alicia wanted more to satisfy her own interest in seeing Esteban attend college close to home. She always wanted Esteban close by. Having him nearby would provide her with a short distance to travel in order to see him and Esteban could conveniently come home whenever it pleased him. Moreover, there were several top basketball teams at nearby colleges. There was the perennial winner, State University, in Lovetville and a rising team at Premier College that was also nearby. However, it was State University and its basketball legacy that Alicia preferred. She took steps to ensure that State University recruited Esteban by steering him toward William Foothead, the aging coach of State University in Lovetville, a neighboring town.

STATE UNIVERSITY AND CHALLENGES

The game against Premier College is a culmination of Esteban's problems. His coach, Mr. William Foothead, is a man from the "Old School" who is conservative, works the players hard and has a "mind of his own." He likes control and wants everyone else to sit back and listen. They have to work much harder and prove that they are worth their scholarship spots. The fitness workout is grueling and the freshmen struggle to keep up. Esteban keeps pushing himself as he does not want to become Coach Foothead's favorite target at practices. Mr. Foothead is legendary for "giving it" (i.e., making life difficult) to players that he believes are unfit or without the perseverance to "suck it up." For him, a Cyclone has to be the fittest basketball player willing to work all day without a breather. His communication is brash and he does not take kindly to challenges to his authority. Right at the first practice, he warned players that high school records and notoriety mean very little at State.

"You are here at the big stage. No more Little League, no more small boy plays or attitudes," he said.

"You may have been a big fish in a small pond, I don't care! You do as I say or you won't be here very long!" he added.

Esteban thought about this and concluded: *I just have to step up my game. I know I can play with these guys. I just hope coach will give me an honest chance.*

The Cyclone's starting center is a junior, David Stone, an inch shorter than Esteban. He is the fittest Cyclone and is always in the gym working out. David is not much of a scorer but he is one of the most aggressive players on the team and the team often rallies around him in the locker room. He is likeable and motivates everyone to give their best. Coach Foothead often relies on Stone to "get the team in line" during difficult times. As Foothead often says to the team, "You guys can go as far as David will take you. You need to listen to him if you won't listen to me." In reality, David's team talks have to be first approved by Mr. Foothead who rules roughshod over everyone including David.

Esteban's play does not stand out as it did at the lower levels but at practices he often scores more easily than David, runs the court better, and defends just as aggressively as David. However, his playing time dwindles steadily as the coach prefers David and relies on him. Esteban is depressed and feels that Mr. Foothead does not like him and that his racial background may have something to do with it. After all, he is not considered White and his only real friend on the team is an African American point guard, Cedric Littleton, who also is struggling for playing time. Coach Foothead regards freshmen players as error prone, unsure of plays, and needing to become physically mature. Esteban and Cedric bear most of Coach Foothead's ire.

To Foothead, Cedric is "not disciplined and is error prone" and Esteban "improvises a lot and relies on raw talent." He told both of them:

"To play regularly for the Cyclones, you must follow my instructions, you must become better."

"Cedric, this isn't Little League. You need to quit giving the ball up to the other team. Use your eyes! If you need contact lenses then get some!"

For Esteban, Coach Foothead also has his choice words:

"Esteban or whatever your name is, this is team ball, son! It ain't one-and-one! Give the ball to the open man or I'll have you running sprints"

"I can't keep repeating myself. If you want to play here then you need to compete the way that I want. I just can't keep trying to get through to your head, son"

Cedric was Esteban's confidant and they frequently discuss Coach Foothead's decisions.

"It's all about race," Cedric tells Esteban. That is how Cedric feels about the duo's predicament under Coach Foothead and he feels comfortable sharing this with his friend, Esteban.

"Coach is still living in the 1960s. Even his game is old. Why does he run slow plays with his guards? Cedric questions.

"Yes, his game is Old School," Esteban agrees.

"If I am on the court, the team is lightning fast and I can get you the ball as we always do in practice and you can work down low with the hook shots. Coach just does not get it," Cedric adds.

"I just do not understand it, I outplay Dave in practice each day and yet I am the one who sits on the bench on game day. It is annoying. I am getting tired of all this. Coach should have long retired," Esteban says.

When alone, Esteban often wonders whether it was the right decision to attend State University. He tells himself, *I could have been at Premier with my buddies… Maybe the coach would have been more likeable.* He feels that the game is no longer enjoyable, at least for him. Moreover, his friends often tell him about the locker room climate at Premier, how happy the boys are and how exciting their game is to watch. He longs for it now. He also remembers that it is not his choice to attend State University but that of his mother and it hurts more at this thought. Despite these feelings, Esteban is confused as he still believes his mother is his best counselor.

But it is not just Esteban, Cedric, and their teammates who wonder about some of Mr. Foothead's decisions; the local media and alumni also inquire about them. During the season, the *Sharptown News Weekly* interviewed Coach Foothead. The reporter wanted to find out why the new recruit, Esteban Cruz, is not starting in spite of the fact that Cruz plays well when he is on the court. Mr. Foothead bristles, "I am the coach here! A lot of times you newspapermen have no clue about how a team is built. First, it is a team and not just a collection of individuals and basketball involves a lot of activities, which, by the way, include defending

Table I Statistical Table for Varsity Players at State

Player	GP	Mins.	PPG	RPG	APG	SPG	BPG	TPG	FG%	FT%	3P%
David Stone	16	36.6	6.0	8.7	0.2	0.1	2.4	2.2	.45	.65	0.0
Jerry Graham	16	34.0	16.2	3.2	1.3	0.6	0.2	1.8	.46	.82	.41
John Langston	16	33.4	14.8	3.0	4.2	0.5	0.1	2.9	.41	.78	.33
Bill Coker	14	28.9	9.4	6.7	2.3	0.9	0.3	1.3	.38	.67	.34
Alf Lamb	16	27.0	8.5	1.7	1.8	1.5	0.1	1.9	.37	.59	.27
Esteban Cruz	10	13.7	6.8	4.2	1.1	0.2	0.4	0.3	.56	.70	0.0
Cedric Wiley	8	2.6	0.2	0.1	0.2	0.3	0.0	0.1	.39	.69	0.0

....

GP: Games played　　　Mins: Minutes per game　　PPG: Points per game　　RPG: Rebounds per game
APG: Assists per game　　SPG: Steals per game　　BPG: Blocks per game　　TPG: Turnover per game
FG%: Field Goal %　　　FT%: Free Throw %　　　3P%: Three point %

and blocking shots. It is not all about shooting and scoring. I have experienced players who are doing the little things and they deserve to start. I would appreciate that you guys respect my coaching decisions and I have won enough here to deserve respect." But the team's statistical table demonstrates otherwise (Table 1). Mr. Foothead stands up from his chair and walks tensely around the room before suddenly stopping and starring at the reporter. He then adds, "Mr. Cruz is an up-and-coming player who has several good years ahead of him. He will be good but right now he is not doing enough to start." He then waves dismissively at the reporter as he walks away. Coach Foothead is not amused by the newspaper inquiry. He feels that the *News Weekly* is simply looking for cheap stories to sell papers and thus has contrived a controversy that is nonexistent.

In any case, the reality is that alumni and boosters are increasingly dissatisfied with Coach Foothead's basketball program at State. One booster threatens to reduce his financial support for the program if changes are not made. He tells the *News Weekly*, "Coach Foothead is a legend alright. However, eras do come to an end and I think it's time to think of a new guy." He is expressing sentiments shared by other boosters and alumni who think that State University could do much better under a new and younger coach. In fact, there was a failed campaign to replace him barely a year ago when a highly regarded recruit transferred from the program after his freshman year.

***

Esteban frequently sends texts to Alicia complaining about Coach Foothead. Alicia, miffed by Esteban's lack of playing time, turns to texting Coach Foothead and complaining. Her texts inform the coach that it is not just her wondering about Esteban not starting. She cites the story in the newspaper and adds that the town is probably wondering about the same thing. In another text she writes: "Bill, I know you are ignoring me. . . I coached before. . . Just do the right thing." Coach Foothead is livid but decides not to respond to the texts and instead he becomes harder on Esteban at practices. He concludes that there is a conspiracy going on among some parents, alumni, and boosters. He will never give in and watch them have the last laugh. In his 25 years of coaching at the university, no parent challenged his management of the basketball team as Esteban's mother is doing. In fact, no university administrator, including the athletic director, has ever done that. This drives him to being defensive and he takes it out on Esteban at practices.

"Hey, kid!" he screams at Esteban.

"What exactly are you doing there? Don't you realize you have to set a stronger screen than that...you have to be a man real fast. . . Get it together because if you won't work hard, then there are no minutes," he adds.

"Coach, you told me not to move on a screen" Esteban reminds his coach.

"So? Use your head, young man," Coach Foothead adds.

Esteban decides not to talk back but continues to work as hard as he can. However, he soon realizes that the coach is getting on him more and more. It is no longer fun.

***

That Esteban now thinks of quitting State University stems from his difficulties with Coach Foothead at practices. Importantly, he feels he deserves to play in the game against Premier College. The situation is tense and becomes worse after the game. Esteban trained very hard and long, spending extra hours in the gym with Cedric. In fact, most of the Cyclones are psyched for the game and several are also in the gym daily before the game. This is a big game, both Esteban and Cedric agree. Even though they are not expecting Coach Foothead to start any one of them, they both expect to play. At least, they want to. The game is also the talk of Lovetville and surrounding towns including Sharptown. Premier College is always a rival but, more recently, the Cyclones have won more than they lost to the Eagles. However, the Premier College Eagles have two freshmen who are starting and the team has lost only once before the game against the Cyclones. One of the freshmen, Isaiah Newcomb, is Esteban's former teammate on a travel team. He calls Esteban two days before the game to talk.

"Look, we are coming to your campus to make a statement . . . are you guys going to stand up or run away?" Isaiah asks jokingly.

"Well, you guys will find out. I just hope there will be no crybabies," Esteban retorts.

As the conversation progresses, Isaiah asks why Esteban is not starting and Esteban has to think quickly and replies:

"It is the coach's decision and I think I am getting to the point where I will start but I am waiting and I hope it will happen soon," Esteban says. But deep inside he thinks, *I am really upset with my coach. He really does not like me and may not give me a chance to start as long as David is still on the team.* That saddens him but he is not about to share his grief with Isaiah.

Sharptown News Weekly publishes a preview of the game and interviews alumni of both schools. State University alumni often speak about their school's basketball legacy and their belief that State will demonstrate this against Premier College in the game. However, Esteban likes the words of one alumnus who tells the *News Weekly*, "We have one of the top recruits in Esteban Cruz and we expect him to be the future of the Cyclones and he has the ability to destroy Premier all on his own." Esteban is motivated by those words and he looks forward to getting on the court and not disappointing State University alumni.

Unfortunately, it is all an anti-climax for Esteban. The coach does not start him as the game begins. He waits to enter the game but the coach never calls his name. Cedric plays and it is just Esteban and Nick, a walk-on who rarely plays, who do not enter the game. Esteban is almost in tears and he never gets up from the bench. Worse still, State University loses the game. He watches as his friend, Isaiah, celebrates with his teammates. It is just too much for him. He wants to be by himself, away from it all, and grieve. At the spur of the moment, he leaves the bench after the final whistle and walks past the locker room and heads home to his mother's house. He has had enough. It is at this point that Cedric stops him.

With teary eyes, he looks past the crowd in the parking lot and he has racing thoughts: *"I am done with this but will a transfer help now? Where would I go? Is Premier an option? What are people thinking? What will my mom think?"* He fails to join his teammates in the locker room and he sends a text to Alicia before he reaches his home. He concludes, "It was best to alert her but not with a call." Coach Foothead is upset and barely notices that Esteban is not in the locker room. However, David notices. David did not play his best but he knows he has to console his teammates and remind them that the bigger prize is the end-of-season tournament. He informs Coach Foothead that Esteban is missing. Foothead becomes more incensed but that pales in significance compared to the loss. But he thinks, *That kid is yet to grow up. Was he absent because of grief from the loss or what was it?* He will find out later.

***

Much later, Esteban thinks about his options and does not want to become a "quitter." His mother, Alicia, is disappointed that Esteban walked out on the team. She makes her feelings known to him immediately after and sternly tells him,

"Son, we are not a family of quitters. . . Your father was. . .but not me. . . and you should never become one."

"Mom, I am not a quitter but I am not stupid either," Esteban responds.

Though Esteban's mother is disappointed, she still wants to support Esteban and is not thrilled by Coach Foothead's decision to keep her son on the bench throughout such an important game. *I am going to show Mr. Foothead that no one "messes with me,"* she thinks to herself. She, however, makes sure not to reveal her next steps. She knows texting Mr. Foothead did not work previously. However, State University's loss does not sit well with several top alumni and boosters of the basketball team and Alicia knows it. She thinks: *It is time to begin a media campaign and I have the experience to build support through social media. My Twitter handle has several hundreds of followers.*

***

But is it best to confront Mr. Foothead face to face? Though Alicia muses that it might be time to use social media, is it? As for Esteban, he is unsure what to do next. Should he contact Mr. Foothead? Is it necessary? If he has to do it, what should his message be?

DISCUSSION QUESTIONS

1. Differentiate among Esteban, Alicia, and Coach Foothead's choices of communication style. Which do you think is more effective in obtaining results?
2. What did Esteban and his mother attempt to communicate with the Facebook page, YouTube, and texting during college recruiting?
3. Should Esteban apologize to the coach and the team? Should he transfer? What should he do?
4. What do you think will be the angle for a news story in the *Sharptown News Weekly* concerning Esteban's walkout from the team? Why?
5. Should Alicia begin a social media campaign against Coach Foothead? Would it be justified? Is such use of social media ethical? Provide your reasons.
6. What role do you think race played in Coach Foothead's decisions concerning Esteban and Cedric's treatment and playing time? Provide your reasons.

KEY TERMS

Relational communication, Family relations and sport, Coach-athlete relations, Organizational leadership.

CASE 3: EVERY DAY IS GAME DAY

Deleasa Randall-Griffiths
Ashland University

ABSTRACT

When her mother's obsession with televised sports collides with family gatherings, Lindsay Walters encounters a complex conflict situation. Her experience studying family communication provides opportunities to explore the issues and help her family find compromise and understanding.

***

OUT TO DINNER

Family is important to Lindsay Walters. On the rare occasion when all of Lindsay's family members are in town, everyone gathers at her parents' home. Lindsay, the youngest of four adult children, lives hours away from her childhood home. Both of her parents still live on the family farm. Lindsay and her adult siblings each have their own active careers. Family gatherings with everyone present are rare events, happening only a few times a year.

"Okay, we are all set for everyone to meet at Rader's Restaurant for "free pie night." I've been on the phone for about an hour, calling back and forth, but I think I have it all arranged so that everyone will be at the restaurant by 6:30." Lindsay excitedly announced to her parents.

"That's great, honey. Is your brother going to be able to make it too?" her dad inquired.

"Yep, he said he was on his way back into town and should be able to get there by 6:30" Lindsay replied.

"Well, if we don't go soon I'm staying home," muttered her mother. "The game starts at eight."

"Staying home!" Lindsay exclaimed. "But, I arranged all of this so we could all be together as a family! You should have plenty of time to get back for the game. Which is more important, spending time with us or watching that stupid game?"

"It's not stupid! Whoever wins this game will move on to the finals and I don't want to miss it!" Her mother retorted. Noticing Lindsay's frustration she added, "Listen, when you retire from a full-time career, not to mention the work of raising four kids, you have earned the right to do whatever you want to do."

"Ellen, for heaven sakes" Lindsay's dad fumed, "turn the TV off and go spend an evening with your family. I swear you follow more sports teams than any man I know!"

"You want to know who moves on to the finals just as much as I do!" Lindsay's mother snapped.

"Yes, I do. But, I also want to spend time with the kids. They're only here a short time, Ellen. For heaven sakes, where are your priorities?" replied Lindsay's dad.

Both Lindsay and her father were exasperated. After all Lindsay's efforts arranging for the family to get together, her mother still saw the beginning of a sporting event as more important than a family dinner. In the end her mother did come to the restaurant and everyone had a good time.

Lindsay's mom was, indeed, late for the start of the game, and made sure everyone in the family knew about it on the drive home. But once they made it home, the men all gathered to watch the game with mom while Lindsay and her sister hung out in her kitchen, enjoying a glass a wine and catching up on their lives.

"What's up with Mom and this newfound love of sports? You see her a lot more than I do these days, is she always like this?" Lindsay asked.

"Oh, she's always loved to stay up on the games," replied her sister.

"Yeah, but since she retired it's getting a bit out of hand, don't you think?" Lindsay countered.

"I have noticed that she is more into it these days." her sister added. "The other day, she was watching one game on TV and had a radio sitting beside her listening to some other high school basketball game broadcast on the local radio station. It was kind of weird."

"And I don't think Dad's too happy about it either. You'd expect him to be the one who is sports crazed, but that's not the case in this house," Lindsay noted.

"You should have heard them last week!" her sister chuckled. "They were at each other's throats about some party Dad wanted to go to, but Mom didn't. Come to think of it, that argument was over a golf tournament she didn't want to miss. She really is getting obsessed, isn't she?" Lindsay's sister half joked.

"It's all I ever see her do anymore. We even had to schedule our shopping trip around some tennis match she was watching," Lindsay added. "It's bad enough that I live 300 miles away and don't see you all very much. Sometimes I feel like Mom would much rather be sitting at Soldier Field than sitting in the room talking with us."

"You're exaggerating, but come to think of it, not by much," Lindsay's sister reflected.

"I know I'm exaggerating. I just miss the way things used to be. I miss our close-knit family." Lindsay confessed. "And I feel like it's my responsibility to say something. That's the downside of studying family communication for a living, you see issues happening, but you don't always know how to help."

FAMILY DINNER

For Lindsay's family, the tradition of large-scale feasts where everyone can be together is the focal point of any family holiday or celebration. Being together and having conversations about each other's lives is the most important aspect of these gatherings. That notion is supported by her father's insistence on lively dinnertime debates about current events.

On one particular holiday, Lindsay watched her father's frustration mount when her mom kept a ball game blaring loudly on TV during dinner. Everyone was seated at the table, her mom purposefully taking the seat that allowed the best TV viewing.

"For god sakes, Ellen, turn that thing off!" Lindsay's dad snapped.

Lindsay's mother did not respond to her husband's request. Lindsay knew it was more than likely a case of her mother not hearing the request, due to the general roar of multiple conversations going on in the room and an intense focus on the TV. After a few minutes, her father tried again.

"Ellen!" Her dad repeated with increased volume and obvious frustration. "Turn that darn thing off! We can't even hear ourselves think with that TV blaring!"

Since she was seated at the table and the remote control was across the room by the easy chair, Lindsay's mom looked up, a little confused and slightly put out. "It's the last quarter and they are tied! I want to see how this ends!"

Lindsay, in an effort to ward off rising conflict, found the remote control and muted the volume of the TV. "Here, this should make you both happy."

Throughout the meal Lindsay was aware of her mother's focus on the muted TV and her disconnection from the various conversations happening around her. She engaged in a lively conversation with her father, but noticed that he too was aware of his wife's distraction.

When her mother had finished her meal she paused between Lindsay and her father, grabbed the remote and snapped, "Okay, I'm finished eating. Now, can I listen to the game?" She made her way back to the television area with an exaggerated sigh.

***

Later that evening, while Lindsay and her sister cleaned up the kitchen, Lindsay's dad came into the room. He grabbed a towel and started drying a large pot, a very uncharacteristic thing for him to do.

"You know, Lindsay, your mother doesn't mean anything when she watches those games. I mean, you shouldn't take it personally. Your mother loves you kids. She just gets all caught up in it, that's all. It's beyond me why she would waste time on TV when she could spend it talking with you kids. She's just set in her ways."

"It's kind of weird, isn't it Dad? Lindsay replied. "I just don't see why she won't turn it off and engage in conversation with us."

"I know, Lindsay. It's frustrating for me too. If you ask me there is nothing more important than focusing on you kids on those rare occasions when you are all sitting right in front of me." Dad added. "I'm used to being replaced by the 'talking sports heads.' It's a daily occurrence around here. But, when I see it happening to you kids, it really makes me mad."

Lindsay could hear frustration and a little sadness in her father's voice. "Have you two talked about it?"

"Not really. She's always watching some game or another. There's no time to ask her anything," Dad sighed.

***

Lindsay struggled to make sense of the tension she saw in her parents' lives. She was very aware that during these large family gatherings her parents were at odds with the balance of TV viewing and family togetherness time. Their power struggle and attempts to gain compliance were, however, ineffective and causing frustration.

Lindsay, having experience in the study of communication and some objectivity as a third-party observer, wanted to help her parents find a compromise that would acknowledge their differing needs, in terms of family togetherness time and television viewing time. Her dilemma is whether or not to intervene on her parents' behalf. If she does intervene, she must decide how to approach her parents, in the spirit of understanding both sides of the debate. From Lindsay's perspective, her parents are experiencing disconfirming messages stemming from differing sets of needs. These events are leading to a power struggle that impacts the entire family. Each party is attempting to gain or resist compliance based on their own wishes and desires. She sees it as her job to help alleviate these issues, but she is not sure how to begin.

DISCUSSION QUESTIONS

1. Can you explain the difference in Lindsay's parents' needs in terms of gender roles and expectations?
2. Can you explain ways in which dialectic tensions are exhibited?
3. What types of power struggles do you see going on in Lindsay's family? How is compliance being sought or resisted?
4. What examples of confirming or disconfirming messages do you see present in this situation?

KEY TERMS

Confirming and disconfirming messages, Power, Compliance gaining and resisting, Dialectic tensions

CASE 4: CONFESSIONS OF A DANCE TEAM:
The Interface of Sport, Dance, and Family Communication

Scott A. Myers
West Virginia University

Jordan Atkinson,
West Virginia University

Hannah Ball
West Virginia University

Dana Borzea
West Virginia University

ABSTRACT

As part of the audition process for a collegiate dance team, three college women must confront the role that family communication plays in their reasons for wanting to join the team. Through self-reflection, the women realize the significance of family communication patterns used in their families-of-origin, and how these patterns affect their self-concept as athletes.

***

"Alright, ladies. Because this is our first clinic, I am interested in assessing your technique and your form. When I count off on eight, I want to see each of you perform a fouette sequence consisting of six turns and a triple pirouette followed by a Calypso, a jeté, and a toe touch. Once you finish, stay in line. Show me that you are serious about joining the Lady Bobcats dance team. Otherwise, I can cut you right now and save both of us a lot of time," said Becky Keyton, coach of the award-winning Lady Bobcats Dance Team.

"Front line, center stage. Back line, move to the side and watch how these techniques are supposed to be performed. Move! Now! Front line, take it from the tippy top. 5, 6, 7, 8 . . ."

***

Moving quickly, Delia Williamson, Vanessa Capizzi, and Erica Edwards are among the 14 young women who comprise the back line (along with the 14 young ladies on the front line) hoping to secure one of 16 available spots on the Lady Bobcats Dance Team representing Mountainview State University. Considered to be one of the elite college dance teams in the nation, the Lady Bobcats have consistently advanced to the final round of competition at the Universal Dance Association National Dance Team championship held each February for the past five years.

Although the Lady Bobcats have yet to capture the national title, their routines in both hip-hop and jazz have been recognized by their peers for their musicality and synchronicity; the team also is well known for their flawless execution and their showmanship. Under the tutelage of Coach Keyton, over the past 10 years, the dance team has risen from being a relatively unknown entity in the dance team world to being one of the top collegiate dance teams in the nation.

Aside from their national reputation as a dance team, members of the Lady Bobcats Dance Team maintain a healthy presence on the Mountainview State University campus. In addition to competing regionally and nationally against other Division I dance teams, the Lady Bobcats perform at all home football and basketball games, pep rallies, and other special campus events. During a typical academic year, dance team members not only are active in campus organizations such as sororities, student government, service clubs, and honor societies, but also serve as officers in these organizations. For the past three years, a dance team member has been elected to the Homecoming Court (although none has yet to claim the crown). And, for the first time in dance team history, a team member was named to the Mountain Society, the highest accolade reserved for a select group of students whose campus involvement embodies the spirit, culture, and passion of Mountainview State University. In Mountainview, where the university is located, they march in the County Fair, Veteran's Day, and Christmas parades and it is a common practice for the coach to send several members to represent the dance team at many charitable events and functions held annually in the town.

***

Coach Keyton claps her hands. "Front line, move to the left. Back line, center stage. Quickly now! If you can't move to the tempo at this clinic, you won't be invited back to the second one because we move faster than this when we're on the field. Take it from the top. 5, 6, 7, 8, turn, turn, turn. . ."

The 14 women from the back line progress quickly through each of their movements. When Erica, who is the last of the back line to perform, finishes her set, Coach Keyton calls all the women together to form a semi-circle around her. "Ladies, thank you for attending this clinic. As you know, this clinic is the first step toward eventually making the Lady Bobcats dance team. For the second clinic, the focus will be on group performance and you will perform a hip-hop routine piece that I have choreographed. Check your email for a YouTube link and make sure you know the routine before you get here. We'll perform the routine at half-time and then move into freestyle. While I am looking for dancers who are technically proficient, I also need dancers who are expressive and artistic, so if you can't groove, that will be a problem."

"A few other things. If you make the team, I expect you to commit 100%. We practice three times a week for three hours at a time. We have conditioning workouts twice a week at six in the morning. Attendance is required at all times. If you miss practice, you are off the team. I also expect you to dress appropriately at all practices. This means tan tights, black booty shorts, and a dance team t-shirt. If you make the team, I will provide you with sneakers for our hip-hop and pom routines and jazz shoes for our jazz routines. Hair should be pulled back in a ponytail. And absolutely no gum chewing. Do you understand?" Coach Keyton says as she points to Delia.

Delia's face turns crimson. *Oh no, I'm already in trouble*, she thinks to herself as she nods affirmatively, all while spitting the gum in her hand.

"If you are one of the 16 dancers fortunate enough to make this squad, say goodbye to your friends, romantic partners, and family for the next 10 weeks. Your weekends will be spent at practice. And if we're going to win first place at nationals this year, we'll need to practice during fall break and Thanksgiving recess, so you will need to remain on campus during those weeks."

"That's it for now. Go home and get some rest because you will need it."

Coach Keyton turns and starts to walk toward the exit when she abruptly stops and turns back to face the dancers. "One more thing. Sometime during the next week, you will be scheduled for an interview. During this interview, you will be asked to tell us your 'story.' Every dancer has a story. What is yours, and why do you want to be a part of the Lady Bobcats dance team?"

***

After the clinic, Delia, Vanessa, and Erica gather their belongings and leave the gymnasium. As they are walking out of the recreation center, they discuss the clinic and their impressions of the tryout process.

"That clinic was tougher than I thought it would be. What do you two think?" Erica asks.

"I don't think it was that bad," Vanessa says. "My high school dance team had a much more difficult first clinic than this one."

"That's easy for you to say, Vanessa. You've been dancing since you were a baby. I only started dancing in high school. That clinic was tough! I'm not sure I'll make it past the second one," Delia states.

"I'm more worried about the interview than the second clinic. What does the coach mean by 'story' anyway? Even though dancing is my life, I'm not sure that would be my story," Erica says.

"I'm not sure what my story is, either. I need to go call my mom. Hopefully she can help me figure this out so I can make the team. Anyone walking back to Towers?" Vanessa queries.

"Nope. I'm waiting for my parents to pick me up so we can go eat at Applebee's," Delia says. "Oh, there's their car now! See you girls later," she says as she walks toward the parking lot.

"I'm heading back to my apartment to go tanning with my roommate, so I'll walk with you, Vanessa. Delia, text us later," Erica says as she and Vanessa begin to walk toward the residential side of campus.

EVERY DANCER HAS A STORY

Looks like Little Williamson isn't that terrible, Delia thinks to herself as she walks across the parking lot and hears a familiar voice shouting nearby.

"So, do we have a dancer in the family or not?" The question comes from Delia's older sister, Summer, who is leaning out of the driver's side window of her parents' car.

"What are you doing here?!" Delia asks with a tone of excited confusion as she opens the car door.

"Mom and dad totally forgot they had their couple's yoga tonight and asked me to come get you," Delia buckles her seatbelt as she continues to listen to Summer. "Oh, and they also told me to tell you to crush it at the baton twirling team auditions!" The sisters simultaneously roll their eyes as they laugh.

"First, I don't know if I made it yet. Today was just the first clinic. I think I did pretty well actually, but now I have to learn a brand new hip-hop routine," says Delia. "Second, there isn't even a baton twirling team. *Those* girls are just a part of the marching band," explains Delia as she mentally attempts to brush off her parents' incorrect well wishes. *It'd be nice if they knew what team I was trying out for*, she thinks.

"Come on, Delia, you know how Mom and Dad are all over the place sometimes and forget things. They mean well, they always do. Mom said to me yesterday she really hopes you're the first Williamson girl to be a dancer!" Summer explains.

Without a pause, Delia responds, "They never forgot about any of your basketball games." Delia knows it is not her sister's fault that her parents cannot remember exactly what team she is trying out for. She knows it is not necessarily her parents' fault either. The support was always there, but Delia isn't convinced that their support actually means that they care if she makes the dance team or not.

"Yes, they have forgotten about my games before!" Summer exclaims half-heartedly. "They've missed at least one or two of my games since I started playing on the junior varsity squad back in high school." Currently a senior at Plymouth College, a private school 20 minutes away from Mountainview State University, Summer has been a starting point guard for the past two seasons and has had several professional league scouts tailing her all year.

Sensing Delia's disappointment, Summer says through her grin, "So, you should probably get something healthy for lunch now, right?"

They both look at each other and simultaneously laugh. "Burgers it is!" they cry in unison.

***

"So, how did tryouts go?" shouts Erica's roommate, Ashley, as Erica walks in their apartment.

"Wow, I'm exhausted, I'm just so glad it's over," Erica replies as she falls onto the couch.

"Tell me! How did you do? I'm sure you were the best," Ashley eagerly remarks.

"I think I did pretty well. My technique was definitely better than some of the other girls, especially Vanessa and Delia. I thought they would have been much better."

"How many girls were there trying out?" Ashley queries.

"There were 28, but a few of them just could not keep up in the group routine. It was sad, actually." Erica continues, "Their leaps, pirouettes, Calypsos, and toe touches were not that great and their timing was even off. But there were a few girls who were really good. Overall, I just thought there was a lack of energy in the group."

"Really? Well, I am so excited for you! You will totally make the team."

"Thanks, I appreciate the support. I couldn't have done it without you," Erica says as she stands up and hugs Ashley. "I guess I'll call my mom and let her know how things went."

Erica calls her mother, but there is no answer. *That's not surprising,* Erica thinks to herself when she gets her voicemail greeting. Erica then sends her mother the following text message: "Hey! Tried to call, but maybe u r busy. Call me when u can. I just had my dance team tryout and want to let u know how it went."

A half-hour later, Erica's mother texts her back: "Hey honey! I have a couple of meetings here in the office so I can't call right now, but I will when I get home this evening. I'm sure you did fine. How did you do on that test last week?"

In her return text message, Erica writes: "Whatever. No big deal. TTYL."

***

Crap. I got back later than I expected. Mom is going to wonder why I haven't called yet. Vanessa quickly dials her mother's number on her cell phone.

Vanessa's mother picks up after two rings. "Hi Doll, I was wondering when I'd hear from you."

"Hi mom!" Vanessa says. "I just got back from the clinic. It lasted a little longer than I expected so I was late getting home."

"Well it's good to hear from you," Vanessa's mother quickly redirects the conversation. "So, tell me, how did it go? I hope you didn't rush the tempo, like I reminded you. Remember, you usually have more time than you think."

"Yes, mom, I remembered. Clinic went really well. Easier than any first clinic I had in high school, honestly." Vanessa responds.

"That's my girl. What's next on the schedule?" Vanessa's mother inquires.

"We have to learn a hip-hop routine for the second clinic and we'll be interviewing sometime next week. Coach Keyton wants us to tell her our 'story,' but I guess that shouldn't be too difficult," Vanessa says.

"Especially considering where you come from," Vanessa's mother agrees. "Well Doll, I'm very excited that everything is falling into place for you with the dance team. Looks like you're headed along the right path. Soon as you know it, you'll be recruited, just like your sister. She sent your father and me tickets to the home game in two weekends. Anyway, I'll let you go so you can practice. Let me know when you get the good news."

"Talk to you tomorrow, Mom." Vanessa hangs up her cell phone and immediately bursts into tears.

***

At the Applebee's near campus, the two Williamson sisters are seated at a booth and barely glance over the menus. Their parents had taken them there for dinner every month for as long as they can remember. Delia's ringtone goes off as the waitress comes to take their orders.

"I'll have a cheeseburger with fries," she quickly orders before she answers the phone. "Hi Mom," answers Delia followed by, "Hey Dad." Their parents love the speaker function of their phones. "Nope, I won't find out for another two weeks." A few more questions, a side story about her Dad's nerves during tryouts for Plymouth College's track team, and 10 minutes later Delia finally hangs up the phone.

"See, I told you they care about how the dance team tryouts went," Summer says in an I-told-you-so manner.

"It's because they feel bad for me. Poor Delia, never really excelled at anything. So, let's just support her in something else in which she'll probably just be average," Delia says mimicking her parents' voices. Delia pauses and then says, "I took one summer dance camp and now I think I can step in the spotlight as a member of the dance team. Who am I trying to kid?"

Summer attempts to answer the question and positively remind her sister that she does have the ability to make the team, but Delia is not looking for an answer. Delia, in a matter-of-fact tone, continues.

"I have participation trophies. I am not the topic of the stories Mom and Dad tell their friends. I have never been in the newspaper. I am just Summer Williamson's sister," Delia's eyes focus ahead of her. "You're even on the wall here!" Delia exclaims as she points to a photo of Summer's high school basketball team taken the year they won the state championship.

Summer waits a moment to make sure Delia has said all that was on her mind and patiently asks, "Are you done?"

Delia nods.

"Yes, you are my sister and I am so grateful for that," Summer replies. "You've always been there for me and I will always be there for you. But, you're not just my little sister. You're not just average Delia. You're the Williamson sister with the most rhythm, biggest heart, and best hair, of which I've always been jealous. You're going to kick some butt during these tryouts. Regardless if you make it or not, you took a risk that I would've never had the courage to take. You've already won."

***

Erica and Ashley get in Erica's car and start driving to the tanning salon for their daily visit. After dancing and singing along to their favorite song, Erica impatiently says, "Girl, I am so ready for the tanning bed. I need some color!"

Ashley asks, "Did you talk to your mom about your tryout? Was she excited?"

"No, she couldn't talk. It's no big deal though, I'm used to it. She's busy, I guess."

"Well, I'm sure she will call you later."

"Yes, but I wanted to tell her about it now. It kind of bothers me that she can't take a few minutes and call."

At this point, Ashley's phone rings and it is her mother. She says to Erica, "Hold on just a bit, my mom is calling."

Ashley proceeds to have a five-minute conversation with her mother about her latest calculus exam score, her tutoring session, and how she needs to come home and visit soon.

While Ashley is on the phone, Erica starts thinking about her own family situation. *Ashley's mom calls all the time, I wish my mom would call, even just once in a while. I mean, today was a BIG day for me and being on this dance team means everything. My mom knew that and the fact that she has not called really bothers me.*

By the time Ashley gets off the phone, they have arrived at the parking lot of the tanning salon. "Sorry about that, but you know how my mom is," Ashley states. "Are you ready to get our tan on?"

"Actually, can I just vent to you for a minute?" Erica asks before they get out of the car. "It's really bothering me that my family hasn't called me to ask about my dance team tryouts. I know you don't know my parents, but they are the 'cool' parents. Like, they always let me do what I want. But the problem is we just never talk about anything. When I was younger, it didn't bother me at all. Mom would always trust me and let me stay at my friends' houses on the weekend. My parents were not really that involved in my schoolwork either. They couldn't care less that I was a dancer and they rarely came to games and competitions to support me. Dancing and sports mean nothing to my parents and I'm sure that's why my brother quit playing football. In my family, everybody does their own thing, you know?"

Ashley stops her and asks, "Wait a minute. How is that a bad thing?"

"It kind of sucks. Of course, it has benefits because I don't have my mom breathing down my neck about my calculus class like you do. However, it's really frustrating sometimes because it makes me think they don't care. I know they do care, but that's just the communication in our family. Everybody does their own thing."

"I know trying out for the dance team means so much to you, and you are totally going to make it. But I'm sure your parents are just really busy today. I know they care," Ashley remarks.

"Thanks for the support, Ash. This does bother me from time to time. I just need to accept that my mom and dad are just not as involved as some parents. One thing for sure is I am much more independent because of my parents. Oh well, I need to get over it. Let's get in there and tan," Erica states as they both get out of the car. "I've got to get home soon and learn this new dance routine on YouTube. Oh, and Coach Keyton said that we'll be having interviews where we tell our dance story. I've got a lot to say about that, too, because dance is everything to me."

***

Vanessa's new roommate, Jamie, had been sitting on her bed on the other side of the dormitory room playing on her iPad and couldn't help but hear Vanessa's conversation with her mother.

Well, this is awkward, Jamie thinks to herself. She debates whether she should pretend that she hasn't noticed Vanessa crying on her bed. Jamie looks up from her iPad and over at the sobbing Vanessa and decides to ask what's bothering her. "Vanessa, what's wrong?"

"It's nothing . . . I don't really want to talk about it," Vanessa replies.

"Not to be nosy," Jamie notes, "but from the sound of your conversation, everything is going really well with the dance team. Clearly something else is going on. Why are you so upset?"

Vanessa lets out a sigh, wipes her nose on the back of her sleeve, and laments, "I really messed up today during clinic. I didn't point my toes during my first fouette. What if I don't make the team? My Mom will be *so disappointed.*"

Jamie, slightly confused, attempts to comfort Vanessa. "Whenever I talk about intramurals, you mention how the team looks like so much fun. . . Worst-case scenario, you join my intramural soccer team instead of doing the dance thing. Best part is, there are no tryouts for intramurals."

Vanessa, looking taken aback, responds, "You don't understand. I *have* to be on the dance team."

Jamie puts down her iPad. "Yeah, but do you *want* to be on the dance team?"

"I don't know if I feel like getting into this conversation. . . ," Vanessa says, coolly.

"It sounds like this is really bothering you. Come on, you'll feel a lot better if you vent," Jamie reassures her. "I vented to you earlier this week about my bio lab partner. I basically owe you one."

Vanessa lets out another sigh. "Fine. But it's complicated. Like I said, I *have* to be on the dance team—dance is basically a family legacy," Vanessa explains. "My mom always tells me stories about my grandmother and grandfather, who were a famous ballroom dance couple. They toured the country together and performed everywhere. When my mom was a kid, she traveled with them, watched them practice, and imitated their dance moves. My mom pursued her own professional dance career until she injured herself. It broke her heart that she couldn't continue to dance professionally—and actually she'd kill me if I told you that—but she opened a dance studio and has been running it for over 20 years now. And she has been coaching me in dance pretty much since I could walk."

"That's amazing," says Jamie, listening attentively.

Vanessa continues. "Of course, both of my older sisters are dance prodigies, with dance scholarships for their colleges. And about a year ago, my oldest sister was recruited to be an NBA dancer. I have never seen my mom more proud than she was when she got that news from my sister . . . or really any time she gets to brag about the recruitment story. Basically, there's a lot of pressure for me to make the dance team here. What am I supposed to tell my own kids someday if I don't make the team?"

"I don't think it's healthy to be that stressed about dancing. Maybe you need to tell your mom how you really feel," Jamie suggests.

Vanessa furrows her brow. "I don't see how bringing that up to my mom would be helpful."

"Why not?" Jamie challenges. "This is *your* college experience. You only get one chance to enjoy it. If you're worrying yourself sick over pointing your toes, I can't imagine what you'll be like before competitions."

"I appreciate the advice, Jamie," Vanessa starts, "but I can't just go ahead and make a decision like that myself. My mom knows what's best for me. And that involves setting myself up to have a great dance career. I have to do better at the second clinic. There's no other option. I'm going to go start practicing."

AND THE NEWEST LADY BOBCAT IS . . .

Two weeks later, the second clinic commences. As Delia, Vanessa, and Erica walk into the gymnasium together, their minds are in three different places.

Delia can't help but focus on her nerves. *Just don't forget the hold in the last eight count. Always use the orange door for spotting. Don't mess up the first transition. Remember, pop left, hold, pop right, left, hold, right, Calypso.*

Vanessa feels nervous as well, but for different reasons, as her mother's coaching reminders kept entering her thoughts: *Don't rush the tempo, Vanessa. Slow it down. No mistakes. Keep the legacy alive.*

Erica, on the other hand, feels quite confident about her ability to perform the hip-hop routine. *I've got this! I know this routine like the back of my hand. I'm flawless!*

"Alright ladies, line up in the same formation as you did in the first clinic, Coach Keyton says. "When I count to eight, I want to see the front line first. We're going to mark it half-time before we pick up the tempo and take it from the top. On my count. 5, 6, 7, 8, go . . ."

***

After the hip-hop routine is over, Delia, Vanessa, and Erica sit on the gymnasium floor, anxiously awaiting the results of the judging.

"I'm so nervous I could puke. I have a lot riding on this," Vanessa says.

"Me, too. This is the most nervous I've been in a long time. I just hope all three of us make the team. Think how much fun we'll have together," Delia replies. "Fingers crossed!"

"Shhh! Here comes Coach Keyton," Erica states as she motions to Vanessa and Delia to stand.

Coach Keyton walks to the center of the gymnasium with an envelope in her hand. "Ladies, please gather around. Thank you for auditioning for this year's Lady Bobcats dance team squad. After consulting with the judges, I have determined which of you will join our team. When I call your name, please step forward. Melinda Tinnell. Rania Davidson. Mindy Epstein. Susie Alderton. M'shelle Davis . . ."

Realizing that Coach Keyton has called 15 names but none has been theirs, Delia, Vanessa, and Erica exchange glances and each wonders if her name is going to be the last one to be called.

This time, I'll be able to answer Summer when she asks me if there's going to be a dancer in the Williamson family, thinks Delia.

What am I going to tell my mom if I don't make the team? thinks Vanessa.

Maybe this time my mom will pick up when I call with the good news, thinks Erica.

"And last, but not least, the final member of the 2015-2016 Lady Bobcats dance team is . . ."

DISCUSSION QUESTIONS

1. Which of the four family types best characterizes each dancer's family?
2. Based on their family type, what recommendations would you offer to Delia, Vanessa, and Erica on how they should inform their family about whether they made the dance team?
3. Which function of family storytelling is present in each dancer's reflections on her family interactions?
4. How do these storytelling functions contribute to Delia, Vanessa, and Erica's identities as dancers?
5. What role should family communication *about sport* play in an individual family member's decision to pursue participation in a sport?

KEY TERMS

Family communication patterns, Family stories

CASE 5: CALLING IT FOUL
An Ethical Dilemma on the Tennis Court

J. D. Elliott
Clemson University

John Spinda
Clemson University

ABSTRACT

The Aiken Open, a prestigious tennis tournament, was shaping up to be a coming-out party for George Bright in the state junior tennis scene. After making a surprise run to the semifinals of this tournament, Bright ran into an opponent who used dubious tactics to cheat the honor system that is often employed in junior tennis. This case examines the ethical quandaries faced in such a situation.

BACKGROUND

On an otherwise quiet Sunday afternoon at the Odell Weathers Tennis Center, a boisterous round of applause filled the warm, sun-drenched day. With a polite smile George Bright shook the hand of another defeated opponent, but there would be no more opponents on this afternoon, as Bright had captured the Becker Open junior championship. His opponent shook his head and quipped, "Where did you come from? I was winning these tournaments all the time until you showed up! Either way, good match." Bright in his typical reserved demeanor replied, "Thanks, I am sure you'll get me the next time we meet."

George Bright was quickly becoming somewhat of a local junior tennis legend. Although the 14 year old had only played in a few tournaments, he dominated local talent and several outlets expected big things from the relative newcomer. Bright had quickly grown a big frame that he used to his advantage, with a high-powered serve and forceful ground strokes. Bright won and he won big. Close matches were not his forte. After winning a pair of Division III tournaments, such as the Becker Open, Bright craved an opportunity to become more visible in the state rankings. "I think I am ready to play in the Aiken Open, what you think?" Bright asked his coach after a practice session.

His coach cautioned, "George, you should be aware that this tournament is not Division II, but is also a really significant tournament that is going to draw great players your age from far and wide. Do you feel like you are ready to run with the big dogs?"

"Well, I have beaten Thomas and Schechter, and they are pretty prominent players at the state level," replied Bright, "so I should be competitive, right?"

"You got my support George," said his coach. "So I guess I shouldn't put these balls away yet, we need to work on your backhand."

SETTING THE STAGE

A few weeks later, it was time for the Aiken Open. Bright could feel his hand tremble a bit as he went to start his first serve of the tournament on a set of local courts he grew up playing on. He stopped, closed his eyes, exhaled deeply and uncorked one of the best serves of his young career. Bright's opponent barely moved from his stance as the ball bounced by for the ace, making a solid "thud" as the ball struck the mat at the back of the court. The air of confidence from this great start carried Bright to a successful first match, then again, and again, until only four of the original 31 players remained after three days of play. Bright beamed inside when he saw how proud his coach and family were at the way he was playing. However, he remained focused, as only two matches stood between him and an unexpected championship in his first Division II tournament.

Upon looking at the bracket as he arrived at the main court, he saw he was matched up with John Smith. Bright thought to himself, *No way, it's the same John Smith whom I whipped at the Diamond Lake Invitational a few months ago.* Sure enough, Smith came in right behind him and Bright recognized him right away. The two had faced off in the Diamond Lake Invitational, a Division III tournament, several months prior, where Bright defeated Smith handily in the finals. The familiarity of their opposing style of play developed a little bit of a rivalry between the two players. Each player remembered his last meeting, Smith wanted to avenge his loss and Bright hoped he could march easily into the finals of his first Division II tournament.

As noted earlier, George Bright relied on a power game to overwhelm opponents, which is precisely what he had been doing for the entire Aiken Open tournament to this point. However, his opponent was the polar opposite. John Smith was a winner, but he lacked the size and power of his opponent. Smith relied on grit and determination and rode a strong mental game to wear down his enemies. It was the first semifinal in a Division II tournament for either player, but both had grown accustomed to winning the easier Division III tournaments. With only three Division II tournaments the whole year, an opportunity to play in the finals was crucial for both players as it would vault them to much higher overall rankings for junior tennis in the state.

In the small world of youth tennis, nothing was a secret. Weaknesses of opponents were bandied around in casual conversation over the course of a weekend. Everyone knew the guy who threw his racket across the court, yelled curse words at the top of his lungs, or was disqualified for poor behavior even if you had not played a match head-to-head, but the worst rumor thrown around was the word "cheater." In highly competitive tennis where the player calls the lines and can subsequently determine the outcome of a point, cheaters are common. Different players have different strategies for dealing with these players, but no matter the court, tension is always higher when an alleged cheater is involved. Once someone is labeled a "cheater" it is almost impossible to shed the tag and opponents are constantly wary of every call even if the right call was made.

Smith was notorious for "bending" the lines in his favor. Bright had heard the rumors even before his match at Diamond Lake, but the first meeting was such an ugly defeat that he did not bother questioning any calls from Smith. This time was different. Before Bright was unfamiliar, he had yet to leave his mark on South Carolina junior tennis. This time Bright knew his style and that he could cheat to gain an advantage. As he laced up his shoes he thought to himself, *no matter what, do not let this punk win by cheating you.*

When the court opened, the two rivals began warming up. Both opponents were joking around to cut the obvious tension but both knew what was at stake, a chance to play in the finals of one of the bigger tournaments in the state. It was the calm before the storm. Once that first serve was hit, all cordiality would be thrown aside and both players would be in a battle for the finals.

GAME TIME: CHAOS ENSUES

The beginning of the first set was fairly ordinary. Both players held serve and neither had much of a chance to break. It was the complete opposite of the previous meeting where Bright broke Smith early before taking a commanding lead that he would not relinquish. The pressure was clearly on Bright playing in front of family and friends. "Out," yelled Smith as Bright hit another unforced error; he was clearly nervous, which lead to easy points for Smith.

When the first set finally reached a six game to six game tie, it was time for a tiebreaker to decide which player would claim the first set. In a tiebreaker, the first player to seven points winning by two points wins the set. Each player serves the ball for two consecutive points before the opposing player gets two consecutive serves to make sure no player gains an unfair advantage in the tiebreaker. Bright had a 4-2 point advantage in the tiebreaker when Smith called out the wrong score. Smith had given himself a point claiming that Bright was only up 4-3 points. *I could have sworn…it was 4-2,* thought Bright. Flustered by the apparent mistake, Bright hit the ball out and then in irritation called out, "Hey John, I think you confused the score before that point."

"Nice try George, it was 4-3 and you just shanked that one, 4-4 is the score!" After the two argued for a few minutes, Bright conceded the score before returning to play.

Shake it off, Bright thought to himself, *don't let him rattle you!* Bright came back strong and won the next two points for a 6-4 advantage. Full of confidence, Bright closed his eyes, took another deep breath, and prepared to use his powerful serve to get the seventh point to put the first set away in his favor. "6-4, set point!" yelled Bright as he prepared to serve. The thump from his racket was a sweet sound to Bright; he knew he just crushed this serve, just as he visualized it seconds earlier. But Smith never moved, he looked back with confusion and said, "Really, George? Trying to take a point away from me in such a big tiebreak…I don't think so man, the score is 6-5."

It was the second time Smith gave himself a point in the tiebreaker. Bright felt the hair on his neck stand up and his face become flush with seething anger. "Whatever John, 6-5, if you say it is." Bright was ready to burst out of his skin as he exclaimed "6-5, set point!" However, he had let Smith get the best of his emotions. Bright ended up double-faulting to tie the tiebreaker score to 6-6. Smith would grind out the next two points, pumping his fist after winning such a big tiebreaker and the first set.

"Awful," Bright muttered under his breath. He couldn't shake the rush of emotions that accompanied losing the set because of the two points Smith added to his score. Smith had just cheated him out of the first set in arguably the biggest match in his young career. *Enough is enough*, Bright thought, *he will not cheat me out of any more points.*

In the second set, Bright won the first three games and broke Smith's serve putting him in the fast track to winning the second set. The games were not close enough even for Smith to argue points. After a few competitive games, Bright was up 5-3 and just needed to hold serve to win the second set and force a pivotal third set. To begin the game, Bright ripped an ace, a serve that just found the corner just out of the reach of the diving Smith. Pumped to win the crucial opening point, Bright moved to the other side to serve the second point of the game. Once he reached the other side, he realized Smith had not moved. Realizing the confusion, Smith told Bright, "Man, you really need to get your eyes checked, that serve was out." The serve looked clearly in to Bright who asked Smith, "No way, if that was out, show me where the ball missed, please." Bright was convinced he could talk his opponent into conceding the point. "I don't feel like I need to do that, it was clearly out," replied Smith, "C'mon man, it's time for your next serve." Bright had no words, he was just shaking, his anger and adrenaline froze him up and he said nothing and simply walked back for the second serve. Bright swallowed, regained some level of composure and went back for the second serve. "Out!" yelled Smith as the second serve was well off course. With this double fault, he had a quick shift from winning the opening point of the game to losing it. The clearly rattled Bright lost the game and Smith won back his break.

On the changeover between games, the Bright knew that in order to keep his cool, he must win the next game and take the set before it potentially came to another tiebreaker, and more anticipated cheating. At times, tennis is a very mental sport and the less-polished Smith was excellent at winning the mental battle, which often leads to victories over higher-ranked competition. A break of Smith's serve would still seal the second set and could potentially be a huge blow to his psyche, which could linger into the third set, boding well for Bright. A loss in this game could lead to a tailspin as Smith would have all the momentum and a dejected Bright could lose what remained of his composure.

After winning the early points in the game, Bright just needed one point to seal the second set. On a long rally where Bright was moving Smith from side-to-side, he took his chance. Bright unleashed a forehand down the line clearly inside the line to win the second set. "Yes!" Bright shouted his jubilation as he suddenly felt the iron grip of the anxiety and anger melt away from his thoughts. "Not so fast," said Smith, "that ball was wide and that is my point." "That is a bunch of crap!" said Bright, "are you really going to make me get a rules official for this, seriously? You need to play by the rules, John, I've had enough!" This idea obviously worried Smith who replied, "Easy there, if you really feel that strongly, take the dang point! Sorry you feel like you needed to steal a set there, Buddy." Rules officials were scattered throughout the courts to watch play just in case one of the courts had a controversial play. They also assisted in disputes if they were called by a player. Most calls are made by the competitors on the court, but in severe situations the rules officials could take over the calling of the game.

Smith's comments did not bother Bright one bit. He already felt cheated out of the first set and refused to let Smith cheat him out of another set. With tensions already high from the confrontations, the match was now tied entering the final set. With most of the other semifinals from the other divisions coming to a close, spectators migrated to the high intensity Boys 13-14 semifinals. In addition to spectators, several local reporters covering the tournament came over to watch Bright, one of the few hometown boys remaining in the tournament.

One set remained to decide it all; the winner was finals bound. Serves flew, curses were yelled and testosterone was abundant. Like a storybook ending, the two players groundout the three-hour match until the score was tied at six games apiece. A tiebreaker in the final set would decide the winner. Smith had won the controversial tiebreaker in the first set and Bright was determined he would not let him cheat for any more points. The tiebreaker was even at 5-5. If either opponent could win two consecutive points, they would win the marathon match. This epic conclusion had drawn a serious crowd with several rules officials watching the final points. Bright nailed a first serve in the corner, just out of reach of Smith. "6-5, match point," a focused Bright barked out with a steely look in his eyes, ready to finally end this match that sometimes felt like a nightmare. But not so fast; Smith called the ball out, forcing Bright to make a tough decision with the match on the line.

CONCLUSION

One of the few sports without officials to enforce the rules, tennis relies on the honor system. An extremely competitive sport on the youth circuit, "cheaters" are common and, most of the time, a dishonest player has developed an unsavory reputation and most players know when they are playing someone who bends the rule to their advantage. Some common practices are confusing the score and the most obvious form of cheating is calling close balls out. Also, given the culture of youth tennis, young players do not want to earn a bad reputation as being a "whiner" or poor sport.

Bright had several options as the match wound down. His opponent was guilty of manipulating the score and miscalling balls out, which initially did not rattle Bright, but as the problem reoccurred, tension mounted between the two players. The two had already developed a rivalry that made each point even more crucial. In a delicate situation, Bright does not want to make the situation worse, especially in front of the hometown crowd. But at the same time he cannot continue to be cheated out of crucial points.

DISCUSSION QUESTIONS

1. How do you believe Bright should handle the remainder of this match? What advice would you give him?
2. Should Bright directly confront Smith and possibly "cause a scene" that may lead to either or both players being viewed negatively, or should he seek out an official to help with the situation? Why or why not?
3. Given all of the worries and concerns about parents overstepping boundaries in youth sports, what role do you believe the parents of either player should play during this particular dilemma?
4. Is there a particular communication practice that you feel Bright should use to solve this dilemma? What communication behaviors would that involve?

KEY TERMS

Sportsmanship, Ethical dilemma, Conflict resolution

CASE 6: SKATING ON THIN ICE:
Diffusing Competitiveness in Figure-Skating Friendships

Erin E. Gilles
University of Southern Indiana

Shannon M. Brogan
Kentucky State University

Kimberly A. Sipes
Kentucky State University

ABSTRACT

In the cutthroat world of figure-skating, balancing competition and camaraderie can strain relationships. Three girls' paths intersect at the US Figure Skating Championships, known as the Nationals. Natalie and Maria, long-time friends who met through figure skating, face a relationship threatened by an up-and-coming brash skater, Mayako. And, relations are further strained as the trash talking migrates from the rink to social media. Natalie and Mayako have both been rumored to have been offered a sponsorship with a leading athletic gear manufacturer, but performances at the Nationals may determine the outcome. Will the heat of battle melt the icy relations created by scathing online posts?

***

IceSktrUSA, the online forum frequented by competitive figure skaters and skating enthusiasts, was abuzz as the US Figure Skating Championships, known as the Nationals, were approaching. Natalie Clark, from her home in Des Moines, Iowa, nervously clicked through the pages of speculations and commentary from site visitors. At 17, she was blonde, petite, and considered the sweetheart of American figure skating. Despite this supposed affection, the online comments were brutal. Not affiliated with any official skating organization in the United States, IceSktrUSA was individually hosted and did not filter the posts for hateful messages or spam.

"Clarkie is why sk8ing is booooring ☹"

"Why can't that blonde skank skate in time to her music? Is she too dumb to count?"

"If she gains any more weight she'll break the ice!!! Tubby = no sk8"

"Americas gunna lose in Olyumpics if Natalie C is ur best hope"

"Natalie is such a blonde ditz."

There were positive comments, too. But they were not enough to keep the tears from coming as Natalie felt the harsh words pile up. *Don't they know how hard I practice or what my diet is like? I haven't had candy or soda in over a year!* Natalie knew that if anyone would understand it was her best friend, Maria Rodriguez. Just two months older than Natalie, Maria was also a competitive figure skater. They had met years ago in regional competitions and training camps. Plus, they were both members of Team USA, those skaters selected to represent the United States in international athletic competitions. In fact, this year's Nationals would determine if they would qualify for the US Winter Olympics Team. Natalie hit Maria's name in her favorites list, and the phone beeped as the call connected. They were miles apart, as Maria lived in Colorado Springs, Colorado with her coach and his wife, but they found time to stay connected.

"Hey, girl! Long time, no see! When are you coming to visit?" Maria asked in a breathless jumble.

"You know it won't be until after Nationals in January," Natalie sighed. "Coach won't let me off the ice until I've got more revolution in my spins. I'm still under-rotating."

"You know that you're not balancing on the right part of the blade," Maria said. "Keep practicing, it'll come together. You sound sad, what's up?"

Natalie felt like she was being too sensitive, but if anyone would get it, it would be Maria. "Well, I've been on IceSktrUSA tonight and they're trashing me again," Natalie said. "I don't get it. Why are people so cruel? I would never do that another athlete."

"I told you to get off of that vile site! They are so dumb there! They don't know a bracket turn from a Mohawk!" Maria laughed. "You won your regional competition and you're ready for Nationals. You practice night and day! Plus, you're the one with sponsors hounding you. Are you really talking to Trident Bladz?"

"I know," Natalie answered. "You're right." Blushing, Natalie mumbled, "I got a letter from Trident Bladz, but you know that they focus more on other sports. It's probably nothing. I think I'm just worried about seeing Mayako. You know how she is when she gets around skaters who are as good as she is on the ice. She thinks she's better than everyone else, but we're all Team USA." Natalie was referring to Mayako Otsuko, who had just turned 15. Mayako lived in California with her family and trained with one of the top coaches in figure skating. She was a snobbish socialite who had been known to hang out with pop singers, pro athletes, and actors. She also badmouthed fellow Team USA skaters in her social media accounts. Last month, she had called Natalie a "one-trick pony" who had to "hold Mommy's hand to get on and off the ice." Mayako's followers found it hilarious. Natalie did not.

"If she gives you any trouble this time, we'll handle it," Maria promised. "Don't forget, we're older than her and we've been to Nationals before. She's a baby. She just qualified this year! Besides, Nationals are four whole months away."

"True," Natalie replied. "I feel better already. Mayako cares more about being seen in the celebrity gossip sites than skating! I'm just being too sensitive. Thanks for listening to me vent. Get some sleep. Talk to you soon!"

THE COLD SHOULDER

Natalie shivered as she got out of the car in the parking garage at the arena for the Nationals. It wasn't the cold winter air; she was used to that after so many years spent on the ice. She was nervous about seeing Mayako. She was even more nervous about seeing her than skating in front of the judges or the audience. In the last four months the online aggression from Mayako had intensified. The attacks were getting more personal and less about skating. Last month Mayako posted that Natalie "was too ugly to find a man to skate pairs with." The month before she had bashed Natalie's coach and said that he was wasting his time with "a wooden toothpick with no sense of artistry." The last comment was when she said that Natalie's sequined costume was chosen to distract the audience from her face. Natalie wanted to tell her parents about the comments, but she was afraid that they would call Mayako's parents. That would make things even worse. *What if they make me quit skating? I could never do that! Why am I so freaked out? She's two years younger than me!*

Natalie felt like she would calm down when she saw Maria. After all, she was her best friend. Then again, they hadn't texted much lately, and every time Natalie called Maria rarely answered. *Was she being distant or just devoting every minute to practicing?* Natalie and her parents entered the arena and headed for the check-in area. The lobby was packed with ice skaters; some Natalie knew, some she had seen in previous competitions or on TV, and some she had never met. In the swirl of the crowd, Natalie spotted Maria. She started to call her name, but then she stopped in her tracks…Maria was walking with Mayako. Maria looked in her direction, then turned her head and laughed at something Mayako said. *What just happened? Why is my best friend with my enemy?*

NAVIGATING THE NATIONALS

After the skaters checked-in they headed to the auxiliary rink to look at the practice schedule. Maria and Mayako were looking at the schedule together. Natalie arrived as the other girls were leaving the schedule board. Natalie's heart pounded as she walked up to them.

Natalie said, "Hey Maria. What time are you practicing?" Before Maria could answer, Mayako responded, "She practices at 1 PM and I practice at 2 PM. The schedule says you practice after me at 3 PM, but you may want to request extra practice time because we all know that you could use it." Mayako poked Maria in the arm and laughed. Maria nervously giggled and walked away with Mayako.

As Mayako walked away, she turned around and looked Natalie in the eyes. "Guess what, Natalie? Did Maria tell you my big news? Trident Bladz is interested in signing on as my sponsor." Maria noticed the tears filling Natalie's eyes, but she didn't say anything.

Before meeting her coach, Natalie went back to her room to change her clothes and get herself mentally prepared for her first practice. Around 2:30 PM she headed back to the ice rink.

When she arrived, Maria had finished her practice and was watching Mayako practice. To avoid further conflict, Natalie sat on the other side and played on her phone to keep her mind occupied. Against her better judgment, she clicked on the IceSktrUSA site. Immediately she noticed another post and she couldn't believe her eyes.

"It looks like that blonde b**** won't be getting a contract w/ Trident Bladz."

"Trident Bladz will announce their upcoming sponsorship on Fri. Watch out blondie, this 15 yr old is coming 4 U!"

Like Katy Perry says, "We got it on lock . . . West Coast represent."

After reading the comments, her heart was in her throat and her heart stung with tears. *I was counting on a sponsorship this year. My parents need help paying for my training.* Natalie told herself that she was not going to cry anymore. *I've got to leave it all on the ice. I can do this!*

"Time to lace-up, Natalie," Coach said. "It's our turn in the rink."

GAME ON

On the day of the competition Natalie woke up feeling anxious, yet determined to show everyone that she deserved the Trident Bladz contract. When she arrived at the skating rink she had about an hour to warm up. Coach informed her that she was the last skater in the competition so she needed to stay focused and ignore everything that was going on around her.

Coach said to Natalie, "I know that you are concerned about the Trident Bladz contract and although I want that for you, too, our goal today is to win so that you will be ready to qualify for the US Olympic Team."

Natalie smiled and said, "Thanks, Coach, I always know that I can count on you to keep me focused. Let's win this!"

***

After the competition, Maria cautiously approached Natalie, who was standing with some other skaters in the locker rooms. Natalie could tell that Maria wanted to have a serious conversation, so she stepped away from the group of skaters. "Listen, Natalie, I'm sorry about what happened here at competition. I wasn't being a good friend."

"I don't understand what happened," Natalie said, shaking her head. "We've both been burned by Mayako. How did you two suddenly become best friends?"

"She's been texting me a lot lately, and she invited me to some parties, too," Maria said. "I guess I got sucked in by all of the glamour. She was going to introduce me to all of her famous friends. But deep down, she's really an awful person and I can't stand her anymore. She even told me that my choreography was amateur." Maria touched Natalie's shoulder. "Can you forgive me? I miss talking to you about training, boys, and school."

Natalie didn't say anything for a minute. She said quietly, "I've got to think about it. You really hurt my feelings, and right before Nationals, too!"

***

The Trident Bladz representative, Bill Harrison, approached Mayako after the winner had been announced. "Ms. Otsuko, do you have a few minutes? I would like to speak to you regarding the Trident Bladz sponsorship offer."

Mayako smiled and applauded her good fortune. *This is it. I am going to be the face of figure skating for Trident Bladz. I'm going to be on TV and get rich!*

Mr. Harrison and Mayako went to an empty room in the arena. He congratulated her on her performance and then told her that they needed to discuss the sponsorship contract.

"Mayako, you are a talented skater. However, our sponsorships decisions are decided on more than mere athletic ability. Trident Bladz is looking for a well-rounded athlete, teammate, and role model for our customers. In fact, one element of our Code of Ethics states, "Winners put their teams ahead of themselves. Winners don't take shortcuts. Winners play with honor." Mayako looked unhappy, and said, "I play by the rules. I like to win. I know the rules of figure skating. So I am not sure what you mean, Mr. Harrison."

"Trident Bladz is concerned about your use of social media and the comments you make about your teammates," Mr. Harrison said. "We have been following IceSktrUSA and we are concerned about how you would endorse our brand. We want athletes to represent the shared values of our company, but you are very critical of the other Team USA members."

"My online followers know that I speak the truth," Mayako rolled her eyes. "Can you get to the point, Mr. Harrison?" Mayako asked.

"It is also concerning that you publically posted that you were going to be signed by Trident Bladz," Mr. Harrison cautioned. "Although we were interested in you, the deal was never finalized. This may be embarrassing for you, Makayo. I'm sorry, but we have decided to sign another athlete."

"Whatever," Mayako said flippantly. "It's your loss. I've got tons of other options. You'll be sorry when I win gold."

DISCUSSION QUESTIONS

1. What strategies could Natalie and Maria use to be successful competitive athletes while maintaining a friendship? How can Natalie separate her professional and personal feelings about Mayako during the competition?

2. Should an athlete's online persona affect their ability to be a corporate spokesperson? How could Mayako have responded to the news about the Trident Bladz contract from Mr. Harrison without closing the door to future endorsements?

3. Do you believe that an individual's social media posts should be considered in a business setting? Do you think that Mayako is protected by the First Amendment Freedom of Speech?
4. Do you consider online criticism of athletes to be a form of bullying? What advice would you offer Natalie to help her handle the comments she received from IceSktrUSA?

KEY TERMS

Social media and sport, Corporate sponsorship, Athlete-athlete relationships, Interpersonal communication in sports

CASE 7: GOING HARD IN THE PAINT:
A Case of Coach-Athlete Violence

Shannon M. Brogan
Kentucky State University

Erin E. Gilles
University of Southern Indiana

Erin Gilliam
Kentucky State University

ABSTRACT

Head Basketball Coach Bruno Withers is demanding on the court with his players and at home with his son, Barrett Withers, whom he is grooming to one day be a professional basketball player. For years they have worked together relentlessly and mercilessly to prepare Barrett for a Division I college team with a transition to an NBA team. After an auto accident that comes with a severe prognosis, can Coach Withers transition back from coach to father?

***

On a hot summer afternoon in July, 13-year-old Bruno Withers was sweaty, sore, and worn out. He had been practicing on the hot asphalt basketball court for the last four hours without a break. He dropped down under a nearby shade tree, panting.

"Get up, boy," his father called. "Quitters don't win."

"But, Pa, I'm thirsty," Bruno complained.

"There's water in the truck, but you can have that when you start hitting those foul shots," his father replied.

Quietly, Bruno stood and stretched. He started a slow jog back to the foul line, and his father bounced the worn ball to him. Bruno looked up at the basket and prepared for his shot. He squinted against the harsh glare of the sun as he released the ball, but it went wide and missed the backboard.

"Another airball, son?" Bruno's father growled. "We've been practicing these for months and you're not getting any better. Your little sister shoots better than you! Don't you want to be team captain next year? No son of mine is going to embarrass me like this!"

"I can't play with this pressure from you," Bruno said. "I'm always better when I'm practicing with Coach." This throat felt thick. He was tired and was trying to suppress the tears that were forming. Bruno dragged the back of his hand across his eyes. He hoped his father would think that he was wiping sweat away.

"This is pressure?" his father asked. "What do you think it's going to be like when you are playing in college? Stop being a sissy. You're almost a man now, and too old to cry."

"Yes, sir," he said sullenly. "I'm ready to try again now." Bruno held the ball aloft and took a deep breath. He took a shot, closed his eyes, and heard the soft swish of the net. He exhaled and knew that his father would back off, for now.

A MISSED SHOT

Since the late 1980's Coach Bruno Withers has been Head Men's Basketball Coach of the Fighting Tigers at a large private university in a major metro area in the northeastern United States. Coach Withers is credited with bringing home six regional titles since his career at the school began. Although the team is the pride of the school and is competitive in its division, Coach Withers has gotten some criticism over the years because his own basketball career was undistinguished. Coach Withers lives for basketball. Growing up in a small, rural town, Coach Withers was a standout point guard on his high school team. Despite rounds of visits by recruiters, Coach Withers was never made an offer by a Division I or II school.

Coach Withers knew that his height was part of the problem. In spite of years of fervent hope, Coach Withers never hit a major teenage growth spurt. And, while his 5'10" stature was fairly average for his high school team, he was rather short for college basketball. After a round of rejections that crushed Coach Withers, he went to school and played intramural basketball and every pickup game he could while he earned a bachelor's degree in physical education and health. He worked at the athletic facility on campus and was friendly with the players and coaches. Coach Withers never missed a chance to talk team strategy. Coach Withers was a permanent fixture in the gym and weight room. If Coach Withers could not play the sport himself, he knew that he would strive hard to coach basketball as a career.

Upon graduation, Coach Withers returned and accepted an assistant coaching position at a university near his hometown. His stellar reputation at his former high school made him a shoo-in for the job. Coach Withers transferred his relentless passion for basketball into his coaching career, and just four years later when the head coach retired Coach Withers was offered the position. Now a fixture on campus and in the town, Coach Withers has a reputation as a tough-as-nails taskmaster. Although he is demanding, his players respect him and he gets their best performance. He has sometimes been compared to other aggressive coaches in the media. As long as the wins kept coming, the university did not sanction Coach Withers for his behavior. Coach Withers seemed proud of his media reputation.

"My coaching style instills fear in opposing teams," Coach Withers was quoted as saying in an article in the local paper. "I consider it to be a badge of honor."

Some notable headlines about Coach Withers are:

- Fighting Tigers Fight With Coach
- Tiger's Coach Ejected for Language
- Brutal Training Camps Exhaust Tigers

RAISING AN MVP

Coach Withers' wife, Brenda, and son have been in the front row at every game. Coach Withers has instilled the love of basketball into his son, Barrett. Since he was a toddler, Coach Withers has practiced with him and taught him the fundamentals of the game.

Coach Withers applied his coaching strategies to his gameplay with Barrett as he grew older. Sunday afternoons were spent reviewing game tapes and reading the weekend sports pages. Instead of bedtime stories Coach Withers would quiz Barrett on offensive and defensive plays. The walls in Barrett's room were lined with posters of his favorite basketball players. Barrett's basketball education was not limited to strategic fundamentals, but also included a stringent athletic regimen. While other kids had chores, Barrett's life revolved around basketball.

Barrett, then a fifth-grader, was sitting home alone on his bed watching cartoons one winter afternoon. Coach Withers, who was typically not home until after 6:00 PM each weeknight, came home early to meet a repairman. Surprised not to see Barrett out on the court practicing, Coach Withers hunted for him inside.

"Barrett, what's going on in here?" Coach Withers barked.

Barrett, who had his mouth full of potato chips, tried to answer. "I'm just watching this show and having a snack. I'm about to do my homework," he lied. "What are you doing home this early?"

"The furnace is acting up, so a repairman is coming. You know that you aren't allowed to watch TV until after practice time and homework!" Coach Withers reprimanded. "And you're in here eating junk food. You know the rule: Food stays in the kitchen. And, did you really drink three cans of soda?"

"Uh, well, yeah," Barrett mumbled. "I'm hungry and thirsty. Mom doesn't care."

"Well, I do," Coach Withers replied emphatically. "You're supposed to be training. Training means choosing practice, exercise, and good fuel instead of lounging and empty calories. Why aren't you taking this seriously?"

"Geez, Dad," Barrett whined. "You had me on lay-up and suicide drills for two hours yesterday. I missed a movie with Chad and Trevor. It's cold out and even your team doesn't have to practice outside. It's not fair. Plus you make me go to all those dumb basketball camps in the summer. Trevor is on the team and his Dad doesn't make him shoot free throws before dinner."

Coach Withers looked at his son's room. Basketball posters lined the walls. Couldn't he see that he was so lucky to have a father who could push him to greatness? Barrett might be in the Hall of Fame someday, but not with this attitude. His own father would never have let Bruno get away with this insolence!

"That's enough now, son," Coach Withers said sternly. "I won't have this backtalk. You're grounded for two weeks, and I'm taking the TV out of your room. Get out on the court now. I'd better hear that ball bouncing. Once the repairman leaves, I'll be out to run drills with you. Expect double tonight. C'mon, lace-up now." Coach Withers turned off the TV and grabbed the bags of chips and cookies.

Knowing he was defeated, Barrett got up to grab his basketball shoes. Not for the first time, Barrett wondered what it would be like to have a different Dad.

A TECHNICAL FOUL

The biggest issues came when Barrett entered his teenage years and sought more time with his friends. One evening when Barrett was 18, he asked to end his practice session early to go to a movie with some of his buddies. Coach Withers berated him and criticized his performance on their home basketball court.

"You just played a terrible game," Coach Withers said, raising his voice. "You're still missing lay-ups and foul shots. Your shooting won't get you into a D-1 school. And I'm not even going to get into your defense tonight."

"I'm the best player on my team," Barrett said. "I've had recruiters calling my coach since my junior year. Besides, I'm only 18. I need a life outside of basketball. All I do it run, lift, shoot, and do homework. It's my senior year and you're ruining it!"

Withers bounced the basketball angrily. "Since you don't give a damn about basketball, go to the movie. The best you can hope for is riding the bench in an overseas team."

"You only care about basketball," Barrett yelled. "I'm tired of being yelled at like this. It's not my fault you didn't make it to play college ball. It's not fun anymore. Just leave me alone!"

Coach Withers threw the basketball at his son's head just as Brenda was coming outside with water for Barrett. Barrett ducked, ran inside, got his car keys, and roared out of the driveway. Brenda tried to calm Coach Withers down, but she couldn't get his anger to subside. Brenda took off in her car after Barrett.

GAME OVER?

In his aggravated state, Barrett was trying to put distance between himself and his father before he said anything else he regretted. Although he loved basketball, he didn't want the pressure of living his father's dream. His father had his entire life planned out, down to which school Barrett should attend. But he never asked him if that's what Barrett really wanted. Barrett drove too fast around a curve and lost control of his car. Barrett was driving 65 mph in a 45-mph zone when the car began to veer off the road. The tires squealed as they left the pavement, and Barrett tried to swerve back on the road. The last thing that he remembered was hearing the crunch of glass and metal as he hit an oak tree.

Brenda arrived minutes later and found Barrett unresponsive in his car. She called an ambulance and then Coach Withers. Brenda rode with Barrett to the hospital, with Coach Withers arriving shortly thereafter. After an extensive examination and testing, the doctor met the parents in the hallway outside of Barrett's room to discuss the results of the EKG.

"He is one lucky boy," the doctor said solemnly. "The accident will leave him with severe bruising and a cracked rib, but the most important issue is the heart abnormality we found."

"What are we looking at?" Coach Withers asked. "Is he still going to be able to play basketball? He can't lose his shot at a D-1 school."

The doctor looked aghast. "Bruno, I've known your family for years and our kids are on the high school team together. But this is serious. This goes beyond basketball."

"Can we see him?" Brenda asks, her eyes full of fear.

"Yes," the doctor says. "But just for a few minutes. He needs to rest."

Coach Withers mutters angrily, "I've worked too hard for this. I'll take him to any specialist no matter what it costs. We'll get him back on the court in no time."

"Bruno, did you not hear the doctor?" Brenda asked, raising her voice. "It's time to quit being a coach and start being a father. This isn't one of your players, Bruno, this is your son!"

DISCUSSION QUESTIONS

1. How much pressure should a coach put on his players? Did Coach Withers treat his son like a college-level athlete starting at a young age?
2. Can motivation cross the line to aggression? Please provide examples.
3. Would you play for Coach Withers? Why or why not?
4. Should Brenda Withers been more involved in decisions relating to Barrett's participation in sports?

KEY TERMS

Family relations and sports, Parent as coach, Sport as achievement, Verbal aggression in sports

PART 2

TEAM COMMUNICATION AND SPORT

INTRODUCTION

One of the alluring aspects of many sports is the fact that, as an athlete in the sport, you are part of a team. Team sports often consider themselves a family. People who have not grown up with a close family life might embrace the family of their sport team as the only family they have. Teammates become like siblings and coaches are often parental figures. Thus when something affects one member of a team, often it can affect the whole team. The cases in Part Two look at various ways teams deal with issues of inter-team conflict, leadership, ethics involving injury, decision making (what is best for the team versus what is best for the individual athlete), how outside factors of one person's life affect the whole team, and how athletes deal with the teammate/competitor boundaries.

Issues surrounding injury and practice time are often at the forefront of team communication. One recent issue of contention among NFL football players is the way head injuries have been handled by the NFL administration. For the NFL, this has become a public relations issue, which we will address in Part Three, but for the players who see their present and former teammates suffer, the issue can be one that affects the team as a whole. This is not just an issue in pro football. Many college and high school athletes suffer from concussions as well.

This also leads to questions of how practices and injuries are handled within teams at all levels. There is evidence that concussions are more likely to occur at practices.[1] In a case with the Ohio State Buckeyes, one of their scout team members, Kosta Karageorge, committed suicide during the 2014 season. While a coroner's report could not verify head trauma in the autopsy, Karageorges' mother revealed that Kosta had sent her text messages saying that concussions were affecting his mind and OSU did verify he had suffered concussions.[2] Tragic events such as this one affect not only individual players and their families, but the team as a whole. Questions begin to arise about how practices are handled and when a player's injury should take him or her out of practices and games.

Some of the cases in this section deal with issues of whether amount and times of practices are fair and whether players who have suffered an injury should continue to play and practice. The need of a coach and some players to win games can sometimes be achieved at the price of other players' health and well-being, whether that be of body or mind. This is not to say that all team sports are full of strife and people who do not care about the welfare of others.

Team sports also give athletes a chance to grow in their leadership capabilities. While not every player will get a chance to be a team captain, as they advance in the sport, they can become mentors to younger teammates and become leaders within their position group. For instance, in the 2015 National Basketball Association's (NBA) championship, while the

Cleveland Cavaliers did not end up winning, LeBron James was able to lead the Cavs' "B Team" (due to the loss of several "A Team" players to injuries) to two wins in the six-game series making the championship a challenge for the Golden State Warriors.[3] James himself believed he needed to go away and learn under the leadership of veteran Heat players to be able to come back to compete for a championship with Cleveland.[4] Even though he was able to help lead the Cavs to a 2007 NBA Finals bid, he realized he did not have the experience to lead a successful run all by himself. You will see a young wrestler face a similar situation in Case 12 of this section.

Sometimes something that affects one team member can lead to a negative effect on a whole team. And how the team deals with that can help or hinder an entire season for one or many. Take two cases of Major League Baseball (MLB) players suspended for illegal performance-enhancing drug use. When Alex Rodriguez was suspended, the New York Yankees kept his locker for him. When he came back in for Spring Ball in 2015, his locker and place among the team were intact, even though his drug use and subsequent suing of the MLB and a Yankees team doctor could have detrimental effects on the team as a whole.[5]

But, when it comes to Josh Hamilton of the Anaheim Angels, who was suspended due to substance abuse, the treatment is a different story. Hamilton's locker was reassigned and he had been effectively "scrubbed from the Angels' clubhouse."[6] One could certainly argue that illegal drug use is grounds for banishment from the team, but at the same time, when the team is often like your family, to have this treatment in such a time of need could be even more detrimental to the athlete's recovery. These are examples of what teams often have to deal with when something affects one member.

The issue affecting a member does not have to be one with such negative connotations. For instance, the case in Case Ten deals with how the religion of one member of the team affects the team as a whole. But often, it is bad decisions, like illegal drug use, that can get in the way of team success. Case Eight tells a similar story about a star high school running back in the height of his senior year.

As you work through the cases in Part Two of the book, be sure to think continually about group and team communication concepts, such as:

- importance of team roles, norms, and rules in keeping a team oriented toward a goal;
- leadership and how leaders develop in an athletic environment;
- ethical treatment of athletes;
- relational dialectics and other issues of conflict

REFERENCES

[1] Dompier, T. P., Kerr, Z. Y., Marshall, S. W., Hainline, B., Snook, E. M., Hayden, R., & Simon, J. E. (2015). Incidence of concussion during practice and games in youth, high school, and collegiate American football players. *JAMA Pediatrics*, 169(7), 659–65.

[2] Associated Press. (3 March 2015). Kosta Karageorge had concussions. Retrieved from http://espn.go.com/college-football/story/_/id/12434907/coroner-says-ohio-state-buckeye-kosta-karageorge-killed-self-had-concussions

[3] Schmitz, B. (10 June 2015). LeBron returned to Cavs as a mature leader. *Orlando Sentinel.* Retrieved from http://www.orlandosentinel.com/sports/orlando-magic/magic-basketblog/os-lebron-james-returned-mature-leader-20150610-post.html

[4] Ibid.

[5] Mathews, W. & Marchand, A. (5 October 2013). Alex Rodriguez files two lawsuits. Retrieved from http://espn.go.com/new-york/mlb/story/_/id/9768073/alex-rodriguez-sues-mlb-ped-investigation

[6] Brown, T. (11 April 2015). The Angels have turned their back on Josh Hamilton when he needs them most. Retrieved from http://sports.yahoo.com/news/the-angels-have-turned-their-back-on-josh-hamilton-when-he-needs-them-most-081942196.html

VOICE OF A PRO

James P. Tressel
President, Youngstown State University

"Concern for man and his fate must form the chief interest in all technical endeavors, never forget this in the midst of your diagrams and equations." –Albert Einstein

"They don't care how much you know until they know how much you care." –Dr. Lee J. Tressel.

The philosophy that we tried to abide by with our 25 teams at Youngstown State and Ohio State was crafted by trying to live by the two quotes/thoughts above that adorned our staff meeting room walls. Every decision we made needed to keep those two thoughts in mind. It was our belief

95

that our students must know that we cared more about them, more about their preparation for the future, than we cared about their ability to perform on the field. When they truly knew and believed that, it was easy to help them reach their potential on the field. Having moved into the world of higher education as an administrator, I have found that the same is true when dealing with faculty, staff, and students. First and foremost, everyone needs to know that their leaders care about them. So, then specifically how do we go about this task? I have found that building relationships through extensive communication is the key. Finding out what are the person's dreams, goals, and especially their opinions is the beginning of the dialogue and relationship that will convince them that we know what they want, and we are here solely to help them be all that they can be.

The industry of sport is booming. Through the increase in exposure from multimedia in the past thirty years, the number of persons interested in being a part of this exciting environment is staggering. The "law of supply and demand" is not in favor of the individual, and the ability to differentiate oneself is highly competitive. I have often recommended to students that, if they want to be in a position to work with student-athletes or professional athletes, it is tremendously helpful to study education, communication, and psychology. There is no substitute for the knowledge of human behavior in competitive environments and how to best connect, inspire, and motivate. When it comes to the business side of sport, developing competencies in business, management, marketing, and communication is essential. In some cases I have felt that the "sport management" majors, while doing a wonderful job of identifying the work ethic needed, at times do not provide the depth of core knowledge that is needed to prepare the individual for the competitive arena they will face in the job market. Liking sports and wanting to be a part of the excitement of competition that you have admired is not enough to prepare one for the scarce number of opportunities in this industry. Although of course work ethic is crucial and success in this field cannot happen without it, I have grown to believe that development of knowledge competencies, curiosity for constant improvement and knowledge, grit, and selflessness are really the difference-makers when competing at the highest level.

In terms of advice for the individual seeking employment in the industry of sport, be prepared to start at the bottom, working for little compensation, and take advantage of every opportunity to show that the organization cannot do without you. In addition, networking with people in the field is paramount. Above all else, be a great listener. Many students, parents, and even fans feel as if they are well educated in the field of sport due to the tremendous amount of information disseminated in the media sources of all kinds. It is important to have a great handle on what people whom you are working with think. Connecting with their thoughts and ideas is the beginning of meaningful dialogue and true connection. You will be amazed with what you can learn from them!

James P. Tressel serves as the ninth president of Youngstown State University in Youngstown, Ohio. Tressel, who grew up in northeast Ohio and graduated from Berea High School in 1971, became vice president for Strategic Engagement at the University of Akron in May 2012 and was promoted to executive vice president for Student Success in December 2013.

He previously was head football coach at Ohio State between 2001 and 2010, where his teams won the national championship in 2002 and Big Ten championships in 2002, 2005, 2006, 2007, 2008, 2009, and 2010. As head football coach at YSU from 1986 to 2000, Tressel's teams won four Division I-AA national championships. He also was executive director of Athletics at YSU from 1994 to 2000. Prior to YSU, Tressel was an assistant football coach at Ohio State, Syracuse University, Miami University of Ohio, and the University of Akron.

He earned a bachelor's degree in education from Baldwin-Wallace College in 1975 and a master's degree in education from the University of Akron in 1977. He has published two books: The Winners Manual: For the Game of Life *(2008) and* Life Promises for Success *(2011).*

Tressel has a long list of awards, including the American Football Coaches Association National Coach of the Year in 1991, 1994, and 2002.

CASE 8: VICTORY ISN'T EVERYTHING

Latent and Articulated Dissent as Forms of Player Backlash on a Winning High School Football Team

Corey Jay Liberman
Marymount Manhattan College

ABSTRACT

The Copeland Cavaliers have become one of the greatest high school football teams in the history of New Jersey, though has the "win at all costs" mentality of the head coach impinged on the loyalty and determination of its players? Team members must now figure out how best to communicate their dissent in a way that ultimately leads to organizational change or else they may find themselves in a situation not well-known to them: defeated.

***

The Copeland Cavaliers football team has won 303 of its last 330 games: a winning percentage of just under 92%. They have won 12 district titles in the past two decades and have been state champions five times in that same stretch. In their small New Jersey county, the Cavaliers have, since 1992, achieved many state records, including, though not limited to, the following: most throwing yards by a quarterback in a single season (6, 233 yards in 2009), most rushing yards by a running back in a single season (2,298 yards in 2011), most consecutive games with at least seven defensive sacks (61), most players joining Division I football schools upon high school graduation (an average of nine per year), and most consecutive seasons atop the league's division (14 seasons in a row). In Copeland, fans live and breathe black and tan: the color of the Cavaliers' uniforms.

The team, including starters and backup players, consists of a total of 41 players (22 of whom comprise the offense and 19 of whom comprise the defense) and a total of 8 coaches. From the outside looking in, it seems as though, behaviorally and communicatively speaking, all 49 constituents of the team get along, working harmoniously to win the team's next state championship. During interviews, players and coaches oftentimes comment about such things as camaraderie, drive, motivation, synergy, hard work, dedication, and devotion. If one were merely to attend games and read the weekly sports column, the relationships between and among players and staff of the Copeland Cavaliers would seem nothing less than congruous, compatible, and, in a sense, congenial. From the inside looking out, however, things are much different than they appear. Although players are afraid to admit that there is a huge problem, especially considering that the town of Copeland supports them so much and any negative image in the mind of the public could impinge on their success, there is. His name is Ryan Roth and he is the head coach of the Cavaliers.

Coach Roth started coaching the Copeland team back in 1988, 26 years ago, when the team often struggled to achieve a final season record of 6-6. The town brought in Coach Roth because they knew that he would bring with him a much-needed energy. He came from a family of football players and coaches (his grandfather played football in the Big East conference and later coached a college team in the Big 12 and his father played in the Patriot League in college and then coached in the Big Ten for 32 years before his unfortunate and untimely death) and he, himself, was a tight end for a college in Division II. Players like and respect Coach Roth, without question, but there are certainly things about him which make communication difficult. "I could not ask for a better coach," explained Bradley Wright, the team's star defensive end, "but his whole life is about winning. In fact, every single meeting, whether it is with one player or with the entire team, ends with him saying 'win, dammit, win.'" "It would be awful to have a coach who was not all about winning," said Chase Albanese, the team's quarterback and one of its three captains, "but there comes a time when other things become more important. When we are afraid to talk to Coach Roth out of fear that he will yell at us or bench us, that becomes a huge problem."

The Cavaliers were 4-0, atop their division, and had outscored their opponents by a total score of 147-42. The team's players, however, were at their tipping point. As long as they played their hearts out and gave it their all on the field, Coach Roth was complimentary and in a great mood. However, even if the team was ahead by a score of 35-3 (as it was against the Rumsfeld Rockets), he interacted with his players as if they had done something wrong and even disrespectful. It was the nonverbal "I cannot believe that you gave up that field goal and we no longer have a shutout" manifestation decoded by many of the Cavaliers that led to feelings of mediocrity and disenfranchisement. During the "locker room talk" preceding the fifth game of the season, Coach Roth said "you guys have played good football recently, but you can certainly play better." He continued by saying "I expect you to run faster, hit harder, and score more. Whatever you have been doing, do it with more tenacity. In order to be great, you must portray an image of greatness. Right now, your record speaks louder than your actions. Go get them and I will see you at the half." The Cavaliers won the game against the Hillsdale Hawks by a score of 28-14, but this victory created angst for Coach Roth, illustrated in his ". . . I am disappointed and I hope that you perform better next Saturday" end-of-game speech.

LATENT DISSENT AMONG THE CAVALIERS

In the days following the game, verbiage about Coach Roth permeated the halls of Copeland High School. The players on the Cavaliers assumed that by "trash-talking" about their coach to each other, it would somehow provide a certain sense of social cohesion. From lunchroom gossip to after-school chats to in-the-hall comments to between-class texts, there were few, if any, of the players who did not get their turn to make a snide comment about Coach Roth and his leadership strategies. "What kind of high school head coach tells his team to do better after a two-touchdown win and after having played their absolute best?" asked Jake Halton, the team's starting wide receiver, who caught seven passed for 59 yards and a touchdown in the victory. "A coach who clearly doesn't give a crap about his players," responded Dan Frost, the team's starting center. He continued by saying "in all honesty, if this was not my fourth and final year, I would question whether or not I had the desire and drive to be part of this team again next year. I really feel sorry for the freshmen and sophomores who have to deal with him for the next several years. Our school and town see a great team play every Saturday morning, but they have no idea what we have to go through day in and day out." "I never even told any of you this because I did not want it to piss you off," said Troy Robinson, the outside linebacker, who led the team with six tackles the last game, "but I injured my left foot in last Wednesday's practice. After the three trainers took a look, they decided that it would probably be best if I stayed off of it for the next 48-72 hours to reduce the swelling. Guess what Coach Roth said? He said, and I quote, 'the trainers have told me that there is nothing broken or fractured, so if you do not plan to come to practice and play in Saturday's game, you can plan to sit on the bench for the remainder of the season.' My foot is still hurting, but I am afraid to mention it to anyone at this point." "Do you guys remember what he did last year when we fumbled the opening snap of the game, causing that safety against the Rumson Riders?" asked Jim Doherty, the backup running back for the Cavaliers. "Oh yes," answered Thomas Roberts, the starting left tackle, "he extended our next practice for three hours and required us to wear those 'we might look like football players, but we play like the cheerleading squad' shirts over our pads. He made me look and feel like a fool. He always does." Even Scott Lumber, the backup right guard for the Cavaliers, said, ". . . Coach Roth is the reason that I have come to hate this game so much and I have only been on the team for six week."

Communication between and among players, off the field, was oftentimes consistent: 80% was framed around the team's chances of winning and making it to the state championship game and the other 20% was framed about Coach Roth. Each and every Friday night, as part of a cultural, ceremonial event, the Cavaliers congregate at one player's home, whose family is gracious enough to invite the entire team (no coaches, just players) for a two-hour dinner, coupled with an opportunity to merely have some recreational fun with one another. All players are required to be home by 10:00 PM on Friday evenings and either Brian Wacklund or Seth Ferguson, the two assistant coaches, will phone their homes to be sure that they are abiding by this rule: mandated, of course, by Coach Roth. In addition to the dinner and the recreational activities, an inspirational team speech is offered by one of the team's three captains: Chase Albanese (the starting quarterback), Jacob Lacoste (the starting running back), or Matt Montgomery (the starting left tackle). This week, it was Matt's turn and, in addition to getting his fellow teammates pumped up for the next day's game against the Pittstown Pirates, a comparatively weaker team, and congratulating all of the stars from the previous weekend's victory, he made an important announcement regarding Coach Roth:

> "I think that it is clear that we are all on the same page about Coach Roth. Is he a good coach? Yes. However, the way that he deals with us players is atrocious. He tells us to play when we are sick or injured. We score 35 points and he wonders why we did not score 36. He thinks that every time that our quarterback gets sacked it is a result of a

weak offensive line rather than a strong defensive attack. We are barely congratulated for our extreme successes and we are always drilled for any on-the-field mistakes that we make. I think that we will also agree that the worst thing about this is that we are afraid of him. We are afraid to tell him to treat us better. We are afraid to tell him to treat us like deserving, hard-working players. We are afraid to tell him to stop treating us like we do not matter. This fear is not only coming from the underclassmen . . . it is coming from all of us. Truth be told, I think that this fear is warranted because, unfortunately, he is a scary guy to have to speak to. But, as you know, when we bitch and complain and make fun of Coach Roth with each other, it is fun and it makes us laugh and for some strange reason it makes us feel good. The problem, though, is that it never leads to change. Well, we are ready for this change. As you know, Chase, Ryan, and I are graduating this year and hopefully heading off to play college ball. That means that three of you underclassmen are going to emerge as the captains and leaders of this great team next year. And, believe it or not, of the 41 of us on this team, only 15 are graduating. This means that 26 of you, and all of the players who make it to the varsity level next year, are going to have to deal with Coach Roth and his bullshit if we do not do something now. Before tomorrow's game, Chase, Ryan, and I are going to meet Coach Roth in his office and tell him everything that is bothering us and the changes that he needs to make in order for us, the team, to feel better and more excited about playing for him. If you are with me and think that this is a great idea, please give me a "Hell yeah" at the count of three.

It was clear, based on the uniform communication of "Hell yeah" on behalf of the team members, that all were in favor of Chase, Ryan, and Matt directing their complaints directly to Coach Roth.

ARTICULATED DISSENT TO THE HEAD COACH

It was 9:00 AM on Saturday morning: three hours prior to kickoff of the game, yet one hour after Coach Roth arrived at his office. It was, for one reason or another, part of his routine. Why he needed to arrive on campus four hours before each home game was an enigma to all, but, like everything else, no one questioned it. Matt, Chase, and Ryan were overtaken by a myriad of different, and conflicting, emotions that morning (about both the forthcoming game and about their forthcoming discussion with their head coach): fear, anticipation, excitement, hope, anxiety, anger, and confidence to name a few. Chase knocked on the door and, in a rather loud, agitated voice, Coach Roth told him to come in.

"Hello, Coach," greeted Chase.

"Good morning, gentlemen," replied Coach Roth. "How are my three captains feeling this morning? Are you ready to kick some ass today?"

"We are feeling great, sir," responded Ryan. "We are going to try our absolute best. We had a great week of practice and we are confident that if we keep to the game plan, we will bring another victory to our squad."

"That is what I like to hear," said Coach Roth. "So. . . what can I do you for," asked Coach Roth.

"Well," began Matt, "this is not an easy conversation to have, Coach, but the three of us feel that it is necessary. Let me begin by saying that the three of us love you and think that you are a coach who clearly is the best and wants the best for us."

"I certainly don't like where this is going, fellas," interrupted Coach Roth.

"It's just that our team thinks that you sometimes consider your needs before ours and put winning before all else," claimed Matt.

"I don't understand what you are getting at here," Coach Roth indicated.

"Let me give you an example, Coach," Ryan stated. "Do you remember our recent victory against Williamstown?"

"Of course," replied Coach Roth. "Chase, here, threw for 425 yards and four touchdowns. He made the top headline in the local news and that was a day that the national scouts were in town. It is likely that this game, alone, earned him a spot in one of the top football schools."

"Yes," answered Ryan, "but in that game, Seth Danielson hurt his calf muscle after receiving a vicious hit on the field. After taking an injury timeout, you asked him, in front of us and the trainer, whether or not he wanted to sit out for the series. When he seemed to question if he wanted to sit out, you said, and I quote, 'what kind of player would want to sit out when he has the chance to score on a drive like this.' He was hurt. He could barely walk. He was afraid that he would do more damage. And the worst thing of all is that we were up by 28 points at this juncture in the game. You did not care about him. It was for the game's statistics. You did not care about how he felt."

"That is not true at all," exclaimed Coach Roth.

"Did you happen to reach out to him over the course of that next week to see how his calf was healing?" asked Chase

"Well, no," replied Coach Roth, "but I had my assistant coaches and trainers do it."

"Seth was so furious about this decision, Coach," said Ryan. "I really think that you should have handled this situation differently.

"So what are you saying, gentlemen, that I handled this situation poorly?" asked Coach Roth.

"This is why we are here," responded Chase. "Since we are the three captains of this team, we assume that you respect us and think highly of us. We told the team that we were going to come speak with you about the things that we, as a team, are pretty much fed up with regarding your behaviors. As you know, we all love to play football. We love to win. But when winning becomes more important than everything else, including health and family and relationships and school and pretty much anything else in life that matters, then the glory of winning is impacted."

"This is how I was coached when I played," replied Coach Roth, "so I know what works and what does not work. My strategy makes you work harder and run harder and play stronger and hit better and throw longer and run faster and win by more. I am not going to stop this."

"The problem is that we want you to stop this," explained Ryan.

"It is absolutely killing us," added Chase.

"I think that we do the things that you tell us and abide by your rules and demands out of fear, rather than respect, Coach Roth," stated Matt. "The three of us are graduating in eight months. But the underclassmen will be here for another two or three years. We cannot let them suffer through this. You think that because we are football players, that your comments do not get to us. Well they do. There is a big difference between respect and fear, coach. It is time to try a different coaching strategy.

At this point in the conversation, Coach Roth had a certain look overtake his face: one that none of the three captains had ever seen. It could best be described as a face of contempt. It was clear, at least in that brief moment, that he began to see himself in a different light and through a different lens. It was, perhaps literally, the first time that any individual was ever fearless enough to directly communicate discontent to Coach Roth. Perhaps he finally realized the flaws of his ways. Perhaps he finally realized that he was not immune to imperfection. Perhaps he finally realized that it was fear, and not respect, that created the social condition of obedience on behalf of his teammates. The meeting ended when Chase indicated that it was time for his team to hit the field for pre-game stretching and practice and that he and the rest of the Cavaliers would see him in the locker room for the 11:45 pep talk.

Coach Roth shook the hand of each captain as they left his office, but no additional words were exchanged.

After a rather long and intense pre-game practice, which included strenuous drills for both offensive and defensive units, the team met in their home locker room to fix their pads and prepare for Coach Roth's pep talk. The 41-player squad gathered in their perfectly created circle, bent on one knee, as Coach Roth stood in the center. He began his pep talk by saying "I hope that you all had a great evening last night and I am looking forward to a great game today." He continued by saying "We are going to do something a little different today."

With their helmets off and their spirits high, Matt, Chase, and Ryan looked at each other and smiled with triumph.

DISCUSSION QUESTIONS

1. What are the positive and negative effects of latent dissent from a sport communication perspective? Do the positive effects seem to outweigh the negative effects? Please be sure to use examples from the case study to support your major claims.

2. In order for articulated dissent to be an effective communicative tool for change within the sport world, what are the necessary prerequisite and/or co-requisite variables? Which of these variables are most important? Please be sure to use examples from the case study to support your major claims.

3. Other than the strategy used by the three team captains, what other way(s) could the team have approached Coach Roth in an effort to increase the likelihood that he would change

his style of coaching? What about this particular strategy would have been effective and would there have been any particular negative ramifications associated with this decision?

4. Assume that Coach Roth decided to respond negatively to the articulated dissent provided by the three team captains. What could this have done to the relationship(s) between and among the head coach, the assistant coaches, and the players on the team? How could this have impacted the rest of the season?

KEY TERMS

Articulated dissent, Conflict, Latent dissent, Relationships

CASE 9: WHEN WINNING ISN'T ALWAYS WINNING

Patrick J. Carey
Clemson University

John Spinda
Clemson University

ABSTRACT

When a star player makes the mistake of a lifetime, Coach Joe Romano is left with a decision that will determine the fate of a record-breaking season and whether his childhood dream will ever be accomplished.

***

BACKGROUND

"What's the move, Joe?" asked Phil, his assistant coach, as the emotional rollercoaster of this story was finally reaching its climax. In the 15 years they had worked together as coaches of Breaking River's ice hockey team, this is the first time Joe could sense fear in his assistant's eyes. Any guilt that should have been felt at this point had already been flushed from his mind along with the trust and respect he had for the captain of his hockey team. Although emotions were racing through his mind, Coach Joe Romano knew his decision still had to be made based on facts and logic.

After staring out the window blankly, Joe said, "Well, Phil, I know what I want to do. But I just keep thinking back to six years ago, picking up the Sunday paper on that freezing morning and reading the headline "2 goals and 3 assists: Williams Carries Team to Playoffs." I was expecting to see this Williams boy playing for one of the powerhouse traveling teams, not a Pee Wee phenom who was only in seventh grade." Joe continued, "For cryin' out loud, he had better stats than our entire top line that season! I knew right then, that morning, that a state championship might possible for us if we pushed hard recruiting him and he chose Breaking River to play high school hockey. I still can't believe we got him on board."

RYAN WILLIAMS: THE GAME CHANGER

Sitting nervously at his locker before his first game as a freshman, Ryan Williams closed his eyes and took a deep breath. He silently told himself, "You can do this, Ryan, just play your game." Coach Romano came into the dressing room and said, "It's time guys, let's start this year off great! Michaels, you are centering the starting lineup between Steward at left wing and Williams at right wing." With that, the 14-year-old Williams put the last wrap of tape on his shin guards, laced up his skates, and exhaled. "Where are you from anyhow, Kid? A hat trick . . . in your first game? Unreal," remarked Steve Michaels, Breaking River's senior captain and Williams's linemate. "Alright! Great game guys, big win to start the year!" remarked Coach Romano, "this is for you Ryan," tossing a puck to the freshman sensation that read "Breaking River – 6, Beechwood – 5, October 28, 2006."

It was clear from his very first game in a high school uniform, Ryan's talents were exceptional. "He just sees plays happen before they even develop," said Coach Joe Romano to friends during Williams's freshman season. "I know he's only 14, but he very well may break our goal record this year if he stays focused." Sure enough, the dynamic right winger broke the school's goal record his freshman year and again as a sophomore. His consistent multi-goal games were the talk of the town and earned the team respect throughout the conference. "For the first time in my head coaching career, we finished back-to-back seasons in the top third of our conference," said Coach Romano. Ryan singlehandedly put the school's hockey program on the map and opened up new recruiting opportunities throughout the county. Applications for the private school rose and some of the top players began choosing Breaking River High School.

Coming into Ryan's senior year, the team was ranked number one in the conference and was considered a favorite to win the state championship. The top line, anchored by the senior right winger, was one of the most potent in the state. The local papers and fans began looking for the hidden secrets behind their monumental turnaround, but Joe's simple answers always began and ended with the "our star winger and team leader, Ryan Williams."

"Hey Coach, more great news! I got scholarship offers from Michigan State and Ferris State today!" Ryan said as he excitedly came into Coach Romano's office, dripping with sweat from a fierce workout. With his rising point totals and work ethic, top Division I college teams were recruiting the 5'11" 190-pound captain. "Wow, so many offers coming in, I hardly know where to begin," remarked Williams to his coach and biggest supporter. Over the course of four years, the two had come to respect and trust one another immensely. When Ryan was not in class or at the rink, he could almost always be found sitting across from the coach in his office above the locker room. The two conversed about everything ranging from future aspirations to family pressures. Ryan's overbearing parents, two of the best lawyers in the area, were always pushing him to train harder, so Joe's office became one of the only places where he was able to let his guard down.

As the regular season ended, Breaking River's 18 wins, 4 losses, and 2 ties put them in first place in the conference. The star right winger finished up another great season and the team was playing magnificently. Breaking River High School was getting attention from all over the state and rumors of an imminent state championship berth began circulating. "Look, guys," said Coach Romano, "they don't give titles in newspapers; they are earned in the weight room and on the ice! Let's get focused, we know what we've got in front of us Saturday!"

Their semi-finals opponents, the South Hills Warriors, had a set of defensemen that was being compared to a New York City skyline and one of the steadiest goaltenders around. Six of their players had already committed to Division I colleges and their legendary coach had accumulated more state championship rings than Coach Romano had above .500 seasons. Joe knew that only a great week of practice and a top performance on Saturday would allow them an opportunity to play for a championship.

THE BIG BUILDUP . . . AND LETDOWN

It was an exceptionally warm Thursday for late winter. As Joe Romano sat down in his chair, a feeling of suspense that only came with a championship opportunity sent shivers down his spine. The semi-final puck drop was 30 hours away and the anticipation was killing him. Breaking River's athletic director visited Joe's office and asked, "How are you feeling, Coach?" "Good . . . I feel good," said Joe, "Our practices have been crisp all week, these boys look hungry to go get after it." "Great! Well, if you need anything, you know where to find me," said the athletic director as he left Joe's office. Next in was Phil, Joe's longtime assistant coach and close friend. "Look, I know you want to make sure we got everything down solid, Joe, but these guys are going to need fresh legs if we hope to win Saturday. I think we should just have a light skate after school and keep these guys loose," said Phil. "We'll see, Phil," said Joe. But after thinking about his assistant coach's recommendation of a light skate that Friday, Joe felt like a light skate made sense and seemed right after all of the hard work from the team.

Joe began Friday morning the same way he did every day before a game, picking the forward lines and defensive pairings. The "bzzz" sound coming from his cell phone pulled the coach out of a deep focus. A text from Ryan read, "Coach, won't be in school today, but will be at practice. See you then." Joe thought it seemed a little strange that Ryan's parents would allow him to miss school, but the trust he had for his star winger made it hard to respond with anything other than "Alright." The morning went on pretty uneventfully with the exception of a teacher stopping by with what seemed like hopes to get a few of his players in trouble. "Joe, three of them fell asleep on their desks this morning and remained lifeless even after all the students left the classroom," said the teacher, "I know it's a big week Coach, but you got to let these kids know this isn't acceptable, okay?" Joe responded "C'mon now, this is the first time you've come to me with this all year. Also, I don't know about you, but I can remember taking an occasional nap in high school . . . especially during biology," adding a wry smirk for effect. "What are we going to do with you Joe?" said the biology teacher as she rolled her eyes and smirked back.

It was just after lunch when his phone buzzed again. This time the name showing up on his phone was a former high school football teammate named Wade. Wade was a local police officer who lived, breathed, and died Breaking River hockey. They often talked about strategies for upcoming games and how great the team had become. However, it was a little surprising to see him calling in the middle of the day.

Immediately upon answering the phone, Joe could sense the call was not about hockey strategies.

"Joe, Ryan Williams and his girlfriend just left the station about an hour ago. Ryan was pulled over on his way to school this morning after swerving into oncoming traffic. He was charged with a DUI, registering a .09 BAC, and the girlfriend was charged with underage drinking."

The line went silent for a few seconds as the coach sat in utter disbelief. *How could this have happened? His All-State winger was drinking before the biggest game of the season?* Joe's next thought was about the text he had received a few hours earlier and how his captain should be arriving at the school soon. "I have also heard from officers that there was a party at Ryan's house last night and they believe most of your team was there." *My Team? How could that be? The biology teacher had said . . .*

"However, there is good news. An hour after we brought him in, Ryan's father showed up. That man must be one heck of a lawyer. After talking with the chief for no more than twenty minutes, the chief had us unlock their cell to let them go. That was the first time I have ever seen a DUI culprit set free and the neither of them received even a fine! A bunch of the officers are a little annoyed with the chief's shady deal, but we all know what would have happened if word had gotten out. It looks like the stars were all lined up for you, my friend. Good luck tomorrow!"

"WHAT'S THE MOVE, JOE?"

"Well, thanks, Wade, I appreciate you letting me know," said Joe, who could not have disagreed more with Wade's final words. How could Wade think he should be feeling lucky? It was now two o'clock in the afternoon, 23 hours before the biggest game in the school's history, and his star winger was recovering from a night of partying. The player he had become so close with those past four years had betrayed him. Not only did he throw a party two nights before the game, Ryan drove to school still drunk and put his entire senior year, not to mention the life of his passenger and everyone on the road, at risk!

What made matters worse was the new sanctions the school had on drinking and driving. The year before Ryan began attending Breaking River, two fatal drunk driving accidents occurred within a three-month period. Both of the deaths were students who played sports at the school and their deaths left the student body an emotional mess. The school took it upon themselves to work with the police to put a stop to drinking and driving. By the end of the following year, a new rule was passed. Anyone caught drinking and driving, convicted or not, will be suspended from school for three days and face a minimum two-week suspension from athletics. The semi-finals were the next day and the championship was the next week . . . If the school got word about his arrest, any hope of Ryan playing in the games would be lost.

Joe thought about the two students who had broken the rule and received the full punishment. Clearly they were not the captain and star winger on the hockey team. Within five hours of his arrest, the charges of a major crime were dropped and the story was squashed. If Joe had not received that phone call, he might not have even found out about the party or the arrest.

All respect for his captain was lost. Now the question on Joe's mind was whether he should do what was right or go after the dream he had been working to achieve ever since his years as a high school hockey player. With over twenty scouts projected to be at tomorrow's game, many of them there to see Ryan, how could his captain choose to throw a party? The betrayal he felt swayed him back and forth. He needed to hear it from the guilty party himself.

Ryan strolled into Joe's office around 3:55 P.M., as he normally did before practice. Joe always admired his ability to forget mistakes. It was something that had enabled him to become the elite player he was and this skill was never more evident than that afternoon.

"Smitty getting bumped up to second line?" said the right winger as he skimmed over the forward lines for tomorrow's game.

Ryan's dissatisfaction was far from the Joe's mind as the coach scanned his captain for any signs of incarceration. Other than the small bags under his eyes, Ryan looked like he did every afternoon.

"Where were you during school today?" demanded the coach.

"The parents were out of town last night. I stayed at my grandmother's house and she asked me to help her around the house this morning."

The lies continued for a few more minutes until Joe could not mask his anger any longer.

"I know you were arrested for drinking and driving this morning. You threw a party last night that most of the team attended and you were pulled over for swerving into oncoming traffic. You have hurt our hockey team, put your senior season in jeopardy, and betrayed my trust! But most importantly, you could have killed yourself or any number of people on the road!"

The last one was the dagger to the heart. The tears that had been pent up for the last six hours were now pouring out into his hands. Finally, Ryan got ahold of his emotions and began recounting everything from the past 24 hours.

"My parents told me they were going to be out of town Thursday and Friday for business. When I told the guys about it, they insisted that I have a few friends over. Since today's practice is going to be a light skate, I thought everything would be fine. Then I woke up late this morning and had to rush. I was pulled over trying to pass a car and knew I was in trouble immediately. I called my father before they could take my phone and he told me to text you. If anyone finds out about me drinking and driving, my senior year will be finished! The chances of me playing in college will be finished! I cannot tell you how sorry I am for this, but you have to let me play. I know I have betrayed your trust, but we have come so far these past four years."

After listening to his pleas, Joe instructed the captain to tell his assistant coach to come into his office and get changed for practice. Phil had been with Joe for his entire career and was one of his most trusted assistants. The two coaches went over every detail of the morning's debacle as if they were a jury presiding over a death penalty case. Joe knew Phil had been close with one of the girls who had passed away in the drunk-driving accidents that had prompted the school's DUI policy, so he would be able to provide an opinion from a different perspective. Phil finally sat back in his chair after contemplating the repercussions of each decision.

"What happens when the boy goes to college and it happens again? Do you think letting him play will teach him anything? As much as I hate to say it, the rule was created to stop behavior like this and a few scouts at the rink should not make a player above the law."

As his longtime assistant and highly admired friend walked out of the office, Joe felt more indecisive than ever. A decision of that importance deserved a night of contemplation.

***

It was eight o'clock the next morning and Joe could hear Phil climbing the stairs to his office. The coach's mind was made up and there was no turning back. In popped his assistant's head, "What's the move, Joe?"

DISCUSSION QUESTIONS

1. If you were in the car with Ryan when he was pulled over, what advice would you give him? Should he tell the truth?

2. Should Coach Joe punish Ryan even though his only source of information came from a close friend?

3. Is there a double standard for athletes? If so, why do you think schools allow it?

4. If you were Coach Joe, what would you do?

KEY TERMS

Coaching, Team rules, Ethics

CASE 10: SPORTS VS. CHURCH
The Dilemma of Choosing Sides

Angela S. Jacobs
Eastern Illinois University

ABSTRACT

Firing someone is never easy. But when it's your best head coach, whom everybody loves, and who is claiming discrimination for not being allowed to attend church, things get downright messy.

***

"I want to thank you all for being here tonight," Tom said. "As you know, we have a tough decision to make." He looked at each of the six board members, weighing his words carefully. "Mitch Anderson, head coach of the 12U Redbirds team, has missed several practices and games. In a nutshell, he has failed to fulfill his obligations as a head coach." Tom watched as one of the board members looked down and shook his head. "A head coach has an obligation to be at all practices and all games," Tom continued. "If that coach cannot fulfill his obligations, then he should not be allowed to coach." Another board member sighed heavily. Tom knew that Mitch was well liked by the players, parents, and many of the board members. "It's our job," he explained, "as the governing body of this organization, to decide if Mitch should continue as head coach."

"Excuse me, Tom." One of the board members said. "It's my understanding that Mitch has only missed a few Wednesday night practices. And that these missed practices were to attend church events?"

Tom nodded his head. "That is correct," he said. "He has also made his daughter, Sarah, miss practice for these church events."

Silence.

"I don't know about you all," Tom snapped, "but that's not the sign of a dedicated coach." He walked around the table. "Mitch has demonstrated that he doesn't care about this team."

"Excuse me," the board member said again. "I don't want to speak for other members, but I'm not sure that missing a softball practice here and there in order to attend church is grounds for dismissal." A few other board members nodded in agreement.

"Sure," Tom smiled. "But we aren't here to address Mitch's absence at practices and games *only*. As many of you also know," he said, "Mitch has been acting inappropriately at softball games. He argues openly with his assistant coach and acts unsportsmanlike at games. Mitch has literally tainted the reputation of this organization with his behavior, and something needs to be done about it."

A few of the board members nodded in agreement.

Tom took a deep breath. "There's one more thing," he said. "Mitch has threatened to sue the Redbirds Softball Organization for discrimination if we release him from his head coach position." Tom tossed a piece of paper onto the table. "You can read all about it in his complaint letter."

***

Mitch ran his hands through his hair and glanced at his cell phone. No missed calls. He walked to the kitchen and grabbed a drink. He glanced at the phone again. Nothing. He walked back to the living room. His footsteps echoed in the quiet room. His hand shook slightly as he held his cell phone. The board was meeting tonight to determine his fate as the head coach of the 12U travel softball team.

Mitch replayed his conversation with Tom over and over in his head.

"Russ can handle practice on Wednesday nights," Mitch had said. "I know it's asking a lot of an assistant coach, but I have confidence he can do it."

"You're the head coach," Tom said, "it's your job to be at practices. Besides," he explained, "we both know Russ Stanley doesn't have your level of expertise."

"But you know this is important to me," Mitch had insisted. "I cannot and will not sacrifice my commitment to my church or my faith. I'm only asking for release for these Wednesday night practices," he said.

Tom had shook his head.

"And possibly a Sunday game here and there," Mitch muttered.

Tom stared at him in disbelief. "Absolutely not," he blurted. "Mitch you're asking way too much here! Softball has to be your priority if you want to be head coach. These girls are relying on you."

"Will you at least consider it?" Mitch had asked.

Mitch wasn't sure why Tom was so adamant about him missing a few practices here and there, especially for church obligations. Tom knew how important church was to Mitch and his daughter.

"There are plenty of girls who would love to take Sara's place on the team," Tom threatened. "We are a competitive organization and not just any girl is allowed to play."

Mitch agreed. It was indeed a privilege to work with this team and this group of talented girls. But he still couldn't understand Tom's stance that it was an either/or situation. "It's either softball or it's church," Tom had said. He also reminded Mitch about the contract he signed at the beginning of the season.

"Coaches and players are required to be at every practice and every game, unless in case of an emergency," Tom quoted from the contract. "Nowhere in these rules," Tom explained, "is church service an excused absence. And let's be honest, Mitch," Tom had said, "this silly insistence on missing practices is hurting a lot of people."

Mitch didn't know how to respond.

"You force Sara to miss practices and then she has to sit out during games. How is that fair to her?" Tom had asked. "She's the best pitcher you have. When she sits the bench, everyone is punished."

Mitch couldn't argue with that logic. He wasn't at all happy with the rules that required Sara to sit the bench for missing practices. He wasn't unhappy about Sara having to sit the bench, per say, he was unhappy because he felt no player should be punished for wanting to go to church.

"Your parents are even calling me, Mitch," Tom had said. "They want to know why Sara can miss practices and still stay on the team. Some of them even blame *you*," Tom said, "for making the team lose because Sara can't pitch."

The last thing Mitch wanted was division among the team and the families. He only wanted what was best for the team. He promised Tom he would consider his perspective.

MAKING THINGS BETTER OR COMPLICATING MATTERS?

The day after Mitch and Tom had met, Bill White, a parent on the 12U Redbirds team, approached Tom.

"Since Mitch is no longer attending Wednesday night practices," he told Tom, "I'd be happy to help out with the coaching."

Tom's initial reaction was to say no, since Bill obviously didn't have Mitch's expertise. But, he reasoned, the girls could probably learn more from him than from Russ, the assistant coach. Without consulting Mitch, Tom approached the board members about Bill. The board unanimously voted to bring Bill on to the coaching staff for the 12U team.

The following week Tom introduced Bill to the team as one of the newest assistant coaches. He also announced that Bill would begin calling all pitches during the games. Mitch, unfortunately, wasn't at practice that evening to hear the announcement, and only learned about it later when one of Sara's teammates tweeted about it after practice.

Tom knew Mitch would be upset about the decision. He was expecting an angry phone call from Mitch trying to argue him out of the decision. But Mitch never said a word to anyone, and he never called Tom or the other board members. He simply showed up at the next Wednesday night practice. This was highly unusual for Mitch and it made Tom uneasy.

CONTRARY BEHAVIOR

Tom soon learned that he had been right to feel uneasy. Mitch began challenging Bill's every decision. Mitch yelled at Bill during games and made off-hand remarks to other parents about his coaching style and pitching decisions. Mitch even began pressuring his own daughter, Sara, to avoid Bill when she was pitching.

"You only need to look at me when you're out there on the mound," he was overheard saying to her. "Don't you dare watch Bill. He has no idea what he's doing out there."

This undermining of the other coach was starting to wear on the other girls as well. Girls were fighting with girls. Some of them felt loyal to Mitch and only listened to him, whereas other girls felt they should listen to Bill. Parents were even fighting with other parents. A few of the parents had called board members to complain about the tension on the team. Two families threatened to take their daughters off the team. Nothing was going well.

One game in particular stands out to Tom about the "new" Mitch.

***

Tom watched as Mitch paced back and forth, throwing his hands in the air repeatedly in frustration. He obviously didn't care for the pitches Bill was calling.

"That's the third batter she's walked this inning," Mitch yelled. "You've got to do something."

The tension was high, and it was only the top of the second inning. The bases were loaded, there were no outs, and Sara, Mitch's daughter, was pitching. Mitch stood beside the fence watching Bill intently. Bill gave the next pitch sign.

"A change-up? Are you nuts?" Mitch yelled. "Are we trying to lose this game?"

"Ball," the umpire called.

Mitch ran his hands through his hair and began to pace. He was nervous about the game, you could tell. But Tom couldn't tell if he was just nervous or if he was angry with Bill for calling pitches. It was the NSA state championship game. They had a lot riding on this game. If they won, they would earn an automatic berth to the NSA World Series. And Mitch was as competitive as they came; he wanted to win. But then again, they all did.

Tom watched as Sara pitched ball after ball. She was struggling to get a strike across the plate. He wondered if maybe he hadn't made the wrong decision after all. Maybe Bill didn't know as much about pitching as he led Tom to believe.

Sara was struggling on the mound and looked on the verge of a meltdown. Tom knew that she was upset and he was afraid she was going to start crying any minute. Whenever she got stressed out in pitching situations like this she usually started crying. He knew her performance would drop once that happened.

"Come on," Mitch shouted to his daughter. "Just have some fun out there. Throw a strike like you know how," he yelled. "Don't worry about those bad calls, just throw like you know how."

It was obvious to Tom that Mitch didn't agree with Bill's coaching style. He and Tom had talked earlier in the year about the strategy of never having Sara throw a change-up on a 2-2 count.

"Everyone knows you shouldn't throw a change-up on a 2-2 count," Mitch had said. "Especially not with Sara. She's never been able to throw a change-up in a pressure situation."

When Tom questioned this, Mitch told him that it's typical for a young girl not to get the strike called on a change-up.

"A change-up" he had said, "was usually a ball. Why throw a change-up on a 2-2 count only to get a third ball called. Then," Mitch had argued, "you force your pitcher to throw a strike right down the middle, and that batter is going to crush the ball. Or worse yet," Mitch had said, "your pitcher struggles to throw that strike and you walk the batter."

Tom couldn't argue with that logic. It was definitely the one thing he and Mitch agreed on. Tom had even gone to Bill and had this same talk with him. He told Bill under no circumstances should he have Sara throw a change-up on a 2-2 count. They had talked about this extensively the moment Bill was brought on to help coach. Bill agreed not to call a change-up in such a situation. But now here they were, Bill had made such a call twice. And Tom was baffled. Why would Bill keep asking Sara to throw a pitch he knew would result in another ball, bringing it to a full-count?

"This coach is killing me," Mitch yelled.

Bill glared at Mitch, then turned back toward the field.

"I don't think this coach knows what he's doing," Mitch shouted to Tom. "He's calling all the wrong pitches at all the wrong times."

Tom didn't respond. He noticed that Bill looked pretty upset by the whole situation. But, worse yet, parents were also looking upset. There was lots of whispering and some agitation from the parents. Some parents had even gotten up and moved away from the fields.

Mitch moved closer to the fence. He was watching Bill closely, but also positioning himself so that Sara could see him. He knew that Sara would look to him for pitching calls.

Another bad call by Bill.

"Ball," the umpire yelled.

Mitch stood up taller behind the fence trying to catch Sara's eye. He was waiting for her to look at him for the next sign. She didn't look at him. Instead, she looked at Bill. He gave her the sign—a rise ball. Tom could see she was on the verge of crying. They hadn't practiced the rise ball very much and she probably didn't believe she could actually throw it.

Mitch looked at Bill. Surely he could see Sara's frustration with this call. *Give her a fastball*, he thought. *Low and outside. Don't make her throw a rise ball.* Sara reared back and threw the rise ball.

"Ball," the ump yelled.

Sara began to cry.

Mitch kicked dirt onto the field.

"Come on, Sara," Bill yelled. "Toughen up and have some fun out there."

Sara looked from Bill to Mitch. Mitch gave her the fastball sign. Low and outside. Bill gave her the change-up sign.

Sara reared back and threw a fastball.

"Strike," the umpire yelled.

Mitch clapped. "See? What did I tell you?"

Bill shot Mitch a look. Tom watched as Bill and Mitch locked eyes. He wondered what he would do if a fight broke out. Mitch looked away and gave Sara another fastball sign. This time, he called high and inside.

Bill yelled at Sara to stay focused on the game and do what she was told. Bill called another change-up.

Sara ignored his call and threw a fastball instead.

"Strike two," the umpired yelled.

"Now we're having some fun," Mitch yelled. He smiled and looked over at Bill. Bill didn't smile in return. Instead, he turned his back on Mitch.

In the end, the team was able to get out of the jam in the second inning. Sara struck out the next three batters thanks to Mitch's help. He stayed close to the fence for the rest of the game. There was only one other inning where they got in a pinch. One of the opposing team's batters hit a hard line drive over the short stop's head and got a double out of it. They got close to scoring when Sara threw a wild pitch over the catcher's head and the runner stole third base. Mitch was able to calm her down and get her back to pitching strikes. She retired the side after that and no runs scored. They won the game 1-0.

Mitch waited for Bill after the game. "Hey, no hard feelings right?" Mitch said as he extended his hand.

Bill shoved Mitch's hand away.

"Hey," Mitch said. "I was just trying to win a ball game for us. If you can't call strikes, then we can't win," he said.

Bill was clearly angry. "You made a fool of me," he snapped. He pushed past Mitch and left the dugout.

"I was just trying to help," Mitch called.

Bill kept his back to Mitch and waved him off.

"Help win a ballgame because you can't do it," Mitch muttered.

Bill kept walking.

Mitch also turned to leave and was stopped by Russ Stanley, the assistant coach.

"You know you really acted like a jerk tonight," Russ said. "I know he's not the greatest at calling pitches, but I think you need to give him a chance."

"No way," Mitch snapped. "This is *my* team."

Tom watched as these events transpired. More than ever, he was convinced that something needed to be done about Mitch.

MITCH'S SIDE

Mitch couldn't believe what he was hearing. Bill White had been asked to step in as an assistant coach? He was in shock. He was even more shocked that the organization wanted Bill to be the pitching coach. *After all my years of dedicated service to this organization,* he thought, *they go and replace me just like that?*

It hurt to know that he could be replaced so easily. What's more, he thought, was that Tom was his friend. He thought Tom understood how important church was to Mitch and his family. They had several conversations about this. And the last conversation Mitch had with Tom, they agreed not to make a decision about anything just yet.

Mitch did feel bad about missing practices and some Sunday morning games, but God was simply too important to subordinate to softball. Mitch and Sara had talked this over and Sara had agreed that God was more important to her than softball.

"I know what my priorities are," Sara had said. "It's God, my family, my schoolwork, then softball."

Mitch had been so proud of her when she said this. They both loved the game of softball, but he believed they had their priorities straight.

Mitch secretly felt bad for being so aggressive toward Bill during games. That wasn't like him. He generally got along with everyone. But Bill was different. He just couldn't shake the fact that Bill had somehow weaseled his way onto the coaching staff. And while no one was saying it, Mitch knew that Bill was replacing him because of Mitch's decision to go to church instead of practice.

After one particularly bad game, where Bill made some horrible pitching calls, Tom had approached Mitch.

"Look," Mitch had said, "I know I behaved badly during the game. There is no excuse for my behavior."

Tom nodded. "We simply cannot have that kind of behavior on the field, Mitch."

"I agree," Mitch said. "It won't happen again."

"I know it won't," Tom nodded. "I am suspending you as head coach until the board decides what to do with you."

"What," Mitch blurted. "Are you serious?"

"I am completely serious, Mitch," Tom said.

"What's my crime?" Mitch demanded. "I yelled at a guy because he's a lousy pitching coach? You're going to suspend me as head coach because I yelled at somebody?"

"It's bigger than that and you know it," Tom said.

"Is it?" Mitch snapped. "Then what's it about, Tom?"

"Families are unhappy with how things are going on the team," Tom said. "And the girls don't know who they should listen to."

"And that's my fault?" Mitch asked.

"You've made choices that have been destructive for the team," Tom said. "I don't feel that you've given me any other choice."

"Are we talking about my actions at the ballpark, or are we talking about something else?" Mitch asked.

"You know what I'm talking about," Tom said.

Mitch nodded. "Yes, I think I do."

"I'm going to schedule a board hearing for next week," Tom said. "I'm going to ask that you avoid contacting any of the players or parents in the meantime. Russ and Bill will handle all practices until a decision is made."

Mitch knew it was pointless to try to convince Tom to think differently. His only hope, he believed, was to launch a formal complaint to the Redbirds' board of directors. The complaint letter addressed the board's decision to bring Bill White onto the coaching staff without his permission, and the board's policy on missed practices due to church obligations. Mitch was most concerned about the board's stance on church. He argued that church should be considered an acceptable reason for missing softball practices and, if necessary, games.

In part of his letter he wrote:

It is my belief that retaliatory actions were taken against me for my decision to participate in church services on Wednesday evenings rather than attend softball practices. I was unjustly stripped of my position as pitching coach, and now from my position as head coach.

I have been wrongly accused of not fulfilling my obligations as head coach. And now, I am being accused of unsportsmanlike behavior for my actions related to questioning my assistant coach during a game.

Nowhere in my contract does it state that I will lose my coaching position if I miss a practice or a game for church. Likewise, my contract does not state that I will be dismissed as head coach if I choose to question the decisions of my assistant coaching staff. Therefore, should the board decide to terminate me from the head coach position, I will file a discrimination lawsuit for unjust and unequal treatment I have received; all stemming, I believe, from my religious beliefs and practices.

***

The board members convened to discuss the matter.

"Based on current board policy," Tom said, "Mitch has acted outside of his obligations as the head coach for the 12U softball team. He has missed multiple practices and games," Tom noted. "He hasn't fulfilled his obligation as the head coach for the team, nor has he acted in the best interest of his players. He has also failed to bring his daughter, Sara, to multiple practices and games, resulting in Sara's inability to start key softball games."

The board listened intently.

"These acts have resulted in decreased morale for the team, and have increased division among coaches, players, and parents," Tom said. "Furthermore," he continued, "Mitch has brought shame upon the organization and division amongst the coaches with his repeatedly unsportsmanlike behavior at games."

He looked at each board member carefully.

"It's time the board acts upon these transgressions," he said.

DISCUSSION QUESTIONS

1. What are the key issues involved in this conflict? Who are the key players?

2. What particular incidents have led Mitch to feel that he has been treated unfairly for his religious beliefs and practices? Do you feel that Mitch has a legitimate complaint against the board for unfair and unjust treatment?

3. What recommendations would you make to the board in order to resolve this conflict? How should the board handle Mitch's missed practices and games? How should the board handle Mitch's unsportsmanlike behavior? What would be the ideal resolution to this conflict?

4. How should religious practices that conflict with sports obligations be handled? Should church be considered an "excused" absence from sporting events? Should sports no longer be played on Wednesdays and Sundays?

5. What recommendations do you have for how families can better negotiate sports practices and attendance at meaningful family events such as church?

KEY TERMS

Church, Youth sports, Families, Sports obligations, Religious practice, Conflict

Alaina C. Zanin
University of Central Missouri

ABSTRACT

A freshman cross-country runner quickly learns that being a teammate sometimes blurs the line between friend and competitor.

***

"On three. One, two, three!" Naomi yelled at the top of her lungs and placed her hand on top of Sadie's and her other cross-country teammates in the middle of the huddle.

"Goooooo Hawks!" Naomi, Sadie, and the rest of the team cheered. Naomi did another strider back to the starting line. She was so nervous. Naomi felt like throwing up right on the grass in front of her. Sadie saw the wide-eyed look on Naomi's face. Sadie gave her shoulder a squeeze.

"You're going to do great. You're ready for this, just think about all the training you put in this summer," Sadie said.

"You think?" Naomi responded skeptically.

"Trust yourself. I believe in you," Sadie said reassuringly.

With those last words, the gun went off and the race began.

WELCOME TO COLLEGE

Naomi and Sadie had just begun their freshman year at Huffington University. They were both recruited to run cross-country and track for the Division I university. They had both been state champions in their respective events in high school and had been given full athletic scholarships to attend school this fall. Naomi and Sadie were both very talented runners. Naomi was better at longer distances, whereas Sadie had natural speed and had excelled at the

800-meter event. During the track season they would compete in different events, but during the fall cross-country season they competed in the same races.

Part of the reason Naomi was nervous for this first cross-country meet is that she desperately wanted to finish first on her team. She thought that being first on her team was a reasonable goal. She had been the number one runner on her team in high school. She had been doing very well in workouts with the team, even though Sadie had been right with her.

Naomi felt a little guilty and selfish for seeing Sadie as competition, especially since Sadie had been such a good friend to her. Their coach paired them as roommates and they had become fast friends—literally. Sadie and Naomi had been spending close to 20 hours a day with each other for the past month including practice, team dinners, and overlapping class schedules. They were inseparable. Naomi genuinely wanted Sadie to do well, but she also wanted to be the best on her team.

**

"Go, just go," Sadie cried and pushed Naomi's arm. "You have to get that girl from Tech."

"Okay, I'll try," Naomi gasped. She set her sights on the runner's purple jersey and picked up her pace. They were in the woods now. Naomi knew they had only 800 meters left to reach the finish line, but she still could not see it. She wanted to beat this runner from Tech, for her team and for herself. She wanted to beat Sadie. She wanted to win. With one last burst of energy, she surged past the purple jersey, out of the woods and onto an open field. She could see the finish line. She was going to do it. Her legs burned, but she dug in, held on and kicked to the finish with her last burst of energy. The crowd cheered as she crossed the line. Naomi collapsed with a smile. She accomplished her goal. She was a winner.

Sadie came in fifteen seconds behind her breathing hard. She had a smile on her face. Sadie gave Naomi a big sweaty hug.

"I told you, you could do it," Sadie said. Naomi was elated. Sadie and she both had fantastic races. Each of them ran their personal best times and their team had beaten Tech by two points, thanks to Naomi's surge at the end.

BEST FRIENDS KEEP SECRETS

After their first meet, Naomi started to notice some changes in Sadie. Sadie began to spend much more time on her own, away from Naomi. She was sleeping a lot more. Sadie started saying no to their nightly trips to the ice cream shop. Sadie started eating lunch by herself. Naomi asked Sadie if she was mad or upset with her for something. Sadie explained that she was just busy with classwork and that the early morning workouts were making her sleepy.

Naomi noticed that Sadie was starting to lose weight. Being a distance runner, weight fluctuation in and out of season was normal to Naomi. Her own body was starting to respond to the increases in training intensity. She was starting to see definition in her abs and arms. So when

Sadie started losing weight Naomi was not alarmed, at first. Sadie was performing well in workouts. As the season progressed she got faster and faster, even sometimes beating Naomi. Naomi assumed Sadie was just eating healthier to be competitive.

One day after class, Naomi bounded into the dorm room and plopped down on their futon. Sadie would not be home for another 20 minutes and Naomi wanted to take a quick nap while their room was quiet. Naomi and Sadie shared bunk beds. Naomi had the top bunk because Sadie was afraid of rolling off in the middle of the night.

From her vantage point on the futon, Naomi could see under Sadie's bed. She noticed there were several plastic bags stuffed underneath the bed frame.

Oh good, she thought, *Sadie grabbed some extra bags to put our sweaty training shoes in*. Naomi grabbed one of the bags to carry her wet shoes to practice. However, when she touched it she could see that the bag was full of vomit.

"Ugh, gross!" Naomi recoiled in disgust. *Sadie hadn't told me she was sick,* Naomi thought, *and why would she throw up in a bag and leave it under her bed?*

Naomi looked back under her bed, there were close to 10 bags all filled with the same vile substance. The sight made Naomi nauseous. She did not do well with throw-up. She sat back down on the futon. Her head spun.

No wonder Sadie's been acting so strangely, Naomi thought, *is she hiding an eating disorder? But she's been running well? Maybe it isn't such a big deal.*

Just then Sadie burst through the door. She saw the bag of vomit open on the floor. Sadie looked at Naomi.

"Oh sorry, I meant to throw that out. I wasn't feeling too great this morning," Sadie apologized, picked up the bad and threw it in the trash.

"I found the other bags Sadie. Tell me the truth, I'm supposed to be your best friend here," Naomi said. Sadie just looked at the floor.

"Promise you won't say anything, you have to promise," Sadie pleaded as her eyes welled up with tears. Naomi bit her lip and gave her friend a long hug. *I can't promise her that,* Naomi thought, *what if she is really hurting herself?*

"Just tell me what is going on and then we can decide what to do," Naomi said.

"I thought it was just going to be one time. I just felt so full after dinner. Disgusting, like a pig. I had eaten way too much. So I just went in the bathroom and stuck my fingers down my throat. I felt so much better after," Sadie said. "I promise I'll stop, just don't tell anyone."

Naomi squeezed Sadie's hand and said, "I promise I won't tell coach, but you have to go see the trainers. You have to get help. If you don't tell them I will."

"That's not fair, Naomi! You don't understand. I just want to be fast," Sadie cried. "You are supposed to be my friend."

"I am your friend. I care about you. And of course I want you to run fast too," Naomi replied. "But this is the wrong way to do it. You could really hurt yourself. We can talk to Veronica tomorrow, she'll know what to do."

"Okay, as long as you don't tell Coach," Sadie sniffed.

***

"Girls, I am glad that you came in to talk to me about this," their trainer Veronica said. "An eating disorder can result very serious health consequences: damage to your teeth and esophagus, heart stress, infertility, not to mention you will not be able to perform your best."

Naomi looked at Sadie. She was not sure if she believed this last part. Sadie had been getting faster and faster in workouts.

"I mean if you are not getting the calories and nutrients your body needs, you could just pass out on a run somewhere," Veronica continued. "I have to tell your coach about this, but I am going to recommend that he allows you to practice."

"What, no!" Sadie protested. "I can handle this on my own."

"Sadie, I am sorry, but I am obligated to tell your coach. It's my job and my ethical responsibility," Veronica responded. "To be allowed on this team you signed a HIPAA release which allows me to share your health information with him. He needs to be able to monitor you during practice."

Naomi felt guilty that she had forced Sadie to talk to their trainer. *Maybe it wasn't such a big deal. Were they going to hold Sadie out of practice? Out of their upcoming meet?* Naomi chewed on her fingernail.

"Listen Sadie, I will make you a deal," Veronica said. "We are going to have weekly weigh-ins. If you go to counseling, and you do not lose any more weight, I will recommend to your coach that you be allowed to continue to practice and compete. Does that sound like a fair plan?"

Sadie was crying now. Naomi gave her a hug.

"It's going to be okay, Sadie," Naomi said reassuringly.

"Look at all of the support you have, Sadie," Veronica said.

Sadie nodded and sniffed, "Okay. I will go to counseling, as long as I can still run."

ON THE SAME TEAM?

The next several weeks were very busy for Naomi and Sadie. They studied for mid-terms together. They raced in a competitive cross-country invitational with some of the fastest runners in the country. Their team had been successful, even though their top two runners were freshmen. Their team was a favorite to win conference. To Naomi's dismay, Sadie had claimed the number one spot for two weeks in a row. Naomi wasn't too upset though because they were both running fast and she genuinely wanted the team to do well. Sadie was integral to the team's success. Sadie appeared to be complying with her treatment plan. She went to counseling sessions and let Veronica weigh her in every week.

Veronica was still letting Sadie practice, so Naomi assumed that Sadie had maintained her current weight, but her other behaviors had not really changed. Sadie was still sleeping all the time. She complained of being cold. She ate most meals by herself. When she did eat with Naomi she noticed that Sadie would only choose a salad without dressing or cooked vegetables. She looked so thin, but so did Naomi. They were long distance runners after all. Naomi had reservations about how well the counseling was working, but she did not want to bring it up again with Veronica. Naomi figured that she was a professional. Veronica and Sadie could work it out; she had done her part. Plus, the conference meet was approaching and the team really needed Sadie.

One day before practice Naomi ran into the locker room. She was so excited about a grade she had gotten on her macro-economic exam. She ran over to Sadie, picked her up and twirled her around.

"Wait, no, what are you doing?!" Sadie squealed. "Put me down!"

"Guess what, guess what, guess what?!" Naomi exclaimed. Just as Naomi set Sadie down, at least ten dollars-worth of quarters fell out of Sadie's pocket and careened to the floor. Naomi looked quizzically at Sadie.

"What are those for?" Naomi asked. Sadie didn't look at her. She quickly started picking them up off of the floor.

"Oh these, nothing. I was just going to do laundry after practice," Sadie said.

"You were?" Naomi eyed her skeptically. "Don't you have a night class tonight? You won't have time to do laundry." Sadie didn't respond.

"Did you have a weigh-in today?" Naomi asked her.

Sadie nodded her head yes. Naomi felt hot with anger. Sadie had been manipulating her weight by putting quarters in her pockets before she went in to see Veronica. *How could Sadie have been keeping this from her? She was just lying to everyone?* Naomi could tell Sadie had lost more weight just by looking at her.

"Naomi. Please, I promise I will stop after the conference meet," Sadie begged. "Please, conference is in one week. Nothing will happen to me. I just want to run for the team. If you tell Veronica, she will make me sit out. Plus, you owe me. You promised Coach wouldn't find out and Veronica told him anyway. Aren't we on the same team?"

Naomi did not know what to do. She felt betrayed, worried, and sad. *Didn't Sadie see that it was hard for her to sit and watch Sadie hurt herself?*

On the other hand, Sadie made a good point. It was only one week until conference and Sadie had been calorie deficient for weeks. The team did need Sadie to run; however, if Sadie did not run, Naomi would be able to be the top finisher on their team again.

Sadie was right. Naomi hadn't been able to keep her promise. She did want to be a good friend. Good friends keep each other's secrets. *But was this secret too big?* Naomi chewed her fingernail. *What was the right thing to do?*

DISCUSSION QUESTIONS

1. Why do you think Naomi felt torn about telling or keeping Sadie's secret?
2. How does the context of a team sport influence an athlete-athlete relationship? How might this type of relationship be unique in comparison to other interpersonal relationships?
3. What types of power bases does Sadie use to influence Naomi? What types of power bases does Veronica use to influence Sadie?
4. Identify the types of roles and identities in this case. What roles is Naomi trying to fulfill? How is Sadie perceiving that role fulfillment?
5. If you were Naomi, what would you do now?

KEY TERMS

Relational dialectics, Athlete-athlete relationships, Bona fide group perspective, Inter-role conflict

CASE 12: WRESTLING WITH TEAM CONFLICT

Joshua Daniel Phillips
Southern Illinois University

ABSTRACT

Tony and his friends have been wrestling together since they were ten years old. At the start of their sophomore year, Tony is named team captain. Tony is thrilled, but soon realizes that being team captain has changed his relationship with his friends. Instead of always joking around on the mat, Tony now has the responsibility of leading his friends, pushing his friends in practice, and making sure his friends are following the rules in the classroom and on the mat.

***

Along the ascending gravel road two miles from home, Tony threw his legs into high gear. "It's not a hill. It's an opportunity. It's not a hill. It's an opportunity." His coach had taught him this mantra and it played over and over in his head. His quads were on fire, but once he made it to the top of the hill, it was a nice long descent for the final mile-and-a-half cool down.

It was the first Monday of November and this was Tony's first long run of his sophomore wrestling season. The high school football regular season had ended Friday and, with his team's 5-5 record, they were going to miss the playoffs. As a football player, Tony played middle linebacker and had bulked up to a respectable 175 pounds However, this year he wanted to wrestle at 152 pounds and had to find a way to lose the extra weight quickly. Wrestling practice started in just over a week and if Tony wasn't down to at least 162 pounds, there was no way his coach would even consider letting him drop all the way down to 152 pounds.

Although some teammates had told Tony just to wrestle up a few weight classes, Tony wouldn't listen. He had to wrestle at 152 pounds so he could get his rematch against conference rival Andy McCoy. McCoy had beaten Tony at the state championships last year and had cost Tony a chance at a medal. Now that McCoy was going into his senior year, this would be Tony's last chance to have his revenge. So Tony kept running. "It's not a hill. It's an opportunity. It's not a hill. It's an opportunity."

ANNOUNCING THE TEAM CAPTAIN

When wrestling practice started the following Wednesday, Tony stepped on the scale in front of his whole team for his first formal weigh-in. The coach looked at the scale and yelled out, "161!" Tony threw both hands in the air like a prize fighter. "Yes!" he thought. He was only nine pounds away from 152 pounds and had three weeks to lose the weight before his first wrestling match. His close friends on the team came forward, began slapping him on the back, and congratulating him. "Wow Tony," Mike said, "You must really want McCoy! We never thought you'd be able to lose that weight in just two weeks. Great job, man. Can't wait to see you tear him up later this year."

The head coach finally cut through all the after-practice chaos. "Okay, men, quiet down. We still have to get through all the paperwork of the first day. So hurry up and get dressed. Meet me in classroom 147 in fifteen minutes so I can get you your permission slips and season calendars. Oh, and we have one special announcement." All 27 guys on the team quickly threw on their clothes, grabbed their gear, and headed down to room 147.

Once they were settled, Coach began. "Here's this year's calendar. Practice will be from 4 to 6 every afternoon and Saturday from 8 to 10 unless we have a meet that day." Holding up a colored piece of paper, he continued, "*This* is for your parents. I made it green so you wouldn't lose it. It's a permission slip that says I own you every day from 4 to 6. If you don't get it signed, then you don't wrestle. So bring it to the start of practice tomorrow or you will be sitting on the bench. Oh, and one last announcement: Team captain."

At this point, Tony and the rest of his sophomore friends were barely paying attention in the back of the classroom. They had their permission slips and that's all that mattered. As far as they were concerned, team captain was about seniority, not talent. As sophomores they had no chance.

"This year's team captain," the coach bellowed, "is Tony Kelly." Everyone was stunned, including Tony. Yet, the decision was not without merit. Tony was the only wrestler on the team who had qualified for state last year and, as a freshman, he did compile a better record than each of the four seniors. But team captain? This was a whole new level of respect and responsibility. Tony awkwardly made his way to the front of the room to shake the coach's hand and receive the "C" emblem for his letterman's jacket. For Tony, it was a pretty great feeling, but as he looked over the room he could see the bewildered, confused, and downright icy stares coming from the older guys. Tony just shrugged it off and returned to his seat in the back of the room.

With that announcement, the meeting was over and all 27 wrestlers headed for the parking lot. When they got out of earshot of the coach, Nick, a senior, grabbed Tony by the back of the elbow and led him around a hallway corner. "That captain title was mine," he whispered so as not to draw attention to the situation. "I don't care how good you think you are, I put in my time and deserved that title."

Nick was bigger than Tony by at least 40 pounds and a good six inches taller. Nick was also a good wrestler who had missed qualifying for the state championships by only one match last year. So, Tony didn't talk back. But in his mind he thought, "Deserve? No one *deserves* anything. I *earned* this title. Why don't you win a few more matches and take it from me?"

When Tony and Nick caught up to the rest of the team in the parking lot, the different grades had already split up: seniors to the senior lot, juniors to the junior lot, sophomores to the sophomore lot, and freshmen to the pick-up lane where they had to wait for their parents. Tony saw his friends Mike, Jeff, James, and Paul all leaning against Andre's car as Andre sat in the driver's seat and played around with the radio.

"What was that all about?" James asked Tony while nodding in Nick's directions. "Nothing," Tony replied, "Nick's just mad because the sophomores are better wrestlers than the seniors." "You're darn right we are!" Paul said. The six sophomores started a playful pushing match until Andre put an end to it by backing up his car. "Sorry guys, I got to pick up my little sister at the junior high, but I'll see you and *our* team captain tomorrow at practice."

As Andre sped out of the parking lot, he rolled down his window, put a fist in the air, and yelled "sophomores rule!" toward the senior parking lot. Jeff leaned over to Tony and said, "Well, that certainly isn't going to help us at practice tomorrow." The five remaining friends had a good laugh, congratulated Tony one last time, and finally headed home.

NEW RESPONSIBILITIES

For the next couple of weeks, not much changed in the wrestling room. Everyone was wrestling hard, cutting weight, and trying to make the starting line-up. The seniors continued to give Tony the cold shoulder, but Tony always found support in his sophomore friends. The only new responsibility Tony had at this point in the season was being in charge of leading team warm-ups. Then, at the end of week three, and right before the team's first match, Tony was called into the coach's office after practice.

"Tony, sit down." The coach was stern. "We have a problem. Your buddy Paul has been acting up in Spanish class. Apparently, he's been disrespectful to the teacher, cutting class, and bullying the freshmen. Do you know anything about this?" Tony became flustered and nervous. Of course Tony knew all about Paul's antics. Tony and Paul were in the same Spanish class and, of course, the coach knew it! Tony couldn't cover up for his friend on this one. Tony stammered, "Y-y-yes-ss coach. I know."

Coach became furious. He stood over Tony and yelled, "Then why didn't you do anything about it! You're the team captain! You're the leader! Does a leader just stand by while his teammate screws around in class, disrespects adults, and picks on younger students?"

Tony's eyes drifted toward his shoes and he mumbled, "No, Coach."

"Well," Coach's tone was softer now, "it's good that you know, but I need you to lead by example. I know Paul is your friend, but you're the team captain. Being a good team captain means confronting your friends and keeping them in line. The reputation of this team is on your shoulders. If Paul is out of line in the classroom, that reflects poorly on your leadership. Do you understand?"

Tony's eyes looked up at Coach and he spoke more clearly, "Yes, Coach."

"Now, our first meet is this weekend and I refuse to start the year off on a bad note. So, go get Paul. He's going to sit out this one."

Tony couldn't hide his shock, "What! Coach, you can't bench him. He's our best wrestler at a hundred and thirty pounds. We could lose if you don't let him wrestle."

But Coach wouldn't listen to Tony's plea. "Tony," Coach said, "Don't put this on me. I'm not the one who sat in Spanish class all semester with Paul and let him screw around. If you want to get mad at anyone, get mad at yourself. You're the captain. You should have intervened sooner before Mr. Ortiz sent me this disciplinary letter. Now, go get Paul. You two are going to sit in my office and you're going to tell him about his one-match suspension."

***

The team ended up losing their first meet by three points. Even worse, the wrestler who filled in for Paul ended up getting pinned by a guy Paul had beaten the year before. If Paul had wrestled, they would have won for sure. When the team returned to practice on Monday after the loss, Tony was now getting the cold shoulder from his sophomore friends as well as the seniors.

"Nice going, Snitch," James whispered in Tony's ear as they ran warm-up laps in the gym. Tony hurried to catch up. "What did I do?" Tony asked. James replied, "You told Coach that Paul was ditching Spanish and that lost the meet for us."

Tony couldn't believe it! James was actually blaming Tony for Paul's suspension. "Wait a minute," Tony was now on the defensive, "I didn't tell Coach anything. Coach got a letter from Mr. Ortiz. I mean, Paul and I are in the same Spanish class. What was I supposed to do? Lie and tell Coach that Mr. Ortiz must have Paul confused with some other jock who skips class and bullies the freshmen?"

"Yeah!" James was blunt, "That's right. You don't rat out your friends. Or maybe you're not our friend any more. You have been hanging out an awful lot with Coach after practice. What are you? His new informant? Is that what you do now, *Team Captain?*"

James had drifted into sarcasm. When the warm-up running stopped and the team got into a circle to begin stretches, James started counting out "One sir, two sir, three sir . . ." every time Tony led them in a new stretch. Tony's friends Jeff and Andre joined in the sarcastic counting. Tony tried to ignore it, but the rest of the team could tell he was frustrated and started laughing at Tony's expense. Tony finally caught Mike's eyes and looked for some support. Mike knew that Paul was a class clown since they first met in the fourth grade. And Mike knew that Paul probably deserved his one-match suspension. But like everyone else, Mike was upset that the team lost. So, while Mike felt bad that Tony was taking all the blame, all Mike could do was shrug his shoulders and look away.

LOSING CONCENTRATION

The regular season had only just begun and the pressure of being the team captain was getting to Tony. He was struggling to keep his weight down and he couldn't focus during his workouts. Not to mention the fact that his life as a wrestler had suddenly become very lonely. The week after the team's opening loss, the team had three away meets. During that entire week, Tony worked out on his own, sat by himself on the bus trips, and listened to his head phones off in some corner during meets. Wrestling was no longer the team sport he had enjoyed with his friends. Instead, Tony was isolated.

Although Tony had won all of his matches in those first four meets, it was obvious to everyone that Tony wasn't wrestling like he should have been. The local paper even mentioned that his "matches had been unusually close against opponents whom he should have dominated." To make matters worse, the team was hosting a big tournament on Saturday and Tony would be placed in the same bracket with his conference rival, Andy McCoy.

McCoy was having a great start to his senior season coming off a fourth place finish at the state championships the year before. He was undefeated and he was winning by big margins. A few wrestling polls even ranked him number one and projected that he would win the state championship in February. McCoy had only beaten Tony by two points last year, but Tony's inconsistent performance in the opening week of the season had all the local sport writers doubting Tony's ability to enact revenge.

Because McCoy and Tony were both undefeated and former state qualifiers, they were placed on opposite sides of the sixteen-man bracket. If they did face each other, it would be for the tournament championship on Saturday night. As predicted, McCoy tore through his first three opponents. Every match ended with a pin in the first period. McCoy was in the championship match and he hadn't even spent five minutes on the mat. Tony's performance was another story. After nearly losing to a second-string wrestler in the first round, Tony found a way to hobble through his side of the bracket. Worse, each of Tony's three matches had gone the full six minutes and Tony was feeling exhausted.

When the finals began around 7:00 PM, Tony walked to the middle of the mat for his rematch against McCoy. As he had done before every finals match since the time he was ten years old, Tony briefly looked to his team's spot in the bleachers for some reassurance. Knowing that Mike, Jeff, James, Paul, and Andre were in his corner always made Tony feel like he could beat anyone. While they had a rough opening week to start their sophomore year, Tony knew that his friends would be there to cheer him on during the most important match of his career. But, to Tony's surprise, his team's section of the bleachers was nearly empty. A few of the guys had left with their parents after they were eliminated from the tournament. Others were hanging out in the cafeteria texting their girlfriends. And some were showering in the locker rooms, anxious to get home. The handful of guys who were in the bleachers were removed and disinterested. And there was no sign of any of Tony's friends.

***

The match was a nightmare. Tony lost 15-6 and the newspaper reported that the match solidified "Andy McCoy's status as the most dominant wrestler in the conference." Furthermore, Tony's loss dropped the team out of third place and out of contention for a team trophy. At this point, Tony wasn't worried about a rematch against McCoy at the state championships. Tony was worried about just *making it to* the state championships and keeping his team competitive in the process.

At school on Monday, James and Paul stopped giving Tony the silent treatment and began to ridicule him openly in class. Jeff approached him in the hallway, put his arm around Tony's shoulder, and said, "Whoa, Champ, I read about the beating you got in the paper. Sorry I missed it, but I was busy texting Molly in the parking lot. Must have been hard out there all alone without the support of your teammates, but you know what it's like not to support a teammate, right? Coach's pet."

Tony had enough. Paul had served his suspension over a week ago and it was time for his friends to get over it, come together, and win some matches! This whole ordeal was a small incident that had become one giant distraction and it was affecting everyone. Tony's performance was terrible, the locker room was hostile, and the team wasn't winning. There were still 25 matches left in the season, and if Tony had any hope of beating McCoy in a rematch at the state championships, then he had to mentally move past this conflict. If the team had any hope of regaining unity and salvaging the season, then Tony had to figure out a way for all 27 wrestlers to confront this tension, quickly.

DISCUSSION QUESTIONS

1. Tony is facing conflicts with the seniors and with his friends. What does this situation suggest about the relationship between team conflict and seniority? About team leadership and friendship?

2. Tony feels stuck somewhere between a teammate and a coach. Who should Tony talk to about his struggles in transitioning to team captain? If Tony does decide to tell his coach, what types of repercussions might he face from his friends and the seniors? Can Tony talk to his coach without further eroding his friendships?

3. Based on what you know about small group conflict, how should Tony and his friends address this conflict? How should Tony and the seniors address this conflict?

4. It is sometimes said that leadership is a lonely position. Do you believe that Tony and his friendships are permanently changed now that he is the team captain and has a different responsibility in the group? How might these relationships be changed for the better? How might they be changed for the worse?

5. Have you ever been placed into a position where you had to lead your friends? What were your experiences like? Did you notice a difference in your relationships with your friends after you were placed in a leadership position?

KEY TERMS

Small group conflict, Interpersonal conflict, Leadership, Team captain, Group roles

CASE 13: COMMUNICATING PAIN

Negotiating the Tensions of Leadership, Toughness, and Injury

Taylor Anguiano
Mountain View High School and Boise State University

John G. McClellan
Mountain View High School and Boise State University

ABSTRACT

Leilani is a star volleyball player, team captain, and dedicated student. During her junior year, she suffered a foot injury. Hesitant to communicate her pain for fear of being perceived as weak or being benched, she played through the pain and tried to manage it on her own. However, her delay in receiving care eventually warranted a more extensive surgery. During her arduous recovery, she felt abandoned by her team and coach who seemed to blame her for not being tough enough and hiding behind a little pain. Upon her recovery, she began developing the same injury on her other foot and found herself in a similar position; struggling to determine when and how to talk about her pain while balancing her roles as celebrated athlete and team leader—to be tough, yet responsible to herself, her body, her team, and her family.

***

"Nurse! Somebody get a nurse in here!" Mrs. Kiakona cried, "Leilani, Honey, please stop!" A few moments later a nurse in pink scrubs walked through the door into the small hospital room, in no apparent hurry despite Mrs. Kiakona's tone. "Why is she banging her foot like that? Is she having a nightmare?" The nurse reassured her that Leilani was simply experiencing prolonged numbness from her surgery. As Leilani lay on the bed, she was groggy from anesthesia.

"Leilani, can you hear me?" the nurse asked. "You must stop banging your foot on the bed. You wouldn't want to reopen your stitches, would you? Leilani?"

She began to open her eyes, and looked around in confusion. "Where am I?" Leilani muttered.

"This nurse is going to take good care of you, Honey. You're out of surgery, but most of your lower leg is still numb. Just try to relax, okay?" Mrs. Kiakona sat on the edge of Leilani's hospital bed and ran her fingers through her hair.

As the nurse left, she said, "You have been out for almost three hours, but surgery went well without any complications. I'll be back to check in on you periodically. Keep resting."

As the fogginess of the anesthesia cleared, Leilani turned her head and asked her mom, "Did the girls leave already?"

"What girls, Lei? Your father went to grab a snack, and Makena and I have been here waiting for you to wake up. I'm sure your friends will stop by the house after practice tonight." But Leilani looked away feeling dejected. She anticipated being greeted by friends and teammates after her surgery. And she began to tear up. After all, it was Monday afternoon; volleyball's day off from practice. They had no excuse! She had visited each of her four other teammates at the hospital when they had surgery. And Coach Keeno didn't even wish her well before surgery—though she didn't really expect him to. She was devastated.

Just then, Meghan knocked on the open door. "How are you, Leilani?" she asked with a sense of sweetness and care. "Look what I brought you—an ice machine from school. What do you think?" Ever since her first visit to the training room, Leilani always liked Meghan, and seeing her gave her a sense of solace. Meghan was happy to hear all went well and after chatting for a while about rehabilitation plans, she left saying "Hey, when you get released from this place, come see me every day to check your incision sites and we'll get started on your rehab when you're ready." As Leilani's dad walked in and greeted her with a smile, Leilani sunk back into her hospital bed and began to think about the last year, her pain, and how things might have ended up differently.

A TEAM LEADER

It was the first week of practice of her junior year. Leilani was excited to be back with her team after the summer break. Coach Keeno greeted her with "How's our MVP? Ready for another season? We're going to need you to be tough this year and push everyone out there!" Leilani sprang up. "I'm on it!" she replied. As she ran onto the court, her team greeted her excitedly and she began to lead them through basic drills.

Leilani's first two years in college were filled with the rigors of being a student-athlete, and she made it look easy. As she ran through basic drills, Leilani felt great. Spending her days in strength training, at practices, and traveling for matches was everything she dreamed of when she was recruited. Not only did she become the star sophomore who led her team to their first conference championship, but she also enjoyed being a college student. Leilani quickly gained a reputation for being committed to winning, earning good grades, and leading by example—both on the court and in the classroom. She had clearly emerged as the team's leader.

As Coach Keeno watched Leilani guide practice, Meghan, the head athletic trainer for the volleyball team, walked onto the court. Barely looking up from his notes, he said with pride, "She's the real thing – she's got it all."

"Yeah, but she has a lot on her plate," Meghan replied.

He looked up and said, "She's is going to take us to the championship, again."

Meghan responded with, "She *is* really passionate about the game." But Meghan's enthusiasm belied her knowing that Leilani's drive originated in her desire to make her family proud by being the first in her family to graduate from college. Meghan often thought that Coach Keeno put too much burden on his team leaders and simply saw her athletic, 6-foot-2 stature that exemplified the ideal all-star outside hitter. She was more than that.

Yet, as Leilani spiked the ball with a strong left hand, Coach Keeno whispered to Meghan, "She is a diamond in the rough."

"And a hardworking student, too," Meghan responded softly as she walked past.

Meghan watched Leilani as she crossed the court. It was evident why she led the conference in kills and aces last season; but she saw more. As she heard Leilani shouting words of encouragement to her teammates, and saw the girls' positive responses, she knew Coach Keeno was right. Leilani had developed into not only a consistently valuable and skilled athlete, but a supportive, and reliable teammate as well. "Nice job, Captain!" Meghan yelled as she walked by the court. After Leilani was named team captain this year, Meghan playfully referred to her by her well-deserved title.

After practice, Leilani grabbed her bag and began walking out of the locker room when a teammate said, "Hey! you going to join us?"

"Not right now, I have to get to the bookstore."

"You are always putting your head in the books!" her teammate laughed.

"I know, I'll join you later, but I need to get on top of things."

"Why is she always so focused on school?" another teammate whispered. "She can't stand the possibility of not being an overachiever."

"But you would be letting *us* down, Captain!" her teammate yelled after her – it's Kylee's birthday after all!"

"I know, maybe I'll buy her a book?" she joked. "I'll see you later!" Leilani replied as she kicked open the door.

"I wish I could do it all, like her," someone said.

"If you do *half* of what she does, you will be doing just fine," another teammate replied. "She just never quits! Which is good, 'cause we can't have *her* quit."

When she walked outside, Leilani's phone rang, "Hey Dad!"

"How was the first day?"

"Great, it is good to be back, it is going to be a good year."

"It will be a *great* year," her dad replied with pride, "I'll be there for your first game."

"You are always there for me, Dad," she said thinking about how he had attended every home match since she was a freshman.

"It's going to be a tough year, though," she declared.

"And you can do it," her Dad said calmly.

"But I have all upper-division courses, and Marketing 429 is going to be a killer."

Her dad offered a simple proclamation: "It's supposed to be hard. If it wasn't hard, everyone would do it. The hard is what makes us great."

"I know, I know!" she had heard him say his favorite quote from *A League of Their Own* to her way too often. "But I just don't know how I can do it all, and I don't want to let you down."

"Don't you ever worry about me, you only need to worry about letting yourself down – I will always be proud of you, no matter what!"

"I love you, Dad," Leilani said with a smile. However, she couldn't help but think it was her dad's unconditional support that made her always strive to be a positive example and encourage others to do their best.

"Love you, Lei," her dad said as he hung up the phone. Yet, as Leilani's dad set the phone down, he hoped she would find the balance between pushing herself to perform at higher levels and working hard to be a good student. After all, she always managed to finish at the top of her class each year.

As Leilani walked across campus, she was feeling good and happy to have her family's support. And when she heard her teammate call up to her, "Hey, Lei, wait up, I'll go with you..."

"Great!" she said and stopped; feeling appreciative of her new family. With a smile Leilani waited.

"Then we can go together to Kylee's thing."

"Thanks, sounds perfect!" she said feeling lucky to have such a good group of friends on her team.

***

Before the start of their fourth match of the season, Coach Keeno yelled instructions as he watched the warm up. They look good, he thought. After arriving four ago as head volleyball coach, he finally felt his early efforts to recruit quality players with the potential to be coached, and win, were paying off. They became champions, but they needed to keep it up. As Leilani collected the team to bring them in after warm up, he watched her from across the court. He thought to himself that he had always been impressed by her strength and skill as a player. From the day she committed as a scrawny high school junior, he knew his program would benefit from her athleticism and leadership. It was that combination of strengths that was the most significant reason his team was able to win their first conference championship. He was happy his top recruit chose to join his team. But now he needed her to help translate what she had to the younger players, and make the "full package" athlete—skilled player, dedicated competitor, and successful student—something that exemplified all his players.

As warm up finished, Coach yelled, "Bring it in! Alright, like I said, you are facing a tough team. Watch for tips, and track the left-side hitter. Don't guess on those blocks. And follow Leilani's lead out there, she's got what it takes!"

Leilani smiled a bit awkwardly, "Thanks, Coach." As she turned to her team she said, "We've got this, we just need to stay focused and communicate. Everyone talk it up, and be aggressive!" As they ran out to take the court she shook off the pressure of her Coach's expectations—and began to play.

THE PAIN

In the middle of their fall season, Leilani and her teammates were doing their best to keep their heads above water. During a visit to the training room, Leilani told Meghan, "I hate the way we're playing. We've lost four in a row and I feel like we're in a downward spiral. I don't know what it'll take for us to break out of this."

"I know," Meghan replied, "but either way we still have to keep you healthy."

That's exactly what an athletic trainer would say, Leilani thought. She could tell that Meghan knew the season was taking its toll on everyone's bodies. One starter was injured and out for the season and others were feeling banged up and all were visiting the athletic training room more often.

After losing their fifth game in a row, Coach Keeno brought the team together in the film room to discuss what he thought was the issue. While he was calling attention to several particularly embarrassing plays, and some moments of apparent "sluggishness" on the part of the team, one player mumbled, "that hurts." Coach yelled in frustration, "C'mon ladies, it always hurts more when you lose!" And he put his plan in place. "From now on we will be focused on strength training and film analysis! And during practices we will run drills over and over until they are perfect! We have to do something to address the apathy, laziness, and what only seems to me is a clear lack of effort from this team!" As Leilani listened, she thought about how much effort she was putting into the games and practices. She fidgeted in her chair. And instinctively reached down to massage the dull ache and pinching she had been feeling recently in her foot.

Later that day, she met Meghan in the training room, "How you feeling?"

Thinking about the dull ache that was bothering her after matches and had transformed to a sharp pinch every time she jumped and landed, Leilani replied "Good. Well, mostly."

"What's wrong?"

"Oh, just sore from practice, bummed that our winning season has deteriorated, and not sure how to live up to Coach's expectations."

Meghan responded, "I know you are tough and I'm sure you will get back out there and rally the team."

"Yea, we'll get through it." Leilani hoped she could distract herself from the pain and focus on ways the team could turn their season around.

"But you have to take care of yourself, or you won't be able to turn things around for the team," Meghan said sharply.

"I know, I will. I'm seeing you more often anyhow," she said.

"Alright, take care." Meghan muttered.

As Leilani stepped out of the room, she felt bad. She had always trusted Meghan and spent lots of time talking with her about balancing school and athletics. She knew Meghan would always do what is best for her to stay healthy. She turned, thinking, *I'll go in there and tell her.* But she stopped. *No, I'll tell her if it gets bad,* she thought. *I can't let my team down because of a little pain. Besides, if I communicate any pain beyond the typical muscle soreness, I might lose playing time. I'll let Coach and my team down.* She turned around and said to herself, "I'm going to be tough—for the team—for me."

***

With her obligations pressing on her shoulders, Leilani grew increasingly anxious. Her body was beginning to feel more than the typical wear and tear at this part of the season; the sharp stings grew more frequent. She knew something wasn't right with her foot, but she tried not to show it. After all, the team was facing so much pressure as last year's conference champs. If their captain showed any signs of weakness now, the last few weeks of the season would be in jeopardy.

As the last weeks of the season progressed, the team was winning again, and Leilani felt her toughness was paying off. "Way to go! Keep it up! Keep following Leilani's lead! Play tough!" yelled Coach Keeno. Leilani was playing well and the team was rallying around her efforts.

As she walked off the court, Leilani winced, "ouch."

"You okay?" a teammate said with concern.

"Yeah, just felt weird for a moment," Leilani shrugged off the pain that had been intensifying. "It's nothing." She still couldn't talk about her pain. She knew she was tough, and she thought how this type of pain was probably a normal part of competing at the elite level. And pushing through pain seemed to be making her a better athlete—especially when her team and coach were counting on her to be a motivating force to close out the season. "Let's keep going!" she yelled to her team. She didn't want to let them down. She didn't want to be weak. She didn't want to disappoint. And it was paying off.

But Coach Keeno noticed a spark was missing from her step. Seeing Meghan in the hallway, he called, "Hey, have you talked to Leilani lately?"

Caught off guard, she said, "Oh, yea, I guess. She's been in the athletic training room a few times this week, but not for anything specific. Why?"

Coach Keeno paused for a moment, "She just seems a little unfocused. I was wondering if she had mentioned anything to you about being stressed with school or anything else off the court," he explained.

"I'm sure she's just exhausted from our travel schedule. It hasn't allowed for much rest so far. Lei is usually good about allowing her body to recover. And final exams are coming up; so I'll let you know if I hear anything."

When the season ended, the team finished third in the conference. It wasn't the championship everyone wanted, but it was a good year. And Leilani's focus immediately shifted from athletics to academics. She had final exams to prepare for and wanted to keep her grades up.

At the library, a teammate saw her with her leg propped up on a chair with an ice pack covering her foot. "Hey Lei, you okay?"

"Yea, I'm just trying to study for a final on Thursday."

"No. The ice. You okay?"

"Oh that, just trying to recover and be ready for sand season."

"Well, you've always been tough, and I'm sure we'll bounce back with sand season. We are so much better in sand, anyhow."

"That's true."

"Good luck on your final."

"Thanks," she replied. But as Leilani put her head back into her notes, she couldn't concentrate with the lingering pain in her foot. But she tried. For two weeks, she iced it and took Advil religiously. However, she didn't experience positive results. When her final exams were done, the pain became overwhelming and she decided to see Meghan.

***

After an extensive evaluation, Meghan looked at her and said, "Okay. I think we need you to see a physician. We probably need to get an X-ray and MRI. I think you have multiple bone spurs due to repetitive impact." Leilani looked down.

Meghan asked, "How long have you been in pain?"

Leilani responded, "maybe since just after the middle of the season." Meghan frowned. She was upset as this type of injury was unlikely to have an acute development, and was probably an overuse injury that had worsened over Leilani's volleyball career. She thought back to her conversation with Coach Keeno and felt like she should have caught this.

"I know you are tough, but I wish you had talked to me sooner about this pain. Let's see what the doc says," Meghan said worriedly.

Immediately following the physician visit, Meghan's suspicion was confirmed but the doctor also explained that Leilani's Achilles had begun to fray.

"So what is the plan?" Leilani asked Meghan tentatively.

"We are going to get you scheduled for surgery in a week to remove the bone spurs and repair your Achilles tendon," Meghan explained. "The timing of the procedure is more pressing than I had originally anticipated. The accumulation of so many bone spurs initiated the fraying of your Achilles, which is at high risk of tearing completely. A few more weeks playing might have been the last straw not only for your Achilles, but for your volleyball career as well."

"Will I be back for sand season?" Leilani asked.

Meghan stated sympathetically, "I'm not sure. I am pleased that this is not as bad as it could have been, and recovery is possible. And I'll help you through rehabilitation. We'll be in a good place to get you ready for your final year of volleyball."

THE REACTION

Leilani was devastated. Now on crutches, she fumbled as she picked up her phone and saw she had three missed calls from her dad. Before she could dial his number, he was calling for a fourth time. "Dad?"

"Hey, kid? You okay?"

"No." She told her dad everything.

"But there is some good news, right? Meghan said that they found the bone spurs and that it surgery can help, right?" her dad said hopefully.

"Yea, I guess," Leilani replied.

"And what did Coach say?" her dad asked.

Leilani explained that Meghan decided it would be best for her to explain her injury to the coach, "She knows more about the technical stuff about my injury and can tell Coach what to expect regarding her recovery and potential future playing time."

"Sounds good, Lei. We'll be there, just let us know what you need from home."

"Thanks, Dad, love you and ask Mom to call after work." As Leilani hung up the phone, she knew Meghan was on her way to talk to Coach.

***

Coach Keeno's office was quiet. As Meghan had explained the injury and initial rehabilitation plan to Coach, he grew increasingly frustrated with the realization of the potential loss of his star player. He stood up, and sternly spoke, "This shouldn't be a big deal. I endured multiple injuries throughout my career. Not once did I need surgery. She needs to grow up and man-up." Meghan insisted that this was a necessary procedure and tried to convince him that, if all went well, Leilani would be back for her senior season. "You better not baby her!" he squawked back. "She is a tough player. Don't soften her up!"

Feeling accused of treating this injury as more significant than it needed to be, Meghan looked back and said, "This is best for her health, and I'm already preparing to spend more time in the training room with Leilani doing pre-surgery exercises. And I'll see her through the rehab process to prepare her for the next season."

"Just get her ready to play," Coach said as he slumped back in his chair. Meghan left without closing the door.

Over finals week, Coach Keeno kept discussions with Leilani and Meghan to a minimum. He did, however, make sure his desire to not lose his star player was not forgotten. Prior to surgery, he sent Leilani a text message stating: "Better be back for sand season. No excuses!" Other than a few occasional texts with similar messages leading up to surgery, she had no interactions with Coach Keeno over winter break. Although Meghan agreed that it was important for the surgery to happen as soon as possible to offer the best opportunity to allow Leilani to return in time for sand season, Coach Keeno didn't seem to grasp the conditional aspect of her rehabilitation process. Depending on how much damage the surgery would do and the response from Leilani's body, her recovery time could vary between two and six months. As such, there was no guarantee on how quickly her body would recover; not even Leilani was in control of her body's ability to recover. As she prepared for surgery, Leilani had hope that she would be able to be ready for sand season, yet she grew anxious about the real extent of her injury and was concerned that recovery might take longer, and she would be out until next season.

A few days before surgery, Leilani expressed her concerns to a few of her teammates. "What if something goes horribly wrong and I can't play anymore?"

"Lei! Stop it!" her teammate yelled. "You are going to be fine. You are tough."

"I just feel like a failure and I want to be there for you guys."

One teammate looked her in the eyes, "You will be. And no one thinks less of you. You're injured because you pushed yourself for the team, for us."

"And you're an overachiever and you can't stand to fail," someone else chimed it.

"Apparently not" Leilani said as she slumped in her chair.

"You're going to be back in the sand with us before you know it," her teammate said as they got up to leave. "We'll see you after your surgery."

"Thanks," Leilani said as she sat thinking. She knew she had felt this pain at the beginning of conference play, and throughout the whole season she just kept pushing through. Looking back, she recognized she had pushed herself too far. At that moment, she decided she would take the recovery at Meghan's pace. After all, Meghan was the medical professional, and she would keep Leilani from pushing herself beyond her foot's limits. And she was convinced her team would support her; they would be there after the surgery, and through her recovery.

THE RECOVERY

When Leilani was released from the hospital and her doctor cleared her, she began working with Meghan on rehabilitation. "You are doing great," Meghan said. "I'm going to get healthy again," Leilani responded. She had turned the frustration with her team into motivation to show everyone that this injury would not debilitate her.

"This isn't going to take me out," she muttered.

"I know, and we have weeks until your Biodex exam to test your ankle strength, so pace yourself."

Leilani's goal was to come back stronger than before—both mentally and physically. Meghan's rehabilitation program focused on both cardio and upper body strengthening on her days off from foot rehabilitation. Leilani felt she was making strides in the recovery process. "But I've lost so much muscle mass since December, do you think there is a chance to be back for sand season?"

"Let's keep on plan," Meghan responded. However, after eight weeks she took her first Biodex exam and Meghan told her the results, "Lei, you have made significant progress in motion and strength over the last few weeks, but unfortunately the results show you are not yet ready for sand." Leilani looked down. She understood.

***

When Leilani and Meghan met with Coach Keeno to explain the results, he was speechless. Thinking about how he had lost his star player, he was livid. He looked Leilani in the eyes, "I thought you wanted to get better. Why aren't you contacting me to get extra practice time and actually make an effort recovering? Stop using your injury as a crutch. Be an adult. Don't you want to play!?"

Leilani stepped back and softly murmured "Sorry, Coach. I'll keep working on it." She knew her junior year of volleyball was over, but she didn't think Coach's reaction would be like that.

Meghan simply said, "We are working to get her ready for the fall."

Leilani felt like she had let everyone down, yet was more determined than ever to be ready for next season.

SAND SEASON

Leilani attended every practice during sand season. Although she was anxious to play again, she also didn't want to push too hard and set herself back. She was committed to keeping moving forward in the rehabilitation process, and improving her strength without any setbacks. As Leilani cheered her teammates from the sideline, Coach began to encourage her to step into the practice. "Team leaders don't stand around watching teammates," he would say, "Get out there and participate in these defensive drills." She gave an awkward glance and sat down. She was under strict orders from her surgeon and Meghan to stay off her feet as much as possible. Practicing could set her back. She was focused on taming her swelling and keeping her foot from being aggravated any more than necessary. She was becoming quite aware of how foot injuries heal slowly because compliance with staying off the feet is difficult. Standing on the sidelines alone is enough aggravation to stunt her healing process. So she quietly watched practice and grew worried that accumulating too much swelling might slow her recovery process.

Leilani was in a bind. A teammate sitting next to her said, "Shake it off, he just wants you to get better."

"I know. I just wish he knew how much I want to practice, get healthy, and play. But if I do what he says, it will ruin my recovery."

"We are just glad you are here, still working with us," her teammate smiled.

But Leilani wanted more. She wanted to be a leader and serve as positive example. She wanted to show others that she could speak up to Coach and tell him "No, that is too much for my ankle." Leilani replied, "I just don't want you all to doubt me, or think I am being a baby and not contributing."

"We all know you're in a tough spot, Lei, but you'll play in the fall. Just be patient. We know you're working hard to get better."

Then her phone rang. It was her dad. After she explained the bind she faced, her dad said, "As an athlete and a leader, you're faced with hard choices to make sometimes. But . . . it's supposed to be—"

"I know, Dad I know. It's supposed to be hard, if it wasn't hard everyone would do it, and it's the hard that makes us great, blah blah blah" she snickered.

"I love you too, Lei." He replied quietly. "Sounds like you have some thinking to do. Call me tomorrow."

As he hung up the phone, Leilani didn't want to think anymore. Every practice, every day, and every night she lived this tension. Her mind raced. How could she simultaneously be a tough player working to recover and stand up to a demanding coach whose pressure to play might not be the best for her recovery? Being a positive voice for teammates had always been one of her strengths. However, for some reason she felt incapable of saying "no" to her coach. She wanted to say his attempt to be encouraging was too much for her ankle. She wanted to follow Meghan's advice and continue at her pace. Ultimately, she wanted to recover so she could play. Leilani felt that while she could be a voice of encouragement and support her teammates until she was blue in the face, but if she wasn't pushing herself and practicing with them she wouldn't be the leader she wanted to be.

Since the sand courts were off campus and Meghan was not able to attend all practices, Leilani finally decided to join practice for a few drills. She tried to stay off her bad foot as much as possible, and the sand offered a relatively soft landing surface. Her teammates seemed surprised she was pushing herself in practices. Some grew worried, but no one said anything. They all looked up to her and were inspired by her enthusiasm. Leilani enjoyed being back into practices and drills, especially with the weather warming up. When paired with her adrenaline and thrill from engaging in team play once again, Leilani rarely felt pain during practice at all, but after practice was a different story.

Not only was the swelling in her foot increasing, but after two weeks of intermittent practices she was starting to feel a familiar pinching sensation on her "good foot." What now? Leilani anxiously thought. Am I going to need surgery, again? Is this the end of the fall season? Will I need to use my medical redshirt? Will I never again play with my friends and teammates? Will I not graduate in the spring? As her heart sank, she remembered how lonely she felt in the Recovery Room after surgery. Had she put herself through all of this so she wouldn't let anyone down? Did she deserve it? Did they deserve it? As the questions stirred, she grew less worried about being tough. She opened the door and calmly said, "Meghan, we have to talk."

DISCUSSION QUESTIONS

1. Who is responsible for Leilani's injury?
2. How did Leilani make sense of her pain at the initial onset?
3. How did Leilani's knowledge of her team role contribute to further injury?
4. What might her coach, teammates, and athletic trainer do reshape how athletes understand pain?
5. In what ways might pain be more successfully communicated?

KEY TERMS

Pain, Injury, Social support, Rehabilitation, Leadership, Toughness

CASE 14: THE BUCKS WOMEN'S RUGBY TEAM FACES COACHING DILEMMA

Bucks Face Dilemma

Elizabeth Ravaioli
Clemson University

John Spinda
Clemson University

ABSTRACT

In 2014, the College of Ohio's women's rugby team was forced to forfeit their spring season due to the inability to field a team large enough to compete in games. Goals for the season were discussed by the players and then emailed to the head coach; causing a major misinterpretation that resulted in the coach stepping down and effectively dissolving the relationship between the players and the head coach. The following week, the players found out that their now former head coach had accepted a coaching position for the men's rugby team, further embroiling the conflict.

***

The fall of 2011 was not only the birth of the College of Ohio's women's rugby club, nicknamed the "Bucks" after the school mascot, but it was also the start of a rugby "family"; the birth of a tradition.

The Bucks women's head coach, Mark Grazian, sat down at his office chair late Friday afternoon and let out a big deep breath after spending three hours stapling, taping, and tacking up flyers advertising his desire to start a women's rugby team. He wondered to himself how many women would want to play rugby this season. As Mark grabbed a cup of coffee on Tuesday morning, he saw new emails from two students, who were also eager to start a women's rugby club. After a few months, there were enough women to schedule one match. Mark excitedly said to his wife, "well, it's not enough women to field a full team of 15, but it's a start!"

Mark's spirits were buoyed when saw the women's smiles and camaraderie in that first match. Sure enough, the original volunteers told other girls around campus of their new club. The next season the Bucks Women's Rugby team had a full roster and played a complete schedule, earning a 5-1 record. The Bucks have fielded enough players to compete as a full team ever since, but it hasn't always been easy to find players. "The thing that is great about this club

145

team is that no experience is necessary. The women playing on this team are here because they want to be here; they may not be as athletically gifted as a lot of the scholarship athletes, but everyone plays and we *compete* . . . hard. We do what is needed to make sure our club accepts everyone on the team, no matter their skill level."

BACKGROUND

Coach Mark is a 42-year-old Philadelphia native who moved to the College of Ohio three years ago with his wife and three children to pursue his master's degree in real estate development. His rugby career began in 1990 during his freshman year at college and continued even after he moved to Ohio. He immersed himself in the game by taking up assistant coaching positions when his busy schedule allowed. He then started the women's rugby team at the College of Ohio in the fall of 2011. Former players describe Coach Mark's personality as friendly and enthusiastic, yet commanding and inadvertently condescending. One former player said, "Coach Mark is so stubborn and controlling about what he wants that it feels like he wants us to be clones of him and not to play the game ourselves." Fran, the captain of the women's rugby club, approached Mark and said, "Hey coach, we need to integrate tackling drills into practice to better prepare us for the physical games we have coming up the next few weeks." Mark shook his head and said, "I don't think we should" without further explanation. Mark has also been described as impertinent and "standoffish." He once told another Bucks rugby club president, "I feel like I am in a crazy whirlwind spiral with you and I want to get out."

Even though he is controlling and brash, Mark is also immensely knowledgeable about rugby and someone who truly cares about the teams he coaches. He has experience and is invested in the game emotionally. Mark has a competitive nature that plays a role in his tactics as a coach. He is goal-oriented and often asks the Bucks to set personal and team goals before each game and for the end of the season.

Fran, nicknamed "Whitey," is the current team captain. Whitey was born and raised in Charleston, West Virginia, before attending the College of Ohio in 2011. She is a 20-year-old junior majoring in biochemical engineering and minoring in anatomy, biology, and mathematical sciences. Whitey is known for her pale features and notorious red "afro." Rugby became a crucial part of her life in 2011 when she joined the Bucks rugby team and immediately became infatuated with the sport. Whitey would be described as an extremely intellectual person; often using what can be described as elaborate and complex words in her everyday vocabulary. Aside from her intellect, Fran has a very responsible and mature disposition that defies her years; often giving the impression that her life is perfectly balanced between work, rugby, rugby executive council, Alpha Omega Epsilon sorority, and maintaining a 3.8 GPA.

On the field, her Bucks teammates describe her as a passionate and intense rugby player with a niche for leadership and a "hint of crazy." A teammate once remarked, "I really can't believe you are wearing nothing but shorts and a t-shirt today, it's windy and it's got to be 25 degrees, Whitey!" Most people might never see her "rugby side" and only view her as a well-mannered student who is respectful in her daily encounters with students and faculty. But Whitey is also aggressive, especially around her team and those she's closest to. Some may say she is forceful in arguments, in games, or in practice. Overall, she is an intelligent, but strong-minded individual.

WHAT HAPPENED: From the Bucks Players' Point of View

It was the fall of 2013 and Mark was ready to kick off the season with his first full roster. "The schedule is in place and we've had some practices, but, wow, I am not sure if these women are ready to execute what I want them to do on the field," Mark told his wife.

The first game of the season was cancelled the night before the match by the opponent, so Mark yelled out, "we came here to play some rugby, right?" The women on the team all replied, "yes!" Mark then yelled out "alright then, get on either side of the line, we're going to play sevens!"

Sevens is a rugby variant where teams of seven face each other, rather than the usual 15 players a side. After this intra-team scrimmage, Mark told his the team "You all kicked some butt out there! I really think you have got an immense amount of potential, and I am going to train us for nationals" (the top tournament for club teams). Walking back to the dormitories, one Bucks team member said, "wow, I want to have fun and play, but it just felt like this game of sevens and now nationals are being forced on us, and we didn't have any say in it as a team. I mean, it should be fun to do nationals, and I had fun today, but this isn't a scholarship sport and I have 18 credit hours this semester!" As the season progressed, Mark put his focus on nationals, encouraging the Bucks to host a qualifying tournament. At this point, he kicked practices into high gear and asked the team and the executive council to go above and beyond their typical responsibilities to make the tournament happen. The tensions and stress levels became palpable between the team and Coach Mark.

Privately, many women on the team were becoming disenchanted with the experience. "I don't really like the additional workload we've had this fall on us, but I can deal with that . . . Coach thinking what he wants out of this experience is the same as what I want out of the experience this is what is really driving me crazy," remarked a member of the team when asked how the season was going. This player represented the majority of the team, who felt that Mark was confusing his goal with the teams' goals and failing to get input from others before making decisions.

This caused a great deal of conflict as the season and semester wore on. Although the Bucks won the two-day qualifying tournament they hosted for nationals, many players suffered injuries and there was very little time to rest and recuperate. Therefore, the Bucks did not experience nationals the way they had hoped to. "We are at nationals, let's win this thing!" Mark yelled out as his competitive side came out before the first match. But the look on the team's faces after Mark left the room said it all; they believed going there to win was an unrealistic goal due to their lack of experience in the sevens format of nationals. The young Bucks team was looking for validation from Mark after a rough stretch of three straight losing games at nationals, but never received it. Between these losses, Coach Mark would proclaim that, "no one has any sympathy for us and our injuries, let's go get it!" After the last game of the tournament, Mark, along with a few others, walked away from the team without any words of encouragement or concluding statements for the season. Nationals was the last experience the team had together heading into the spring season.

***

After the Christmas break, the team was in turmoil. The captain, Whitey, told a teammate who planned to play in the spring that "we need to either start mending some fences or recruiting, because we don't have enough to field a team right now. Most of the team doesn't want to return for the spring." This foreshadowing came to pass, as due to a lack of players, the Bucks not only forfeited their first match but their entire season as well. The Bucks now had to decide what to do going forward. While eating lunch with a large portion of the team at the school cafeteria, Whitey said, "We need to meet as a team to figure out what to do." Immediately, a number of teammates insisted that Mark not be a part of the meeting. After talking with more teammates individually, Whitey emailed the team, writing, "It seems like the majority of us do not want Mark at the meeting, so I won't invite him."

After meeting as a team, without Mark, they decided they were going to focus on recruiting and try to schedule a few friendly matches versus other local colleges. Whitey had the unfamiliar feeling of nervousness as she prepared to express these new goals to Mark via email. She wrote:

Coach Mark,

We as a team have decided we would like to put 7s on hold. Most of the team has a bad taste in their mouth from nationals. The team felt the transition you made from 15s to 7s was too quick and drastic. We will be forfeiting our 15s season; however, we would like to play a few friendly matches if possible. The team really liked the dynamic of the captain-led practices along with coach-led practices. Please let me know what you think.

Thank you,

Whitey and the Bucks

After hitting send, Whitey experienced the unfamiliar feelings of nervousness and anxiety about how the competitive and standoffish Coach would receive this message. Three days later, Whitey's received the following response:

Team,

Based on the Whitey's email, I think it best I step aside this season. Along with struggling to retain players over the last few years, the team has struggled to retain coaches. Over the past few school years I have committed my time and energy for very little or no pay to try to help the team rebuild and advance. My hope is the team can grow from within this season and embrace the importance of making new players, and coaches, feel like a valued part of a team.

Coach

After Mark sent this email, the team discovered that he had accepted an assistant coaching position with the College of Ohio men's rugby team less than a week later. The team felt betrayed. Whitey's jaw was fully squared as she told another teammate "I can't believe Coach Mark just gave up on us like that, I've got to know more."

WHAT HAPPENED: Coach Mark's Point of View

After the emails were exchanged, Whitey met with Mark to discuss what had happened and hear his point of view. Mark told Whitey, "I truly believed that nationals were a good option for us, even though we were struggling with retaining players. This is why I pushed it so hard; I thought it was best for the team." Mark also admitted that there was an unclear vision for the team, "I just didn't outline the club's goals well and didn't communicate them effectively between the team and you as their leader."

"Well, I will admit it, making nationals like a dream come true for me, Coach," said Whitey.

"Me too," Mark replied with a quick smile, "I guess I thought it would be for the entire team as well."

Training for nationals was demanding and harsh at times, but only because he believed it was a privileged opportunity that any team would dedicate themselves to. Constantly pushing the team to live up to their potential was rooted in the fact that he thought everyone would go the extra mile to get better because he truly believed the team was capable of greatness. Mark admitted that he did not understand the true dynamic of the team. "But," Mark said, "I also felt like you and the team did not value my experience and expertise. I felt like I wasn't being heard or respected as a coach." Mark concluded by saying, "Look, I know what I want, I want to be competitive. This season, the team cannot give me that as a coach. This is why I thought it was best if I stepped down."

WHAT DO THE BUCKS DO NOW?

After the spring, when the Bucks played only a handful of friendlies with nearby schools, Whitey addressed the team as the captain, "Ladies, we have a decision to make. Should we recruit more competitively and ask Mark back to be our coach in the fall?"

After a brief pause, one teammate stood up and proclaimed, "No offense to you, Whitey, because you know I love ya, but I'll quit immediately if he comes back."

"Me too," said another voice, and then another.

Whitey asked with a look of frustration, "So, if I am hearing you all correctly, 3 of 11 of us will quit if he comes back?"

Running the basic facts of the situation in her head, Whitey tried to figure a way out of this situation. *We need at least seven players to compete in "sevens," which is feasible with eight players, and possibly a few backups. Should Mark be asked back? However, most club matches play standard Rugby format with 15 players, which seems very unlikely for the Bucks to obtain, given the difficulty recruiting players, Therefore, we cannot afford to lose three girls because of a coach's perceived persona and attitude.*

Whitey then responded, "Look, I know Mark's negatives sometimes overshadow his positives, but this is my senior year, I really want to play competitive again, and it seems like a good number of you all want to play that way again also."

One teammate agreed, "You are right, I hated the hard practices, but I loved competing and winning." This drew some nods from some teammates and scowling looks from other teammates.

DISCUSSION QUESTIONS

1. Due to the nature of these events, how should the Bucks move forward? Considering the future and the foundation of the Bucks team is in a fragile state, what would be the most stable option for them?

2. Can and should the Bucks salvage the lost relationship with Coach Mark? If so, what steps would you recommend to begin the relationship repair process?

3. Should the Bucks have taken a different course of action during their off-season interaction with Coach Mark? If they had, would the future of the team be the same? Why or why not?

KEY TERMS

Coaching-athlete relations, Organizational leadership

PART 3
PUBLIC RELATIONS AND SPORT

INTRODUCTION

As we discussed in the opening pages of this book, sport is pervasive in our society. Nowhere is this more prevalent than in the news. Every day there is some news about some athlete, team, or sport organization that has either required promotional tactics from public relations (PR) personnel, or will require reaction and perhaps restitution by those same practitioners.

In sport, PR practitioners do a variety of things and many of these endeavors are covered in the cases in this section. One job PR practitioners find themselves doing is creating hype for a sport or sport figure. For instance, sports information directors at colleges will produce whole campaigns for student athletes who are in line for special awards. The Heisman Trophy, college football's most coveted award, is known for the hype and buzz sports information directors (SIDs) help create for their respective student-athletes. These campaigns consist of everything from social media buzz to direct correspondence with the sport media outlets where highlight videos of the athlete are compiled and distributed. Like creating hype for an athlete competing for the Heisman, the first case in this section considers how hype and buzz are created in the world of mixed martial arts (MMA).

These days, the main public relations tool is all the social media outlets available. Four different cases in this section deal with various social media issues one might encounter as a sport PR practitioner. If you find yourself working with athletes on a team, the PR or sports information office will often be responsible for creating a social media policy for their players. This is more likely at the high school and college level than in the pros. But even at the professional level, various sport organizations will often at least want social media guidelines, or even training for their athletes. How athletes and fans use social media changes daily. And things can be said and spread by social media very quickly; thus keeping up with how athletes you work with use the various outlets will be important if you want to practice public relations in a sport organization. New social media content companies dedicated to sport are cropping up now. For instance, Whistle Sports claims to be the "first sports entertainment platform built to engage and activate the new generation of fans and athletes."[1] There are similar "news" content sites such as *HuffPost* and *The Buzz* for general and entertainment news. Whistle Sports is focused on the millennial generation and has over 75 million fans on six different social media platforms.[2] Whistle Sports also partners with nine different professional sport organizations such as the NFL, MLB, and NASCAR.[3]

A study conducted by brand engagement firm GMR Marketing found that more than 80% of people surveyed are more likely to check the Internet for sports news than turn to TV or radio,[4] and half of those are checking Facebook or Twitter specifically.[5] Of those surveyed, 83% said they like to check social media for sports updates during a game and 63% said they will even do it while at the game.[6] New social media apps, such as Periscope (launched in late March 2015), allow sports fans to broadcast what they are seeing AS they are watching it.[7] The use of social media linked to sporting events seems to know no bounds.

Ethical issues are always in the news when it comes to the sport world. Whether it is the Olympic or FIFA officials taking bribes, or athletes doping, gambling, and violating NCAA rules, news about ethical violations occur practically daily. Is it that these things happen more often in the sport world? Not necessarily. But because events that occur in the sport world seem to generate more interest with the public, these stories get more attention than similar events occurring in other areas of our society. Whenever ethics is involved, PR practitioners will be there to help put a focus on one area rather than another (or pull focus from one area to another).

Take the recent FIFA scandal where in May 2015 the US "Justice Department unsealed a 47-count indictment against 14 defendants—including FIFA bigwigs, sports marketing executives, and the owner of a broadcasting corporation—with charges of racketeering, wire fraud, and money laundering."[8] FIFA's president and likely PR staff immediately went on the defense (and in some cases offense). FIFA's general communication in the face of allegations has always been to maintain that the organization is "but a humble nonprofit doing humanitarian work to bring sport to the world,"[9] which was usually recited by the then-president, Sepp Blatter. Although Blatter has yet to be indicted himself at the time this book went to press, he did step down as president. One of FIFA's main PR endeavors before these indictments was to payroll 90% of the movie, *United Passions,* that debuted just after the scandal broke in June 2015.[10] Unfortunately for FIFA, the film did do not well at the box office. According to CBS Sports News, the 29 million dollar project grossed only $918 in its opening weekend.[11]

This is all just to show that doing public relations in the sport world can be a nonstop ride, ever changing, and scrutinized to the fullest. Of course, as those in the collegiate sports information office reveal,[12] it can also be a rewarding position where you get to work with student-athletes on a daily basis building media guides and statistics reports and working with the media in press boxes.

As you work through the cases in Part Three, consider the various guidelines, concepts, theories, and models you may have learned in public relations classes such as:

- image repair/management;
- various stakeholders;
- crisis communication planning;
- media/social media policies;
- framing theory;
- press agentry-publicity model, public information model, two-way asymmetrical model, and two-way symmetrical model of public relations;
- press release, media guide/kit, fact sheet guidelines;
- interviewing guideline

REFERENCES

[1] Whistle Sports. (n.d.). About. Retrieved from http://whistlesports.com/about/

[2] Ibid.

[3] Ibid.

[4] Laird, S. (5 February 2015). How much do sports fans love social media? [Infographic]. Mashable.com. Retrieved from http://mashable.com/2012/02/15/social-sports-infographic/

[5] Ibid.

[6] Ibid.

[7] Periscope. (26 March 2015). Up Periscope. Retrieved from https://medium.com/@periscope/up-periscope-f0b0a4d2e486

[8] McFarland, K. M. 27 May 2015). Everything you need to know about FIFA's corruption scandal. *Wired.* Retrieved from http://www.wired.com/2015/05/fifa-scandal-explained/

[9] Ibid.

[10] Ibid.

[11] Mello, I. (18 June 2015). FIFA film "United Passions" lowest-grossing in US box office history. CBSsports.com. Retrieved from http://www.cbssports.com/general/eye-on-sports/25218330/fifa-film-united-nations-deemed-lowest-grossing-in-us-box-office-history

[12] See Leann Parker's Voice of a Pro in Part Four of this textbook.

VOICE OF A PRO

Jackson Jayanayagam
Senior Vice President of Digital Strategy, Taylor@jacksonjey

Photo courtesy of Jackson Jayanayagam

"Be yourself; everyone else is already taken." – Oscar Wilde

Among the many, many . . . many things that I have learned in my career, this is the one that I have found the most important – *be authentic in everything you do.*

I know it's obvious to "just be yourself" as you have been told by every parent/grandmother/teacher that you have ever come into contact with. But as you begin your career, it can be all too easy to conform and assimilate.

That's not to say that you won't have to adapt and learn new things. Quite the opposite, in fact. Changing with the times is the only way to succeed in your career . . . but doing it with a sense of authenticity and transparency will separate you from your peers.

Authenticity is the quality that inspires, motivates, and drives people to take action based on *your* actions; it's the characteristic that allows you to influence others to follow your lead in times of crisis; it's what will define *your character* and allow you to survive any potential negative scenario . . . even if you are at fault.

Take a cue from every athlete, celebrity, and politician (or NFL commissioner) who has ever made a mistake. Those who sincerely admit responsibility and do what they say they will do to fix it are usually forgiven, by even their harshest critics. But those who try to hide behind semantics and inconsistencies will usually suffer a much more severe backlash, even from a seemingly small mistake.

But as I have learned over the years, authenticity is not limited to who you are and how you act. It is also a critical element of *successful* sports marketing.

In my job, I work with Fortune 500 companies that spend millions of dollars on major sponsorships—including the NFL, NBA, NCAA, Olympics, World Cup, and NASCAR. These brands come to us to help them maximize their sponsorship by engaging fans in a unique and relevant way, beyond traditional advertising.

But when trying to engage with, and speak to, sports fans there are very few "rules," that you can learn from a textbook; and the one that separates a campaign from being a success or a dreaded #fail is authenticity . . . authenticity in the content that you send to the fans and authenticity in the message that you are re-enforcing (in relation to that sports sponsorship).

Because we are targeting such passionate fans, it is critical that every message and every piece of content we distribute is authentic and resonates with the fan . . . and sometimes that means it shouldn't even come from the brand. In fact, we have implemented a number of campaigns where the client's branded content is delivered to fans only by the teams, or the players of their favorite team, via Twitter.

The combination of this credible source (the player/team), relevant content, and right-time targeting (my agency's refined approach to "real-time" marketing) ensures that our client's message to the fans is perceived as authentic to their fandom as well as their experience with the sport.

There are plenty of things that you will learn in your respective careers but if you can learn to do what should come naturally to you, you will be in a unique position to inspire and motivate others; and if you can truly understand how to apply that authentic approach to sports marketing, then you will be just a few years away from becoming my boss.

Jackson leads digital and social media integration across Taylor (a leading sports marketing firm), supporting a number of top consumer brands including P&G, Nike (Jordan Brand), NASCAR, Allstate, Capital One, Diageo, and Taco Bell. He has helped create and implement a number of innovative digital campaigns that span audiences and have leveraged a wide variety of sports and entertainment sponsorships including NCAA March Madness, the BCS, NBA, NFL, NASCAR and CONCACAF. These campaigns have incorporated social influencer and advocacy marketing, real-time content creation and delivery, and mobile marketing.

Prior to joining the agency, Jackson worked with brands such as Old Spice, Dentyne, T-Mobile, and Microsoft to launch various products and help build advocacy among key influencers through social media and digital integration. He also managed fan engagement around various sports sponsorships including the NFL, NBA, and NASCAR.

Jackson has participated in various speaking engagements on panels and at conferences, including SXSW Sports, Internet Week, WOMMA, Sports Business Journal Motorsports Marketing Forum, Advertising Week, PRWeek Digital Roundtable series, Inbound Marketing Summit, The Digital Collective, Publishing Business Conference & Expo, #140Conf, as well as guest speaking roles at NYU and UNC's Kenan-Flagler Business School.

CASE 15: BATTLING THE BIG MO
MMA and the Power of Buzz

Dariela Rodriguez
Ashland University & University of North Texas

Gwendelyn Nisbett
Ashland University & University of North Texas

ABSTRACT

For most people, playing sports as a child was all about having fun. Many people argue that professional sports are all about the money and not about the love of the sport, but that is not necessarily true. Those athletes just have a different goal at the end of the day, a bigger goal. They want a championship. In sports such as football, baseball, and hockey, the road to that goal is paved by wins and losses, arguably in the control of the players. If you play hard and get the wins, no one can take away the chance to win a championship. In other sports such as boxing and mixed martial arts, the road to a championship title is determined by ranking systems and match makers. Performances will bring hype for the fighter and bring momentum to the wave he or she will ride to a title shot.

***

"The winner, and still champion, Jim "The Hitman" Johnson!" The announcer Malcolm Shaw had to scream over the noise of the crowd as Mixed Combat Championship (MCC) President Daniel Jones put the belt around The Hitman's waist.

"A-gui-lar, A-gui-lar, A-gui-lar!" Brandon and Lindsey, who were at the local sports bar to watch the fight with their friends, were big fans of the number one MCC lightweight contender Jose Aguilar, and they were excited to see Aguilar take on Johnson next.

"Brandon! This is it!" Lindsey was practically jumping out of her seat at the bar. "Johnson vs. Aguilar! And the new light heavyweight champion . . ."

"So you think Jones will give Aguilar the fight?" Gina, one of Brandon and Lindsey's friend's in the group, asked. "You know Jones is famous for his ranking leapfrogging. That guy is more interested in money than fair ranking or selecting fighters who deserve the chance. This guy is making match making a joke. Benefits of being president, I guess" Clearly, Gina was not in favor of the politics behind Jones' decisions.

Brandon jumped in, "I don't think Jones can do that this time. I mean, Aguilar is ranked as the number-two contender behind Daugherty, who just got submitted by Johnson. And Aguilar hasn't lost since the last time he faced The Hitman a year and a half ago. And we all know he deserved a rematch for that fight. I still think he beat Johnson in that battle."

"I guess we will see by tomorrow. You know Jones always announces the next match up at the post-fight scrum. Let's get out of here." The group left chanting A-gui-lar as they left the bar.

***

Within the realm of world-class sports there exists an unwritten rule of power and politics that influences the ranking of the top team or individuals in that sport; this is prevalent throughout the nation and, sometimes, the world. The political game influences everything from the preseason rankings in college sports, to the ranking systems in sports such as boxing, tennis, and here mixed martial arts (MMA). The need for ranking teams of players helps to provide an easy-to-understand list of who the top performers are in the sport; however, the process by which rankings and match ups are set is not always as simple as reading a list.

LET THE BATTLE BEGIN

Battles in sport are not always played out on the field of battle, so to speak. It is not uncommon in sports such as tennis, boxing, MMA, and even most collegiate sports for teams to leapfrog over others in the rankings based on more than just a win. Conversely, a successful team can drop multiple spots after just one loss. These circumstances seem to imply that more than just the game outcomes play a role in rankings.

Eager to find out when Aguilar was going to battle with Johnson, Gina got up early on Sunday morning to watch the replay of the press conference to hear Jones make the announcement. Flipping on MCCTV, Gina was shocked by what she heard and immediately called Brandon.

"Can you believe this guy?! Last night Jones announced that he had not made a decision about the next fight for The Hitman! Who on earth would he put up next? This is so not fair!"

Brandon, who had seen the news on Facebook right before Gina called, was scrolling through some of the comments in his newsfeed and noticed a lot of people calling for MCC up-and-comer Mark Hernandez to get the fight.

"Gina, you think Jones is going to put his buddy Hernandez into the next fight? A lot of people are saying Jones will leapfrog him in the rankings to number two because he is undefeated."

"But that shouldn't make a difference; he only has three fights in the MCC. Everyone else in the top five has at least seven and most only have one loss. I can see a Hernandez-Aguilar fight if he wants to see who is worthy, but Hernandez has not beaten a single top-ranked fighter. How will he justify jumping from seven to two?" Gina was now looking at Twitter and saw that a lot of people were making her same argument, but it did look like the fans were also calling for the jump of Hernandez.

"I don't know, Gina. We have seen fighter momentum bring in big pay-per-view revenue for the MCC before. I have seen Jones seeing dollar signs over a promised fight in the past. I would just hate for Aguilar to get the short end of the stick on this one." Brandon did not think things were looking good for Aguilar . . .

Brandon did have a point, when looking at a season of a sport, it is usually not just one game that would make all the difference, it is the accumulation of the season, but there is also some weight to Gina's concern about whether or not it is fair that one game, or one fight, can so impact as season or set of rankings. The media seemed to have a lot of power in creating perceptions about which fighter was a winner and which fighters were irrelevant.

"It's all about media hype," grumbled Brandon.

GAINING MOMENTUM

Within one week, Brandon, Gina, and Lindsey's hopes of a rematch between Aguilar and Johnson were dashed. Daniel Jones had decided to book Johnson versus Hernandez for the biggest fight night of the year, the July 4th Showdown in Atlantic City. It was clear that the media hype surrounding Hernandez had won out.

"How is it that people believe Hernandez is ready for this fight?! Most of Johnson's opponents had twice as many fights before their title fight was granted." Lindsey, who had held out hope that Aguilar-Johnson II would happen, slammed her fist on the table at lunch, not able to get past her anger.

"Daniel Jones loves Hernandez, of course he would show favoritism toward his biggest fan draw. The media pays attention to him because he talks a lot of trash, and the people pay attention to the media. Total bandwagon fans, if you ask me," said Brandon, mirroring Lindsey's anger. "Plus he has a huge following in his home country of Mexico, and you know Jones wants to expand the market down there."

"The MMA TV shows make him out to be a maniac in the cage and Mr. Charisma out of it," argued Gina. "His story is pretty interesting, though. I guess that is why everybody loves him. I can see where he is a big draw for the pay-per-view events."

Gina's comment caught Lindsey off guard a bit. She was just hoping and praying Gina was not buying into the Hernandez hype machine. "Do you really think he can beat Aguilar? Because to get the title fight, I think he should have to work his way up through the top of the ranks, and that means Aguilar, not to mention all the other fighters he is leapfrogging here. He is just riding this wave of fame to the top."

"Jones practically served him up wins by placing him against fighters who never even broke the top ten ranks. He has been handpicked for this and everyone knows it." Brandon, backing up Lindsey's claim, was practically yelling now.

He continued, "Hernandez never fought top-ranked fighters. I just don't understand how one loss for some fighters is a death sentence and others get a free ride to the top by fighting a bunch of has-beens. So much for strength of schedule in the MCC!"

Power Play

Coming up on the end of the season, Lindsey and Brandon were still hopeful that Jones would reconsider Aguilar for the championship fight. They were sitting in their favorite pizza hangout, waiting for the next Aguilar fight to come on the TV. Since Johnson was out with an injury, the MCC match makers decided to have Aguilar and Hernandez both fight; however, they did not create the match up everyone wanted to see, Aguilar vs. Hernandez, instead they matched them up on the same card against two other fighters. Many assumed that MCC President Jones was too afraid that Hernandez would lose to Aguilar and ruin Hernandez' bid for the title. After all, a loss to Aguilar would stop the Hernandez hype train right in its tracks.

"People really doubted Aguilar," Lindsey told Brandon. "But he has been at the top of his game – he's golden."

"And Hernandez dragged in his last fight," laughed Brandon. "Everyone thought he was soooo superior – but he totally flaked. I still do not think he won."

"Aguilar was amazing in his last match," argued Lindsey gleefully. "He is heads above Johnson at this point. People need to get on board and just admit that he is the best and force Jones to make the fight happen!"

"Aguilar has a ton of momentum at this point – he just seems really unstoppable," said Brandon. "I'm so excited his ranking is rising."

"Jones will have to cave now," added Lindsey. "There is no way he can pit Johnson versus Hernandez."

Just then, Gina walked in wearing an "I Heart Hernandez" shirt, to which Brandon and Lindsey threw some serious shade.

"OMG Gina – what are you thinking?!" guffawed Lindsey.

"What?! Don't be haters," exclaimed Gina, a bit exasperated. "Hernandez is the hottest commodity in mixed martial arts."

Gina continued, "Look, my boy Hernandez has momentum – he has the bandwagon support of the media and the fans – just look at the social media buzz. Plus, he's super-hot! He's going to get the title match."

"Ya know who the media hates right now?" asked Lindsey rhetorically. "They hate Johnson. That guy is a has-been – he has no charisma and no support."

"Yeah, Johnson's managers will have a tough time spinning his lackluster image," laughed Gina with rueful glee.

"Oh I totally agree," said Brandon. "Sport is all about buzz. Live by the buzz, get killed by the buzzsaw!"

The Big Fight

"Buzz won out – Hernandez is in the final," sighed Brandon. "I'm so stoked that Aguilar is the co-main event because it is a big spotlight, but I'm so sick of the Hernandez hype."

Hernandez again fought a non-ranked fighter in his last fight, but since it was a first-round submission win, his reputation momentum carried him into the championship. Aguilar had been riding high on a wave of wins and good media coverage, but fans and marketing put Hernandez a rank above and into the championship.

"I think it's exciting," exclaimed Gina. "It really shows you how much press coverage and trending on social media can drive sports rankings."

"The media is powerful and professional sports is incredibly political," explained Lindsey. "Buzz and momentum dictate seasons and championships almost as much as scores and performances."

"It's a victory for Hernandez fans too," said Gina. "We call ourselves 'Hernandez Honeys' and the social media hype over him was amazing . . . how could you not get onboard?!"

"Aguilar's PR team really did a crap job in managing his media coverage," argued Lindsey. "Really, Aguilar is better than Hernandez . . . but it doesn't really matter when he didn't have public opinion and media momentum on his side."

"You can't fight the 'Big Mo'," laughed Brandon.

And with that, the threesome wandered off to catch the championship fight.

DISCUSSION QUESTIONS

1. What role did media influence play in the outcome of the MMA season?
2. How is a momentum narrative created during a season?
3. If you were in charge of public relations for an elite athlete, how would you use narrative and framing to combat momentum against your client? How would you keep a positive momentum narrative?
4. Can fans like Brandon and Lindsey do anything to influence the momentum narrative of the season?

KEY TERMS

Media framing, Narrative, Public relations, Momentum, Framing

CASE 16: BEYOND X'S AND O'S ON THE COURT

Why Social Media Demands a New Playbook for Student-Athletes

Margaret C. Stewart
University of North Florida & Neumann University

Jeffrey B. Eisenberg
University of North Florida & Neumann University

ABSTRACT

This case examines the impact of a Twitter war among student-athletes at rival colleges. The exchange carried out on social media causes wide-reaching effects, prompting administrators to visit the idea of establishing and implementing a social media policy to guide the behavior of their student-athletes online.

***

Monica Malphus, a junior point-guard and co-captain for the Green Valley University Sabers, was eagerly anticipating a competition against rival Kelley College, and she felt the upcoming game was more than an athletic contest. To Monica, this was about making a statement. To her, the game was a chance to prove who was a better team of women. Monica's passion to win compelled her to make her feelings known more publicly.

Four days before the Friday evening matchup at Kelley College, Monica took to Twitter and wrote:

> @MMalphus: Excellence. Tradition. Any1 tries 2 keep us down doesn't know the @GVSabers. We're coming. Counting down to Thurs night @KelleyWBB

Most of the Kelley College's Golden Wave women's basketball team members (10 out of 14) had active Twitter accounts. Unfortunately, freshman Katharine Allen, a power social media user, was the first to see Malphus' tweet due to the included team tag. Instinctually, Katharine was motivated to defend her team. With the home court advantage, a spectacular record to-date, and first place in the conference at stake, this was clearly meant to be a direct and personal threat. All the same, Katharine was feeling confident. *We all know who the top team is*, she thought.

Katharine held up Monica Malphus' tweet with an attitude of superiority. In a quoted tweet, she wrote:

> @KA_Wave: Who now? BConf CHAMPS 12-13 RT @KelleyWBB RT@MMalphus: Any1 tries 2 keep us down doesn't know the @GVSabers. We're coming

With a direct tag to her account, Monica Malphus' phone lit up within seconds. *Are you serious?* A loss is a loss, and her team looking to avoid a third loss in a row to the Kelley College Golden Wave was bad enough, but a nose in the air and a giant "'F' You" online was the final push. *Allen?* she thought. *Who the hell is this?*

Monica found her answer with a quick search of the Golden Wave women's basketball roster. #16, Katharine Allen. Freshman. Guard. Five foot, five inches. Box scores . . . a total of just 25 minutes of game time this season. Point average: 6 for 17 from the field. *Hold on . . . this is who's talking?*

Monica Malphus had enough. If Katharine Allen wanted to talk, she'd better be ready to defend her words on the court. And that, Monica knew, wouldn't be happening any time soon. She tweeted:

> @MMalphus: @KA_Wave @GVSabers @KelleyWBB Should be asking u that question. Don't remember ur # on the court. How's sideline treating u? Let the women play.

Friday's game, Monica Malphus knew, had suddenly become much more than a win or loss. This was going to be a fight.

HISTORY BETWEEN THE SCHOOLS

Kelley College is a co-curricular, Catholic institution located in the United States' mid-Atlantic region. Founded in 1902, Kelley places an emphasis on a values-based, rounded liberal arts education and prides itself on developing students with sound intellectual, spiritual, and emotional intelligence.

For its rigorous academic standards, the College consistently ranks in the top 25 for East Coast Academic Excellence in Higher Education within the "small school" category. Kelley serves 3,200 full-time undergraduate students.

Kelley is home to 16 NCAA Division III intercollegiate athletic teams. Though the Kelley College Golden Wave teams are members of the relatively small Breakers Conference, several teams – most notably men's baseball, men's lacrosse, men's and women's soccer, and women's basketball – have enjoyed frequent success within the conference. Most recently, the men's lacrosse and women's basketball teams won the conference championships for the 2012-2013 academic year, with both teams winning one game apiece in the NCAA Division III tournaments for their respective sports.

Kelley's women's basketball team is a fourteen-person squad. During the most recent 2013–2014 academic year, half the students on the team were seniors, including two team captains. Four juniors, two sophomores, and just one freshman composed the rest of the team. The beginning of that 2013-2014 season began well for the Golden Wave. With an 11-3 record, the Golden Wave team was tied for first in the conference with the Green Valley University Sabers.

The two teams had a short history. Green Valley University only entered the Breakers Conference four years ago, and during their first three years the women's basketball team mostly tread water, finishing each season just barely above the .500 mark. Last year, however, gave birth to an intense rivalry, with Kelley's and Green Valley's teams routinely trading first and second place in the conference throughout the season. Ultimately, the Golden Wave prevailed, as Kelley defeated Green Valley by only a six-point spread to win the Breakers Conference Championship.

To-date in the 2013-2014 season, the Golden Wave and Sabers had played each other twice – both games on Green Valley's campus – and Kelley, despite the visitor's disadvantage, prevailed in both contests. Looking to snap their three-loss streak to the Golden Wave and especially to avenge a feeling of humiliation at home, the Sabers planned to focus on one thing in anticipation of their upcoming game at Kelley College: a decisive win.

But that changed when things took such a nasty turn online.

STUDENT-ATHLETE INTERACTIONS

Kelley College senior and Golden Wave women's basketball co-captain Jessica Bradshaw had been instrumental in her team's recent successes. Consistently shooting 50% from the floor and 80% from the line, she had been the difference-maker in several games over her previous three years on the team. In addition to her numbers, Jessica had grown into a respected leader. Though she was relatively reserved during her freshman and early sophomore years, her laser-like focus and quiet determination had become a point of admiration among her coaches and teammates. Now, in her final season with the Golden Wave, she was a leader who consistently and effectively drove herself and her teammates toward success.

Mondays were Jessica's toughest academic days. In class from early morning through mid-afternoon, she rarely caught a break. So, although she always followed Kelley Athletics' social accounts, the feud between her teammate Katharine Allen and Green Valley University rival Monica Malphus had been in progress for hours before Jessica took notice. She scrolled through the Twitter feed; eight tweets went back and forth between Allen and Malphus.

Jessica immediately began composing a text message to her freshman teammate Katharine Allen.

"Hey Kat. Saw the tweets. Don't worry about Green Valley . . . we r gonna be fine on Fri. Don't engage her more . . . could look bad for the team."

Bad for the team? Getting called out looks bad for the team! Katharine replied:

"She's calling us out . . . tryin to defend the team. You guys owned it last year, she's tryin to put that down. Don't want to let her"

But Jessica knew that an online flame war would get them nowhere.

"If she wants to talk, let her. Pls let it go. We'll settle it on the court :-)"

No sooner had their text conversation ended, though, did Jessica return to Twitter to see another teammate, Meg White, had decided to join the conversation.

Meg White, a senior, had been an integral part of the Kelley College team the past two years. She blossomed into an outstanding rebounder through her freshman and sophomore years, and at five feet, eleven inches tall, she was responsible for many decisive put-backs that may have been the difference in close games.

Meg had also tried to claim a position as a team captain this season, but had not been selected by Head Coach Greg Carson. Meg was no doubt a leader and a talented player, but Coach Carson was concerned that she could be too hot-headed. Her on-court celebrations could be a bit over-the-top, but her frustrations were even more visible. During her sophomore year, she had been called on four separate flagrant fouls.

This could get ugly, thought Jessica Bradshaw. She checked Meg's tweet:

> @Meg_White_62: @MMalphus @KA_Wave @GVSabers @KelleyWBB Think ur lookin for the girls league? U attack us, ull get ur ass kicked out of our house.

While Jessica Bradshaw now turned her attention to Meg White, other members of the Kelley women's basketball team – those who used Twitter and followed their teammates as well as the basketball accounts – began to take notice. Though none of them elected to engage in the exchange of tweets, two players did "favorite" tweets by their teammates Meg White and Katharine Allen. Meanwhile, two members of Green Valley's team joined the online argument in support of Monica Malphus, tweeting in response to Meg White's latest attack and throwing more fuel on the fire:

> @BBallTall: @Meg_White_62 @KA_Wave @GVSabers @KelleyWBB girls league? The only girls I see are too busy tweeting trash to win games

Although some members of the Kelley team were indifferent to the Twitter war, several others – especially the senior members – began to feel frustration at the argument, which lasted well through that Monday afternoon and into the evening. Golden Wave co-captain Jessica Bradshaw, in particular, was feeling the stress. This exchange could really tarnish the team's otherwise solid reputation. Luckily, things settled down by the end of the evening. The responses stopped, and Jessica talked to everyone on the Kelley College team who had tweeted or otherwise engaged in the online conversation. Hopefully, she thought, that would be the end of it; they could avoid further chaos and focus on the game.

COACH'S PERSPECTIVE

Coach Greg Carson had been at the helm of the Kelley College women's basketball team for the past five years. During those five seasons, he led the team to 91 wins and only 45 losses, a very impressive record within the conference.

Coach Carson was respected and well-liked within the community. Though he could be loud on the court, he was known as a more reserved and humble figure around the community. After last year's team record 22-6 run along with the Breakers Conference Championship, Carson famously said only: "It was a great year. So happy for these girls." Moreover – and to the disdain of the Office of College Communications, who could have capitalized on the stories – he regularly got his team involved in both on- and off-campus service projects without telling a soul.

Carson was by no means a tech expert or a huge proponent of social media – he thought such platforms were too narcissistic, at best, and a distraction, at worst – but from time-to-time he did check in on colleagues, athletes, and teams who used Twitter and Facebook. He did so, however, about only once or twice per week. Tuesday morning, then, came as a complete surprise. By 11:00 AM that day, two of his players, Katharine Allen and Meg White, were sitting in his office in the small annex just behind Kelley College's modest arena.

"This probably isn't coming as a surprise to either one of you," started Coach Carsen. "Mike Pierce and I had a pretty serious conversation this morning. Ladies, this is not how we should be starting our day. It's certainly not how our athletic director wanted to start his day. But I'm also not going to pretend to be an expert at this. As members of this team, I place my trust in all of you to work hard and play hard . . . and also to be good stewards of this team. So . . . with that said, why don't you all tell me what's going on with Green Valley?"

Katharine and Meg glanced at each other. The senior, who had only stepped in during the latter part of the feud, chose to speak. "Coach, Katharine didn't do anything wrong. We got an obvious threat from Green Valley. Kat just saw it first. I mean . . . I get it, it's what's on the court that matters, but none of us want them coming here feeling like they own the place. I mean, they're gonna intimidate us on Twitter? We have to let them know it isn't gonna work."

Katharine, the freshman, jumped in. "I know I've only been here half a season. But last year's team has a lot to defend, and by joining this team I made a commitment to do that. And I wasn't attacking her, Coach. I was just sticking up for my teammates."

Coach Carson, Katharine, and Meg continued their conversation, with the student-athletes contending that they were simply defending themselves and that their responses were not meant to be particularly hostile or negative. All the same, Coach Carson's earlier conversation with Athletic Director Mike Pierce illuminated the potential reach of the Twitter war. Not only had these athletes' friends possibly seen the tweets, but so had the official accounts of Kelley College, Green Valley University, and both women's basketball teams. Though the argument luckily had stayed on Twitter, it was a public forum and one that neither Mike Pierce nor Greg Carson wanted littered with team name-calling.

***

For the good of the team, Coach Carson ultimately decided to sit both Katharine Allen and Meg White in the upcoming game against Green Valley. Highly upset, both girls argued that the punishment was unfair. Had they known their playing time was in jeopardy, they noted, they would have withheld from tweeting in the first place. As a result of this contention, Coach Carson decided to call a team meeting before their practice that night to establish ground rules with all his student-athletes and to make sure that the expectations and consequences were clearly understood.

Coach Carson thought the meeting would be relatively straightforward. Address the issue head on, let the girls know they need to use social media responsibly, focus on the positive, and avoid any harsh focus on Katharine Allen or Meg White. But in the meeting, several players began to express their frustrations about their teammates' tweeting and insinuated the meeting was an unnecessary waste of time. Others who saw the tweets felt that, because they were not involved with the dispute, they should not have been subject to new standards or rules because one or two people made poor decisions. The players who did not have Twitter accounts were especially annoyed, feeling they were unfairly roped into something they had chosen to avoid completely.

"Social media isn't hard," said one junior player. "This should all be separate from basketball anyway. We're defined by our actions on the court."

Others chimed in: "We don't all even use Twitter!"

"Let Green Valley say whatever they want. How's it worked out for them?"

"We'll be fine. We're not on social media trying to promote ourselves. We let the game speak, and nothing else."

Coach Carson knew something serious needed to be said. "Ladies. Who among you has visited a school service project with me?" Every hand, besides freshman Katharine Allen's and one sophomore who had been sick during last year's school visit, went into the air. "Ok. How many of you have come with me to the Park Pickup Project?" Coach Carson referred to the combined park cleanup and youth basketball mentoring event at which his team volunteered every September. This time, every hand went in the air.

"Now let me ask you this," Carson continued. "Have I tweeted about it? Have I written newspaper articles? Have I submitted photos to *The Courier*?"

The team stared back at him, with blank expressions.

"No! And not because I have anything against any of those!" said the coach, his tone becoming more serious. "It's because the people who need to know who we are – those we serve and those we play for in this community – they see us already. We go where they go. We're where *they* need support. And they're where *we* need support."

"But the same goes for Twitter, ladies. Your game and your actions speak. You know that. But understand this: *all* of your actions speak. When you tweet, that's a representation of you and me. That's a representation of your teammates sitting on your left, on your right. Everything you do is bigger than you as an individual. That's not a threat: it's a promise, and an opportunity. Let's not blow it."

EXTERNAL IMPACT

The weekend of the contest between Kelley College and Green Valley University also happened to be an Open House weekend for Kelley. Danielle Keller, a high school senior and prospective student-athlete whose parents had friends on Kelley's board of trustees, had been considering attending Kelley after intensive recruiting from Coach Carson. Danielle had been offered attractive opportunities from several schools, including others in the conference, and Kelley was among her top choices. She was hoping that visiting during the Open House weekend, attending some classes during the day on Friday and the big game against Green Valley on Friday night, and then spending the night on campus would help her make an informed decision.

Danielle's parents hoped to make it to the game, too, even though they lived an hour and a half away. While researching ticket information, they came across the team's Twitter handle and did a quick search of the online profile. Unfortunately, this search returned not only tweets published by the team's handle, but also ones in which the team's handle was tagged by others. Scrolling through the recent interactions, they quickly saw the red flags.

More than their disappointment in the quality of behavior displayed online by the student-athletes from both Kelley College and Green Valley University, Danielle's parents were most keenly disturbed by the perceived threat of physical altercations at the game. Concerned for Danielle's safety, they decided not to allow her to spend the night during the visit to minimize unsupervised social activity in case anything arose in response to the online exchange.

Meanwhile, the Kellers expressed their disappointment to their friends on Kelley's board of trustees over dinner on Wednesday evening. They wondered: *Is this common practice among the student-athletes at the school?*

The board members suggested that the exchange was likely overblown and that most of the athletes were extremely responsible and respectful young adults. Nonetheless, they recognized why the Kellers were worried and assured them that the matter would be brought to the attention of key administrators.

ADMINISTRATIVE INTERCESSION

The next day – Thursday, just one day before Friday night's big game – Kelley College President Joe Parker and Dean of Students Don Gorman arrived at work to find an unsavory email from a cherished board member detailing what occurred on Twitter and the outcome it had on some external opinions of Kelley's athletics program. This raised a serious concern. If this impacted one prospective student so significantly, how many others may have been negatively influenced by this?

Immediately, they called a meeting with Kelley College Athletic Director Mike Pierce, to discuss the situation and determine an appropriate course of action. Coach Carson was called in, as well, and shared the action he had taken to discipline the matter. The conversation progressed as to what steps could be taken to prevent these types of interactions from arising again. Coach Carson contended that he felt the students were responsible to mandate their own conduct online, and that this was an isolated incident. AD Mike Pierce had a differing opinion; if it happened once, it would be likely to happen again and, next time, the outcome might be worse. The president agreed.

"Social media isn't going away, folks," President Parker stated. "In fact, the reality is that students will be using these platforms more and more, and in different ways, especially as new programs become available to them. We have a responsibility to our institution to get out ahead of this early in order to maintain our values, demonstrate our integrity, and ultimately protect our reputation."

Dean of Students Don Gorman suggested a ban on social media for students who misuse it in a way that is detrimental to the institution. Immediately, the others chimed in that this was unreasonable, and could have a negative effect on how current and prospective students view the culture of the school. After all, there are countless benefits and opportunities with social media when it is used responsibly, including advantages to athletic and institutional recruiting. Besides, there could even be legal implications to an institution attempting to regulate personal social media. After an exhaustive conversation of options, the group came to two conclusions: 1) they decided to form an official task force and invite a fifth member, a university faculty member who specializes in social media research, to create a well-rounded team; and 2) they would conduct some research about the best approaches for implementing some social media guidelines for their student-athletes.

***

The Task Force on Student Social Media Protocol (SSMP) convened one week later for their first official meeting. Each member presented an executive summary of their research findings. President Parker shared some advice from Professors Blair Browning and Jimmy Sanderson from Baylor and Clemson, respectively. When dealing with negative or critical tweets, these researchers suggested, student-athletes can rely on one of the following strategies: 1) Ignoring the tweet; 2) Using the criticism or negativity as motivation; 3) Blocking users who send inappropriate or unpleasant tweets; or 4) Responding with positive and encouraging sentiments.

Parker went on to share that Browning and Sanderson indicated that educating student-athletes is a key agent, as their research suggests that universities should instill student-athletes with proactive knowledge and awareness as to how to manage and self-monitor their online exchanges. Dean Gorman, however, held firm on his position to sanction students who commit egregious violations online. Citing that Louisville men's basketball coach Rick Pitino has banned his players from using Twitter, Gorman felt that a strict and consequential approach would be the best road to take if they decided to take any action at all.

Coach Carson and Athletic Director Mike Pierce contended that it is better to coach the student-athletes about what is appropriate online, and train them to utilize the platforms constructively. They shared an online resource they found, published by a values-based athletic institute within a university of roughly the same size and with a similar mission and values as Kelley. The publication provided a comprehensive overview about how to teach student-athletes about responsible social networking online.

Dr. Lee Wheng, the faculty member and social media expert, shared that she had previously reviewed this online publication and confirmed the validity of its contents. She asserted that using the information set forth in Browning and Sanderson's study, the institute resource, their own recent experiences, and several other cases involving college athletes and social media that she had gathered for them, the task force would be in a good place to begin drafting their own set of social media guidelines for a student use policy.

At the close of the meeting, the team took a vote. They reached a consensus to move forward with establishing a social media policy to guide the conduct not only of student-athletes, but of all students who represent the reputation and brand of Kelley College. Their next step would be to brainstorm the elements of the policy in preparation for their next meeting.

DISCUSSION QUESTIONS

1. In your opinion, did Golden Wave women's basketball co-captain Jessica Bradshaw take the appropriate course of action in confronting teammate Katharine about the tweets offline (via text)? Why or why not?

2. In your opinion, did Golden Wave's Coach Carson take appropriate action with his team in response to the Twitter war? If you were in his role, what, if anything, would you have done differently and why?

3. How does the role of human perception impact the outcome of Twitter exchanges, such as the one in this case? If you were the Kellers, or other parents researching the school, how would seeing these kinds of exchanges potentially impact your impression of the institution and/or its athletic program?

4. What are some essential elements of an effective social media policy? What recommendations or guidelines do you feel are most important to include?

5. Aside from setting up an appropriate social media policy, what other actions can or should collegiate athletic departments and institutions take to prevent reputation threats on social media?

KEY TERMS

Flaming, Perception, Online reputation management, Social media policy

CASE 17: THE CORPORATE SOCIAL RESPONSIBILITY SAVE

Paul Ziek

Pace University and SUNY–Westchester Community College

Julio A. Rodriguez-Rentas

Pace University and SUNY–Westchester Community College

ABSTRACT

Despite having just won the league championship, stadium attendance for New Jersey Football Club is still at an all-time low. General manager Nolan is already hearing complaints from the team owners. Desperate for attention, Nolan looks to his counterparts in the other soccer franchises and thinks he has found a solution to his problem.

***

Nolan, the general manager of the New Jersey American Soccer League (ASL) franchise, was glad to be attending the ASL's executive meeting in Orlando, Florida just weeks after a thrilling season-ending finale in which New Jersey Football Club beat the Grand Rapids Real in a shootout, 5 goals to 4.

As Nolan walked into the Hotel South's lobby he heard, "Congratulations on the win!" from MJ, the general manager of Cedar Falls United.

"Thanks. Being tied for the last 10 minutes of the game was tough. I could barely sit and watch. But it all came together on free kicks," responded Nolan.

"Yeah. Remember when we won in 2009? It was a blow out! We got to celebrate much of the second half. But, hey, now you get all of the benefits that come with being the cup winner."

"We got some things in mind," Nolan stated as he pointed to his bag. "For the past few weeks we've been planning on a banner raising and some promotional days next year."

Just at that moment, Matthew, the assistant general manager of Grand Rapids Real, walked up to Nolan and MJ and shook their hands. "Hey, great to see you two. I am glad to be here. It's cold in Michigan. We had a great run to the finals but you were ready for us, huh, Nolan. Are you ready to defend?"

"I think so. We have to sign a few of our free agents and develop some of the younger players, but we seem to be set-up pretty well for the next few years. You wouldn't notice from our ticket sales though. We are still not hitting our attendance goals and I'm starting to hear it from our owner," chuckled Nolan.

"Tell me about it. It took us three years to figure out what worked best off the field," MJ explained.

"Maybe we can talk a bit more about that," Nolan said to MJ. "Are you two free after the first round of meetings? I want to do some information gathering on why many of the other franchises are setting attendance records while New Jersey FC is struggling to fill the stadium's lower level for games."

"Yeah, no problem, how about 5 PM?" MJ responded.

"I can do that," answered Matthew.

"Great. Let's do 5 PM in the hotel lounge," Nolan said with a smile.

THE AMERICAN SOCCER LEAGUE AND ATTENDANCE

The ASL was created after the United States successfully hosted the 1994 World Cup. The league started with 12 teams, situated in cities such as New York, Chicago, and Los Angeles. In the early years, the ASL had great financial struggles mostly because teams generated low attendance. The main reason for attendance problems was that the teams played in football stadiums that were not equipped to host soccer games. Over the past 20 years, the league has expanded to over 25 cities with soccer-specific stadiums. The product of this has been a boom in popularity and profitability of the ASL. Yet, even though the average yearly attendance exceeds that of the NBA and NHL, there are still some teams fighting to get people to the game.

THE GM DINNER

Nolan noticed MJ and Matthew standing at the bar as soon as he walked in the door of the Hotel South's Lounge. "Hey guys! Thanks so much for taking the time to meet with me," Nolan expressed as he walked up to them.

"No problem, Nolan. I'm always game for dinner and drinks with guys who understand exactly what I'm going through in my job," responded MJ.

"No kidding," agreed Matthew. "Sometimes it can feel a little lonely in our positions because of all the pressure and no one else who really understands all we need to deal with. That's why I always look forward to these meetings."

As soon as they were seated in the lounge for dinner, Nolan looked at MJ and asked, "how are you getting people in the seats? I was not even close to filling the stadium. Even when we had that five-game winning streak going into the playoffs, we still couldn't get anyone to come out to the games."

"We had the same problem and it took a while to figure out a solution. First, we had to get better on the field. But we had to do it with players that people wanted to pay to see. Then, we started to get more involved in the community—and this is when things started to change," MJ explained.

"We followed that same plan," Matthew agreed, "we rolled out an entire corporate social responsibility or CSR plan. We started a green campaign based on recycling, we started donating leftover food to the local food bank, and we got involved with a kids youth soccer program. After doing all that we started to see a change. More people at the games."

"Look," MJ jumped in, "The NBA has NBA Green, and the NFL has the partnership with Susan G. Komen, so we figured why not take a page from them and develop something similar. Two years ago, we implemented what we like to call the CFSR . . . Cedar Falls Social Responsibility."

Nolan looked at Matthew and said, "None of this crossed my mind. I thought about several promotional events, but nothing like this."

"Listen. These things take time to develop and money to implement, and your staff better be equipped to handle it," warned Matthew.

"Matthew's right. When we were researching this plan we noticed that a few minor league baseball teams had been shredded by their local newspapers for taking up some halfhearted Corporate Social Responsibility attempts. I remember one team had started a green campaign, but was caught leaving the stadium lights on for hours after the game," MJ said.

"Yea, but think of the press and the amount of people we could get interested in going to the games if we did it right," Nolan exclaimed.

THE NEW JERSEY FOOTBALL CLUB'S PLAN

The following week Nolan gathered some of his staff to discuss ideas on how to be more socially responsible. In the meeting sat many of the managers from facilities, ticket sales, and communication. They were the people whom Nolan would charge with designing and adopting a CSR plan meant to enhance the visibility of the franchise with both the community and the media. Nolan looked around the room and started the conversation with highlighting some of the research he had done on CSR in sports.

"So I have been looking into this. Here is what I found," said Nolan. "There are a great deal of CSR programs in sports that we can use as a benchmark. Each NBA team gets involved with *NBA Fit!*, the league's health and wellness initiative. The NHL has the Water Restoration Project where all the water in the arena is tracked and whatever is lost during operation is restored to local streams and rivers."

"Nolan. When you called this meeting I was a confused, but now I am getting a clear picture. You want to create a water conservation plan?" asked Danielle, public relations manager.

It doesn't just have to be about water," Nolan answered. "But I want us to come up with a plan where we do something better for the community. For instance, the MLB started the Reviving Baseball in Inner Cities or RBI program a few years back. So teams like the Dodgers launch their own RBI to serve their own cities. As you can see, there are many different types of programs. CSR seems to be a pretty open concept."

"What do you want us to do then? What types of programs?" asked Danielle.

Nolan responded. "I don't care. I want to get the club more recognition and consequently more people in the seats. I am counting on you and your team to put together a plan that delivers on our increased social responsibility. I also wouldn't mind winning a Beyond Sports Award either."

DISCUSSION QUESTIONS

1. Do you think Nolan's plan will succeed?

2. If you were part of Nolan's staff, would you have gone with the plan? Would you speak against the plan?

3. What type of CSR plan can New Jersey FC adopt that is beneficial to both the team and the community?

4. If stadium attendance increased, ethically speaking would you continue with the CSR plan?

KEY TERMS

Corporate social responsibility, Stakeholders, Public relations

CASE 18: THE TRUTH IS IN THE PHOTO?

The Ramifications of a Photo Posted on Instagram

Allison R. Levin
Social Network Advisors for Professional Sports

ABSTRACT

When an NHL player goes out clubbing with childhood friends, he posts pictures on Instagram. The next morning he wakes to the news that his pictures are all over TMZ and other celebrity gossip sites and he is being characterized as a leader of the Blood gang. Over the next 12 hours, the situation goes from bad to worse.

***

It was a typical Saturday night during the offseason when Patrick's teammate Devan called to discuss their workout plans for the following week.

"What are you doing tonight?" Devan asked.

"I am going to Club Mixx, that hot new place in West Hollywood," Patrick explained. "I really want to see all my friends from the old neighborhood and they are going to meet me there."

Devan immediately expressed concern, "Aren't your old friends still living in Watts? I think you said your best friends from high school are now the leaders of the Blood gang? Are you sure it is a good idea?"

"I'm not worried," Patrick quickly replied. "I got out of that lifestyle and all my fans know how much money I give back to support afterschool clubs and to help others avoid the gang life. I've never hidden where I come from and both ESPN and the NHL network have done stories on my background."

***

The next morning Patrick woke up to a call from his agent Scott.

"Have you looked at the Internet yet?" Scott asked.

"No," said Patrick.

"Well TMZ picked up the photos you posted from the club last night and did a little research. They found that your friends are all leaders in the Blood gang, so they are saying you are a leader as well," Scott explained.

"That's ridiculous, I have never been a Blood, and everybody knows that! It is crazy for anybody to claim that, it's slander," said an irate Patrick.

"The problem is," explained Scott, "that the photos show you dressed like your friends and flashing the Blood gang sign. TMZ is making a big deal out of that. They aren't sports fans, they are just reporting to the masses."

"But my ESPN Outside the Lines story explains why I use that sign; it tells all the kids like me who were taught that sign as a kid and told it was our future that there is another path that they can take. Why are they doing this to me? I don't understand what I did wrong," asked Patrick.

After continuing this conversation Patrick and Scott discussed various strategies that Patrick could use to quell TMZ's story. They agreed to discuss the matter later in the day once they saw if the sports media also picked up the story.

***

The Kings owner John woke up to the same story on TMZ. While he has always admired Patrick as a player, Patrick's background has always been a concern to the team. John immediately got on the phone to the team lawyer Steven.

"Steven, I don't like this story. It is implying that I am allowing the leader of the Bloods to be a role model for the kids of Los Angeles and a leader on our team," explained John.

Steven looked at the articles and explained to John that it was just a TMZ story, but John was still concerned. "It is going to spread to all the sports outlets. And what if it is true? Look at other teams, they have been blindsided by players who were arrested on criminal charges during the season. We are in a tough market, we can't risk the distraction of this story being true," explained John.

"As you know John, Patrick's contract can be terminated if you are willing to execute the buyout option," explained Steven.

"I know," said John, "but his buyout is the equivalent of a year's salary and if the rumors are true, I don't want to give him all that money and face the bad press."

"Well, if we could show cause for firing Patrick, you wouldn't have to pay buyout," said Steven.

"How can I do that?" asked John.

"You have to somehow prove his conduct violates his contract," explained Steven.

***

Two hours later Patrick received a phone call from Scott.

"I've got bad news, Patrick. I just got a call from the Kings, they have decided to terminate your contract effective immediately" explained Scott. "They are saying you violated the conduct portion of your contract, so they are refusing to pay the buyout."

"What! Why? I have done nothing wrong. I attended every offseason training session, met every incentive they set for me; I did everything right! How can they fire me and claim my conduct was bad?" screamed Patrick.

"They are terminating you because of your involvement with the Blood gang," said Scott. "They are using your gang involvement to call you a detriment to the team and justify not paying you the buyout."

"But I am not in the gang, you know that, everyone knows that!" Patrick yelled.

Scott responded, "I know that, but they were upset about the media attention from the TMZ story and looked back over your Twitter and Instagram posts over the past year and decided that there was enough evidence to suggest that you are involved with gang activity."

Patrick was shocked, "But if I am not in a gang and have never been associated with gang activity. How can they possibly claim I am in a gang?"

"They've hired a gang expert who found that you tend to wear colors associated with the Bloods, tip your hat in a way similar to how the Bloods would, drive a car popular with Bloods, and use the gang sign in the end zone when you score. Based on this analysis they believe you have gang connections," Scott explained.

"I don't understand, they know me. I've played for them for five years. I've been a model player and citizen. Not one person on the Kings would ever claim I am in a gang, but they are going to fire me because of some guy looking at pictures of me?" said Patrick. "It doesn't make sense. I grew up in Watts. Of course I am going wear certain clothing that looks gang related, it's what I grew up seeing. The people I admired wore their hats tipped a certain way and wore certain colors. I wanted to be them. I chose different route and got here honestly."

"I understand, but the Kings have made up their mind," said Scott.

"How can they fire me for doing nothing but posting a picture when there are members on the team who have been arrested for domestic abuse, DUI, and drug possession? Plus we have at least one White player who was caught on tape making racially offensive comments and he didn't even miss a game. I feel like I am being singled out because I grew up in a neighborhood where nearly everyone was a Blood," said Patrick.

DISCUSSION QUESTIONS

1. Following the initial release of the TMZ story, if you were Patrick's agent or a public relations specialist brought in to advise Patrick, what steps, if any, would you have taken to respond to the story?

2. When the Kings fired Patrick, what steps would you take to help Patrick get rehired by another NHL team?

   a. What image restoration techniques would you use?

   b. Beyond image restoration, what other steps would you take?

3. Based on the information provided and your personal opinion, make a case for or against the Kings being able to fire Patrick. Provide three reasons to support your opinion.

KEY TERMS

Social media, Image restoration, Preemptive firing

CASE 19: MANAGING SOCIAL MEDIA
Responding to Critics on Twitter

Theo Plothe
American University

ABSTRACT

When a struggling star running back calls out the team's play-by-play announcer on Twitter, the team must deal with the workplace and public relations aftermath.

***

"Can you believe this hogwash?" bellowed an irate Stu Montague, otherwise known as the radio play-by-play voice of the St. Louis Buckhorns. A vein in Montague's temple was throbbing a bright blue in the blue and gold of the Buckhorn team colors.

An exasperated Bud Swanson sat at his large, mahogany general manager's desk, silently shaking his head in supportive acknowledgment of his now-irate announcer.

Montague furiously pointed to his tablet computer, on which appeared the Twitter stream for one Florian "Chicago Flo" Flanders. "These damn millennials," growled Montague. "They just can't be respectful and keep their thoughts to themselves. Do you know how embarrassing this is?" Montague glared accusingly at Swanson.

All Swanson could do was nod his head and mutter, "I know, I know." The Buckhorns star running back had just placed him in an untenable position. The reasons Montague was so irate were the social media missives Flanders had fired toward the team's media representative.

Montague collapsed into the fine leather chair in front of Swanson's desk. The anger dissipated a bit into disbelief and a slight sense of betrayal as Montague said, "You know, I was his biggest defender early on in this season. To think Flo would react like this to a little criticism? It's wholly unacceptable."

***

Florian Flanders arrived in St. Louis with the pomp and circumstance any big-name free-agent pick-up would. He certainly wasn't in town for a lack of performance, having just come off one of the most successful years for a running back in Tampa history. Flanders knew it was just business, he wanted to get paid, and the Swashbucklers didn't want to invest in a 27 year old with five seasons of mileage on his legs in a league where tailbacks are chewed up and spit out at age 30. As such, though he had a signed free-agent contract with the Buckhorns, he clearly felt as if he had something to prove.

Fan expectation of the titles "Chicago Flo" would bring to Mound City and the records he would break in the Dome were nearly as high as the Gateway Arch. For a team that made the Wild Card in Tampa, a moribund franchise if there was one, Flanders had run for 1258 yards and 12 touchdowns. With a better team and a better organization, why wouldn't 'Horns fans (and the media who stoked the fire) expect the sublime?

***

"Look, Stu," Swanson said as he looked at the still simmering play-by-play announcer, "What do you want me to do? You want me to cut a guy just for talking garbage on Twitter?"

Montague bristled. "I'm not saying that," he replied as he stabbed his stubby index finger on Swanson's desk, "But you've got to do something."

Swanson sighed and sat back in his seat. He certainly knew how the 'Horns got here, which made the situation all the more difficult.

Flanders' season got off to a very slow start, fumbling twice in the first game in his new digs, and a rumble soon followed every time he touched the ball in the Prometheus Funds Dome. His 2.7 yards per carry were the worst of any league running back with at least 70 carries. The 'Horns as a whole, and not just Flanders, struggled mightily in the first half of the season, losing their first five games before winning 14–6 over the New Jersey Griffins. In the New Jersey game, Flanders had his best start of the season by gaining 82 yards on 23 attempts, but was pulled late in the game on the winning goal line touchdown.

Shortly after, Flanders hit Twitter in a rage, reacting to fan criticism:

Don't ever question my heart or effort. You should want over achievers! That means they have a pulse and give a damn each game!

—Florian Flanders (@chicagoflow22) October 26, 2014

@djswales33 You talk big for someone who can't count my stax. Keep askin me if I want fries with that #knowyourrole

—Florian Flanders (@chicagoflow22) October 26, 2014

"@hornsfancutie: Glad we're pay you all that money to sit on the bench!!!" You aint payin me shit! I get paid 2 produce. U get paid 2 #STFU.

—Florian Flanders (@chicagoflow22) October 26, 2014

Eventually, Flanders turned his attention toward Montague. Montague had been critical of Flanders' play during the latest broadcast and during his weekly radio show Tuesday nights on WLIS 940.

"@suedegator: @chicagoflow22 Stu tore ur ass up this week! Lol U suck!!!" Like should care what he says? #smfh #bruhplease

—Florian Flanders (@chicagoflow22) October 26, 2014

Don't hate cuz Stu don't know. My pops balled for Fox at MinnieSt and played in the League. Stu? Nuthn. Stu sniffin jock at KSU #bruhplease

—Florian Flanders (@chicagoflow22) October 26, 2014

Stu "applauds that move" when I don't score?! Only scorin Stu knows is getting an extra blazin wing at BDubs when his fatass orders 2 dozen

—Florian Flanders (@chicagoflow22) October 26, 2014

Only redzone that lardass been in is the high blood pressure one. dude smells like bacon on the radio.

—Florian Flanders (@chicagoflow22) October 26, 2014

Ten minutes before Montague walked in his office at 9:30 this morning, popular sports blog *Kissing Shelly Kohler* already had 275,000 views on their Flanders' Twitter story. The Buckhorns media and public relations office had been deluged with requests for comment.

Massaging his temples with his left hand in defeated acknowledgement of the growing PR nightmare, Swanson had much to weigh on his mind in whatever decision he would make: a star player in the midst of a poor season, a hyper-attentive fanbase on social media, and a team ready for a title.

Swanson dialed his intercom, "Hey Julie, I need Flo in my office yesterday. We have to have a conversation about this."

DISCUSSION QUESTIONS

1. How should Swanson manage this situation in terms of the personnel issues? How might he address both Flanders and Montague? Should Swanson penalize Flanders in some way?

2. How should Swanson address this conflict with the media and the Buckhorns fanbase? What can Swanson do to mitigate the negative media coverage?

3. What, if any, changes should the team make to their social media policy in light of this situation? What should be in the team's social media policy?

4. How should Montague, as the "voice of the Buckhorns" respond? What should he say publicly about the incident, or should he respond at all?

KEY TERMS

Social media and sport, Organizational leadership

CASE 20: A SOCIAL MESS

Stacy Smulowitz
University of Scranton

ABSTRACT

When a university coach is encouraged to use social media, his inappropriate sense of humor and unfamiliarity with Facebook gets him into trouble. Fans and relatives of the players push back through social media creating a public relations nightmare for the university.

***

"Did you hear what Coach Ross said about the chicken at lunch today?" asked Lindsay.

"No. What did he say?" asked Jessica.

"Didn't you hear? When we were ordering Coach was in line behind me. I asked whether the chicken was white or dark meat and when the server replied that the chicken was breast meat Coach said 'great because I'm a breast man,'" replied Lindsay.

"And, did that bother you?" asked Jessica.

"Yes, it did. He always makes sexist remarks like that in front of me and the other girls on the team and it makes me feel uncomfortable. Doesn't it bother you?" asked Lindsay.

"I think you're making too much out of it, Lindsay," said Jessica. "I think he's just trying to be funny."

"Well, I don't think he's funny at all," stated Lindsay.

Pam Fender came around the corner into the locker room and, when she overheard the conversation between the two players, she stopped to listen in an area where the players couldn't see her. From time-to-time Pam herself had felt a bit uncomfortable due to the head coach's comments. She had never realized that some of the other players felt the same way. In fact, Pam was in the lunch line earlier that day when the coach had made the remark about the chicken and all the girls on the team seemed to think the comment was funny. Many of them laughed quite loudly and even the server seemed to get a chuckle out of the comment.

Pam walked over to Jessica and Lindsay in the locker room and asked, "Who was funny?"

The girls looked at each other and finally Jessica said, "Oh, we were just commenting that Coach Ross can be very funny."

Pam looked directly at Lindsay and asked, "What do you think, Lindsay? Do you think Coach Ross is funny?"

Lindsay looked at Jessica and then at the floor and said, "Sure do" as she left the locker room in a hurry.

Pam asked Jessica, "Is Lindsay okay?"

Jessica replied, "Yes, absolutely!" and hurried out of the locker room as well.

THE BEGINNING OF THE MESS

Pam had joined the University of the South women's basketball team as assistant coach just two months ago after an exhausting interview process where she met with the head coach, Ross Penderfield, several of the players on the team, and some of the university administrative staff. During her third and final interview, Coach Ross asked Pam to draw a play on his whiteboard. Pam told Coach Ross that she would be happy to do so, but had used several apps on her tablet to create plays. She brought out her tablet and showed Coach Ross some of her existing playbook. He was quite impressed.

Since this was her third round of interviews, Coach Ross asked Anne Flack, the administrative staff member in charge of updating the team's web site, to join him and Pam for lunch. Anne was very good at updating the team's web site, but she had complained to her director just a few months ago that she didn't want to work closely with Coach Ross anymore because some of his comments made her feel uncomfortable.

Coach Ross is a big, burly man in his sixties who is used to people listening to him when he has something to say. He typically dresses in gym shorts and shirt with a whistle around his neck and carries around a clipboard and pen. During lunch Coach Ross dominated most of the conversation. He talked about his wife and children quite a bit and as a result Pam and Anne also discussed their families. Pam and Anne were only in their mid-twenties and were not yet married, but both are in relationships.

"Pam, how do you think things will go with your boyfriend, John, when you are separated by three states?" asked Anne

"Well, that's something we have discussed at length. And, you know, Anne, when I was playing for the WNBA I travelled extensively and we didn't see each other much throughout the season anyway. So we think things will work out just fine," commented Pam.

"So, Pam," said Coach Ross. "Before you and your boyfriend get, let's say, romantic with each other do you pull out your playbook app and tell him where the candles belong and what type of music to play?"

Pam was shocked. This was only the third time she had met Coach Ross and the first time she had met Anne. She felt the comment was completely inappropriate, but she was in the middle of an interview for a job she really wanted. Pam looked at Anne for a cue and saw Anne smiling awkwardly and forcing a giggle. Pam looked at Coach Ross and said, "Oh, too funny, Coach. Too funny."

Three days later Coach Ross called Pam to offer her the job and she was excited to begin a new part of her life. Prior to joining University of the South, Pam played basketball for her college basketball team and then went on to play four years in the WNBA. She was an excellent player and was extremely qualified to coach. As such the women on the team admired her and were excited to be able to train with her. Coach Ross was also excited to have another coach on the team who was younger and female. In addition, he was happy to have someone else who could work along with Anne to help keep the team web page updated.

The team was practicing between the fall and spring semester and staying together in dorms on campus to prepare for their upcoming games. As such their schedule was quite rigorous. Each day the women woke up at six o'clock in the morning and met each other for breakfast. Then they met outside the gym at 7:30 AM for a run and then headed to practice until their break at 10:30 AM, lunch at 1:00 PM. Practice ended each day at 4:00 PM and the women were on their own for the rest of the day.

Being new to the team, the university, and the community, Pam was offered living space in one of the dorms until she had a chance to find her own apartment. At first Pam was hesitant about living in a dorm again, but quickly found out that it was a great way to bond with the women on the team. Frequently, the women who lived in dorm rooms asked Pam to join them for dinner or to see a movie. As such, Pam felt she was developing a nice relationship with the women.

The next day Pam met with Anne to discuss some new ideas about the team web page. Pam was excited about the ideas that Anne had, making the web page more interactive between fans and team members. One area of the new web page design she was especially excited about was a place where fans and team members could post updates through various social media sites such as Twitter, Facebook, Instagram, and Snapchat.

That night as the team and Pam were having dinner together, Pam told them about the new web page additions. The women were as excited as Pam was about the thought of being able to interact with their fans. They decided that they should add each other and Coach Pam and Coach Ross to their list of "friends" on each social media account.

The next day Pam discussed the social media addition to the web site with Coach Ross. "The players are really excited about this new addition to the web site, Coach," said Pam. "Last night they were 'friending' each other and when they tried to find you they couldn't."

"That's not something I've really ever been interested in," said Coach Ross. "I don't have any of that . . . and I wouldn't even know how to get it started or what to do with it if I had it."

"Well, it would mean so much to the team if you started even just a Facebook page," said Pam. "I can help you get it started if you'd like."

"Okay. Why don't we meet for lunch in my office and you can show me what to do," said Coach Ross.

"Great," replied Pam. "The team will be thrilled!"

There wasn't much room in Coach Ross's office by his computer so Pam squeezed in another chair and quickly started the Facebook page.

"Do you have a photo you'd like me to add?" asked Pam.

"I need a photo?" asked Coach Ross.

Pam took his photo sitting at his desk with his clipboard and uploaded it to his Facebook page. Then Pam showed Coach Ross how to add "friends" and information to the rest of the page.

As Pam was working on his Facebook page she accidentally brushed her arm up against Coach Ross's arm. "Pam, I never realized how soft your skin feels," said Coach.

Suddenly, Pam felt uncomfortable. "Sorry. I didn't mean to bump into you, Coach," said Pam. "That was an accident. So, you're all set up and if you have any questions about the Facebook page you can just ask. Time to get to the gym for training." Pam got up, put the chair back where had she found it, and abruptly left his office thinking to herself, *Why does he always have to say something that makes me feel uncomfortable?*

The following week, the team travelled to their game. The team members and Pam were excited to have a chance to use the newly launched interactive portion of the web site and began posting updates. Some of the players posted photos of the bus, other team members, game pictures, and photos of some of the places they stopped along the way. The fans responded to their posts with encouraging comments throughout their travel and the game. It was fun for the team and the fans.

The next week the team travelled to another away game. The social media interaction between Pam, the team members, and the fans continued. As the team arrived at the hotel the day before the game, Jessica asked Pam, "Why isn't Coach Ross posting anything?"

Pam replied, "I'll find out" and went to talk with Coach Ross.

"I'm really not sure how to post or what to say," said Coach Ross.

Pam showed Coach Ross how to post and told him, "Post anything you'd like." She showed him some posts and comments made by the team showing places they went and thoughts they had. "Just have fun with it," said Pam.

On the road with lots of time before dinner, the team decided to go for a walk to explore the new city. As they walked through the city they passed a construction site and some of the construction workers whistled at them and made catcalls. The players rolled their eyes and thought it was obnoxious behavior. The next morning Lindsay found a cartoon of a similar scene and posted it on Facebook asking why men don't know that this sort of behavior is inappropriate.

Coach Ross posted in reply, "I often whistle and catcall when my wife bends over to pick something up from the floor. And sometimes I even put things on the floor to see her bend over. I do this almost exclusively with my wife and also with some good friends, both men and women. I think it's hilarious!"

Pam was sitting at the hotel café having a coffee and talking with some of the players when her cell phone rang. Seeing that it was Anne she excused herself and picked it up.

"Hi Anne! How are you?" asked Pam. "The team is having a great time interacting with fans about their travel and games. This was such a great idea, don't you think so?"

"Well," said Anne in a solemn voice, "I'm beginning to wonder whether or not it is a good idea. Have you seen the post by Coach Ross this morning?"

Initially Pam was excited to hear that Coach Ross had posted because she knew the team members wanted him to post. However, the excitement quickly turned to that same feeling of discomfort that she had experienced several times before when interacting with Coach Ross.

"Uh, no. I haven't looked," said Pam. "Hold on while I quickly look." As Pam read the posts by Lindsay and Coach Ross she felt even more uncomfortable remembering the comment Coach Ross had made about the chicken weeks ago and the conversation she had overheard between Lindsay and Jessica.

"Anne," said Pam, "I see what you're talking about."

"Don't you think that's an inappropriate comment that Coach made?" asked Anne.

"Maybe Coach Ross was just trying to be funny," said Pam.

"Listen, Pam. Since you started working here I feel like we've developed a good relationship, don't you?" asked Anne.

"I sure do. You're great to work with," said Pam.

"Well, do you remember during your interview lunch when Coach Ross asked you if you use a playbook with your boyfriend?" asked Anne.

"Yeah, I sure do," said Pam.

"How did that make you feel?" asked Anne.

"Well, to be honest the question really caught me off guard," said Pam. "I felt really uncomfortable, but I didn't want to blow my chance at the job."

"I've had some similar interactions with Coach Ross," said Anne, "When you are back in town let's meet to talk about how to handle this."

Meanwhile in their hotel room, Jessica came out of the bathroom and saw Lindsay in tears. "Lindsay, what's the matter?" asked Jessica.

"It's this," cried Lindsay showing her phone to Jessica, with the post from Coach Ross open on it.

"Okay, now that's just weird," says Jessica. "But why does this make you so upset?"

"Do you remember the other day at training when Coach Ross threw his pencil across the court? He asked ME to go and pick it up!" wailed Lindsay.

"Sure," said Jessica, "But he certainly didn't whistle or catcall at you. I think you're really being overly sensitive to all this."

"Wow, what a great friend you are," Lindsay said curtly, as she stormed out of the room.

IN A JAM

Pam went back to her room to think more about the events that had unfolded. She wondered if this would have happened if she hadn't pressured Coach Ross to post something. Was she really the one to blame for this? Just then Pam's phone rang.

"Hi Mom," said Pam, "How are you?"

"Honey, I'm doing well but I have to say I am a bit concerned for you," said Mrs. Fender.

"Why" asked Pam?

"Pam, I've been following the posts for your team online and saw what Coach Ross posted in response to your one player. Is he like that all the time?" asked Mrs. Fender.

Pam filled her Mom in on the kinds of things that Coach Ross had said to her in the past and then shared her fear that it was her fault that the post had been made.

SHEDDING LIGHT ON THE MESS

Worried that she had upset Lindsay, Jessica went looking for her. She knocked on a teammate's hotel room door, "Hello?"

She heard a voice inside say, "Oh, it's Jessica," and the door opened revealing nearly half the team – and Lindsay.

"Lindsay, I've been looking for you everywhere," said Jessica. "I'm sorry that I upset you earlier."

"It's all right," said Lindsay, "I was just so upset to begin with. I shouldn't have stormed out on you like that."

"So what's everyone doing?" asked Jessica.

Beth, the player who opened the door, said, "We are discussing Coach Ross's post about catcalls and whistling."

"Okay, so Coach Ross needs a filter," exclaimed Jessica, "I really don't think he meant any harm."

"Well," said Beth, "Many of us have felt uncomfortable by some of the things Coach Ross says from time-to-time. This is just one more example of his inappropriate behavior."

The team members went back and forth expressing their thoughts about the coach's post and previous comments. They were fairly well split between players who felt uncomfortable about the post and comments and those who thought the coach was just trying to be cool.

***

Back on campus Pam and Anne met for lunch to discuss Coach Ross. Anne told Pam all about her previous experiences with the coach and that she had asked not to have to directly work with the coach anymore because he makes her feel uncomfortable.

"And that's one of the reasons for your position here, Pam," said Anne.

"Wow. I had no idea and I actually thought it was just me who felt uncomfortable with some of his comments," said Pam. "Of course there was the time in the locker room when I overheard two players talking about Coach's sense of humor."

"What does the team think about Coach Ross's comments?" asked Anne.

"Well, why don't I find out?" asked Pam.

***

That night when the team and Pam were having dinner, without Coach Ross present, Pam asked the players what they thought about Coach Ross's comments about the catcalls. The conversation became lively as players discussed their differing points of view about the comments. One player in particular had been silent throughout the discussion, Lindsay. Pam asked her directly, "Lindsay, how do you feel about Coach Ross's comments?"

Lindsay gave a careful glance at Jessica and then started to cry as she told Pam about how Coach Ross's comments made her feel. She also shared the story about training when Coach Ross threw his pencil and then asked Lindsay to pick it up. "Do you think that's the reason that Coach Ross's post was directed at me?" asked Lindsay.

Again the conversation picked up. Some team members felt that Lindsay was reading way too much into the whole thing while others felt that she might have a point. Many of the team members on Lindsay's side agreed to pay careful attention to how Coach Ross treated Lindsay and the other members, as well as what he said.

HEADED FOR TROUBLE

The next week the team won a game that put them in the lead in their division. Lindsay made the final score that won the game. Everyone was elated. That night Coach Ross thought he should send the team a message through Facebook telling them how proud he was one more time. The message read, "You bitches played like men tonight. Especially you, Lindsay. See you at practice tomorrow. Coach Ross." Little did Coach Ross know that, instead of sending a message to the team, he had posted the comment as his new status.

Pam was getting ready to go to bed when she saw Coach Ross's status update and was floored. Pam's phone rang. Two calls were coming in, one from Anne and the other from her mom.

As Pam fielded the calls, she saw that the team Facebook page was filling with posts from angry fans and relatives responding to the message from Coach Ross. Players were posting comments as well.

THE LAST STRAW

The next day when Pam arrived at practice the team was there early, and having an intense conversation. Pam walked over to the players.

"What's going on?" asked Pam.

"Lindsay quit the team," said Beth. "She just can't take Coach Ross' comments anymore – last night was the last straw."

"Does Coach know?" asked Pam.

Before anyone could answer, Steven Long, the athletic director, walked into the gym. "Pam, I need to talk with you for a minute. Please come with me to my office. Team, great game the other night. Pam will be right back. Why don't you warm up?" asked Steven.

When they arrived in Steven's office he asked Pam to close the door. "I assume you've seen the posts from Coach Ross?" asked Steven.

"I have," said Pam.

"I had a call from Lindsay's parents last night. They were hysterical. I tried to reason with them, but they told me that Lindsay was quitting the team unless I fired Coach Ross for inappropriate behavior," said Steven. "I talked with Coach Ross last night and he told me he was just trying to look cool and have fun with posting. He also thought his message would only reach the team. He had no idea everyone would be able to see it. We agreed that at least for today he is going to lay low and let you run the practice. Can you do that?"

"Of course," said Pam.

"Great," said Steven. "Now, it's your job to get the team focused on their next game, and not on this mess. Until you hear from me, you're in charge. One more thing, if you're approached by a reporter please say 'no comment' and refer them to me. Now, I have four reporters waiting to hear back from me. I also have a meeting with the university president and public relations director in six minutes."

Pam got up to leave Steven's office and looked back and said, "Okay. Thanks." As Pam left the athletic director's office she wondered to herself, *What do I tell the team? What's going to happen to Coach Ross? Is this partly my fault? What could I have done to prevent this? Should Anne and I have gone to Steven weeks ago with our concerns?*

Shaking her head, Pam, took a longer route back to the gym, walking slowly.

DISCUSSION QUESTIONS

1. You are the public relations director at this university. What do you do?
   a) How do you respond to the media, parents, and team?
   b) What communication tools (social media, newspapers, television, etc.) are effective during a crisis, and how would you use them in this instance?
   c) What else should you do?
2. If you were Pam, what would you do?
3. If you were the athletic director, would you fire Coach Ross? Why or why not? What are the consequences of your decision?

KEY TERMS

Social media, Crisis communication, Collegiate sports

CASE 21: THE CLOSED FILE
Practicing Ethical Communication to Ensure Transparency

Shaniece B. Bickham

Walden University

ABSTRACT

Brett Staller, a rising star rookie athlete, has been asked to serve as the official spokesperson for the Boys Matter nonprofit organization. Boys Matter focuses on keeping teen boys away from a life of crime while providing them with opportunities to engage in life-changing experiences. Brett seems like the perfect role model, but he had a previous brush with the law as a juvenile that has never been publicly revealed.

***

The announcement came as no surprise. Brett Staller is the number one draft pick for the upcoming year's professional basketball season. Brett is, and has been, America's favorite college basketball player for the past four years. In fact, all of the major sports analysts had predicted that Brett would be the first to go on Draft Night. Yes, it is written in the stars, Brett Staller is "the next big thing" in the league.

"Well, well, well," said one journalist with a microphone shoved close to Brett's face. "Your life story reads like a fairytale. You grew up in the inner city where the odds of getting out were stacked against you. And even though you are a great player, your team and school were sub-par when compared to other top-ranked high schools in the area. What makes you different?"

"I'm not different," said Brett. "I am a hard worker and I've been mastering my craft for a very long time. Now, I have a bigger platform to show off my skills to the world."

"I'm just amazed that you were able to stay out of trouble to even make it this far," the reporter continued on. "I can name ten people from similar neighborhoods who were destined to stardom, but never made it because they couldn't beat the odds."

"Well, those people aren't me," Brett responded. "And obviously since I am standing here talking to you, I am not like them."

Brett quickly ends the interview and walks away abruptly, hoping to avoid any other questions that do not focus on his success. As he makes his way through the crowd, he can't help but wonder why the reporter seemed to second-guess him and his accomplishments. Brett worked hard to reach this point in his life and has plans to go even higher in his career.

THE BIG SECRET

Brett's rise to basketball success is not by chance. He has been a "baller" since the age of seven when he first joined his neighborhood playground's team. As a member of the Comiskey Comets, Brett's skills on the basketball court at point guard only improved over the years. He moved from the Comets to the Lafayette Mustangs basketball team at his junior high school, and later played for the Hightower High School Panthers.

Just as he had done on the playground and in junior high school, Brett excelled at basketball with the Panthers. His playing skills garnered attention nationally thanks to videos he uploaded weekly to social media websites. Even before Brett's senior high school graduation, people knew his name. Brett was also able to be very selective about his next basketball destination, having received 50 different college offers. Now, four years later, all of Brett's hard work has finally paid off. From the moment he accepted his new professional team jersey, Brett knew his life would never be the same. Even with his confident attitude, however, a bad decision in Brett's past continues to haunt him.

At 15 years old, just before the height of his high school basketball career, Brett started hanging out with the wrong crowd. The boys in this crowd influenced Brett to experiment with drugs and they even convinced him to commit an armed robbery to prove his loyalty to them. Because Brett was no skilled criminal, he was caught, arrested, and later charged with the crime.

Luckily for Brett, the victim of the crime was an alumna of Hightower High School who didn't want to see Brett's future ruined. The victim informed the district attorney's office that she did not want to go through with a trial, and would support a reasonable plea deal for Brett. As a result, Brett was sentenced only to community service and to pay restitution. His criminal record would also be sealed because he was still a minor.

Brett knew this was the case, but he still remained on edge because, these days, no information seemed off limits if reporters wanted it bad enough. He just hoped his bad decision as a teen wouldn't affect his new career as an adult.

BRETT STALLER, THE ROLE MODEL

Brett's schedule is filled to capacity with photo opportunities, meetings and more press conferences. During a full day of smiling, meeting, and greeting, Brett received a phone call from his agent.

"You aren't going to believe this, Brett," said Tom Laswerger. "Boys Matter wants you to serve as their official spokesperson. It would be a three-year deal that will not only put money in your pocket, but will also give you an opportunity to serve as a role model to young boys in an official capacity."

"I would love to," said Brett. "What are the conditions? I don't want to be just a talking head for the organization, though. I really want to touch the lives of the youth."

"I have all of the paperwork and the language is pretty standard," said Tom. "It just basically says that you are an upstanding citizen with no criminal record or history. I will email the package over so that you can review and sign."

Brett realizes that Tom isn't worried about the specifics of the agreement because he automatically assumed Brett didn't have a record.

"Tom, I don't know how to say this, but I did get in trouble with the law when I was 15. The record is sealed because I was a juvenile, but I am sure Boys Matter would want to know about this," said Brett.

"What? A record?" asked Tom. "Well, you said you were a minor, so it really shouldn't matter. We can go ahead and move forward with signing the paperwork."

Tom is certain that becoming the spokesperson without informing Boys Matter about the juvenile record is the best approach. He doesn't want to put Brett's reputation at risk if he didn't have to. Brett, on the other hand, is not so sure. Brett doesn't feel as though it would be ethical to sign an agreement saying that he had no criminal record and then serve in an official capacity based on that premise. He did, however, believe that his story could be used to show youth that they could overcome obstacles through his role as the spokesperson. By doing this, he wouldn't feel as though he was compromising his ethics or integrity. Brett's hesitancy led to Tom recommending that his sports agency's public relations director, Amy Brighton, examine the situation and advise Brett of next steps.

TRANSPARENT COMMUNICATION

During the meeting with Tom and Amy, Brett explained the details of his arrest and the conditions of the plea agreement. Amy is actually surprised that the story about Brett hasn't leaked yet, especially in the age of gossip blogs and entertainment news websites. Though it hadn't, Amy knows that the chances of the story leaking will increase as Brett becomes more famous and visible in the public.

Amy is a huge proponent of transparent communication through proactive public relations strategies. Amy is also well-versed in PR ethics and knows there is no way that Brett could ethically agree to serving as the official spokesperson without disclosing his criminal record. Releasing information about the record might negatively affect Brett's reputation, however. If the record is disclosed, she would have to 1) determine how this message should be communicated, 2) identify who needed to receive it, and 3) select communication channels that would be most appropriate for delivering the message and reaching the target audiences. These steps are critical to making sure that Brett's reputation isn't ruined before he fully has a chance to establish it.

So far, Amy is only equipped with the information Brett has given her about the case, but she needs to make sure no conflicting information exists in archived articles or other documents. Amy then realizes that Brett's possible announcement about his criminal history will not only be of interest to Boys Matter, but will also have an impact on the basketball league and his fans. Amy also has to consider the implications an announcement of this magnitude might have on Brett's future in the basketball league and the many endorsements that he is currently negotiating.

DISCUSSION QUESTIONS

1. As the public relations director, how would you advise Brett to proceed?

2. If you decide to disclose the criminal record, what key messages would you communicate? Who would be your target stakeholders?

3. Which communication channels would be most appropriate for disseminating the messages to the target stakeholders?

4. If the criminal record is not disclosed, what would be the PR ethical implications of accepting the role of official spokesperson for Boys Matter?

5. What steps would you take to manage Brett's reputation effectively if the record is disclosed? Would reputation management still be needed if the information isn't revealed?

KEY TERMS

Reputation management, Public relations ethics, Transparent communication

CASE 22: HOW DID THIS END UP ON MY DOORSTEP?

A Head Coach is Accused of Physical Assault

Karen L. Hartman
Idaho State University

ABSTRACT

A university's sports information director (SID) must react to a public relations crisis when a video is sent to the local newspaper showing the men's basketball team's head coach physically assaulting a player.

***

Mark could see his coach's lip curl up over his teeth and his eyes bulge as he ran across the court toward him. Mark flinched as he felt Coach Simpson's warm breath on his face.

"If I have to tell you one more time to get closer to the baseline I will not let you forget it!" Coach Simpson yelled at the top of his lungs. His hands were clenched in fists and they both came up in front of Mark's face, seeming to threaten him. Mark knew he better run the play correctly on the next try or he would *really* see his coach flip out.

"Yes sir," Mark replied, taking a step backward to create some space between him and his coach. He dribbled the ball back toward the half court line to restart the play. His teammates got back into their positions, silent as they ran around the court.

This was not the first time Mark had been yelled at – in fact it was a common occurrence to feel the wrath of his coach. Mark and his teammates often discussed at dinner in the university's dining hall after practice how their coach would go off of the deep end. He'd yell, cuss, and even grab them if they did something wrong in practice. Missing a shot, running a play incorrectly, or turning the ball over would often end in a verbal or physical tirade.

"Hustle up, Mark! Get the play going!" Coach Simpson yelled.

Mark passed the ball to his teammate on the wing and started to run the play. After he passed the ball, Mark turned and ran toward the sideline – momentarily forgetting that he was supposed to go to the baseline.

Mark heard a loud, shrill whistle.

"Mark, you idiot! I can't believe you ran the play wrong again!" Coach Simpson shrieked as he charged toward Mark.

Mark was silent as he saw his coach's hands fly out toward his chest. Mark felt a heavy push against his upper body as his coach made contact with him. Mark hit the ground with a heavy thud. He was absolutely furious and wanted to scream at his coach. His actions were absolutely unacceptable.

Mark slowly got up. Not one player made a sound, but instead everyone looked down and tried not to make eye contact with anyone.

"Dalton! Get in and take Mark's position," the coach yelled at another player on the sideline.

Dalton sprinted onto the court, picked up the ball, and yelled out a play as Mark slunk over to the sideline. He couldn't wait for practice to be over so he could leave.

Once the final whistle blew and the coaches dismissed them from practice, Mark hit the showers and changed. He was still fuming over the altercation with his coach and just wanted to get back to his dorm where he could decompress. He was walking briskly as he left the locker room and headed up to the stairs leading out of the gym. Taking the stairs two at a time, he heard someone call his name in a loud whisper.

"Mark! Mark!" the person whispered with urgency. Whoever wanted to talk to him was almost hissing. "Wait up!"

Mark turned around at the top of the stairs, his eyebrows raised in annoyance. Wasn't it obvious he was trying to leave in a hurry? Rushing up the stairs behind him was Chris, the team's graduate assistant. Chris had been working with the team for two years and he and Mark had gotten to know each other fairly well. All of the time spent at practice, road trips, watching tape, meals, and games meant that Mark spent more time with his teammates and coaches than he did his family or girlfriend.

Chris was in charge of helping with travel, assisting in practices, and heading the videotape sessions. In most practices, Chris worked with other assistants to film each practice so it could be broken down and watched later.

"What's up, Chris? I'm kind of in a hurry," Mark responded, clearly agitated he was being stopped.

"Yeah, I know, but listen. What happened today in practice, that's not right, man. Coach shouldn't be yelling like he does and he definitely shouldn't be pushing you – or anyone else."

"Well thanks for your concern, Chris, but that's just how it is," Mark said as he turned and started walking through the lobby of the arena and toward the row of double doors leading to the parking lot. "What am I going to do, say something and get him even madder at me? I'm not going to ruin my chance to play by saying anything. Heck, he could even take my scholarship away if I complain too much."

Chris kept up with him step for step as Mark had picked up his speed the closer he got to the exit. Even though he was a full foot shorter than Mark, Chris was right beside him. It didn't seem like Mark was going to brush him off easily.

"I know, but it still isn't right," Chris said. He took a quick look around and leaned in toward Mark, his voice lowering, "What if I told you I have the whole altercation on film?"

"So? What are we going to do, watch it during the tape session? Discuss Coach's technique as he pushed me?" Mark said sarcastically as they left the building and started walking toward the parking lot.

"No, man, aren't you tired of how he acts? What Coach does is not right. I've been here for two years and I've seen how he treats the players. I have the whole thing on video. Heck, I've got lots of videos where he is out of control. But don't you think he is way over the line? Let's finally stand up to him."

"What are you talking about?" Mark asked, his annoyance with Chris lessening. He was now a bit more intrigued. He *was* sick of how his coach treated him and the other players, but couldn't quite figure out what Chris was suggesting.

"Look, we have the whole altercation filmed. No one would have to admit to where it came from, but maybe the tape could anonymously end up at the local news? That way what Coach is doing could be exposed and he would have to account for his actions. You won't have to do anything."

Mark took his car keys out of his black gym bag and paused as he thought about showing everyone what went on in practice. He didn't want to cause trouble, but he was sick of dealing with the physical and verbal abuse. And maybe this could be an opportunity for others to see what really went on within the team? Mark knew Chris didn't need his approval to send the tape out, but he was glad Chris approached him. This way Mark would have some idea if it did, in fact, end up in the news. Mark turned to Chris who was eagerly waiting for his reply.

"Sure, do it," Mark said. "I won't tell anyone we had this conversation and we'll just see what happens. Hopefully it'll stop Coach from doing this anymore."

Chris nodded in agreement and turned around and headed through the parking lot back to the arena. Mark hopped into his car and drove off in deep thought about the practice and the video.

***

Maria sat at her desk, hunched over with the phone pressed hard to her right ear. She had heard the question the man asked but couldn't quite process what he was asking. She closed her eyes so she could concentrate.

"Hello, ma'am, did you hear me?"

"Yes, yes, I did, but can you please repeat that?"

The man sighed on the other end of the line.

"I'm finishing up a story on Coach Simpson, the men's head basketball coach. We have a video of him pushing a player in practice and we're gonna run a story about his alleged physical and verbal abuse of players. Would you like to respond at all?"

Maria took a deep breath but silently let it out so the reporter wouldn't hear her. She tried to collect her thoughts as her mind was going in a thousand different directions. *Coach Simpson pushed a player? When did this happen? Is there more to the story? How long has this been going on? Whatever happened, this is not good for the university.*

"Sure, I'll make a statement on behalf of the athletic department," Maria responded. She thought for another moment and then said, "Western University and its athletic department is committed to transparency and the highest of ideals. While we are not prepared to reveal details at the present time, we will be prepared to comment as the facts come in."

The reporter thanked Maria and she quickly got off the phone; she knew there was a lot of work for her to do. Maria bit her lip and sat back in her chair as she thought about the story that was going to run and how she had to get as many facts as she could. The media would really be calling once the story ran.

Maria tried to think through the situation before she sprang into action. *This is what I was hired for, I guess,* Maria thought to herself. She had only held the position for six months and was wary about dealing with this type of crisis. There had been several high-profile stories in the news about coaches verbally and physically assaulting players and she was in disbelief that something similar landed on her doorstep.

Well, there's not much time to sit here. I need to get moving.

Maria picked up the phone to call the athletic director's office. She knew she had to give him the heads up that the story was going to run. She needed to be in full response mode.

As she brought the phone up to her ear, she paused as the outer office door swung open and a large man with a scowl on his face burst through the door. The athletic director walked straight to her office space and didn't bother knocking before he entered.

"Maria, have you heard?" he asked, his face a mixture of anger and disgust.

"Yes, I just got off the phone with a reporter from the *Town Gazette*. I guess they're running the story tomorrow. I gave him a quote and was just going to call you."

Maria told him what she had said to the reporter and asked if he'd seen the video yet.

"No, I haven't seen it yet, but we need to get our hands on it. Call whoever you can to get a copy."

"Yes, and we'll need to set up separate meetings with Coach Simpson and the players to get everyone's side. Once we get more information we'll know what we're working with, but we have to act fast. We'll also have to let President McPhee and a few others know about this. As soon as the story hits, the media will be everywhere."

Maria knew things were picking up speed and they were starting to put together a game plan to react to the assault allegation. She just hoped they could do enough to maintain control over the story.

"Let's head over to Coach Simpson's office and see who we can talk to," the athletic director said.

Maria stood up and they both hurried out of the office to get to the basketball arena as fast as they could.

***

"This is ridiculous! Are they really going to report this? Who sent the video? Why am I just hearing about this?"

Coach Simpson looked like he was going to explode. He was at his desk but had raised himself out of his chair and was leaning over his desk with his neck jutted out in disbelief. His face was red, sweat was already beading on his forehead, and veins were popping up all over his body. Questions were streaming out of him with an almost uncontrollable fury. Maria was taken aback by his fiery reaction but was secretly happy that the media didn't see this. The reaction alone would be huge fuel to the story.

"Coach, we need to take a step back and discuss what is in the video," Maria said. "Did you push a player? Do you have a copy of the practice tape the reporter was talking about?"

"No, I am not physical with my players," Simpson said adamantly, angrily falling back into his chair. He took a deep breath and a pause before he continued. "And we should have a copy. We make a few as soon as practice is over so all of the coaches can view the day's tape before the tape sessions. One of the assistant coaches can get it for us."

Simpson pushed a button on his phone and yelled at his secretary to have an assistant coach bring a copy of yesterday's practice tape up to him.

"Okay, well that's a starting point," the athletic director said. "So you're saying you have never verbally or physically assaulted any of your players?"

"No, absolutely not. I mean I yell at times and I might get in someone's face if he messes up, but *assault*? No way. That's not how I treat people."

"Well, there must be something the press got that is making them run the story. Think hard now. Anything at all?"

Coach Simpson was quiet as he looked up at the ceiling. "There's nothing, I swear."

Simpson paused but looked like he still had more to say. Maria waited to see if the silence would make him say anything else. The athletic director sat quietly in his chair.

Simpson let out a loud sigh.

"Yesterday I might have run into Mark Carter, one of the guards on the team. It was toward the end of practice and I was fired up."

Maria noticed that Simpson's anger was starting to dissipate as he started to recount what happened.

"And . . . .?" the athletic director asked, clearly not in the mood for Coach Simpson to take his time while he told the story.

"And I might have accidentally knocked him over," Simpson said, not making eye contact with either Maria or the athletic director.

"The kid just wasn't running the play right," he continued. "He gets a full scholarship and can't run a simple play correctly."

Simpson's voice was starting to rise again. "Yeah, so I was angry and I was yelling and when he ran the play wrong again, I couldn't believe it. I ran over to him and just when I was getting to him, I lost my balance, fell against Mark, and he fell onto the ground."

Maria and the athletic director didn't say anything. Maria jotted down a few notes to remember Coach Simpson's version of what happened.

Maria was finishing up her notes when the door opened and an assistant coach walked in with a videotape in his hand. Coach Simpson took it and walked over to a television in the corner of his office and popped in the video. As it began to play, showing the warm-up drills from the beginning of practice, the athletic director became clearly agitated.

"We don't have all day, Simpson," he barked. "Get to the part the press is gonna talk about!"

Simpson fast forwarded the video and looked up at the same time to both Maria and the athletic director. As the sound of spinning tape filled the room, Simpson's demeanor changed. No longer was he the fired up, bulging eyed man she was dealing with just a few minutes ago. Instead he looked a bit scared and his eyes seemed almost to plead with them.

"I just lost my balance, I swear," Simpson said. "I love these kids. I would never do anything to hurt them. I just want them to win, to know what it feels like to be a champion. We don't have time to be losers and I coach to motivate, not beat anyone up. Anything I do, I do out of love. I simply lost my balance. I should have apologized to Mark after practice, but I didn't get a chance to – he left so quickly."

The Athletic Director didn't respond and Maria wasn't sure what to think. Was it all just a matter of tough coaching and Simpson losing his balance? If that was the case, then maybe it wasn't as clear-cut as she thought.

Maria was deep in thought as the whirring sound of the tape slowed down and then stopped. Simpson pressed the play button and the video showed the players scrimmaging against each other. They watched a few minutes of the team running plays and prepping for their next game. Mark was on the video and she could see that Coach Simpson was visibly riled up with him. The next thing she knew, Coach Simpson's voice filled the room.

"Mark, you idiot! I can't believe you ran the play wrong again!"

Maria watched the video as Coach Simpson raced toward Mark.

***

Maria was ready for the press conference. The media advisory was sent to every relevant journalist Maria could think of; the location and time were set; and the chairs, podium, and microphones were all ready.

That morning she woke up early to get a copy of the paper. The story made the front page of the sports section: *WU's Men's Basketball Coach Accused of Physical Assault*. And then the phone calls started coming. Local and state reporters were mostly calling, but there had been a couple of national outlets looking for statements and more information.

Maria had been at her desk all morning taking calls, providing statements on behalf of the athletic director, and finalizing aspects of the press conference. As she picked up her cell phone and laptop to leave her office, she thought back to yesterday.

After meeting with Coach Simpson and viewing the video, she had met with the players on the team. She was particularly interested in speaking with Mark to get his side. He and the rest of the players had a much different version of the story than Coach Simpson provided. The players told her and the athletic director about a long history of verbal and, at times, even physical abuse. They were afraid to say anything because they didn't want to lose playing time or their scholarships.

Maria was frustrated when she left the meetings. She knew it wasn't her decision as the SID to deal with whether the coach was fired or retained, but she did know she needed to provide advice about what messages to give to the press and how to manage the PR crisis. She would need to think quickly and work with the athletic director and other members of the university to help strategize an appropriate response.

This morning she felt better. She met with university media relations personnel along with the athletic director yesterday evening to discuss the situation, and this morning, once she had a better idea of the reaction the story was getting, she decided to set up a press conference to answer questions and make the athletic director available. Someone needed to serve as a spokesperson and he was in the best position to do so. The president knew what was going on but was going to stay out of it until he was really needed.

"Don't want to make too big a deal out of it unless we need to," the president had told her. Maria wasn't quite sure she agreed with him, but he was the boss.

Maria had at least an hour before the press conference started but wanted to get there to ensure everything was ready. She also needed to prepare the athletic director for the press conference. Of course they had already discussed ways to approach the press and respond to the situation, but she needed to ensure they were on the same page with everything.

Maria made her way to the athletic director's office and he motioned to her to take a seat as he wrapped up a phone call.

Maria sat down and waited as he finished up. The athletic director put the phone down and rubbed his forehead.

"Okay, Maria. What do I need to say?"

***

The athletic director walked on the stage toward the podium and turned to face the reporters. Dozens had shown up from both the local and state media outlets. Maria stood at the back of the room and looked around as the athletic director walked onto the raised platform. Every eye seemed to be on him as he cleared his throat to make a statement and answer questions. He adjusted the microphone and began his statement as the cameras clicked and the reporters hurriedly jotted down notes.

DISCUSSION QUESTIONS

1. What advice or key messages should Maria give to the athletic director effectively handle the press conference effectively?

2. Coach Simpson and the players had two different viewpoints about the incident. How would each viewpoint change the way Maria could respond?

3. Do you think Maria was adequately prepared for the crisis? If yes, why? If no, what could Maria have done differently to be more prepared?

4. Now that Maria needs to deal with the PR crisis, what PR tactics beyond the press conference can Maria utilize to manage the repercussions?

5. What do you think of the statement Maria gave to the reporter from the *Town Gazette*? Was it an appropriate response or would you have crafted it differently?

KEY TERMS

Relationship between sport and media, Crises in sport organizations, Coach-athlete relations

PART 4

ORGANIZATIONAL COMMUNICATION AND SPORT

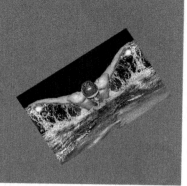

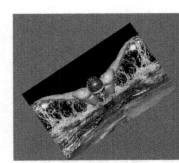

INTRODUCTION

Organizational communication is the perfect discipline for case study analysis because we tend to equate organizational communication with business-oriented communication, and certainly that is the case much of the time. But there are many aspects of organizational communication that one might find outside the business world. Although many of these cases in Part Four do involve the business side of sport, some revolve around rules and norms within a sport organization and will give you the chance to negotiate the intricacies that working in a sport organization entails.

Real-world examples of such cases abound. For instance, during the writing of this textbook, there are a number of sport leagues vying for new arenas and threatening to pull their teams from a city if demands are not met. The St. Louis Rams and San Diego Chargers both are looking at moving to Los Angeles. Were that to happen (and the behind the scenes negotiating in each city to try to make it not happen) the logistics that would need to occur to make it a successful move (or to make sure the move does not happen and a new arena is built in the current city) would be detailed, involve a lot of contract lawyers, and would require impeccable organizational communication among all facets of the organization. Although we do not have a case considering this issue, there are two cases in this section that look at contract issues in sport communication.

Every sport has many rules of the game, which may make us forget that outside of the game every sport organization has sets of rules as well. Sometimes these rules are unwritten and more of a "norm" or "expectation;" other times the rules are strict and have organizing bodies to monitor members of an organization to ensure that they are abiding by the rules. Take the National Collegiate Athletic Association (NCAA) and the many rules they impose on American collegiate sport. The idea behind the rules and regulations is to make collegiate sports fair for all players at all NCAA schools. Thus if one school has wealthy alumni willing to give a lot of money to a certain sport program to pay for the best athletes, that school can't benefit from that sort of gift when another school might not have that kind of support. But in reality, there are great discrepancies between schools in terms of facilities and what different schools can offer their athletes. In January 2013, the NCAA finally acquiesced to the fact that they cannot control the variability among the member schools (such as facilities and resources such as wealthy alumni) and they deregulated some two dozen of the rules that had been hard for them to regulate.[1]

Rules that did not change in collegiate sports are those regulating athletes and their grades, scholarships allowed, number of players and coaches, and money given directly to athletes. Case 26 gives you a little insight to one of these issues that has often shown up in the real-world news. That is the case of athletes being given grades that were not earned so that they could play.

Other organizational issues involving athletes include how coaches determine their rosters and who plays what position. Just like in any corporate organization where sometimes people are shifted to new positions and new titles are given, so too does a coach have to weigh all his or her options and determine when to cut someone or move him or her to a new position. The first case in Part Four deals with this very matter.

Hiring is another point of interest (and often contention) when it comes to organizational communication and sport. Whenever a popular sports team is in need of a new coach, the fans will likely give their two cents in many forms, which could include phone calls, letters, social media, and even downright verbal threats. For instance, when Rutgers University hired its first female athletic director, Julie Hermann, in 2013 following the scandal of coach abuse going on in the men's basketball team, many state legislators and university donors argued against the hiring.[2] Some questioned her ability to govern the Rutgers' Athletics Department based on allegations that she was an abusive coach when coaching volleyball at the University of Tennessee.[3] In addition, they were concerned about a sex discrimination lawsuit against her and the University of Louisville in 2008.[4] Case 24 depicts a similar situation for you to unravel.

So far we have been discussing organizational issues concerning sports-oriented organizations. But what about when sport becomes a problem within a corporate business? Case 27 gives you the chance to tackle this subject. Although that case deals with the consequences of office personnel feeling obligated to be on the company softball team, there are other ways sport can become a major factor in organizations that otherwise have nothing to do with athletics. For example, there are often office pools for March Madness or the Super Bowl for anyone interested in participating.

Any time leadership is involved, that is also a concern for organizational communication scholars. Certainly many athletes and coaches are considered leaders for their team and within their communities. In their 2015 article, "Sports Teams as Organizations: A Leader-Member Exchange Perspective of Player Communication With Coaches and Teammates," Cranmer and Myers used leader-member exchange theory to investigate how former high school athletes perceived their relationships with coaches versus teammates.[5] Cranmer and Myers found that "athletes with in-group relationships with coaches report more satisfaction and symmetrical communication with coaches, and more task cohesion, social cohesion, and cooperative communication with teammates."[6] Studies like this are helpful to keep in mind while you are analyzing these cases. Consider the interpersonal relationships within each case and how the variables of a case might affect the different characters and the ultimate outcome.

Other sport organizational communication concepts to consider as you contemplate the cases in Part Four include:

- interdependence within a sport organization or between organizations;
- organizational culture, including assimilation into and cohesion within a sport organization;
- a sport's organizations norms and roles for members;
- organizational networks, communication flow, and chain of command;
- contract law and labor relations;
- leadership styles;
- and internal crises management

REFERENCES

[1] Belzer, J. (21 January 2013). NCAA rule changes open door for escalation of college athletics arms race. Forbes.com. Retrieved from http://www.forbes.com/sites/jasonbelzer/2013/01/21/ncaa-rule-changes-open-door-for-escalation-of-college-athletics-arms-race/

[2] Eder, S. (28 May 2013). Rutgers athletic director faces new questions. *New York Times*. Retrieved from http://www.nytimes.com/2013/05/29/sports/new-rutgers-athletic-director-was-at-center-of-sex-discrimination-suit.html?_r=)

[3] Ibid.

[4] Ibid.

[5] Cranmer, G. A., & Meyer, S. A. (2015). Sports teams as organizations: A leader-member exchange perspective of player communication with coaches and teammates. *Communication & Sport*, 3(1), 100–118.

[6] Ibid.

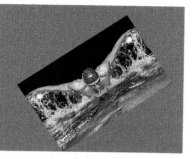

Leann Parker
Director, The Ohio State University Athletic Communications

Photo courtesy of Kirk Irwin

When it comes to getting into communication management in athletics, the earlier a student starts gaining experience, the better. Athletics encompasses so many different fields that a student may go into an internship set on one area and then realize they are more interested in pursuing something different. Talking to staff throughout a department will expose a student to everything that goes into running a department and the sporting events that department hosts.

No matter where a student is working, or what his or her job description is, they should also be willing to help out with whatever is needed (as well as whenever possible). Don't be too good for any task. There are many opportunities to volunteer at local and conference events, and making the effort to work those events is helpful to getting your foot in the door with a new group of contacts.

In terms of actual communications work, students should focus on learning the ins and outs of the profession . . . for ALL sports, not just their favorites. The more sports students are familiar with, the more job opportunities will be available. Although athletics communications entails much more than statistics, stats are still part of the job. It is worth the time to become comfortable with the scoring systems for as many sports as possible. Developing interviewing skills will help improve both feature writing and video creation. Looking at other schools for examples and best practices is helpful to generate content for your own programs. If you see something that you think would work for your program, don't be afraid to suggest it to the full-time contacts in the office you are working in.

In a job like mine, I work with student-athletes every day. Other communication management type positions may not have regular access to athletes. If you are fortunate enough to work at the college level, being involved with student-athletes will be a rewarding experience; and it will be important to build relationships with them so that you can do your job successfully. One of the keys to developing good relationships with student-athletes and coaches is spending the time getting to know them. There is always work that needs to be done, but making the effort to get to practice, to make the trip to the coaches' office, to find free time during a road trip, goes a long way in getting to know both the student-athletes and staff. The best way to get to know someone is just to talk – and listen to what they say. Everyone has a story; it's just a matter of taking the time to really get to know them by talking and asking great questions. It's also helpful to listen when your coaches and student-athletes do interviews. You never know what you might find out and you can always ask more about a topic after the interview is over.

I also work with the media on a regular basis and that would likely be an important part of any position that involves communication and sport. Developing a good relationship with the media takes time, but is worth it. It starts with being responsive to their requests in a timely fashion. Even if you can't help with each one, being honest about what is and isn't possible up front is good practice. Treating all media with respect, from student to national reporters, is important. Everyone has a job to do, so understanding where they are coming from, and having them understand where you are coming from, always works better when you have a good relationship.

Leann Parker handles all media relations duties for the Ohio State men's hockey, men's lacrosse, and women's tennis teams, including coordinating media requests, producing media guides and game notes, updating the OhioStateBuckeyes.com web site and the teams' social media accounts, handling statistics, and overseeing the press box. Her role also encompasses communications duties for special projects including the athletics hall of fame and academic success stories for the department. She acts as the operations manager for the athletics communications office, including oversight of student employees and fulltime staff members.

Parker has been with the Ohio State Athletics Communications office since 1999-2000. After a year as a graduate assistant, she moved into an assistant athletics communications director position the following year and was promoted to associate director in 2005. She was named director in October 2012. She was the recipient of the Doyle Smith Sports Information/Media Award from the United States Intercollegiate Lacrosse Association in 2013 and was named the 2004 Central Collegiate Hockey Association SID of the Year.

Prior to coming to Ohio State, Parker was a full-time intern in the James Madison University sports media relations office and served as an assistant ticket director for the Frederick Keys in the Single A Baseball Carolina League. During college she interned with the JMU sports media relations office, at the Metro Atlantic Athletic Conference, and with the New York/New Jersey MetroStars (now New York Red Bulls) in Major League Soccer.

A native of Metuchen, N.J., Parker earned her bachelor's degree in kinesiology with a sport management concentration from James Madison University in 1997 and her master's degree in sport management from Ohio State in 2000. She and her husband, Eric, also a graduate of JMU, have a son, Devin. The family lives in Lewis Center, Ohio.

CASE 23: TO GAIN OR NOT TO GAIN, THAT IS THE QUESTION

Michael W. Kramer
University of Oklahoma

ABSTRACT

Cory was a highly recruited high school football star who found himself red-shirted during his freshman year. Then, after almost no playing time during his next year because he was third on the depth chart, the coach asked him to gain weight and change positions in order to help the team and improve his chances of playing. There were no guarantees, of course, as he considered his choices.

***

Cory did not expect to find himself in this predicament. His football career was supposed to turn out quite differently. As he considered what to do, he reflected on how he had gotten to this point.

As a high school athlete, Cory was a successful multi-sport athlete in football, basketball, and track, but he stood out from his peers in football. As a defensive end, his speed and strength made him almost impossible to beat. Most teams rarely ran or threw to his side of the field, or if they did early in the game, they quit after being unsuccessful a few times. He made the all-conference team his sophomore year and all-state his junior and senior years. As a result, he was highly sought after by college recruiters.

Cory received literature from dozens of Division I universities whose coaches contacted him one after another, all within the NCAA rules, of course, or at least they mostly followed the rules. When it was time to plan campus visits, there were really only two schools Cory was interested in attending. One was the large state university in his home state. He remembered what Coach V told him more than once, "Our two best defensive ends will have used up their eligibility at the end of this season. You'll have a great opportunity to compete for a starting position your very first year with us."

The other university was a private one. When Coach Dan talk to Cory, he emphasized, "We have one of the highest graduation rates among Division I programs. A few of our graduates go on to play professionally, but most pursue careers in other areas like business, computer science, even an occasional doctor. We'll give you the opportunity to get the education that will give you a start on whatever career you pursue, football or otherwise." Cory knew the figures, that only two or three percent of college football players ever signed a professional contract and some of those never played, and so Coach Dan was telling him to think about what he would do after he played his last college game.

But Cory also knew that almost every year the state university's team was nationally ranked and played in a bowl game. Each year some of its players were drafted into the NFL. The opportunity to be in that elite group was more than Cory could resist, and so on national letter of intent day during a ceremony held at his high school, he signed on to play in his home state, close enough that his family and friends could come to see him play. Coach V called him that day and said, "You've made the right choice. You won't regret this decision." At the time, Cory thought his decision would launch his college career and then his professional career; he was on his way to the NFL. Two years later, Cory was not so sure.

***

When he arrived in midsummer to begin fall practice with all of the other new freshmen, Cory was surprised that he did not stand out like he had in high school. There were other athletes who were as fast as he was, or bigger, or stronger. Whereas in high school he was always on the A team during any scrimmages, he was splitting time with six other defensive ends including Kenny, a junior who confided to Cory after one practice, "Coach hinted to me that this is finally going to be my year to start, now that Johnson and Bartles have graduated." Then there were two sophomores and two other freshmen who wanted to play defensive end, too.

At the end of one practice when the three freshman defensive ends were putting away equipment along with the other freshmen, a tradition that had gone on for years, one of them, Jason, commented, "When Coach told me he thought there would be a position for me my first year on the team, I didn't think he meant equipment supervisor." The three of them laughed, but it hurt too because Cory realized that Coach V used the same line on everyone. He was not so special.

With about two weeks to go before the season opener, Cory had concluded he wouldn't be in the starting line-up. In fact, he wasn't sure that he would get to play at all. But when he was called into Coach V's office after practice, he was hoping for good news, not the news he got.

Coach V started off in his usual friendly manner. "Come on in, Cory. How's it going?"

"Okay. I'm getting used to things."

"Are you finding your way around campus?"

"Yeah, it's pretty easy–haven't got lost yet.

"How's your dorm room? Got a good roommate?"

"It's going pretty good. My roommate isn't around much, but he seems okay."

"What do you think about practice? Harder than you expected?"

"Yeah, a little, I mean, but I knew it would be tough. I prepared for two-a-days all summer."

"Good for you. I can tell you're a hard worker. It shows in practice."

"Thanks, Coach. I do my best."

"Now I want to talk to you about an option that I think might be good for you and the team. We have more depth at defensive end than we expected this year. So we're thinking about red-shirting you this year instead of playing you."

"Really? Redshirt?"

"You see, if we redshirt you, well, that way, in a year you'll be better prepared to contribute to the team. You'll have a whole year of practice and training. That'll help you build up your strength. Then, you'll get to play spring football. Together, that'll give you a head start on the fall season. That will be better for you and you will be able to contribute more to the team. You'll still have four years to play and we're committed to keeping that promise to you."

Cory didn't remember much else about that conversation or the ones that followed. There was talk about how if someone was injured or didn't work out, they might bring him into a game and burn his redshirt year. The coach emphasized it was important for him to continue to work hard at practice just in case. But in the end, he was redshirted his entire freshman year. That meant he attended all practices and training sessions, just like everyone else. He just never got to travel with the team or play in any games. He did get to stand on the sidelines in uniform for home games, but that's as close as he got to playing. He told his parents and friends not to come to home games, but some did anyway because they had already bought tickets. It was nice to have them around after the game, but it would have been a lot better if they could talk about how he played.

And, of course, he had to attend class and stay academically eligible to play, just in case. He didn't do great, but he did manage to get mostly Cs in his classes the fall semester.

During spring practice, Cory was pleased to at least make it onto the depth chart. In the spring football game, the inter-squad game, he actually got to play for a few snaps. He thought he played pretty well, making one assisted tackle and knocking away one pass that came in his direction, but his position coach, Dave, gave him the same "way to go" that he gave everyone who did something good.

When fall practice began, Cory was third on the depth chart for right defensive end. That rarely changed and so he spent the first few games watching from the sidelines. It was fun cheering his teammates onto victory in the early games of the season, but it would have been more fun to play and no one was going to notice him if he didn't get to play. When his family asked him about not playing after each home game, he could only say, "I'm working my way into the game. I'll get my chance," but he wasn't so sure.

After a year on the team, he knew now not to expect to get to talk Coach V. He only interacted with the starters or if he called you into his office. But after watching the first six games from the sideline, he finally got the courage to ask Dave one evening after watching game films, "What else do I need to do to get into the game?"

Without hesitation, Dave responded, "You know, a lot of freshmen think they're going to come in here and start right away. Almost never happens. Too much talent around here. You're doing the right things, getting better, getting strong. Don't be discouraged. This is really only your first year. You'll get your chance. And when you do, you'll know you're ready, at the top of your game."

Cory was discouraged, but he tried not to show it. He continued to do his best at practice and Dave even seemed to give him a little more encouragement after their talk—or at least for a couple weeks until things seemed to go back to normal. He did get into three different games late in the season. Two were blowouts where he was on the mop-up squad. The other time, a starter was injured and his replacement got the wind knocked out of him and so he got in for two plays. At the end of the season, Cory had played a total of 16 plays and assisted on one tackle.

In the meantime, between practice, training, and traveling to away games, Cory was not doing all that great in his classes and he was having trouble finding a major. Either the material wasn't interesting to him or the standards were too high. He couldn't believe you had to have a 3.0 to declare a business major. When the fall semester ended, after three semesters in college, he had 39 credits and a 2.2 GPA, no major, and 6 minutes of playing time.

Entering spring football, Cory was optimistic. The starter for his position had finished and graduated. This year was going to be different. Still there were six players vying for two positions and on national letter of intent day, two highly rated defensive ends signed up to join the team. He thought, "They're only freshmen. Coach probably made them think they'll start right away, but they'll find out soon enough. This is going to be my year."

At the end of one of the spring practices, Dave asked Cory to meet him in Coach V's office. Cory was surprised since it had been a long time since Coach V had talked to him personally. He wondered what it would be about as he sat down in the large chair across from the coach. This time he took in all of the pictures of former players who were now in the NFL, a dream of his that seemed to be becoming more and more out of reach for him. Dave stood by his side. There wasn't much small talk this time.

"How's it going for you, Cory?"

"Okay. I think I'm doing good this spring. I think I can get more playing time this year."

"Yes, we've noticed that you have shown improvement. We know you're a hard worker." Then Coach V got to the real point of the meeting. "Cory, we've been thinking about making a change. We want to do what's best for you and the team. You understand that, don't you?"

"Yeah, Coach, I understand."

"Well, it seems like we're going to be deep in defensive ends next fall what with who's already on the team and our new recruits. You've probably noticed that."

"Yeah, I realize that, but I think if I keep improving, I'll be a starter."

"You certainly can try for that and maybe you'll make that, but we have another idea."

At this point, Dave joined in. "We think that you would better serve the team if you switched to a different position. We're thinking you'd make a good guard and we're pretty thin on guards."

"Guard? I'm not really big enough to play on the front line, am I? Some of those linemen weigh 280 pounds."

Coach V took over again. "You're right. You're not big enough, right now. But you've got all summer. With the right regimen of diet and exercise, you can put on say 30 or so pounds and then you would be big enough. You'd have a better chance of playing more as a guard than at end, plus you'd be filling a hole we have in our defense."

"But I'd have to learn a whole new position."

"You're smart. You're hard working. We can't promise you'll be a starter, but we think you have more potential as a guard."

"So you want me to gain 30 pounds this summer?"

"Yeah. Thirty pounds isn't that much. And you can start learning the new position during the rest of spring practice. Of course, it's your decision. It's your choice."

Cory didn't remember much of the rest of that conversation either. There was advice on eating to gain weight, about learning the new position, and about how this was the best for the team and for him. He also recalled having seen some other players try to change positions over the last two years. Although he remembered one who was successful, others continued to ride the bench and some others seemed to have disappeared from the squad altogether.

This was not the choice he expected to be facing after two years on the team.

DISCUSSION QUESTIONS

1. Is it appropriate for coaches in football or other sports to ask athletes to gain or lose weight (in addition to football, consider gymnastics and wrestling)?

2. What resources give coaches unequal influence or power in college athletics? What influence or power do players have in college athletics?

3. How is the coach using deep structure power in this situation? Consider issues like unquestioned assumptions (legitimacy), naturalizing the present, and representing sectional interests as universal.

4. Hegemony is typically defined as the process of willingly participating in your own oppression. How is Cory participating in his own oppression in this situation? Does he have other options?

5. How do societal myths like "you can be anything you want to be" contribute to Cory's dilemma?

6. How does the referent power of professional athletes in general contribute to Cory's dilemma?

7. What should Cory do?

KEY TERMS

Resource dependency, Referent power, Legitimacy, Naturalizing the present, Hegemony

CASE 24: HISTORY OR HUBRIS
A College Golf Program Reaches a Crossroads

John F. Borland
Springfield College

ABSTRACT

A selection committee charged with hiring a new golf coach at a storied college program in the Deep South must choose between a proven winner with a shady past and an unproven coach with a potentially troubled future.

***

"Were we able to get the police report on the 2010 incident involving Coach Bastion?" yelled Jeffrey Jackson, the athletic director for State University, from his spacious office overlooking the football field.

"Yes, we did," answered Jackson's administrative assistant, Shirley Wilson. "They just faxed it over a few minutes ago." Wilson and Jackson had worked together for 25 years, but Wilson had been at the college for 31 years. Besides Wilson, the only other Black employees in the athletic department were the head coaches for the men's and women's track and field teams and two assistant coaches for both the men's and women's basketball teams. State University's athletics department had always been run by White men as had its successful golf teams.

The issue of race was weighing heavily on the athletic director's mind that mid-August morning. Although he was White and had nearly all White administrators and coaches working for him, he was taking seriously the calls made by national media and representatives of the National Collegiate Athletic Association (NCAA) and the Black Coaches and Administrators (BCA) organization to consider more diversity in hiring. In fact, Jackson had an opportunity staring him right in the face.

A LEGEND RETIRES

State University had parted ways with its head golf coach in May, following an embarrassing fifth-place showing in the conference tournament. Hunter Brown had coached at State University the previous 27 years as head golf coach. His teams had won three national titles – one in the early 1990s and two in back-to-back seasons (2003, 2004). His fellow coaches and State University alums marveled at Brown's ability to communicate with young student-athletes and "stay current" in his teachings. Even though he had gotten older, his ability to coach ever-brasher young men remained of high quality. However, over the past five years, Brown's teams had been competitive but never vied for another national title. There were never any loud calls for Brown to step down – people respected him too much for that – but Brown's wife and two sons suggested that he might actually enjoy retirement and spending more time with his seven grandchildren. Brown himself admitted to Jackson in late April, after a 20-stroke loss to State's in-state rival, that perhaps "the game is passing me by." Two weeks later, on a Saturday afternoon, a grim-faced Jackson called a news conference attended by local and regional media and announced that Brown would step down after the season.

The next day, a Sunday, Jackson's voice mail and email inbox were inundated with messages from prominent alumni of State University "suggesting" who the next golf coach should be. "Geez," Jackson thought to himself. "The body isn't even cold yet, and they are already talking about a replacement."

Jackson had always been friendly to alumni because he knew the kind of influence they have with the dollars they donate to the college, but he didn't feel they should have any influence in the hiring process. He had been at State U long enough to accumulate plenty of social capital, and he realized that he wouldn't risk his own firing if he ignored requests from powerful alums. He and the university president had a warm relationship. His job was secure. While he thought about what to do next, his cell phone rang. It was the university president.

"Good afternoon, Jeff," crooned Sally Alfreddson, State University's 13th president in its illustrious 155-year history and its first female president. "So, have you heard from the alums yet?"

"Of course," Jackson said. "You think they could have waited a few days."

"Never," Alfreddson replied. "They think they're the most important people on Earth. Let's not wait too long to start our search. When you get your committee together, please let me know who will be on it. Go ahead and write the advertisement or have one of your associate directors do it. I'd like to see it, of course. The school will pay for the advertisement to be run in any three places you ask. I don't want to pay for a search firm on this. Let's do it ourselves."

"Will do," Jackson said, "I'll keep you posted, Sally."

"And, Jeff, one more thing," Alfreddson said, "let *us* hire the best person for the job with minimal alumni influence. The golf program is a staple here, but WE are the decision makers on this. Well, I'm preaching to the choir. Bye."

THE SEARCH TO REPLACE A LEGEND

Jackson had never had to put together a search committee for a golf coach because Coach Brown had been here longer than he had, but he certainly had put together other search committees to hire other coaches. It was important to have a variety of voices on this committee along with diversity. Jackson tapped four people at State University to be on the search committee, along with himself: Associate Athletic Director Bill Byers; men's track coach Phillip Shegley; communications professor Sarah Jacobs; and the senior women's administrator, Jessica Soldich. He had three men and two women on the committee, one Black man on the committee (Shegley) and a professor from the communications department who could help everyone listen to one another and understand different viewpoints. The head golf coach hiring was particularly important for State University. The college did not compete that well in the men's revenue sports of football and basketball. Despite some lean years recently, golf still had the potential to bring in prize recruits and wins for State U.

The city and state in which State University was located had changed demographically over the past 10 years. The city population reflected more diversity with the Black population moving from 34% to 43%. The state also saw increases in both Black and Hispanic residents. In fact, a Black gubernatorial candidate recently garnered 38% of the vote in an election, the highest ever by a non-White candidate in the state's history. Jackson had noticed changes at State University as well. More student-athletes of color were playing a diversity of sports, including golf, tennis, and volleyball.

The search committee work went well. There were a few disagreements, but with Jacobs' background and her ability to get others to listen to one another, acrimonious incidents were mostly averted. Jackson praised her in his head. He had picked her for a specific reason. Her golf knowledge was good as she was married to a former golf pro, but it was her ability to get people to communicate effectively with one another and leave the personal politics at the door that really emphasized her contribution. After the grading of prospective candidates and more discussions, the committee eventually settled on four candidates.

Jackson thanked the committee members for their hard work and said he would call the four finalists to find out if they were still interested in becoming the next head golf coach at State University. "This process has lasted very long, and it's quite possible that some of our finalists could be finalists for other jobs. I will contact all of you through email when I have more information."

On his drive home, Jackson weighed the four finalists, and he concluded that the committee had come up with the best four from the big initial pool of candidates. Although he was proud of the committee's work, he was less than pleased with an exchange between Associate AD Byers and SWA Soldich. The two did not agree on the quality of one of the candidate's body of work. Byers had the candidate rated somewhat low. Soldich had him rated the highest of the four candidates. The candidate currently coached at a Division III school. Soldich said, "It does not matter if it is Division I, II, or III. If you can coach, you can coach at ALL levels."

"It does matter," replied Byers. "It's a completely different sport from Division I to Division III. We are the top level of competition."

"Golf is not like football," Soldich said. "You are making too much of the difference here. Do you have an issue with the candidate for some other reason?"

"Never mind," Byers said. "Forget I mentioned it. Let's drop it."

As troubling as that exchange was, it was not as troubling as what Jackson read on his cell phone as he pulled into his driveway. Byers had texted him to say that two of the committee's four finalists had already accepted jobs elsewhere. They had called the office to withdraw their names. Jackson could not believe his final pool had just been slashed from four down to two. He could not believe this had all happened in the past hour. He reached into his briefcase to secure the applications of the two remaining candidates.

He pulled out his cell phone and dialed Roger Bastion, one of the remaining finalists. Coach Bastion, who was White and well-known nationally, answered after three rings. "Hello."

"Coach Bastion, this is Jeffrey Jackson calling from State University. We are interested in inviting you to campus for an on-site interview to possibly become the next golf coach of State University. Are you still interested in the position?"

"I sure am!" Bastion almost yelled into the phone.

"Excellent, Coach. My assistant Shirley Wilson will be in touch to work out the travel arrangements. We want to do this soon, say in the next two weeks."

"That sounds great," Bastion said. "I will clear my schedule. I'm surprised it took so long for y'all to call me."

"OK, I look forward to meeting you in person, Coach."

Jackson hung up and called the second remaining candidate, Wilfred Lidson. Jackson was not as familiar with Lidson, the Division III coach, but liked what he had seen on his resume. He had also seen him on television give an interview after his team had won the Division III championship and was well aware that State University had never seen a job candidate like him in such a high-profile coaching job.

Jackson repeated the same information to Lidson that he had to Bastion about travel arrangements and the importance of doing the interview soon. Lidson was agreeable to the terms. Lidson closed the call by saying, "I'm surprised and humbled to have received your call, Mr. Jackson, and I look forward to our meeting."

Jackson hung up and sighed. "We are entering unchartered territory," he said aloud as he entered his front door. "And everyone is going to have an opinion."

The next day, a Saturday, Jackson walked out onto his front porch to retrieve the newspaper. Saturdays were typically slow news days, but a headline below the fold on the front page of the sports section caught his attention: "State University Job Search Pits Proven Winner Versus Unproven Black Candidate."

Jackson's ears burned. Not only did the headline miss the point, but how did they get this story so fast? Was there a leak on his committee? While eating breakfast that morning, Jackson got a call from the school's sports information director, saying that the story had taken on a life of its own on Twitter and fan Facebook pages. State University golf student-athletes and former State U golfers were talking to local media, singing the praises of Bastion and chiding the selection of Lidson as a finalist. Jackson asked the SID to send some of the more inflammatory Twitter posts to him through email so he was well-versed on the situation. The SID asked if his office should release any information about the job search because the media would want answers.

"Hell no," Jackson said. "We are in the middle of a job search. This is a personnel matter. We will do this search without help from the media."

The Tweets were about what Jackson expected:

"Bastion is a winner! So what if he bent the rules a little? Who hasn't in college athletics?"

"Lid who? The guy doesn't even coach at the Division I level. And then there's his complexion."

"AD Jackson is clueless. Neither one of these guys can hold Coach Brown's clipboard. State U continues down the path of no return."

"Gotta go with Bastion. He's a winner. Lidson coaches in the Little League; we need a man, not a boy."

Jackson was instantly glad that his athletic department had instituted a ban on Twitter use for their student-athletes during the academic year. He was worried about what some of the golfers might say.

AND THEN THERE WERE TWO

Lidson was an up-and-comer, but unproven at the Division I level. He was male, Black, 40 years old, and had won two national titles at the Division III level over a 13-year coaching career at the same school. Bastion was also male, White, 52 years old, and had 28 years of Division I coaching experience at three schools in competitive conferences. Although he had never won a national title, his teams had consistently finished in the top 10 of the final collegiate golf rankings – except for his last team. For the past two seasons, he was unemployed after being fired from his previous job after he was photographed at an after-tournament party on the campus of the school HIS TEAM had just lost to. He was pictured with a drink in his hand surrounded by young women (some below the drinking age) who also had drinks in their hands. Some "selfies" were taken with the coach and the young ladies – all with alcohol in their hands. Later that night, Bastion was stopped by police and later charged with a DUI after leaving the party. He was fired after the season, and did not coach in the team's conference tournament. In addition, schools that Bastion had worked at had recruiting violations that led to some NCAA investigations. Despite all this, Bastion was still a proven winner at the highest level, and he had scored high on all categories on the committee's rubric – except for the infractions area, although a lot of the violations could not be directly linked to him.

If Lidson were hired, he would be the first Black head coach of golf in the school's history, but a hire like this would be controversial. Despite the change in demographics in the state, change still came slowly at State U given the lack of diversity in the athletics department and on the faculty. Jackson wanted to leave a lasting legacy of turning around the golf program before he retired. In addition to the head coach search, he had another project brewing in athletics: A new, on-campus workout facility for student-athletes that was state-of-the-art with two full-length football fields, an indoor driving range for the golf team, golf-swing analysis software, an indoor track and Olympic size swimming pool. The $40 million facility would have top-of-the-line scouting and film rooms, a cafeteria for the student-athletes, a large athletic training room and all of the latest in workout equipment. Jackson had recently seen the blueprints for the facility, and the new building was going to be stunning. It would be the nicest athletic department in the conference. It was to be named the Hunter Brown Athletic Complex, after the former golf coach, and half of the $40 million price tag was being supplied by former golfer and State U's most supportive alum, Dr. Mark Justinburger.

The day before Bastion, the first candidate, was set to visit, Jackson called him to see if he needed transportation from the airport. "I'm all set," Bastion said. "I have my ride all taken care of." It was at this point that Jackson received the police report from his assistant about Bastion's after-tournament party incident and DUI. He wanted to make sure he knew everything.

The next day, Bastion was scheduled to meet with AD Jackson at 9:00 AM. A few minutes after 9:00 AM, Jackson heard laughing outside his office. One of the laughs sounded familiar. "Well, Jeffrey! Look who I found out in the hallway!" Jackson turned around to see Dr. Justinburger escorting Bastion through the door of the AD's office. Jackson smiled but felt uneasy. He wondered if Justinburger had been Bastion's ride from the airport.

After some small talk, Justinburger got up to leave, turned to Jackson and said, "Now take it easy on our next golf coach, Jeff. Don't let your committee treat him too harshly. We need a winner in our new building." Justinburger winked at Bastion as he turned to leave.

The rest of the day – and Bastion's visit – was unimpeded by alumni influence. The current golf student-athletes treated him warmly, and Bastion soaked up the attention like a king holding court.

A week later, there was no such royal treatment for Lidson when he visited campus. The golf student-athletes were nowhere to be found. Time had been scheduled for Lidson to visit with them, but none of the golfers showed up at the scheduled place and time. Jackson was furious. He apologized profusely to Lidson. Lidson smiled and said, determinedly, "That's OK. I think I would have to win over a lot of hearts and minds if I came here. I'm ready to do that."

After Lidson and Bastion made their visits, the committee reconvened, and Byers was the only member of the committee who favored Bastion. Jackson did not put forth a vote (he would if there had been a tie), but it was 3-1 in favor of offering Lidson the job, and, if he refused, not to offer Bastion the position at all. Bastion's manner was a turn-off to some of the committee members. "He seemed too cocky," Soldich, the SWA, remarked. Jacobs, the communications professor who analyzes communication for a living, did not like the way he talked over the committee members in the main question-and-answer session. "He does not know how to listen. He hijacked the proceedings."

"But he doesn't have to listen!" Byers boomed. "He's the boss."

"The president is the boss, and she is his boss. In fact, I'm his boss," Jackson said.

Byers continued, "The golfers don't want Lidson."

Soldich countered, "Since when do they get to pick the coach?"

Byers: "You don't think they should have any influence?"

Soldich: "No, I don't. They are going to be gone long before Coach Lidson leaves here."

Byers: "This is naïve. If Lidson is hired, we will lose alumni support."

Soldich: "Or we just might create a new culture, something we have been needing at State University for a long time."

Jackson was troubled by this exchange although he appreciated frank conversation. He was more troubled by Bastion's over-confidence, not to mention his evasiveness. Jackson had to ask him difficult questions about his past indiscretions, particularly the drinking incident. Bastion was unapologetic. "That was in the past. I'm ready to start thinking about the future. I can turn around this program. I have done it in other places. You're asking me about drinking? You should be asking me about winning."

Lidson, on the other hand, was humble and thrilled to have the opportunity to move up to such a storied program. And he was hungry. When asked about his ability to deal with being the first Black head coach at State U, he did not shrink after hearing the question. "It would be an honor. I want to be a role model for my players and for young Black men at the college who might be pursuing other things besides athletics. I realize this would be a milestone, but ultimately I don't want to be seen as the first Black coach, I want to be seen as the coach who followed the legendary Hunter Brown and did things the right way, as he did."

So, it was settled, Jackson told the committee. "Lidson will be offered the position. If he turns it down, we will not offer it to Bastion, and it will be a failed search."

Roughly three hours after that statement to the committee, Jackson's office phone rang. It was President Alfreddson. "Jeff," she said. "Justinburger just called me. He is threatening to pull his funding on the new athletics facility if we don't hire Bastion."

Jacskon said to Alfreddson, "This has become bigger than a job-search committee issue. What do you recommend we do?"

DISCUSSION QUESTIONS

1. If you were Jackson and the president gave you the power to proceed in any way you wanted, what would you do next?

2. In your view, was the makeup of the search committee appropriate with regard to having a diversity of voices? Did it possibly provide a different level of communication than the usual "winning is the most important thing" argument?

3. When a controversial decision is about to be made in professional or college sport, normally a torrent of responses quickly begins to dot the social media landscape. Should decision-makers bother reading any of this chatter, as AD Jackson did, to stay informed?

4. Five committee members essentially made the decision for this important hire. What other groups should have a say in the hiring of the coach, if any?

5. If Lidson is hired, what methods should the college and the athletics department utilize to put a positive public relations spin on this historic hiring?

6. If Bastion is hired, what methods should the college and the athletics department utilize to put a positive public relations spin on this hiring given his past indiscretions?

7. If Jackson and Alfreddson cave to alumni pressure, what would this communicate about the culture of Division I athletics?

KEY TERMS

Diversity, Social media, Job search, Communication

CASE 25: FOULING OUT?

Raúl J. Feliciano Ortiz
SUNY Oneonta

ABSTRACT

A basketball head coach is faced with a difficult decision when he overhears a secret conversation between his assistant coach and his most valuable player.

***

"Here's what you asked for last week. That's all I can give you for now," whispered Toney James, the assistant coach of the SeaMonsters.

"Man, I knew you would come through, Coach! I really appreciate this!" Diego Salgado, the SeaMonsters' starting point guard replied, a little too loudly.

"Shhhh! Keep it cool, Diego. You can't tell anybody about this. You know that, right?"

"I know, Coach. You have my word."

"And you know what happens if somebody finds out?"

"Yes, Coach. I could get suspended, lose my scholarship, get thrown out of the team, yada, yada, yada. I got it. Don't worry about it."

Seamus O'Healy, the SeaMonsters' head coach, had gone back into his office to retrieve his playbook. As he crossed the team's locker room, he heard some whispering near Diego's locker. O'Healy had enough coaching experience to know that whispering in a deserted locker room was usually a sign of trouble. He stayed back and hid behind another row of lockers where nobody would see him. He heard the entire exchange between Toney and Diego.

Oh God! No, Toney! Why are you doing this? And why in the world are you doing it now? thought O'Healy as he watched both men exit the locker room.

As soon as Salgado and James left, O'Healy went to his office and closed the door. He paced in front of his desk for a while and suddenly, without thinking about it, he slapped the desk lamp as hard as he could and let out a frustrated groan.

"Why do these things always happen at the worst possible time? Why can't it happen during the offseason? No! Of course not! It has to happen just when we're on the verge of making the postseason!" O'Healy muttered to himself.

THE DISCIPLINARIAN

Before he became the head coach of the State University SeaMonsters, one of the most storied programs in Division I male basketball, Seamus O'Healy had made his mark at a smaller university. He had taken the Twisters from Grand Canal College to back-to-back "Final Four" appearances in the Division II national tournament. This was an amazing feat considering that Grand Canal College had only been playing Division II basketball for ten years, and had never been to the postseason before O'Healy joined the program in its sixth year.

But it was not only O'Healy's winning ways that put him on State University's radar. It was also his reputation as a great "disciplinarian."

Before O'Healy was hired, twenty-seven Grand Canal basketball players had been detained by the police. That amounted to 30% of the players in those first five years of the program. Ten of those twenty-seven were charged with felonies. Also, the program itself had been fined several times for "undisclosed NCAA violations."

At the end of the Twisters' fifth season, the Grand Canal College Athletic Department finally fired their coach. Even though the program had been a disaster from the beginning, the athletic director felt he owed it to the coach to let him try to fix it. After all, he had been the driving force behind bringing basketball to Grand Canal in the first place. Nonetheless, the felonies and the violations continued to pile up and the administration finally replaced him with O'Healy, an experienced high school basketball coach who had several state championships under his belt.

O'Healy, like other great coaches, made an impact in his first year. In his rookie season, the Twisters had a .500 winning percentage, making it the first non-losing season in the program's history. By his second year, the Twisters posted their first winning season ever, and by the fourth year they were two points away from making it into the national championship game.

But the Twisters would have never been in that position if they had not taken care of their off-the-court issues. O'Healy had made it very clear from the start that his players needed to be serious about the team if they wanted to play. He kicked four players (two starters) off the team during the first month of practice.

"There is no place in this team for those who don't respect the rules!" he used to say constantly.

During that first season, the team only had eleven players on its roster, as opposed to the customary fifteen. In one memorable occasion, the Twisters had to forfeit a game because seven of the eleven players had been suspended by O'Healy for not keeping up with their schoolwork. By his final year with the Twisters, all of his players had passing grades and none were in trouble with the law. It was a real Hollywood ending! This balance of discipline and success made O'Healy a hot commodity in the coaching ranks.

***

State University was one of the premier collegiate basketball programs in the nation. SU's SeaMonsters had won six national championships and were considered one of the perennial powerhouse teams in the postseason. Unfortunately, the program had fallen on hard times. They had failed to make the NCAA tournament for two years in a row and had not made it past the initial round in their last two appearances. The last straw, however, was the NCAA sanctions. Their previous coach had been found guilty of recruiting violations and of covering up for players who were taking money for autographs and team memorabilia. The NCAA is very clear in those matters: Student-athletes may not receive any type of money that does not come in the form of an athletic or non-athletic scholarship previously approved by the university.

These were hardly the kinds of problems O'Healy faced at Grand Canal College, but after the NCAA suspended State University from the national tournament, the administration thought they needed to send a clear message with their new hire: they were taking the suspension seriously and they had brought in someone who would clean up the program.

Unfortunately, O'Healy had not been quite as successful with the SeaMonsters yet. During his first season, the SeaMonsters were still suspended by the NCAA, so they could not play in the national tournament. Regardless, they would not have been invited; they had a subpar record that first season (and the next one). Now, however, they were close to earning a last-minute invite thanks to their freshman guard, Diego Salgado. Salgado had become the top scorer in the conference tournament and had the SeaMonsters poised to win the conference championship. A win in their conference would certainly earn them an invitation into the national tournament.

ET TU, TONEY?

"I know you're giving money to Diego," said O'Healy as calmly as he could.

"What?!" asked James nervously.

"Don't deny it, Toney. I saw you in the locker room."

"Oh, God. Listen, it's not what it seems like–"

"No? So he had an incomplete game of Monopoly and you lent him the bills from yours? Is that it?"

Toney was so nervous he could not even laugh at O'Healy's lousy attempt at sarcasm. He stood there petrified, in silence, for a few seconds before trying to explain.

"Yes. I gave him some money, but it wasn't like a bonus or a bribe or anything like that. Diego's mom was laid off recently, and they can't make ends meet with the dad's salary alone. He came to me to tell me he was thinking of dropping out to see if he could help his parents financially. I told him I could *lend* him some money that he could pay later, once things stabilized."

The thoughts raced across O'Healy's mind as he heard Toney's explanation: *Yeah, sure, a "loan." Can't you see the kid is playing you, Toney? He preyed on your compassion and is off to buy himself a tablet or a console game or another one of those gadgets the kids like so much.*

"Why didn't you come to me first, Toney? And, are you 100% sure that he is telling you the truth?" O'Healy asked.

"To be honest, I didn't know what to do. I just thought it would be best to shield you from the situation to avoid putting you in a difficult position."

"But, Toney, that's exactly what you've done! Now what am I supposed to do? Just forget I ever saw this?"

"This was a one-time thing. It's never happened before, and it's not going to happen again. And yes, I believe him. I'm sure he *will* pay me back and it will be like nothing ever happened. Let's not ruin our season over this."

O'Healy sat quietly in his chair and just stared at Toney, as if trying to figure out whether to fire him right there on the spot or just yell at him some more. But he was too confused and conflicted to do anything at that moment.

"Just . . . get out of here for now. I have to think about what I'm going to do," said O'Healy in a low grunt.

"Trust me: this is not worth ruining our season over."

"Just go! Go!"

As Toney left his office, O'Healy sat there staring at the ceiling. He was thinking about all the difficult decisions he had made in his time as a head coach. He was thinking about Diego and how he had carried the team on his back during the conference tournament. He was thinking about the increasing chatter in online fora calling for his job. The SeaMonsters fans were *not* very patient. It had been four years since they had last gone to the national tournament, and even though three of those misses were not his fault, the fans were restless and were already calling for his head. Plus to be honest with himself, he had to admit that the team was not performing up to his standards. This was an opportunity to finally create some goodwill for himself, and maybe buy him a little more time to right the ship. If he came forward now, he would lose Diego, and that could be his undoing.

"I can't deal with this now. I have to get the team ready for the next game," muttered O'Healy to himself.

THE FINAL STRAW

It had been four days since O'Healy confronted Toney James in his office. The SeaMonsters had beaten their opponent in the semi-final match of the conference tournament to set up a big championship game against their in-state rivals, the Robots of West State University. O'Healy had forced himself not to think about the incident for the moment. He was just going to coach the team for now. He would deal with James and Salgado later.

When the team finished their last practice before the big game, O'Healy went to his office to pick up his briefcase. As he made his way through the locker room, he saw a few of his players congregated around Salgado's locker. They were all admiring something that Salgado was showing them. O'Healy couldn't make out what it was at first. When one of the students moved, he saw Salgado was wearing a thick gold chain around his neck. He had never seen him wearing that chain before.

O'Healy got very anxious. His thoughts were racing: *Great! This is exactly what I thought was going to happen! He took Toney's money, he used it to buy gangbanger jewelry, and now people are going to start wondering how the hell he got it. This is definitely going to trigger an investigation, and it's all going to come back to me!* He needed to find Toney, quickly.

He left the locker room and went back to the court. As he was making his way through the tunnels, he ran into Toney.

"Toney, did you see the gold chain Salgado's wearing?"

Toney sighed and let his arms drop.

"Yes, I saw it. Don't freak out. It's not what you think."

"No? So he didn't buy that with the money you gave him?"

"Nah, man. It's just an unfortunate coincidence. His uncle, his mom's brother, passed away a couple of days ago, and he left him that chain. His uncle was also a ball player and apparently he had promised to give it to him one day."

"That's *very* convenient timing, don't you think? And how do you know all this?"

"You think you're the first one to freak out? I already had my freak-out this morning! I saw it before the guys started practicing. Salgado came in wearing it, so I asked him. I knew his uncle had died because he told me when it happened. They just gave him the chain last night, after they went through his uncle's things."

"Listen, Toney, this is bad. Okay? Even if I believed the story, which I'm not sure I do, people are going to start asking questions. The money might come up."

"How? How is it going to come up if the chain has nothing to do with the money?"

"That's what you say, but I'm not so sure. Honestly, I think the kid's been playing you since the beginning."

"You need to calm down, Seamus. The kid is telling the truth. I know what I'm telling you. He's using the money to pay the rent on his parents' house and some food for his little brother and sister. He's going to pay it back. It's really not an issue."

"And I'm just supposed to take your word for it!? Put my career on the line based on the word of a coach who might be getting conned by his own players!?"

"Okay, fine. Do what you want! Go and accuse the Latino kid whose uncle just died of hustling his coach out of some money so he can go and buy some gangsta chain. We've worked together for six years now. I thought you trusted me more than that."

O'Healy couldn't believe his ears. Was Toney insinuating what he thought he was insinuating? How dare he! O'Healy didn't even bother answering. He turned around and started walking toward his car. He was hurt, worried, and confused. He opened his car door and sat in the driver's seat without turning on the ignition. He just stared at the arena. *What am I going to do?*

DISCUSSION QUESTIONS

1. What do you think are the choices available to Seamus O'Healy in this scenario?
2. What are the possible consequences for each of those choices?
3. Why do you think Toney makes the distinction between a loan and a bribe/bonus? Does that distinction change your perception about the incident?
4. Why do you think Toney brings up Diego's ethnicity? Do you think it's an important consideration in this situation? Does Diego's ethnicity factor into your own reaction to this case?
5. If you were Seamus O'Healy, how would you resolve this case?

KEY TERMS

Employee relations in sports organizations, Organized collegiate sports, Group roles and norms, Ethnicity in sports

CASE 26: I'M A STAR. GIVE ME AN "A."

Julio A. Rodriguez-Rentas

State University of New York (SUNY)–Westchester Community College

Regina Pappalardo

Mount Saint Mary College

Paul Ziek

Pace University

ABSTRACT

Lisa is excited for the final project for her investigative journalism class. Off to uncover a topic, it turns out to be something more scandalous than she thought. Lisa is faced with an ethical decision. Should she report it and tarnish her university's reputation, or be known as the college snitch?

***

Lisa Rogers sat fidgeting in her chair, itching to get going. She had an idea that couldn't be beat; she just knew it. So when her journalism professor called out, "Alright class, are you ready," Lisa leapt from her seat as if being sprung from a starting gate.

Professor Mendez called out after her, "Don't forget to email me with any questions. Remember, this is 40% of your final grade!"

Lisa bee-lined straight to her dorm room to get her camera and iPad. She already knew that she wanted to investigate the Edgemont University Lions basketball team. Being the editor-in-chief of the *LionPrint* student paper, she knew she could get easy access to what she needed. All these ideas were flowing in and out of her head. *Get to Lions Den Arena*, Lisa told herself as she scurried to the basketball arena. She was sure that for her class final project she would do an investigative report of the average waste a typical Lions game produces.

The campus was beautiful in the spring, with winding paths through serene study gardens branching off of wide thoroughfares lined with red and white flowers–the school colors, of course. To think, as spring comes into bloom, waste from the school's 10,000 students was disappearing somewhere. But where? Lisa jotted down some notes on her iPad while sitting outside the arena.

Looking up from her tablet, she saw a porter and jumped at the opportunity.

"Excuse me," she called out to the man. "Can I ask you a few questions?"

"Who? Me?" asked the porter, Reggie.

"Yes. Hi, my name is Lisa. I'm the editor-in-chief of the *LionPrint* student paper. I'm working on my final project for one of my classes – it's a report on how much waste a typical Lions game produces."

"Waste?" asked Reggie puzzled. "You mean, garbage? Um, well, tons!"

"Hmmm . . . tons, you say? Can you get me an actual number? Is there a company that hauls the trash away? Who's in charge and how much money do you spend on removal?" Lisa could feel herself rushing through her questions, not giving the porter a chance to answer.

With each question, Reggie took a half-step back. He finally held his hand up, prompting Lisa to take a breath. "I'm Reggie. What's your name again, Miss?"

"Lisa." Her fingers tapped her iPad. Was he going to cooperate or not?

"Right. Yes, sorry about that," said Reggie. "You have a lot of good questions. Questions that I'm sorry to say I don't have the answers to. My supervisor's name is Tom Jackson. He's not around today, but if you come back tomorrow morning, you'll catch him."

Not a complete rejection and something of a lead. She thanked Reggie and watched as he disappeared around a corner.

This might be a huge undertaking. How was she going to measure the amount of trash and carbon waste a game produced? Just then, Lisa noticed a door that was ajar with a sign that read *recycling: authorized personnel only*. Undaunted, Lisa looked over her shoulder, and in a stealth move worthy of 007 himself, she passed through the door.

Great. No one is here, she thought. Inside the massive room she noticed separate piles of glass and plastic. *So, this is where everything ends up. I wonder where it goes from here?* Taking another step into the room, she noticed a piece of paper stuck to her shoe. Lisa read it and recognized an assignment of a basketball student-athlete. The top header read: Independent Study Final Paper. She was a little surprised to read "final paper" since there seemed to be only one paragraph on the page. Lisa looked around her feet to make sure there weren't any other pages from that assignment on the floor. What was even more surprising was the letter "A" written in red pen, as if an instructor graded it.

A worker pushed a garbage can down the hallway outside the recycling room. Frozen, Lisa drew a breath and crossed her fingers that whoever it was would keep on walking. She glanced around the room, ready to dive behind a nearby mountain of plastic bottles, blood pounding in her ears. *Please, please, please*, she silently begged no one in particular, the worker in the hallway, anyone. The can rumbled down the hallway and away. Not wanting to risk being discovered, she shoved the paper in her camera pack and, heart still pounding, slunk out of the room and hurried from the building.

DID THIS REALLY HAPPEN?

The entire way back to her dorm, Hays Hall, Lisa kept checking over her shoulder. She turned down Pride Avenue even though she always took Rose Way. She remembered hearing that people under surveillance try to vary their routes so they won't get caught. *You're being ridiculous . . . and paranoid,* she thought. She couldn't quite shake the thought that someone had seen her.

Hays Hall was one of the newer dormitories on campus. The builders went for a modern concrete and steel, industrial structure more fitting of an architecture or engineering school, not a liberal arts college. She always preferred the Manor House, with its fieldstone exterior and rose gardens. Perhaps that was due to her more creative side. Her thoughts turned to the paper she found. She was not thinking creatively now; in fact, she couldn't think what that paper could be. She pulled open the tinted glass and steel door, her sweaty hands slipping on the steel and nearly dropping her camera bag. Her friend, Drew, called out from the booth . . . something about an ID, giving her the business. She waved and headed straight for her room.

When she had first moved into this room, she had been uneasy about not having a roommate after spending two years in a triple, but now she was never more thankful to be by herself. She pushed the door closed and flipped the lock, threw her bag on the bed, and carefully pulled out the paper.

An "A"? Really? The paragraph read like her fourth-grade paper on Rosa Parks. Lisa chuckled. Mendez would have ripped this to shreds if she had turned this in. Heck, her fourth-grade teacher would have done the same. Something was up, of that she was certain.

A knock at the door startled her. After tucking the paper back into her bag, she crept up to the door and peeked through the peephole. What did he want? She unlocked the door and only opened it a hair when Drew pushed in past her.

"What you got in here?" He looked around the room. It was in its usual tidy state. How a college student as overbooked as Lisa maintained such a neat room was beyond Drew. Then again, there were some things about Lisa that always confused him.

Lisa glanced at her bag, hoping Drew would leave it be. "Why? What are you . . . conducting some sort of search for contraband? I have a case of fruit snacks under my bed to buy you off with."

He laughed. "Nah. Not today." He plopped down on the bed next to her bag, papers–including the paper–partially spilling onto her comforter. "You seemed like the devil was after you, so I thought I'd see if everything was okay."

"I'm okay." Could she trust him?

"Really?" He put his hand on the bag, leveling his eyes at her. "This is me, Lisa."

They'd known each other since orientation when Drew helped her find her way out of the catacombs–the study, relaxation, and eating areas under the student center. They hadn't dated, just been very close friends. He was on the lacrosse team . . . he might have some insight. There could be a bigger story here.

"Okay." She shut the door. "You know I have to do that investigative article for my journalism class, right? Well, I didn't get anywhere with a porter over at the arena, but I did see an open door." She sat next to him and pulled the paper out of her bag. "The room was nasty with all this trash and recycling, but I found this paper." She handed it to him. "In what world is that an A?"

Drew read the paper and laughed. "This has got to be a joke."

"Drew, what if it's not? What if professors are just passing athletes? This could be huge. Have you ever run into this?"

"No way," he said, handing the paper back to Lisa. "We'd get our butts kicked if we attempted to hand something like this in. I've never known anyone on lacrosse who had this kind of deal." He leaned back against the wall. "Doesn't mean it couldn't happen. Basketball brings in a lot more money and students than lacrosse does. They also win more championships . . . contenders nearly every year. What are you going to do?"

"Well, there's nothing I can do with just one piece of evidence and no context. I wanted to be an investigative reporter. Now's my chance."

"I could make some discreet inquiries," he offered in a phony accent. Lisa declined . . . for now. So, Drew wished her luck and went back to the booth, but only after Lisa made him promise not to say anything.

Lisa decided her first move would be to speak with a faculty advisor. She trusted her own, though Lisa wasn't 100 percent sure he would have any more knowledge about student-athletes and any "deals," as Drew put it, than they might have.

Lisa didn't waste any time. She looked up her professor's office hours on her class syllabus. "Nice!" Lisa said to herself as she checked the day's date and time. Professor Clark was in his office for another half hour. Lisa rushed out the room and straight to Professor Clark's office in Halfin Hall.

When Lisa got to the outside of Professor Clark's office she saw his door was ajar. *Knock, knock.* "Professor Clark?" Lisa said as she slowly opened the door.

"Hi, Lisa, how are you?" asked Professor Clark. "I'm OK," Lisa said hesitantly, "I'm working on the project, but I found something that I need your feedback on." Lisa held the paper out in her hand. "Let's take a look," said Professor Clark as he grabbed the sheet from Lisa.

Lisa explained how she found the paper and revealed her concerns. "Well, Lisa, I don't have much information on this. This is the first I've heard of this."

"What should I do Professor?" asked Lisa.

"Well, I think you should continue with this and pursue any lead you find. I know this could be big . . . and scary," he told her, "but you should find out the truth. Seek the truth and report it–the number one principle in the journalist's code of ethics. I'll help you in any way I can."

Lisa tapped Drew to make his inquiries on the down low and discovered that yes, this did happen a lot with the basketball team, but of course, no one wanted to go on the record. How could she blow the roof off this story without a source to quote?

About a week later, Lisa received an odd text. "Catacombs. 1:30 today. I have what you need." She shot off a text to Drew, thinking he was jerking her around. It wasn't him, but he offered to be backup for the meet. He would be in the cafe seating area if she needed him.

Ever since that day at orientation–when Drew rescued her from the catacombs–Lisa avoided the place. It always smelled like French fries and pizza but with back notes of body odor, cigarette smoke, and bleach. She descended the stairs, searching every face for a clue. Who was this person and how would she find him . . . her? After nodding to Drew, who was seated with some lacrosse teammates, Lisa moved from the larger of two cafe seating areas down a red-and-white painted cement block hall. Students bumped their way past her when someone tugged on her arm and pulled her into a conference room. The door shut securely behind her and, before she could scream, she recognized her source. It was the assistant coach of the basketball team, Joe MacNamara.

"I heard you've been asking a lot of questions about the team," he said as he moved away from Lisa. He towered over her, but then sat down in a chair at the table as if knowing his size intimidated her a bit.

"Word gets around, I guess." She sat down as well, in a spot closest to the door. The lights were dim in the room, with a flat-screen TV on the far wall and a dry erase board next to it. There was another door, but no windows. Her heart was still pounding from being pulled into this room, but as she took in her surroundings and what this meeting meant, fear gradually turned to excitement.

"We watch tape in here," he explained quietly, then paused. "You should be careful. The team and the coaches, the administration, and the school all have a lot to lose."

Lisa could tell that Coach Joe had not quite made up his mind to say anything, was feeling her out. Would she be courageous enough to take this story all the way? "The students are the ones losing right now, Coach, and I think you know that. Otherwise you wouldn't be here."

He smiled. Joe liked her, could see her as a really good newswoman someday. "So where does that leave us? You know I can't just spill it."

"Well, I guess that means 'on the record' is out."

Joe laughed, nodded, and shifted in his chair. "How about I give you a few names and you take it from there? My name and involvement stays out." He stood up and walked toward her. "I mean it . . . completely out."

Lisa held up her hand in acceptance of the terms. "I understand. Completely out. No involvement. I know enough about protecting a source."

Yes, she would be good someday, on her way, Joe thought. He gave her four names–two students, a parent, and a professor. "That last one," he said about the professor, "told Coach

Robbins he was out of play. I guess his conscience or ethics or whatever got the better of him finally. It wasn't an amicable divorce, either."

Lisa opened her iPad, typed some notes down next to the names, and then looked up at Coach Joe. "How do I contact you again?"

"You don't." He went to a door on the far side of the room and flipped the lights up all the way. "Stay a while. Get some studying done." Then he disappeared through the back door.

What do I do first? Lisa's mind was racing through various scenarios. If these four (FOUR!) sources all talked she could . . . wow . . . bring down the basketball team, coaching staff, administration, perhaps even the school. She pushed the iPad away from her. As she went through every step, carefully, logically, Lisa arrived at the same outcome. Doubt started to creep into her mind, slowly replacing the enthusiasm and excitement of only moments ago when Coach Joe was present. She packed up her things, shut the lights, and exited the room. Fewer students crowded the hall now, study groups replacing lunch circles in the seating areas.

Drew walked up to her, but she waved his questions off. "I'm fine," she called, and repeated "fine" under her breath. The two friends took the usual way back to Hays Hall, Drew staying behind at the dorm security booth to start his shift. He was worried about her, but knew she would tell him if something was really wrong.

Once in her room, Lisa threw her bag on the floor. She pulled out her tablet and stared at the names. Then without any hesitation, she began to write.

***

Professor Mendez stared at the draft in his hands, looked up at Lisa, then down at the draft again. "Shut the door," he said. Once the door clicked shut and Lisa was seated again, he asked her, "They all corroborated this? You have the evidence?"

She nodded.

"Where did you get these names?"

"You know better than to ask me that, Professor," said Lisa. "I can't give up my original source."

Mendez tossed the draft on his desk and leaned back in his chair. "Well, there's already some buzz. The university PR office has contacted me to see if I know anything. Of course, I said no. Now," he paused with a smirk on his face, "well, now I know a lot."

"Do we print it?" Lisa asked nervously.

"Heck, yeah, we print it. And then we brace for the backlash." Mendez softened a bit, seeing the nerves on Lisa's face. "We'll be fine. You've done your work and a damn good job, too. I'm going to confirm your sources, fact check a few things, and then we'll print." He gestured to the door and Lisa opened it, gathered her things. "Needless to say, you'll get an A–a real one–on this project."

She laughed. "Thanks, Professor."

Lisa walked from her professor's office a little straighter, a little taller, with purpose. *So this was what it feels like*, she thought, *to file a story, a good story, a hard-earned story and receive the approval and praise from my editor.* She couldn't wait to see it in print.

A woman with a blond bob stepped in front of her. "Lisa Rogers?"

Lisa took a step back. "Can I help you?"

"May I have a word with you," the woman asked, gesturing to two empty chairs in the corner of the atrium.

There were several students seated in the atrium, plenty of people walking around. The mid-afternoon sun shining through the skylights cast a warm glow in the vast space. She glanced back toward Professor Mendez's office. *Please come out. Please come out.* No luck. Lisa nodded, followed the woman to the chairs.

"Hi, Lisa. I'm Meg Peterson, executive director of public relations here at the university. You've been a busy girl," Meg said. "And you're going to cause a lot of work for me and my team very, very soon, I fear."

"I'm not sure what you're talking about," Lisa replied. This must be the woman who contacted Professor Mendez.

Meg sighed. "Ah, yes, well. Here's what I need from you. A copy of the story, when it will run, a list of your sources, and contact information for each of them."

Lisa slowly shook her head, trying to come up with the words to respectfully tell her no, but Meg held up her hand, putting a stop to anything Lisa might say. "Don't bother saying no. The university's reputation, and frankly, your own as a student and a reporter are on the line. Here's my card. You have until tomorrow morning to get me the information I need." Meg stood and left the atrium.

What does Lisa do now?

DISCUSSION QUESTIONS

1. Would you have thrown away the "Independent Study Final Paper" after finding it in the trash?
2. Would you contact campus police and report the harassment by Meg Peterson? Do you trust Professor Mendez to defend your work?
3. Would you still print your article, even though it would tarnish you college's reputation? Would you change your final project topic if you were Lisa?
4. Would you give your sources up? Why or Why not?

KEY TERMS

Crisis communication, Reputation management, Public relations

CASE 27: PEAK PERFORMANCE

Stephanie Martinez
St. Edward's University

ABSTRACT

North Point Autos has a company softball team originally created by the owner as a fun way to blow off steam and build unity through sport. But is the softball team actually an unpaid, forced work obligation that causes resentment and takes away from family time?

***

Jason Roxford, car salesperson of the year (for the past four years) for North Point Autos, looked at his text messages and sighed. His wife Amelia was angry again and Jason knew she had a right to be angry. Jason had just told her that morning that he was going to miss another family dinner on Sunday. Jason put his head in his hands and rubbed his temples. He contemplated taking another swig from the bottle of Mylanta heartburn medicine in his drawer, but decided he was too young to be this stressed over something so silly. He could not believe he was getting headaches, having stomach problems, and losing sleep over softball. Yes. Softball.

Jason used to love playing softball. A year ago when his car dealership's owner, Bob (Smitty) Smit, decided to create a company softball team (North Point Mavericks) to compete in local games, he was all for it. It started off being a blast. Smitty played in the games too. When the dealership's team had arrived for the first game, they had all joked that it was the first time they had seen the owner without his signature Stetson hat, suit, and cowboy boots.

FRIENDLY RIVALRIES

North Point had a friendly rivalry with another dealership. They all played and went out for beer and barbeque after the first few games. Softball started as a great way to have fun and blow off steam. At first, on Monday mornings, everyone enjoyed reliving the game from the previous Sunday as they drank coffee and ate donuts before the company's team meetings began. Jason had played baseball in high school and had been pretty good at it. Jason started off really

239

enjoying the games, and Smitty liked to call Jason "his secret weapon." Little did Jason know at the time: The volunteer softball team would soon become a continual Sunday obligation.

Sundays were the only day of the week that North Point Autos was not open. As a salesperson, Sunday was literally the only day Jason was not at work, on call, or on his cell phone calling, texting, emailing customers and future customers. It was the only day Jason unplugged to spend what his wife called "quality time' with his family. So, Jason was torn. He loved his job and was really good at it, but he was thinking about looking for a new job or even a new career. His wife was angry. His kids were angry. And softball was no longer just a fun game. Softball was destroying his life.

After receiving the latest text from his wife about missing another Sunday dinner, Jason looked bleakly out the window of the dealership. He didn't even mind it was a slow day and no one was looking at any cars. Samantha Carrizales, one of the sales managers, stopped by his cubicle and chuckled at the expression on Jason's face.

"Let me guess?" she said. Jason groaned out loud.

"You think if I broke my arm or leg I could get out of this game?" Jason replied.

Samantha stopped laughing. "The fact that you are contemplating breaking your bones in order to get out of the game could be the bigger issue," she replied.

"I know. I know," he continued. "But I really need to get out of this week's game or I am going to end up in divorce court. I think even the dog is mad at me. I need to do something," he said and then paused as if trying to think of what else he wanted to say.

"Wellll . . . ?" Samantha prompted.

"Well," he continued, "How do I tell Smitty without him going off the deep end? The last time I tried to get out of a game, he gave me a two-hour lecture on 'being a team player,' and 'taking one for the team,' and my personal favorite was how he did not want me to 'drop the ball' and let the whole dealership down."

"What are you going to do?" Samantha prompted.

"I don't know. I only got a lecture when I tried to skip a few months ago. Did you know Don got put on Internet sales full-time last month right after he skipped the game? Don figured he would just ask for forgiveness instead of permission like me. Well he did ask for forgiveness, but the next thing you know his hours on the floor were cut and he was strictly Internet."

"I knew Don was put on Internet sales, but since he is a part of Rob's team, I hadn't talked to him about it, but I do know that I am soooo happy I don't play softball and never agreed to do it," Samantha said.

"Exactly," said Jason. "No one would have agreed to play if we had known we were signing our lives away."

"I know." Samantha said.

Jason looked over his shoulder and whispered, "I know I am not the only one thinking about looking for a new job. I haven't done anything yet, but I have been thinking about it, Samantha. I do know I can't keep this up. You have to do something and quick."

Samantha knew that she and the dealership did not want to lose Jason. He was one of their best salespeople and just a great guy to work with at North Point. She couldn't say the same thing about everyone. She knew if things kept up the way they were, they were going to lose all their good people. Jason and Samantha spent the next twenty minutes thinking of ways to approach Smitty. They decided it might be best for Samantha and Rob (the other sales manager) to approach the owner. Samantha was hoping that sales figures might help show that, while the softball team had started out as a morale booster, lately it had done the opposite. Samantha knew that, while Smitty loved his softball, he loved sales even more. At least she hoped he did.

Later that day, Samantha stopped by Rob's cubicle.

"Hi Rob. Do you have a minute?" asked Samantha.

"Sure. What's up?" answered Rob.

"Well we have a little bit of a situation. You know the softball team?"

"Yes?" prompted Rob.

"Well, I have been getting some push-back from some of my team. They are tired of playing softball on Sundays and feel like it has become a work obligation rather than voluntary," said Samantha.

"Huh. I haven't heard anything from my people," said Rob.

"I looked over our sales figures and while we are not down for this quarter, we have not increased as much as we wanted. I think this softball issue is taking a toll on our numbers. We need to talk to Smitty about this situation," Samantha continued.

"Go ahead, but since my team is not complaining, I think you need to handle it on your end." Rob crossed his arms and leaned back in his chair. "Honestly, I love the softball team. I look forward to it every week."

Samantha left the meeting with Rob feeling frustrated and knowing she was on her own. She wasn't sure if Rob was in denial, or if he really hadn't heard any complaints. Then again, perhaps he simply didn't want to confront their boss since Smitty was notoriously hard headed. Samantha knew she was not going to sleep well tonight.

TEAM MEETING

Samantha was nervous at the next morning's team meeting. Since she had talked to Jason yesterday, she knew it was past time to confront Smitty. Her boss was just very abrasive. Samantha knew this abrasiveness was how he had built this dealership into the largest in

Texas, but he was losing good people. Just this morning, Don had resigned. He took a job with a competitor. Now Jason was considering leaving. Team morale was in the toilet.

As the sales meeting broke up, Samantha grabbed a cup of coffee and a donut for courage and to avoid the inevitable confrontation ahead of her. She knew she needed to be firm, but compassionate. Samantha knew Smitty loved his softball team. He bragged about it all the time. Samantha wondered if his softball fixation might be a part of empty nest syndrome. Both of Smitty's boys had grown up in Texas football, graduated, and moved on. Smitty and his wife had been huge boosters of the high school football team while their boys had played. Neither one of their sons was playing college ball so Smitty had put his all energy into the company softball team.

Samantha finished her donut and then walked to Smitty's office. She knocked on the door.

"It is open," Smitty hollered.

Samantha opened the door and walked deep into the office. Smitty was sitting at his desk talking on the phone. He gestured for Samantha to take a seat on one of the chairs opposite the desk.

"Oh it is a bet. If you win, I get your box tickets to the UT/Oklahoma game and if I win, I get your tickets," Smitty chortled into the phone.

Samantha had a sinking sensation in the pit of her stomach. She knew Smitty sometimes bet on the Sunday softball games, and now he was betting his beloved University of Texas Longhorns tickets for the biggest game of the season on the outcome of Sunday's softball game. This meeting just got even more stressful. She felt a trickle of sweat go down her back.

"Ok. Ok. We will see," Smitty continued. "I gotta run. I have a meeting. Yep. See you all on Sunday."

Smitty put down the phone with a thump and smiled as he crossed and rested his arms on his stomach. "He has no idea what is waiting for him," he said. "I am really looking forward to Sunday."

Samantha sighed. "We lost Don this morning. He just resigned."

Smitty shook his head. "I know. He is going to work for Crown Motors. I could not believe it after all his years here. We are a family."

Samantha looked directly in Smitty's eyes and said, "I am afraid we may lose Jason."

Smitty smacked his hand down on his desk and stood up. "What? What are you talking about? He is our number one salesman. We cannot lose him."

"I know," Samantha said.

"Well why in the heck would he leave?" Smitty asked.

"I can tell you in one word." She paused.

"Well?" Smitty prompted.

"Softball."

Smitty abruptly sat back down.

Samantha waited. She knew the first person who spoke up here was going to lose this conversation, and she was not going to lose.

After a couple of minutes, Smitty loudly cleared his throat and said, "What do you mean? How could the softball team possibly make Jason leave? We all have fun. We are a team. Heck, he had his peak performance last week. He hit two homers."

"Don left because of softball," she said.

"No Don left because he didn't want to do Internet sales," Smitty stated.

"No Don left because he couldn't go to softball a month ago and you put him strictly on Internet sales the next day. He thought it was a punishment, and I am not saying it was or was not a punishment, but that is what Don thought. He left because he thought after all his years here you were punishing him for not going to the softball game."

"Heck no," Smitty continued. "Ok. I admit I was not happy that he missed that game. It was an important game."

"They are all important games," Samantha interrupted.

"It was an important game, but I did not punish him for not being a good sport," he said.

"You just said he was 'not a good sport,'" Samantha stated. "I know you are passionate about the softball team, but saying Don was not a 'good sport' is not going to help our team—Our team here at work."

"Ok fine. But I did not punish Don. I needed someone strong on Internet sales. I thought he was my man. I was wrong," Smitty admitted.

They both paused for a few minutes. Samantha figured they both were trying to figure out where to go from here.

"Now tell me about Jason," Smitty demanded.

"Well his marriage is falling apart because he keeps spending time at the softball field on Sunday instead spending time with his family. His wife is threatening to take the kids and move to Dallas to be with her Mom," Samantha replied.

"Are you kidding me?" Smitty said.

"Jason has had it. And it is affecting his job performance, and he is not alone. I did a quick informal survey at today's meeting and two other people on your softball team said they have had fights with their families because of the time spent away at night for practices and on Sunday game days," Samantha continued.

Smitty sat in stunned silence.

"Also, I asked the entire sales staff at this morning's meeting if they still enjoyed playing softball and not one person raised their hand," she added.

Smitty took off his Stetson, set it on the desk, and rubbed his eyes. "Well, I just cannot cancel the season. Let me think about it."

Samantha stood up knowing she was dismissed. On her way out, she said, "I know you love the team, but is the team good for our dealership anymore?"

DISCUSSION QUESTIONS

1. Do you think Jason let his feelings about the softball game linger for too long? How would you have handled the situation?

2. Although the softball game could be considered a part of one's social life, in this case the game went from social to part of Jason's work life. Should organizations be able to impose extracurricular activities on employees that cut into their personal lives?

3. Why do you think Smitty was so clearly out of the loop on what was happening in his own business?

KEY TERMS

Occupational and sport identity, Culture, Team building, Leadership, Fandom, Sport metaphors, Sport and hazing, Sport and betting

CASE 28: SACRIFICE AND WINNING
The Difficult Reality of Players, Management, and Contracts

Stephen Puckette
Clemson University

John Spinda
Clemson University

ABSTRACT

As seriously as professional sports are taken in the world, often people forget that it is first and foremost a business. When decisions have to be made, they are not only sports moves, but business choices as well. Athletes are just as much employees as they are sports figures, and their lives outside of the sport are just as relevant as the one in it. This case study will look at an upcoming offseason for a star basketball player named Dalton who faces a tough decision about his pending free agency and future contract. There are many factors involved in this decision including the general manager, Ray, and the owner, Mark. Making a salary-related decision in the professional world involves losing as much as it does winning and this case study seeks to explore the complex difficulties involved in this process.

***

There are many ways to measure a lifetime. Generally speaking most people will look at their life in terms of money or relationships or places lived or if they've ever sung "Seasons of Love" in their high school choir, or cups of coffee. But when looking at the lives of athletes, perhaps the best way to view a life is in windows because that's how most observers chronicle sports. A constant focus of any commentary for a championship level contender over the years is, "How much longer will their window remain open?" Now—putting aside the perplexing metaphor of using a window as a metaphor for opportunity when the reality is that there is probably a perfectly usable and open meta-door in this meta-room that our athletes are probably intelligent enough to use—we use these "windows" to measure these opportunities throughout a career. However, from an athlete's perspective, the windows of a career are only part of a much larger window, the window of life.

And it's the focus on these windows which drives a lot of conflict in today's professional sports world because everyone sees them differently. Athletes are going to view their years at the pro level within the broader picture of their lives. For many, this will be the period of their lives when they will make the majority of their earnings. Some prepare themselves well, others do not, but the reality is that once you hit your mid-30s, "Father Time," who remains undefeated, starts to break down the body and no matter how you try to fight it, he'll win. Although fans and teams may love and support their players to the bitter end, the reality is that eventually it all fades away. This is what can make contract negotiations so testy; athletes are looking out for themselves and management is looking out for the team.

BACKGROUND

Easing into his seat at the podium with slumped shoulders, Dalton takes a deep breath and adjusts the microphone. The weight of another early playoff exit, unmet expectations, and his looming free agency only add further discomfort to the throbbing he's felt all season in his lower back. In many ways, though, he will feel relieved to finally get some rest. His mind flashes back to just a few years ago when he re-signed to man the middle for the Virginia Beach Bombers, back when he was loved without question and his back could still bear the daily grind of playing center. In front of him sits probably two dozen individuals whose credentials range from the local news to a prominent fan blog and even a second-tier reporter from a major sports network who's followed him closely for the past several years. Despite their differences in background, their questions are all going to sound the same to him. Just by glancing at his Twitter mentions from the past few days he already knows full well what to expect. Another All-NBA nod and the farthest he can make it is the first round? Does he still think he's a superstar? Is his back going to limit him going forward from being the player he was just two years ago? Is he going to stick with his hometown or risk being labeled a traitor for chasing a ring or more money? They all claim to want to know the truth, but "I don't know" evidently isn't honest enough and his agent's stern gaze reminds him of that.

Dalton has long been the face of the Bombers, but the franchise is at a crossroads. Different teams have different standards. For some teams it's championships or bust. For others it's making the playoffs. For others . . . well they don't really care. Perhaps the worst place to be in the NBA is pretty good. Ideally you want to be a contender, a move or two in the next few years away from being a contender or blowing everything up and rebuilding. But being pretty good is a no-man's land and for the majority of Dalton's career that's what the Bombers have been. They've made the Conference Finals twice, one was a lopsided series against the eventual champs and the other was a competitive seven-game series. Other than those two seasons, Dalton has only advanced past the first round one other time and hasn't advanced in five years. And, while the fans love him, this is also one of the most popular franchises in the league and they are starting to agitate for another championship banner to be hung.

ISSUES OFF AND ON THE COURT

Part of it is the talent. There's only so much you can do when your best teammate since getting here was washed up. He's expressed to the media every way possible short of just saying they're terrible, but still nothing from management. He could try his hand at recruiting some new teammates again but everyone he talked to last time knew that the Bombers had no chance. It's only gotten worse since then.

A rookie reporter pipes up with a well-worn question about Dalton's relationship with his coach, Sam. Pursing his lips, Dalton forces out a terse reply about his focus on the team winning. "Even though Coach and I don't always see eye-to-eye, we both have the same goal in mind." "Don't always" is an understatement and everyone knows that. The sideline videos and locker room rumors have been something he's had to address all season. . .Sam is widely regarded as a sound defensive coach—although the numbers would disagree—and although the team was successful in his first season, they've dropped off considerably since then. Dalton would love for nothing more than to see yet another coach go and for management to get someone who gave him more freedom to play the way he wanted to. . .The trouble is that Sam has two years left on his contract, which means the team is stuck with him unless they want to swallow their pride and money—mainly the pride part for this franchise.

Dalton can tell the media are growing a little frustrated with his platitudes. He scans the crowd impatiently, hoping that they realize they won't be getting anything good today. He locks eyes with one person, however, a man he's never been able to read no matter how hard he's tried. This man is the team's general manager whom many would describe as a "lapdog" of a general manager. This GM is good friends with the owner and really does everything to keep the owner happy, which often means signing the splashiest names he can fine for way too much and inevitably having it not work out. Dalton smirks as he pictures the GM wearing a bejeweled collar with a leash being held by the owner. The old owner was once regarded as the best in the league, if not in sports, because he was able to put the franchise in a position for success year after year. However, as he got older he seemed to care more about the perks of being an owner rather than trying to win. Regardless though, he was an owner who was beloved by players and coaches. He had a great personality and would cater to their needs. But, halfway through Dalton's career, the owner died and was replaced by his son, Mark.

Mark is nothing like his father and is described as spoiled, entitled, and petulant by just about everybody. He's exactly everything Dalton hates about the billionaire owners. Upon receiving the team he fired just about everybody and set out to make a name for himself which meant getting rid of several people Dalton actually got along with. Many would argue that Mark's main focus is himself and then the team. This is especially true with personnel decisions: Mark has to have his way in everything. The more the media describes him as incompetent the more it drives him to keep making the decisions so that people will respect his genius. The first few years of his ownership were a spiral of actions and reactions resulting in the debacle of this season where the team woefully underperformed. Finally, in an indirect admission of surrender, Mark hired a new team general manager and promised to cede control to him. This new general manager , Ray, is a widely respected person in the league. He is 12-year veteran who then did several years as an analyst and TV personality before moving to a team to be in charge of player operations. He's regarded as being a calming influence and possesses a great understanding of not only the game but of people as well.

DALTON'S DECISION

It's clear though as the team is headed into the offseason that nobody in the franchise is happy with where they are. Unfortunately to complicate matters, this offseason will be tricky. Dalton is currently in the fourth year of his five-year contract with a player option for the fifth year. For Dalton it's an interesting decision. A new Collective Bargaining Agreement (CBA) has been created since his previous contract and, unfortunately for Dalton and the players, the max contract money is not the same as it used to be. So if he did opt out he would not make as much money as if he were to ride out the remainder of his contract. The catch is that if he does opt out then he will enter Restricted Free Agency and if he wanted to leave the Bombers for another team they would have the ability to match the contract and keep him. If Dalton chooses to remain for the rest of his contract then he will go into Unrestricted Free Agency and can choose wherever he wants. Another card that the Bombers have in their pocket though is that they can offer Dalton a five-year deal worth around $115 million; whereas anyone else can only offer him a four-year contract in the mid $90 million range. His agent has also floated the possibility that with a massive cap hike looming there's a chance he could make even more.

As a 30-year-old center this will probably be Dalton's last chance at "big money." Although he hasn't been ready to admit it even to himself, the fleeting notion that he's no longer who he once was is becoming more and more apparent. Getting out of bed after a hard-fought game can be its own battle, and it's even harder when you're on the road in a hotel bed. It's just not easy to play at the level he's been accustomed to. Of course, based on his production and the reality in the NBA (that is, if you're over seven feet and can "walk and chew bubble-gum at the same time" you can get a deal), then he'll probably still be in the league well into his late 30s. But after this next deal he very likely won't be the same player. He could play out the rest of his contract but that would run the risk of another year of wear and tear on the body, which could threaten an injury that would affect a long-term contract.

Based off of what his agent has been pushing for, it seems the best option will be to test the market. It's clear that Dalton can't carry a team by himself anymore. Although the end of the road is still far away, his legacy is something that's become increasingly important over the past season. He's come to terms with the fact that he may never make everyone happy, at least winning a championship could shut out most of the complaints from his critics. To make the dream a reality, though, there will need to be changes. The first issue is the coach. Sam was hired in large part because Mark wanted him after consecutive seasons of deep playoff runs. It's clear though that he isn't working at this point. For Dalton, the best option would be to get rid of him and let Ray put in his own people. This will be an interesting test between Ray and Mark as it will be a chance for Mark to prove whether or not he's turned a corner in letting his staff do their jobs. To fire Sam would not only require Mark to pay him the remainder of his $4 million dollar contract but also force him to swallow his pride. If Mark refuses, it will not only upset Ray but Dalton's chances for returning, the fans, and the media as well.

If Mark does choose to fire him, then the next step in replacing Sam will be difficult as well. Dalton will want a say in the decision. For, as great as Ray is perceived to be, there are worries that he will favor one of his former media buddies, who is untested, for this position. If Dalton doesn't agree with the choice then he could up and leave. It will also reflect poorly on Mark, Ray, and the Bombers though if this new coach is a flop.

To complicate matters further, other teams are looking to poach Dalton and can do so convincingly. One team, the St. Louis Spirits, is lacking at center but if they could get Dalton then they would be immediate contenders. Plus living in St. Louis would actually make Dalton more money than one would expect due to the state not having an income tax. For as much as people complain about how much he makes, most of them don't realize how much he loses to taxes and other financial obligations like his extended family. The Seattle Supersonics are another intriguing choice for Dalton. Although probably not as ready for a championship run they have a former assistant for the Bombers as their head coach whom Dalton remains close to. The Sonics also have some young talent that far exceeded expectations this season and will likely have a top-five pick in a loaded draft that could land them a key piece for a championship run in a few years if Dalton is willing to wait. Another reality for Dalton is his wife is getting tired of Virginia Beach. For, as much as he hates dealing with an upset coach or reporters, dealing with an upset wife might be the hardest because she's actually someone he truly loves and respects. If she doesn't like the new deal he gets from the team and he still takes it, he'll never hear the end of it from her. One positive he's come to realize though is that for the most part it seems the fans will still support him no matter where he goes. This at least makes it a little bit easier to consider other options.

By and large, Ray and Mark have made it increasingly clear over the past few months that they want to retain Dalton by whatever means possible. But the unspoken truth is that if he really wants a championship to happen, it will mean he will have to make sacrifices himself; not just sharing the ball but financially as well. Due to some previous poor management decisions, there are several salaries clogging up space for the next season. But after that the Bombers will be open to sign some quality talent. However, if he signs the max contract it will seriously compromise the Bombers' chances at getting other superstar talent. This means that he will likely have to take a self-imposed pay cut if he wants the Bombers to be a contender. But, he also knows that, given his age, his back, and the chance that the team's moves in the offseason might not work out, he won't have a chance to make big money again.

CONCLUSION

Winning at the professional level takes sacrifice, as anyone will tell you. However, the idea of sacrifice is far different from the reality. Sacrifice involves pride and money, neither of which is in short supply at the professional level, and these two often take precedent over winning. Of course, even if you play your cards right, there's no guarantee of success. Luck plays a role as well. No matter what choices Dalton, Ray, and Mark make, there will be consequences and unforeseen results. In sport, winning is defined by victory on the field or on the court, but in life winning is much more subjective. Ultimately, the choices these three will make will be defined by whose interest they are choosing to serve and what each party means by "winning."

DISCUSSION QUESTIONS

1. What strategies can be used to clarify a lot of perceptions in this case, which may actually be misperceptions?

2. If you were Ray, the new general manager, and wanted to sign Dalton, what would you communicate to him and how?

3. How should Dalton express his feelings to the new general manager and to the team owner?

4. What public communication strategies can high-profile athletes use successfully to allow fans to see their perspective in a given contract or free-agency situation?

KEY TERMS

Management-athlete relationships, Perceptions and communication, Professional athletes

CASE 29: BUT IN THE END, IT WASN'T ENOUGH

Jason S. Wrench
SUNY New Paltz

ABSTRACT

Sport contract negotiations can be the beginning or end of one's professional career. What happens to a player who loses one opportunity to play professional ball only to find out that his chances of ever really getting back in the game start to disappear?

***

"Let's start by discussing the elephant in the room," Scott Levinson said as he looked across his desk. "When I first started in this business, I knew nothing about sports, let alone baseball. I shared an apartment with my best friend in high school's little brother. He had come to Smithville University on a baseball scholarship and stayed in the dorm for a year and then roomed with me while I was going through law school. During his senior year, he started getting scouted and he turned to the only lawyer he knew for advice. Now 23 years later he's in the MLB Hall of Fame and I have a client list of 107 baseball players coast-to-coast." Scott paused for a second letting what he had just said sink in. "I would not be sitting here today if you hadn't been coached by a long-time friend of mine. Let's face it, you've dug yourself into a hole over the past three years because of horrible decision making on your part."

"Hey, that's not fair . . ."

"Not fair, let's talk about what's not fair," Levinson flatly responded. "It's not fair that I'm sitting here today with you wasting my time on what appears to be a man who has continuously self-sabotaged his own career. You passed up contracts from not one, not two, but three major league baseball teams because you didn't like their offers. Most college baseball players would have jumped at a contract that first year, but you decided to be greedy. Not sure what the hell happened those next two years, but you kept saying 'no' and you kept seeing your chance of making a career at the game disappear. Now you're playing for an independent league team making $1,000 a month."

Matt Boras hung his head, not finding any way to combat what Mr. Levinson was saying. He just kept looking at his hands sitting in his lap, wondering, *How did it get this far?*

"Now," Levinson's gruff voice refocused Boras' attention to the imposing figure sitting in front of him. "Here are my conditions on temporarily taking you on as a client. First, you will be working with one of my junior associates, Stephanie Little. Two, you will do what Ms. Little tells you to do when she tells you to do it. Three, the two of you," Boras gestures to Matt's parents sitting on either side of him, "will stay out of this completely."

"Now wait a second, you listen to me . . ." Boras' father started to say.

"No!" Levinson barked, "You listen to me." Levinson started looking Boras' father directly in the eyes. "If you want to see your son play ball, then you need to stop giving your son 'advice' and let him make his own decisions. Trust me, I know how your 'advice' tanked his last three negotiations and I will not put up with that kind of nonsense at my firm."

"Then we'll just go somewhere else."

"Please do," Levinson said flatly, "and your son will never see the inside of a professional ball field unless he's bought tickets or is cleaning it." Levinson waited for a few beats before continuing, "And Four, my commission rate will be 5%."

"What!?" Boras' parents should in unison.

"This is madness," his father yelled.

"Highway robbery," his mother added.

"Come on son, we're leaving." Boras' father grabbed him by the arm and started to lift him out of the chair.

"No, I'm not going," Boras said in a whispered voice that contained years of anger behind it. "I want to play. You two killed my chances for the past three years. Now, this man," gesturing toward Levinson, "is willing to ensure I get a shot this time. So no, I'm not going with you. I'm not listening to you. I'm not going to be your puppet anymore."

Boras' parents just stood looking from Boras to Levinson in a state of shock. Finally, Boras' father grabbed his mother gently, saying, "Clearly, we're not wanted here anymore. You've both made that abundantly clear."

Boras' parents started leaving Levinson's office when his mother turned around and said, "Honey," locking eyes with her son, "we'll see you back at home. I hope you know what you're doing."

HEY, ROOKIE! YOU WERE GOOD

Matt Boras was one of the kids who knew from an early age that he wanted to play baseball. Some of his earliest memories involved him and his father sitting in front of the television watching the games. His father, though not athletically inclined himself, had a real passion for baseball. He never liked those "other" sports like football or basketball because only baseball was the true "American" sport. Matt always remembered his father saying, "There's a reason why baseball is called 'America's favorite pastime'!"

As soon as Matt could carry a bat and hold a glove, he was playing every summer. He started off playing tee-ball and quickly moved on to the pony league and rose through various ranks starting at age five with the Shetland League all the way through Palomino League. Although he could have kept playing for one more year with the Palomino League when he graduated from high school at 18, he decided it was time to really focus on college baseball.

Matt was scouted by Division I teams all across the country. His parents drove or flew him to many of universities from UCLA to the University of Florida to check out their programs. But Matt was determined to go where he thought he would be the most challenged, so he ultimately signed with the University of Louisiana, which was ranked #1 at the time for Division I baseball teams. Both of Matt's parents were schoolteachers, so they decided to pick up their Iowan lives and move to Baton Rouge with Matt.

As a kid who had grown up in rural Iowa, so Baton Rouge was the first large city he had ever lived in. He started off as a second-string pitcher and didn't see too much play during his freshman and sophomore years. The coach had warned him early on that the pitcher, Daryl Jones, was a "monster" who was rarely injured and could pitch multiple games without tiring. As luck would have it, Jones tore his rotator cuff at the beginning of the season of Matt's sophomore year. Instead of admitting the amount of pain he was in, Jones just kept plugging away. However, the team's trainers started figuring out something was wrong and eventually forced him to go see an orthopedic surgeon at the university's medical school. Jones' rotator cuff had been put beyond any form of sane limits, so he ended up needing rest and cortisol injections. The surgeon warned Jones not to play anytime soon if he wanted to avoid surgery.

The team was completely dismayed when Jones told the team he was out for the rest of the season.

"Who's going to pitch now?" asked first baseman Ricardo Rodriguez.

"The coaches are in a meeting right now. It's too late in the season to recruit a new pitcher, so they're looking at the second-string guys to see who is prepared," Jones responded. "Basically, I've been told that we're not having practice today while the coaches make their decision. Instead, all of you should hit the weight room."

Within 30 minutes Matt was asked out of the weight room and told he would be stepping into Jones' shoes for the rest of the year. The coaching staff had been impressed with Matt's ability to keep plugging along without making waves over the previous year and a half. Too many college athletes think they cannot be replaced coming out of high school, so they often get angry when forced to a second-string position for the first couple of years on the team. Matt, on the other hand, clearly just had a love for the game and was glad to be part of the LSU team.

For the rest of the season, Matt garnered some impressive statistics. He had a .301 batting average and IP = 114, BB/9 = 4.15, SO/9, = 9.06, and ERA = 2.59 pitching stats.[1] Overall,

Matt's sophomore year ended up being a resounding success. He quickly became one of baseball's names to watch.

MAKE THIS DREAM COME TRUE

Matt's junior and senior years flew by in a whirlwind of classes and baseball. During his senior year his starts stayed consistent and he was scouted by a number of different teams. Along with the different team scouts Matt started fielding calls from a number of different agents. As Matt was busy finishing school and the season, he left a lot of the decision-making power to his parents. His parents met with the agents initially and Matt really only got involved after his parents gave an agent a thumbs up. As the season and semester were quickly ending, Matt and his parents decided to go with Roland Salazar.

Salazar was impeccably dressed and very slick. Although Salazar's background was primarily in football, he had started representing a number of baseball players over the past five years.

"Going with my firm will ensure that you have a lot more individualized attention. We only represent seven baseball players for a reason. We could easily recruit more, but we like to focus on a select clientele, unlike some of those larger people mills," Salazar informed Matt when they first met. Both Matt and his parents liked the idea of a more individualized approach to being an agent. Many of the larger agencies told them flat out that the names above the door generally only work directly with the top 5 to 10 percent of their talent. So right before the early June draft, Matt signed with Salazar.

***

On first night of the draft, Matt sat between his parents on a couch looking at a large screen TV in the living room of their house. All of his coaches, family members, and friends were sitting on every possible seat in the room. Matt was wearing the customary LSU polo and jeans. As the draft began to air on the MLB Network live from their studio in Secaucus, New Jersey, Matt sat in silence waiting to hear what his fate would be.

"In the third pick, the San Diego Padres select Jose Garcia. A left-handed pitcher from the University of North Carolina. Raleigh, North Carolina. The Chicago Cubs are now on the clock."

Matt was happy to see that Jose had been drafted so early. He'd known Jose since the two were kids. Although the two never played together, the top-tier players tended to know each other. Matt also knew that Jose's stats were admittedly better than his, but not by much. Matt could feel the sweat forming on his palms and rubbed them off against his jeans. *Stay cool,* Matt thought to himself. *Just remember, Salazar expects you to get picked up tonight.* In fact, all of the predictions figured Matt would be somewhere in the top 20 if not the top 10. *Just keep it together.* Admittedly, he hadn't slept in two days. He was hitting the gym three times a day trying to drain some of his energy, but he just couldn't sleep. *You're going to draft, it's just a matter of where.*

"In the eighth pick, the Pittsburgh Pirates select Matthew Boras . . ."

Matt's dad turned and embraced him and he could feel his mother's arms embrace him as well. He just sat there frozen for what seemed like an hour before he felt himself burying his head into his father's shoulders as tears started streaming down his face. He had worked so long and so hard to get to this point.

The rest of the night was a blur. At some point, Salazar called to congratulate him and tell him that he'd be reaching out to the Pirates in the morning on his behalf to start contract negotiations.

SURE, KID. WATCH OUT YOU DON'T GET KILLED.

The negotiation clock was officially ticking. Now that the Pittsburgh Pirates had officially offered him a contract, he had to sign on the dotted line by July 15th or face becoming a free agent.

The first contract was what was anticipated. The contract stipulated that Matt would earn $3.47 million over two years, which was pretty common for an eighth pick in the league. However, Matt's parents weren't completely happy.

"What do you mean he only gets a $3 million bonus?" Matt's dad questioned, sitting in Salazar's office. "At his point in the draft, he should be getting at least a $3.4 million bonus."

"You've got to remember that the Pirates only have a $6.2 million draft bonus pool. Your son is getting almost half of what they have."

"Maybe so, but from what I've read online, those above him and below him are getting at least their immediate salary as a bonus. If the Pirates want our son, they're going to have to compensate him," Matt's dad barked.

Matt sat in the room watching his agent and dad go back and forth like this for a while as they created a strategy to get him what he "deserved."

***

Over the next three weeks, the negotiations between Salazar and the Pirates grew in intensity. As the negotiations lingered both Salazar and Mr. Boras dug their heels in deeper determined to get Matt a "fair" contract. On July 14th at 11:00 PM, Salazar called to tell Matt that the negotiation with the Pittsburgh Pirates had officially fallen through.

"Don't worry Matt," Salazar said. "These things happen. I'm sure there are a number of teams who will gladly snatch you up now that you're a free agent. I'll start making the calls first thing tomorrow and see what we can get going."

"Thanks, Mr. Salazar. I know you've really worked hard for me thus far. I know you're just looking out for me . . . like my father."

***

Matt kept his hopes up, but the offers just didn't roll in. He was finally drafted by one of the independent league teams called the Corn Rebels in Normal, Illinois. Unfortunately, he ended up having a disappointing season, so his prospects were not nearly as bright as they had been the previous year in the draft. This time, his father had encouraged him to drop Salazar as his agent and go with a newer agent named Nikolas Daly who seemed more intent on making his son a star. Nevertheless, he was chosen as a 62nd pick by The Mariners and was offered a $1.25 million contract over four years and a $260,000 signing bonus. Once again, Matt found himself in the middle of a contract negotiation.

"That number is insulting!" Matt's dad barked. "How can his prospects go from $3.5 over two years to $1.25 over four years in just one year?

"It's the reality of the business, sadly," Daily started explaining. "Your son had a better year his last year of college than he did with the Corn Rebels."

"Maybe so, but his stats weren't that far off the mark."

"Again, it's the nature of the game. The different major league clubs want to see growth from year to year, and Matt just didn't give them growth. In fact, Matt looked less impressive as a whole."

That evening Matt and his parents sat around the kitchen table. Matt's father was livid.

"I just don't see how you can drop so far because of one perfectly normal season?" his mother questioned.

"That's just it, Mom, the season wasn't normal for me. Sure I had a decent season. In fact, it was a better than average season, but 'better than average' just isn't want the major leagues want."

"Well, even if you had an 'average' season," his father responded, placing an added emphasis on the word "average." "That still doesn't explain why their offer to you is so low. Other guys in your league are getting deals."

"Trust me, I've looked," Matt responded. "I know all too well what other guys are getting and what I'm not getting. Sadly, the situation is what it is." Matt looked from his father to his mother before saying, "I think I should just take the offer."

The shock and outrage that quickly was expressed on both of his parents' faces was immediate and startling. "We did not sell our house in Iowa and move to Louisiana and then to Illinois so you could settle!" his father yelled as a grabbed a dinner roll and chunked it across the kitchen. "We've given you so much, and this is how you repay us!?"

"Matt, I'm with your father on this one. I just think it's in everyone's best interests here to be level-headed and negotiate harder."

Looking at both of his parents, he could see how much this really meant to them. Right then and there, he knew he would to call his agent in the morning and ask for a better contract. Even if the voice in the back of his mind kept saying, *It's your contract, not theirs.*

***

Once again, the contract ended up falling apart at the last minute and Matt found himself without a team. The Corn Rebels were not enthusiastic about keeping him, so they refused to even look at him again. This time, he was seen by only a handful of teams and most of them simply were not interested. Instead, he ended up playing in the Nippon Professional Baseball League, commonly known as the Japanese Baseball League. He ended up playing in the Pacific League for the Tohoku Rakuten Golden Eagles in Sendai, Miyagi, which was the newest team to enter the league. His new agent said he didn't work with the Nippon League, so he was dropped as a client.

Matt had a better year than he had with the Corn Rebels, but still not as good as he had when he was at LSU. Overall, the Japanese fans were pretty amazing, but having to relearn a sport he loved was harder than he had expected. The biggest challenge as a pitcher was learning to pitch with a baseball that was wound tighter and harder. When he first started practicing, he could clearly tell the difference in the hardness of the ball as he caught it in his mitt, but over time he grew to work with the new ball.

At the end of the year, it was once again time for him to rethink his options. By this point he'd already gone through two agents, lost two opportunities, and wasn't sure what to do. He finally broke down one night and called up his college coach. On the third ring, someone answered.

"Hello?" a woman's voice came over the line.

"Is Coach in?"

"Just a second," he heard Coach's wife waking him up.

Great! What time is it there? He looked at his watch and saw that it was 6:00 PM. *So, Louisiana is 13 hours behind us, which would make it 5:00 AM.*

"Hello," a groggy voice said as he came to the phone.

"Coach. I am so sorry to call you this early in the morning. I totally forgot about the time differential."

"Matt Boras? Is that you?"

"Yeah Coach."

"Honey, I'm going to take this call in the study."

Matt could hear Coach hand the phone to his wife as he went into the study and picked up the phone there. "Got it," Coach said into the phone. Matt could hear the light clicking sound as his wife hung up the phone.

"I am so sorry to call you this early," Matt began again.

"Don't worry about it, son. I'm generally up right around this time of morning anyway. So, why did you call? I'm guessing it's not just to talk about the weather in Japan."

"Oh, you know where I am?"

"Of course I know where you are. I know where all of my former players end up. Keep a logbook in my office and track them every year. The big donors like that kind of information."

"Well, sorry I've been such an utter disappointment, Coach."

"You're not a disappointment, boy. Clearly, you've made some dumbass decisions since you graduated, but you're not a disappointment. So again, what can I do for you?"

"I need a sounding board. I can't talk to my parents. You remember how they are?"

"God, do I ever. And people think stage parents are bad because they've never met a sport parent before. And your parents were in a league all by themselves."

"Tell me about it," Matt responded. "So, I'm looking at going into my third draft this year. I still need to find an agent."

"I may be able to help you there. But if I do this for you, you cannot screw it up this time. This could be your last real shot at an MLB contract. Unless you want your career to stop before it ever gets a chance to start, you need to start humbling yourself and realize that you're no longer the 'it' kid you once were."

"Trust me, Coach. If the last two years have taught me anything, it's that this business doesn't care how good you were in college. The teams only care about how good you are now and whether they think you're worth the effort to make you better."

IT WOULD KILL SOME MEN TO GET SO CLOSE TO THEIR DREAM AND NOT TOUCH IT.

Matt met with Stephanie Little of Levinson Sport Associates shortly after his meeting with Scott Levinson. She once again laid out Mr. Levinson's rules for Matt.

"If I see or hear from one of your parents, you will no longer be my client. Is that understood?"

"Yes ma'am."

"Right answer. So, let's see what we can do. Let's start by you telling me how we got to this point."

Matt was surprised that she didn't have more information on his history, but he dove into the long drawn-out saga of the past two years. "So that's my story."

"Good, it matches with what I've learned already."

"You mean you already knew this?"

"Of course I knew this. I just needed to know if you realized what your situation is right now."

***

Over the next two months, Stephanie Little shepherded him through the draft process for the third time. This time, he was picked up by the Philadelphia Phillies in the third round. The contract offer was $510,00 with a $512,00 signing bonus. Once again, his parents were really upset by such a low-ball number, especially after his stats had improved over the previous year in the Nippon Professional Baseball League. Matt did his homework and realized that most of the players from the previous year's draft were getting paid only slightly higher than his offer. His parents told him to reject the offer outright and get a better one this time because his luck was changing. He thought he should negotiate for at least what last year's draft picks were making. He hated these decisions. *Of course, that's how I got here. I never made any decisions. I just let everyone around me make them.* Matt picked up the phone and punched in Stephanie Little's cellphone.

"Hello?"

DISCUSSION QUESTIONS

1. Where do you think the communication has broken down over the past three seasons?

2. When it comes to the previous negotiations, who is most responsible: Matt, his agent, or his parents? Why?

3. Knowing what you know now, how should Matt handle this negotiation?

KEY TERMS

Contract negotiation, Player-agent communication, Family communication

[1] IP – Number of innings Pitched; BB/9 – Base on Balls over 9 Innings; SO/9 – Strikeouts over 9 Innings; and ERA – Earned Run Average

PART 5
THE CULTURE OF SPORT

INTRODUCTION

The "Culture of Sport" encompasses many areas of study. For our purposes, the cases in Part Five focus mostly on the demographic issues of gender, sexuality, race, and religion in the sport industry. But we also have cases that involve fan culture. When we look at the culture of sport, we are investigating more nuanced aspects of the sport world. For those of you who are taking classes on the rhetoric of sport culture, these cases will likely resonate with what you are discussing in such classes.

Issues in this section demonstrate how sport affects culture and how an ever-changing culture can affect sport. Real-world events that would fit into this section of the book include stories such as Augusta National Golf Club finally opening its doors to female members in 2012.[1] Certainly the campaigning against the club by a number of elite athletes and the decision making that went on behind the scenes would make for a great case to analyze. Similarly, instances of letting women in to play a variety of male-dominated sports (and visa versa— men to play female sports) would make for great case studies. Case 33 provides just such a case for you to contemplate.

Another real-world case that cases in this section might remind you of would be the media storm surrounding a gold medal Olympian, formerly known as Bruce Jenner, as she transitioned to become Caitlyn Jenner in 2015. Although this transition itself has nothing to do with sport, the way that American society communicated about an American sport hero as she transitioned has everything to do with sport communication. You will get to consider a similar situation in Case 34 of this section.

Race and religion are two other factors that are important to consider when discussing the culture of sport. Some have argued that sport itself is inherently conservative and helps to consolidate patriotism, nationalism, and racism.[2] Then again it has some inherent properties that make it a possible instrument of integration and harmonious race relations as well.[3] How does sport consolidate racism? The most apparent example comes in the inequity of African Americans represented in the upper echelons of the sport industry. When so many of our amazing athletes are African American, but then are not represented in the levels of management and ownership where the major decisions are made, it begs the question: Who is profiting from the athletic performances of African American athletes?[4]

At the same time, sport can bring races together. Nelson Mandela knew this when he used the South African National Rugby Team and its 1995 season as a way to help the people of South Africa bond during his first years as their president.[5] When players and fans from many backgrounds and races come together as a team or to root for a team, they get to experience a common goal and camaraderie with people from other races that they may not have had a chance to experience before. Thus, the sport world can often open up a new world for some people and help them look past differences such as skin color. Cases 32 and 37 give you a chance to examine race relations and (in Case 32) religious differences in the sport world.

Ethical issues concerning the culture of sport abound. What is fair for all involved in a sport is often a point of contention. These ethical issues often involve race, sex, ableism, and other demographic aspects. The cases in Part Five give you the chance to ask yourself about fairness versus tradition. You can delve into the intricacies of dealing with individuals and their needs while also trying to meet the expectations of fans and the community. Having the chance to discuss these issues with fictional cases will help you to intelligently discuss them when real-world cases occur with similar events during your own careers in the sport industry.

As you read these cases and begin to discuss ways to approach solving the problems laid out, consider the following concepts that you might have been learning about in your sport communication class as you talk about sport culture:

- Diversity issues (race relations, stacking, stereotypes, tokenism);
- Organizational culture;
- Hegemonic masculinity;
- Myths, heroes and ritual in sport;
- Gendered language in sport;
- and sexual disparagement (and use of social media in such disparagement)

REFERENCES

[1] Crouse, K. (20 August 2012). "Augusta National adds first two female members." *New York Times*. Retrieved from http://www.nytimes.com/2012/08/21/sports/golf/augusta-national-golf-club-to-add-first-two-female-members.html?_r=0

[2] Jarvie, G., & Reid, I. (1997). Race relations, sociology of sport and the new politics of race and racism. *Leisure Studies* 16, 211–219.

[3] Ibid.

[4] Ibid.

[5] Getz, A. (9 December 2009). The real story of 'Invictus.' Newsweek.com Retrieved from http://www.newsweek.com/real-story-invictus-75669

Michele Tafoya
NBC sideline reporter for *Sunday Night Football*

Don't think like a man. Don't think like a woman. Think like a reporter.

That was the rule I gave to myself as I entered the business of sports television and radio.

I got into the business at a time when people would categorize women as "female sports reporters." Such classifications still exist in the minds of many, but they never existed in mine. My goal was to compete with all.

Naturally, women were scrutinized for their knowledge and presentation far more than any man–regardless of his experience or talent — ever was.

That critical observation, although unfair, was a reality I knew I would have to deal with, just as a pilot must deal with rough air.

So I prepared, did my homework, and never left a question that I knew my subject matter as well as anyone.

Basketball legend John Wooden once said, "Failing to prepare is preparing to fail." I took those words to heart and reminded myself of that necessity every time I began to tire of my research. (As an aside, I recommend Wooden's books for all sorts of wisdom and encouragement.)

I think the combination of accepting reality and being prepared to overcome obstacles, no matter how unjust they appeared, was essential as I was starting out.

Advice? Remind yourself that you are not working against the industry, you are working within it and therefore must be ready for its hurdles. Be confident that you will overcome the challenges. They are, after all, learning opportunities.

There are countless examples of people who have broken stereotypes, defied traditional roles, and succeeded in sports broadcasting. Look to those examples for inspiration rather than looking for excuses in the stories of those who did not fare as well.

Michele Tafoya is the sideline reporter for Sunday Night Football. Tafoya joined NBC Sports Group in 2011 and, in addition to her Sunday Night Football work, she was a sports desk reporter for NBC during the 2012 Olympic Games in London. Tafoya has won two Sports Emmys for her NBC sports reporting.

Prior to joining NBC Sports Group, Tafoya spent more than a decade at ABC/ESPN where she saw her profile rise steadily since 2000 through a variety of on-air roles, most notably as a reporter for Monday Night Football and ESPN's NFL studio programs.

Prior to ABC/ESPN, Tafoya worked for CBS Sports from 1994 to 2000 as a game reporter and studio host for NFL, college football, and college basketball telecasts, as well as hosting CBS' late night Winter Olympics programs in 1998.

Earlier in her career, Tafoya worked as a host and Minnesota Vikings sideline reporter for KFAN-AM in Minneapolis (1994–1998). During that time she also served as a Minnesota Timberwolves host and sideline reporter for the Midwest Sports Channel and play-by-play commentator for Big Ten women's basketball and volleyball. From 1995–1998 she was a sports anchor and reporter at WCCO-TV in Minneapolis. Prior to her roles in Minnesota, she worked for WAQS-AM in Charlotte (1993), where she was the first female analyst to call UNC-Charlotte men's basketball games.

A native of Manhattan Beach, California, Tafoya graduated from the University of California at Berkeley with a degree in mass communications and earned her master's degree in business administration from the University of Southern California.

CASE 30: TIGER TROUBLE

Carlee Tressel Alson
Independent Communications Strategy Contractor

ABSTRACT

The daughter of a successful college men's lacrosse coach refuses to shut down her racy blog, risking the reputation of a program that has done much to repair its image in recent years. When the sports information department tries to avoid another black eye for the men's lacrosse program and the university, they learn there's much more at stake than just appearances.

***

"You will take down that site or I will come over there and take it down for you!"

Coach Rod Riley punched the End Call button. "I swear that bull-headed girl is going to be the death of me."

Bull-headed, thought Sports Information Director (SID) Kim Stark. *The apple doesn't fall far from the tree.*

"We may need to take a different approach with this," Kim said. "It sounds like your daughter doesn't respond well to being told what she should or shouldn't do."

Coach Riley snorted. "You could say that again."

"Respectfully, Coach, I think 'The Tiger Tamer' is just a play for your attention," Assistant SID Brian Feester added.

Kim, Coach Riley, and Brian looked at the webpage projected onto the wall of Coach's office. It was difficult not to notice the header, which featured an illustration of a leggy auburn-haired woman wearing tiger-striped stockings and a black garter belt. Above the waist, the figure had on cat-like eyeglasses and not much else. Her right hand clutched a long whip.

The header art was just the beginning. "The Tiger Tamer" was the personal diary of a semi-anonymous character who called herself "Miss T." and recounted with biting wit the

266

explicit details of her romantic encounters on campus. Her favorite pastime was to "hunt tigers"—male and (occasionally) female student athletes at the school. Each entry was steamier than the next.

Glancing away, Coach removed his blue Tigers ball cap and rubbed his temples. "She's always been one to say or do anything for attention. Now how do we get her to shut up?"

A FAMILY AFFAIR

The bold and brash "Miss T." was, of course, Tanya Riley—Coach Riley's twenty-year-old daughter. Tanya was a sophomore at the school where the Tiger men's lacrosse team was enjoying an excellent start to their season. When Kim first caught wind of the salacious blog and who might be behind it, she and Brian worked on gathering all the information they could about Tanya and compared notes.

"She transferred from an Ivy League school over the summer," Brian reported. "Apparently, she partied a little too hard her freshman year and flunked out, so now she's enrolled where her dad can get a pretty nice tuition discount."

"She probably wasn't too happy about being forced to transfer," Kim said. "Tanya and Coach haven't had the best relationship. Riley and his wife split when Tanya was in elementary school, and since then, Tanya has always lived with her mom. She would travel to one or two of his games each year, but that's about it. Essentially, she's watched her father's rise in the college lacrosse world from a distance."

"She's also watched her father go through three more wives in just about ten years," Brian added.

"Good point," Kim said. "We're all aware of Coach's interest in women—whether he happens to be married at the moment or not."

"Imagine how that has been for Tanya."

Kim wanted to empathize, but she had no time for childish stunts—especially when the reputation of her lacrosse program was finally on the mend.

NINE LIVES

Four years ago, Tiger men's lacrosse was in serious crisis. Not only was the program found to have committed multiple NCAA violations, but two members of the team were found guilty of sexual battery and assault. The players were expelled from the university and found guilty in a criminal trial.

As a result of the crises and the way they were handled, the director of athletics (AD) and the entire coaching staff were fired. The SID was fired, too. Shortly after, Kim was hired to take over the position. It was truly an opportunity of a lifetime for Kim. She had always dreamed of heading up sports information for an athletics powerhouse.

On her first day on the job, the president of the university, the vice president of marketing, the outside public relations firm that had been hired by the university, and the new AD made it quite clear that Kim's department would be the crucial link between the recovering men's lacrosse program, the media, and the public at large. Additional embarrassments to the program—or the university—would not be tolerated.

In the intervening three years, the media had begun to let go of the program's past misdeeds. Thanks to the new coaching staff and the tight ship Coach Riley seemed to be running, the Tigers were winning and staying out of trouble. The public's memory of the program's past ugliness was beginning to dim.

THE CAT'S MEOW

In Coach Riley's fourth season, the Tigers went undefeated in the first six games. There was talk of winning the conference and securing a top seed in the tournament.

Just days before the team's first big conference game, The Tiger Tamer blog had a sudden surge in popularity thanks to a particularly eye-popping recap of Miss T.'s exciting evening with two men's lacrosse players that included artfully suggestive photos of athletic-looking bodies wearing team-issue helmets.

Students all over campus shared the post and speculated about who Miss T. was and how she had managed to hook up with so many Tiger athletes—lacrosse players included. There were many theories about Miss T.'s real identity, but one in particular caught fire: Miss T. was Coach Riley's daughter. It was too scandalous a rumor not to spread, and spread it did—all over social media.

With minimal digging, Kim was able to confirm that Tanya was indeed the creator and content manager of the Tiger Tamer blog. Although nothing she was doing was illegal or in violation of university policy—she claimed she had her romantic partners sign waivers giving her permission to write about them and anything that happened, as long as real names and identifying details were withheld—it reflected poorly on the student-athletes who got involved with Miss T., the programs, and Coach Riley.

READY TO POUNCE

Back in Coach's office, Kim was losing patience with the Tigers' "no-nonsense" leader.

"Coach, we don't have much time to control this story," she said.

"You heard me try to reason with her," Coach Riley said, "but she's hell-bent on making me and my team look foolish."

"I'll talk to her," Kim said. "Brian, see if you can arrange a coffee date for 'Miss T.' and me."

***

Kim arrived early and found a table near the back of the coffee shop. She scanned the room. It was filled with students hunched over their laptops and phones. *Please don't be tweeting or reposting Miss T.'s latest entry,* Kim thought.

She was surprised by how readily Tanya had agreed to meet with her. Kim credited Brian, who had a real gift for finessing people. He wasn't a smooth-talker; he was genuine.

"You should've become a therapist," Kim teased one day shortly after they had begun working together.

"It's amazing what a little listening will do," Brian replied.

Kim mostly forgot that bit of wisdom as she waited for Tanya to sashay through the door. Thanks to the sexy cartoon on the website, Kim had an idea of who to watch for. She tried to make eye contact with any girl wearing a low-cut top or extremely short shorts.

It would be difficult not to give Tanya a piece of her mind. Tanya needed to realize that whatever sort of daddy issues she was playing out could end up hurting many more people than just her father, however arrogant and preoccupied he could be.

"Excuse me."

A short young woman in a button-down plaid shirt and loose-fitting jeans stopped at Kim's table. "Are you Kim Stark?" she asked.

"Yes. Are you . . . Tanya?"

"I am." She stuck out her hand. "Nice to meet you."

Kim tried not to look incredulous. Short strawberry blond hair and freckles and androgynous clothing—this was not the Miss T. she had imagined at all. Kim was staring.

"I . . . I'm sorry," she said, catching herself. "It's just that I was expecting . . ."

"You were expecting Miss T.," Tanya said. "My work must be convincing."

"To say the least," Kim said. She was still recovering from the surprise. "I appreciate your willingness to meet with me about the site."

"Sure. What about it?"

"I think you already know that we—the Department of Athletics—are concerned about the content on The Tiger Tamer. We think it reflects poorly on our student-athletes."

"Why? Because it confirms that your student-athletes are having sex in their free time?"

"No," Kim said, her temper rising at Tanya's snarky attitude. "Because the content is sensational and exploits our student-athletes and their reputations as role models."

"Role models?" Tanya snorted. "Do I have to remind you that two men's lacrosse players were charged as *criminals* for *raping* multiple female students at this school?"

"That was four years ago, Tanya," Kim said. "As you may know, the Department of Athletics has adopted a zero-tolerance policy and there has been no reported sexual misconduct since."

"The key word is *reported*," Tanya said. "Sexual violence is still a huge problem here."

Things were beginning to crystalize for Kim. Tanya wasn't just acting out against her father; she had a broader agenda. Kim knew it was best not to further rile an angry activist type like her.

"I'm very sorry to hear you say that," Kim said. "I truly hope that's not the case."

"Trust me, it is. All of a sudden, the lacrosse team is winning again and people forget that the culture hasn't changed. Sure, the most brazen perpetrators are behind bars, but that doesn't change what goes on every weekend."

"With The Tiger Tamer, aren't you just adding to that culture?"

"Absolutely not. The site is about giving women their sexual power back. It's also a parody of the college hook-up culture . . . You didn't think those stories were real, did you?"

"Those photos look awfully real," Kim said.

Tanya laughed. "I have some very generous—and fearless—volunteers."

Kim was scrambling to get her head around everything she had just learned. "So you're reporting on these fictional escapades to empower women and make people aware of the ongoing issues with sexual violence on campus."

"Basically, yes."

"Why target athletes?"

Tanya's face darkened. "Like I said, certain programs aren't as good and wholesome as they might appear."

"What's your opinion of the men's lacrosse program?"

"It's awesome," Tanya said. "Yeah, they're all really great."

"Come on, Tanya. It's obvious you're harboring some ill will toward the team or your father or both."

"Look, my relationship with my father is none of your business," Tanya snapped. "I know you're here to tell me to take down the blog, but it's not going to happen."

"I'm not *telling* you to do anything," Kim said, remembering Coach Riley's unsuccessful threats. "I'm just asking you to think about how your method of bringing attention to important issues may have unintended consequences."

"I don't care about the reputation of our precious lacrosse team, if that's what you mean."

"What I'm saying is that your father's reputation is at stake—and so is your own. You're asking for attention you don't necessarily want."

Tanya stood up, her face a deep red. "You have no idea what you're talking about."

She rushed out of the coffee shop.

IT'S PERSONAL

"How'd it go?" Brian asked when Kim returned.

"Let's just say it could've gone better."

She recounted the conversation. Kim's frustration was quickly turning into panic. It would only be a matter of time before a national sports gossip website would pick up this juicy story about Coach Riley's naughty daughter. The damage control would be excruciating—especially if Tanya continued to post.

"Did Tanya say why sexual violence prevention is so important to her?" Brian asked.

"You know how college kids are. They pick a cause and throw themselves behind it just because they have the energy and freedom to do it."

"I don't know," Brian said. "This one seems personal."

***

Through what Kim perceived to be a small miracle, Brian convinced Tanya to have coffee with him the next day. In his email to Tanya, he promised he wouldn't badger her about the blog. He said he had some questions for her about the campus social scene in general and the way student-athletes, in particular, engage in it.

"That's a nice angle," Kim told him, "but you're wasting your time with her."

While Brian had coffee with Tanya, Kim started drafting an official statement addressing the blog. She knew it could go viral any moment, and they had to be ready with a response from the department of athletics.

Brian returned to the office two hours later. His expression was grim.

"I told you it was going to be a waste of time," Kim said.

"It wasn't a waste," Brian replied. "Unfortunately, things are worse than we thought."

"How could they be worse?"

Brian took a deep breath. "Tanya was sexually assaulted earlier this semester—by someone on the men's lacrosse team."

Kim was stunned. "Does Coach know? Did she report it?"

"Tanya says she tried to tell him, but when she explained the circumstances—that she was very drunk at a house party off campus—and named the player who assaulted her, Coach wouldn't hear it. He told her that she should not have been drinking and that the player she identified would never do what she claimed he did." Brian sighed. "She didn't end up reporting it, but she told me she wishes she had. She thought the blog would make her feel better—it hasn't."

Kim recalled her last words to Tanya in the coffee shop: *You're asking for attention you don't necessarily want.* She felt awful.

Before Kim could even begin to think about what to do next, Brian's phone rang.

"It's Tanya," he said. He picked up. After a brief greeting, he listened.

"Tanya, that took a lot of courage," he responded. ". . . I understand . . . Yes. Thank you for telling us."

Brian hung up. "She went to campus police and reported the incident. She's deciding whether to go to the local authorities, too," he said. "It was considerate of her to give us a heads-up. She definitely didn't have to."

Kim sat down, struck by this new information. *Just two hours ago, we were trying to avoid minor embarrassment over a silly little blog,* she thought, *and now this.*

She focused on getting her head around the situation and deciding what their next step should be. One thing was clear: It was a whole new ballgame.

DISCUSSION QUESTIONS

1. What should Kim and Brian do with the new information from Tanya?
2. How might Riley's identity as a coach influence his role as a father?
3. Suppose Coach Riley comes to terms with Tanya's experience. How should he communicate with his team about what happened and its implications, if at all?
4. How might Kim and Brian have approached the blog problem differently?

KEY TERMS

Family relations and sport, Crises in sport organizations, Gender and sport identity

The Potential Influence of Sport and Gender Socialization on Athletes' Reactions to Injury

Gregory A. Cranmer
West Virginia University and Indiana University-Purdue University Indianapolis

Maria Brann
West Virginia University and Indiana University-Purdue University Indianapolis

ABSTRACT

After taking a hard hit on the football field, David, a high school star athlete, must determine whether to communicate his suspected injury to his coach. David recalls the competing messages he's received about masculinity and responsibility regarding health in sport as he makes this difficult decision.

***

It is a brisk Friday night late in November. Throughout Greenville, Texas, members of the community gather in the parking lot of the local high school. As the sun slowly sets and disappears from the sky, the weekly ritual known as Friday night lights begins. Off in the distance, Daryl Stadium is illuminated with giant stadium lights, which reflect off the empty bleachers making the stadium look more like a shining city on a hill than an arena that will soon be the site of athletic combat. The Greenville High School Yellow Jackets (i.e., the local team) end their warm up and head into the locker room as the stadium opens to the public.

Students, parents, and other fans slowly begin to trickle into the stadium and take their seats on the cold metal bleachers. The fans wait for the game to begin and attempt to get comfortable by placing blankets and cushions on the bleachers to sit on. Some head to the concession stand to buy snacks and hot chocolate. In the air, there is a palpable sense of anticipation for an exciting night of athletic competition. With each passing minute, the tension and excitement in the stadium builds among the crowd as echoes of the fans' cheers can be heard from a distance. However, tonight's game is not just any ordinary game. Tonight marks the beginning of the high school football playoffs throughout Texas. This year, Greenville has fielded a team that is capable of making a run deep into the playoffs, but these expectations can be dashed with a single loss – making tonight's game crucial. This reality is not lost on the players.

Within the bowels of the stadium, the fans' cheers can be heard by the team as they make their last preparations in the locker room. A senior wide receiver, David, sits on a bench trying to stay calm. The thought crosses his mind that he could potentially be playing in the last game of his high school career tonight – if his team loses. He feels the immense pressure to win because all week teachers, parents, and members of the community have made it clear that they expect a victory. Further, as the team captain and one of the best players on the team, he knows that his teammates are looking to him to lead them to victory. He believes the stakes of a game have never been higher. The tense but quiet locker room is interrupted by the slamming of their head coach's office door.

Coach Smith walks into the locker room and David calls for his teammates to take a knee and listen. Their coach's pregame speech ensues:

> "Now men, you have a hell of an opportunity to prove your worth tonight. This is not just a game. This is so much bigger. You are representing this town, your parents, yourself, this team, and me. Do not leave this field tonight with any regrets. You are accountable to each other to give your best and anything less will result in defeat tonight *and* for the rest of your lives. I want to see you play this game the way it is supposed to be played – like men – because tonight, that is what it is going to take to win. Football has a way of revealing courage. It separates the men from the boys. That other team across the field tonight thinks they are going to walk into our house, in front of our families, and take what is ours because *you* are not man enough to stop them. So, it is real simple tonight. Are you going to back down? Give up? Quit when you experience a little pain? Or are you going to go out there, smack them in the mouth, and show them they don't have the fortitude to play with us? That they are not tough enough to handle what we are going to dish out for 48 minutes straight? Let's go kick their ass, men."

The team, including David, responds with a raucous display of enthusiasm as they get up and head toward the tunnel to take the field. On their way, David and his teammates smack each others' helmets and shout phrases like "Let's go" to get pumped up. As the team is seen starting down the stadium tunnel, with the lights gleaming off their helmets, the fans erupt into a frenzied applause – standing on their feet, clapping, shouting, and whistling. The team stops and bounces up and down in a massive huddle at the end of the tunnel waiting for the cue to enter the field area.

Once Coach Smith gives them the okay, David and his teammates break from the huddle and run onto the field tearing through a big paper banner held by the cheerleaders that reads "Beat the Cowgirls" (i.e., a twist on the mascot of their opponents, the Cowboys). The stadium erupts and David quickly realizes that Coach Smith was right that this is more than just a game. The entire town has turned out to root on the Yellow Jackets. The stadium is above capacity (15,000 people) and louder than ever before. David looks into the stands and sees fans in the student section holding signs that read "Protect this House" and hears the crowd join the cheerleaders chanting the normal pregame cheer during the coin toss: "Let's get fired up. Get rough, get tough, get mean. Let's get fired up and roll right over that team!"

As the game begins, a back-and-forth battle ensues for the first half. Toward the end of the second quarter, with time running out, Coach Smith calls in the last play of the half. He decides his best chance to gain an edge is to call a trick-play that could get the ball to David in the end zone. He shouts from the sideline: "Eagle, double razor, 35" (i.e., a trick-play that will result in the halfback pretending to run a sweep, only to pull up and throw a pass back across the middle of the field to David).

David immediately recognizes the play and says to himself, *Stay calm. Set your block before you release.*

The team heads to the line of scrimmage knowing this is their last chance to score during the first half. The players get in their positions with sweat dripping from their brows and a fiery desire to score in their bellies.

The quarterback yells, "Hut, hut, hike!" Then, he tosses the ball to the halfback. David makes contact with a linebacker, releases his block, and begins his route. He heads across the middle of the field and quickly realizes that he is open. He throws his hand up to get the halfback's attention once he reaches the end zone. The halfback stops running and throws a tight spiral toward David. With each rotation the ball gets closer and closer to David.

David puts his hands up, and thinks to himself, *Focus on the ball. Watch it come into your hands. The team needs this touchdown.* However, just before the ball reaches David, an oversized safety from the other team arrives out of nowhere with a ferociously punishing hit that blindsides and knocks David to the ground. The force of the blow dislodges his helmet and sends it bouncing out of the back of the end zone.

David sees black for a second but quickly comes to his senses, only to realize that, instead of catching the ball, he got knocked to the ground. He is not sure exactly what happened but does have a ringing headache and is experiencing slightly blurred vision.

He begins to think to himself, *Damn, I should have caught that ball. Where did that guy even come from?* As David attempts to get to his feet, he quickly realizes that something is not quite right. He knows he got his bell rung and feels off, but he is not sure of the extent of his potential injury.

A teammate jogs over and helps pick David up, teasing, "Quit milking it, Dave. Get up already." David complies and heads to the sideline with the help of his teammate.

With the first half over, the team begins to leave the field for half time. As David follows his teammates down the tunnel toward the locker room, he begins to realize he is confused about what happened to him. He sits down on a bench and tries to decide whether he should tell Coach Smith or a trainer about this headache. As he contemplates what to do, he tries to remember what he has learned about sports injuries and thinks about what his coach and teammates would expect him to do.

ATHLETE-COACH INTERACTIONS

Coach Smith begins his half-time speech by yelling at players who missed assignments or made mistakes during the first half. As he berates his players, David flutters in and out of focus. Unable to concentrate on the speech, David instead begins to wonder what Coach Smith would tell him to do regarding his headache.

David immediately thinks back to a practice that occurred two weeks prior to tonight's big game. During that practice, a teammate hurt his shoulder and did not want to play anymore. Coach Smith responded by calling a team meeting, where he lectured the team on the nature of football injuries. David recalls him saying:

> "Boys, football is a tough game. You are going to get 'hurt' often. It is part of the game. You will never be 100% healthy playing this game. If you are, you are not playing the game the right way – like a man would. So you need to learn to play through minor bumps, bruises, and soreness. On this team, we have an expectation that you will play through some injuries, and most of you already have. It would require a pretty significant injury to justify not playing. It comes down to knowing the difference between being hurt and being injured. If you are injured and you cannot play, that is one thing, but if all you are is hurt, you need to push through that discomfort. Do not be one of those quitters who gives up because things got hard, and is forced to look back and wonder 'What if?' Remember pain is temporary, but pride lasts forever."

David also remembers Coach's post-game speech from the previous week when he touted a teammate's ability to play through an injury. Coach Smith told his team:

> "Hey y'all, how about John tonight? He had enough heart for all of you. He breaks his thumb, but did he quit or ask to be taken out? No! He played through it like a warrior, like a true champion. This is what I have been trying to tell you – champions learn to overcome adversity and say 'yes I can' when their bodies tell them 'no you can't.' All of you will have to man up like John if we are going to make a run deep into the playoffs next week. And let's not forget, that is what we are here to do – win football games. And not just any games, we want to win important games. If you are on the sidelines, you are not helping the team accomplish that goal. Instead, you are letting the team down, this town down, and yourself down. Do not look back in 10 years and have regrets that you did not tough it out when things got difficult."

Although Coach Smith often preached toughness and David recalled several speeches touting the ability to play through injuries, David feels conflicted regarding whether to inform someone of his condition because Coach Smith also frequently discussed making responsible and healthy decisions. David particularly remembers a team meeting that was held by Coach Smith earlier in the season. During this meeting, the athletes were instructed to make responsible decisions regarding their health:

> "Men, part of playing sport is building up one's body. We need to make health-conscious decisions regarding what we are eating and how we are working out. You need to take care of your body because then it will take care of you. This means that I want you to eat right. Get

your rest. If you are sore or banged up, see the training staff. We need to be icing, stretching, and resting. We need you to be able to perform at a high level when those lights come on and we take that field. So I want you working out during the scheduled workouts, but do not do too much additional individual training. We do not want you to be unprepared, but we also do not want to put ourselves at risk for further injury by overtraining either. We need to listen to our bodies and make smart decisions."

David is called back to reality as the team erupts in a loud roar; Coach Smith finishes his half-time speech and the team gets up, puts their helmets on, and heads back to the field. David is still not sure what he should do regarding his headache. In his state of confusion, he approaches his friends and teammates John and Billy to ask for their advice.

TEAMMATE INTERACTIONS

David cautiously turns to his friends with a worried look on his face. He motions them closer, trying to be quiet so his other teammates and the coaching staff would not hear him.

"John, Billy . . . Something isn't right. I really don't feel so good. My head is killing me, and I feel like I'm going to puke."

He then takes a big gulp to clear his throat and a few deep breaths. David is fearful of how his teammates may respond, but he hesitantly suggests that he doubts if he can play in the second half.

Billy immediately replies, "Man you have to play. We need you! Without you, we don't have a shot at winning this game. You owe it to us to stick this out. If not, and we lose, it could be your fault."

David slowly nods as Billy's statement reinforces the responsibility that David already feels to his teammates. He thinks to himself, *Billy is right. I am the team captain. I need to be there to lead my team.*

But Billy continues, "And if we do find a way to win without you, your spot in the line-up next week will not be guaranteed. Coach Smith is always telling us that none of our jobs are safe and that we are always competing for our spots. Do you really want to end your career on the bench?"

David shakes his head to indicate that he does not want to finish his playing days as a reserve. He feels terrible.

But just then, John quickly chimes in, "Yea bro. You need to quit being a pansy and suck it up! We have all played through injuries at some point this season. I do not care if you are scared of getting hit again, you need to man up and quit being such a little girl. Now let's get out there and win this game."

John and Billy turn around and begin to walk out of the locker room. On his way toward the field, David reflects on his teammates' statements. He thinks to himself, *Billy made some good points. I made a commitment to my teammates; they look up to me and expect me to lead them to victory. The younger players are counting on me. I cannot let them down.*

David also knows that this could be his last game ever and that there are only 24 minutes left to play. Although his desire to win and keep his starting spot are undoubtable, he is still not sure if he can play through his potential injury.

Despite Billy's well-made points, John's insults are on the forefront of David's mind. He is in shock that his friend and teammate would say those things to him and thinks, *Does John think I am faking this? Why would I make this up?*

Even more important to David, he feels that his toughness and masculinity are being questioned by his teammates. It is clear to him that his friends expect him to play through this injury and will consider him a weakling or coward if he cannot compete.

He wonders, *Will Coach Smith or the community members still respect me if I cannot play? They often talk about how football separates the men from the boys* (i.e., a common phrase that his coaches and teammates would say during adverse situations). *Would not playing mean I am less of a man? Will my classmates make fun of me on Monday during class if I decide not to play? Will girls still want to go out with me? I cannot be labeled a chicken or a sissy.*

David feels extremely vulnerable at the thought of his potential inadequacy; this feeling is quickly accompanied by a need to prove himself. David considers few things worse than having his toughness, courage, and strength questioned. He heads to the field with a renewed intensity and is intent on playing in the second half. However, his resolve is shaken when he takes the field and is called over to the sideline by his parents.

PARENTAL INTERACTIONS

As David jogs onto the field with his teammates, he sees his parents leaning over a fence close to the field. They call him over with concerned looks on their faces. His mother attentively asks, "David, are you okay? You got up really slowly after that last hit."

David replies with a half-hearted nod, attempting to indicate that he is fine. However, he is merely trying to put his mom at ease.

Being his mother, David's mom sees through her son's disingenuous attempts to reassure her, and she begins to ask a series of questions, "Does your head hurt? Can you see okay? Do you feel nauseous? Did you go to the trainer?"

David feels overwhelmed with her questions and does not know what to do or how to answer them. He replies, "Mom, I think I want to play. The team needs me to win. This is the playoffs."

She immediately replies, "David, winning is not everything. Having fun and your health should be the most important things on your mind. If you are hurt, you need to say something. This is a dangerous game, and there are serious life-long consequences that can result from playing when you are not able to protect yourself to the best of your ability. I need you to be honest with me right now David Michael [his middle name, which indicated she was very serious]. Are you hurt?"

David pauses. He knows if he tells his mother that he is hurt she may tell the coach or the trainer and the situation could quickly slip out of his control. However, he does not want to lie to his mother either. He looks to his father out of desperation, hoping for some help or instruction.

At this moment, David's father finally chimes in, "Susan, he said he was fine. Stop babying him."

He then turns to David and says in a stern tone of voice, "I know you got your bell rung, but you need to suck it up, dust yourself off, and get back out there. You are the man out there. Your teammates, Coach Smith, and I are counting on you."

David nods slowly. He is slightly disappointed, as he was half-hoping that his dad would understand that he is not feeling like he is able to compete.

Sensing his son's hesitation, David's father reinforces his previous statements by asserting to David, "You got to toughen up, ignore the pain, and do your job. Life is going to throw a lot of adversity your way. Being a man means finding a way to overcome that adversity and still get the job done. You are not being asked to do anything that others have not already done. All the greats have played through pain. If you want to be great too, you will need to play through this as well. Now get back out there and make me proud!"

David looks at him and nods, "Yes, sir." He then turns and begins to jog toward his teammates and the sideline. As he makes his way over to his teammates, he thinks about what his father just said about the greats of the game.

MEDIA INTERACTIONS

David recalls growing up and hearing stories from his father and uncles about how the older generations of football players were tougher than the "kids these days." He remembers watching old football games on ESPN Classic with his dad and cousins while growing up. Those games often touted athletes' durability and willingness to play through injuries, including head injuries, as impressive feats of toughness and dedication to their teams and sport.

In particular, David thinks of his dad's favorite football player, Troy Aikman (i.e., the starting quarterback for the Dallas Cowboys throughout the 1990s and someone whose on-field accomplishments were revered by his father). Growing up in Texas, David idolized Aikman. His garage and room are still filled with posters, magazines covers, and newspaper articles featuring the legendary quarterback. David also recalls hearing and reading about tales of Aikman's toughness and ability to play through nearly a dozen concussions during his career – including a game-winning performance in Super Bowl XXX. These feats have elevated Aikman to legendary status among Texas sport fans, including David's family, and have shaped his perception of what an ideal football player does.

He also thinks to himself, *Most of my NFL heroes have played through injuries and even concussions without much difficulty. In fact, several players (e.g., Super Bowl XLVIII Champion and Seattle Seahawk corner, Richard Sherman) have recently claimed that despite playing with head injuries they do not feel like they have suffered any negative side effects. If they can do it, maybe I can as well.*

As David attempts to reassure himself, he also thinks of the materials that he has read regarding potential head injuries in sport and the long-term side effects they can produce. Specifically, with the increased attention that head injuries in football is receiving in the media, the Greenville School Board required all athletes to complete an educational training program prior to being cleared to play this season. This training program included reading Christopher Nowinski's groundbreaking book (i.e., *Head Games: Football's Concussion Crisis from the NFL to Youth Leagues*) and attending several seminars that were meant to help athletes recognize when they might be experiencing a potentially traumatic brain injury.

David immediately begins to recall the lessons he learned before the season started. He recognizes the chances that he has potentially suffered a concussion are legitimate because he knows he has several of the symptoms (e.g., feeling dazed and confused, experiencing a severe headache, hearing a ringing in his ears after a hard hit, feeling nauseous). Further, he knows that concussions are common in football as nearly 60,000 high school players are diagnosed with at least one concussion every year.

He also recalls the potential long-term effects highlighted during the school board's program. The doctors said that there is a multitude of side-effects with concussions, including memory loss, additional headaches, depression, increased rates of suicide, or difficulty concentrating on rudimentary tasks. David knows that the training advocated telling a coach or a trainer immediately upon experiencing the first symptoms, but he is not sure what to do.

CULMINATION

David continues to contemplate what to do. His coach, friends, and father seem to emphasize player toughness and have encouraged him to play through the pain. He does not want to disappoint them. He also feels the need to prove himself on the gridiron like the immortalized greats who played before him. Further, he wants to convince his friend John that he is not a sissy and that he can play the game like a true man.

However, David still is not sure whether to tell a trainer or coach about his potential injury or play through it. He feels conflicted because Coach Smith has encouraged players to make responsible and health-conscious decisions, and the team's preseason educational program outlined the risks associated with playing with these types of symptoms. David then looks over to his mother in the stands who is clearly concerned, and he knows that his mom is usually correct when she senses something is wrong. He struggles with a decision. As the team gathers for Coach Smith's last instructions prior to the start of the second half, David's mind continues racing.

He is contemplating how he should proceed, but just then Coach Smith barks at him: "David. You hear me?"

"Um. . . . Yea coach," He replies. He pauses because he has not been able to focus and is not really sure what Coach Smith has been instructing the team.

Coach Smith gives David a puzzled look because he suspects that he is not focused, but the second half kickoff is under way. It is now time for the Yellow Jacket's offense to take the field. Coach Smith looks at him and says, "David, everything okay? Are you ready to get back out there?"

DISCUSSION QUESTIONS

1. What do you think David should do regarding whether he should report his suspected injury? What aspects of the above case study would affect your decision (e.g., the fact that it is a playoff game or David's senior year; seriousness of injury; the communication David received from friends, parents, etc.)?

2. At what point, if ever, does an athlete's autonomy over his/her own body and his/her ability to play end? Explain your answer.

3. How did David's attempts to enact his and others' expectations of appropriate gender performance manifest in this case? Do you think these aspects were consistent with larger themes in sport or society? Explain.

4. How might this case or your answers to the previous questions differ if the sport, sex of the athlete or coach, or the age of the athlete were different? Explain.

KEY TERMS

Masculinity, Norms, Gendering, Injury

CASE 32: INTERFAITH DIVISIONS AT SOUTHERN STATE UNIVERSITY

Jason Moyer
Malone University and Luther College

Thomas C. Johnson
Malone University and Luther College

ABSTRACT

The intersection of faith and sport, specifically college soccer and evangelical Christianity, presents a series of questions for coaches, players, and spectators. When leaders (including coaches, captains, and the team chaplain) at Southern State University explicitly connect the two forces, faith-related dilemmas rise to the surface.

***

It is a steamy August morning as 45 athletic men fill Southern State University's newly constructed Smith Athletics Auditorium in Macon, Georgia. On this, the first day of soccer practice, players from all over the country sit anticipating a season of work both in the classroom and on the field. Although excitement fills the room, it is a nervous excitement for many of the players new to the school, the soccer program, the town, the southern culture, and the idea that for the first time in their careers, they might not be the best players on the team. Their hope, though, is that they will be good enough to play in front of the 2,500 Senators fans that fill Dalton Stadium for each home game.

Head Coach Jamis Harvey is the first person to address the audience.

In his signature twang, Coach Harvey declares, "Men, in respect for the heritage of our soccer program we must begin our time together with a prayer."

Before introducing the team chaplain, he declares, "We are members of a soccer family that keep each other responsible to our common goal. Above all we must have faith that we can succeed this season. Without faith we are nothing. And we need to remind ourselves that faith comes from God."

Harvey pauses and gestures to his left. "Gentlemen, this is our team chaplain, Bill Webster."

"Good morning, Senators. Please join me in the Lord's Prayer . . .

Our Father, who art in heaven,
hallowed be thy name, thy kingdom come,
thy will be done,
on Earth as it is in heaven.
Give us this day our daily bread
and forgive us our sins,
as we forgive those who sin against us,
and lead us not into temptation,
but deliver us from evil,
for thine is the kingdom and the power
and the glory, forever. Amen."

Following the Lord's Prayer, Coach Harvey introduces assistant coaches, covers practice logistics, and mentions other first day type of material. He then closes the meeting.

"Gentlemen, it's our time, each and every day we get up and go to work, to give glory to the Lord each time we make a play on the pitch . . . each time we win or lose. It's our time, Senators. Let's hit the field!"

Practice begins for the season and all seems well, but the marriage of college soccer and evangelical Christianity at Southern State University is readily apparent.

THE EVANGELICAL CHRISTIAN

Coach Harvey's introductory meeting hits the right note for incumbent senior starting goalkeeper Johnny Russell. When practice ends he gathers the team leaders of the Fellowship of Christian Athletes (FCA) to thank God for a practice without injury, to pray for their season, and to begin organizing their first social event of the season.

"Before y'all run off to the showers we need to sort out when we're going to have our yearly peach cobbler event. If you're new to this group, Mr. and Mrs. Fairfax have hosted the FCA soccer players at their home every year. It is a fun event, you can bring a date, and eat the best peach cobbler you'll ever taste!"

Johnny's roommate, junior Ben Halloway, a midfielder on the soccer team, responds, "Let's have it next Saturday night after our inter-team scrimmage."

"Sounds fine to me," replies Johnny.

Sophomore Robby Cedric raises his hand as he starts asking his question, "Is everyone invited or is this just for Christians? I'm sorry, but I've noticed a lot of unchristian stuff happening in our locker room . . . swearing, taking the Lord's name in vain. And, I've even seen a Muslim praying in the corner. Do we invite everyone? And, if we do, what are Mr. and Mrs. Fairfax going to think?"

Cutting Cedric off, Johnny indicates, "We don't exclude anyone from our FCA activities. All are welcome."

With a smile and a chuckle, Ben resolves Robby's concern by clarifying, "Don't worry about it. Anyone can decide to come, or *not* come."

Robby and Johnny catch one another's eye and exchange an agreeable nod.

THE SOUTHERN BAPTIST

On the morning of the intra-team scrimmage, Johnny approaches first-year defender Elias Barnes to invite him to that evening's FCA event.

"Elias! Hey, FCA's first social event of the season is tonight. Can you make it? We'd love to have you! Bring a lady!"

It takes everything Elias has not to roll his eyes in disgust at Johnny.

"Possibly. Let me see what I can do, Johnny."

Elias is less than thrilled by the invitation. For his entire life, Elias has spent countless hours in the front row of a small country church that preached biblical inerrancy. As his father, Teddy, often repeats, "God made this book simple so that anyone, no matter their station in life, could plainly read it."

When the time came to choose a college, Teddy pushed hard for Elias to follow in his footsteps and attend Cardson College, a school devoted to the Bible and its teachings. Elias paid lip-service to the idea, but ultimately knew Cardson was a non-option. Why? Because ever since Elias realized he was gay (at the age of fifteen), he despised rhetoric aimed at demeaning homosexuality and knew Cardson to be a place where such language was accepted, if not celebrated.

When he was younger, Elias committed his life to Jesus Christ and he wants that to continue. However, he doesn't know how to be Christian and be gay at the same time. He chose Southern State because he thought it would be a secular institution that would allow him to figure out his internal confusions.

The FCA event feels like his first real test. He wants to fellowship with a Christian community, but he knows he will be looked down upon if the soccer team knows he is gay.

As he walks back to his dorm room, he thinks, *Ok, how do I handle this now? If I don't attend, am I pushing myself farther from my religious beliefs? If I do attend and don't bring a girl, will people know that I'm gay? If I do attend and do bring a girl, is that fair to anyone, particularly her?*

He is in disbelief. *Maybe I did choose the wrong college.*

THE MUSLIM

Growing up in San Diego, first-year forward Abdul Hammad experienced a few incidents of prejudice against him and his family, but they were relatively minor. As a proud Muslim, he was surrounded by like-minded Muslims, as well as Protestants, Catholics, Jews, Buddhists, and atheists. For Abdul, freely exercising his religion felt natural.

After several weeks of falling in line and listening to the Lord's Prayer at the end of start of each practice and before each game, Abdul reaches his breaking point. He decides to approach team captain and starting defender, Bill Jenkins.

"Hey, Billy. What's up? Can I talk to you about something?" asks Abdul.

"Abdul, how are you? What's going on?" replies Bill.

"Umm, I'm doing well. I'm ok. But, there's something I need to talk to you about. We're supposed to come to team captains with issues, right?"

"Yes, most definitely."

Abdul swallows hard and pauses for a moment. "Well, I'm struggling with the praying. You know, like, we pray before every practice?"

"Yeah, most of the guys are Christian so it's just a good opportunity for us all to connect with Jesus Christ. I'm not all into the FCA stuff that Johnny and those guys do, but it's good for the team. Coach wants us embrace it, as well."

"Ok, but you know I'm Muslim, right?" responds Abdul.

"Well, yeah, of course. So are Anthony and Aamir. It's all good!"

Abdul takes a deep breath and looks to the sky for a moment. *It wasn't all good.* He had spoken with Anthony and Aamir about the praying. Their response, to his surprise, was to just let it go. *How could they just let it go? Why weren't they uncomfortable?* Abdul wonders.

"Yeah, I talked to them."

"What did they say?" asks Bill.

"They said that's just how it is."

"Look, this is who we are, Abdul. We're about playing soccer and praising Jesus. It's what's important to us."

We? Us? Abdul thinks, *well I'm me and I'm not Christian, I'm Muslim.*

Bill puts his hand on Abdul's shoulder and smiles. "Abdul, man, this isn't something worth fighting. You don't want anyone thinking you're all high and mighty on radical Islam, you know? Let it go, man," Bill declares.

Stunned by Bill's reference to radical Islam, Abdul thinks, *a moment of silence might work just as well,* but refrains from sharing. Instead, he sheepishly nods and replies, "Ok."

A FINAL WORD

Evangelical Christianity is intertwined with the culture of the men's soccer team at Southern State University. It is no surprise that players in the religious minority find this to be more of a problem than do players in the religious majority. When faith is used to bring a team together it might have an opposite, divisive effect for those involved.

DISCUSSION QUESTIONS

1. Explain each player's perspectives on the issue of religion. What makes each of them unique?
2. What are each player's options? How might they navigate their specific faith-related dilemmas?
3. What other sorts of characters can you imagine in this soccer program? What questions might they ask about the relationship between soccer and religion?
4. Should sport and religion mix at all? If so, under what conditions?

KEY TERMS

Communication apprehension, Religion, College soccer

CASE 33: GRIDLOCK ON THE GRIDIRON
Gender Issues in Football

Nancy J. Curtin
Millikin University

ABSTRACT

Lauren is a sixth grader living in a small town. She is athletic and interested in sports. With the encouragement of her friends, Lauren wants to play on the football team. In trying out for the team, she encounters some gridlock on the gridiron.

***

"Mom, I want to play football. Can I try out?"

"Lauren, I don't know. Let me talk to your dad about this."

Lauren was a sixth grader at Stockton Elementary School, located in the small town of Stockton. Football begins in sixth grade and continues in seventh and eighth grades. The junior high football program is believed to be a "feeder" program for the high school football program. Lauren had always been athletic and interested in sports. She regularly played soccer and flag football at recess, in teams that were mainly made up of boys. It was because of her participation in these games that her male friends encouraged her to try out for the football team.

"Hey, Lauren, you're pretty fast and can outrun a lot of boys," remarked Connor, a classmate who played often in these games during recess with Lauren.

"Yeah, Connor's right. And when you throw, you don't throw like a girl," chimed in another classmate, Javon.

Lauren instantly felt proud. She was getting complimented on her athletic ability from these boys. *And then she wondered if she would feel the same way if girls had said these same things. Would she still feel complimented? Would the compliments mean anything different if they were said by girls? Does it mean more to her since boys said it?*

Lauren concluded the conversation by saying that she might try out for football but wasn't sure.

Even though Lauren indicated that she "might" want to try out, she instantly knew she wanted to try out for the football team. After all, this was the first year in school that students could participate in a school team sport. No more YMCA games . . . this was a bigger deal . . . playing for the school . . . and playing *real* football—no more flag football.

THE COMMUNITY OF STOCKTON

Lauren grew up and lived in Stockton, a small farming community. The community tended to be more conservative. People adhered to traditional gender roles. Sure, girls played sports and women worked outside the home, but even then, gender traditions still prevailed. For example, girls played on all-girls teams. This would be different. Football had been and still was a male-dominated sport. She had not heard about any other girls *even wanting* to play football. At recess, she was the lone girl playing flag football.

THE FAMILY

Lauren's family included her mom, dad, and two younger siblings, a brother and a sister, all living in the same household. Lauren wasn't sure what her parents would say to her wish to play football for the school. While she always felt her parents were supportive of her, she wasn't sure if this would be "too out there" for them to support.

"Lauren, your dad and I talked about you wanting to play football. Honey, we just don't think it is a good idea. We don't want you to get hurt. And you will probably be the only girl on the team. Girls just don't play on the football team. Why don't you try out for the volleyball team? It would be much safer, and you'll be with other girls," asserted Lauren's mom.

"But Mom, I want to play. And the boys said I would be good at football. They want me to try out," refuted Lauren.

"THE REVERSE PLAY—THE DECISION IS REVERSED"

A week went by and Lauren was still observably disappointed with her parent's decision. Unexpectedly, at supper on Monday evening, Lauren's mom initiated the football topic.

"Lauren, your dad and I have discussed it more over the weekend. We have decided to let you try out for the football team. We will support your interest and trying out for the football team."

"Thank you so much!" shouted Lauren, "I'm going to see if the guys will start practicing with me tomorrow!" as she ran off to text her friends the news.

THE TRYOUTS

At tryouts, Lauren, not surprisingly, found she was the only girl trying out for the team. There were about 20 boys trying out. While she had heard that there was the possibility that there would be no cuts—that all would make it who tried out, she was relieved. Still, she wanted to prove to herself that she was a good player and could handle the sport. Lauren felt like she had to prove herself even more since she was a girl. At times, she felt like "one of the guys" playing, but then at other times, it was apparent that she was the lone girl.

During some of the tryouts, Lauren was playing defense. She was playing hard, tackling the offensive players using all her muscles.

As she was lined up on the defensive line, ready to tackle, she heard the coach yell to one of the players on offense, "Come on, are you going to let yourself get beat by a girl?"

Lauren was more determined than ever to tackle the offense. Coach's comment caught her off guard, but she forged on, trying to tackle the players.

"Come on, don't let a girl beat you down!" continued the coach.

Lauren was surprised. She figured that it would be the boys, not the coach, who might be saying negative comments. Instead, she found her peers to be supportive and encouraging of her on the field.

***

After tryouts, Lauren's mom picked her up and, on the drive home, inquired about tryouts. Lauren wasn't sure if she wanted to tell her mom about coach's comments. After all, Lauren didn't want to hear an "I told you so" from her mom. She figured that her mom probably anticipated some negative comments; that was probably one reason her mom was hesitant to let her try out for football.

Lauren simply remarked, "It was fine" in response to her mom's inquiry.

TRYOUT #2

At the next tryout, Lauren continued to show her determination to prove to herself that she was a good player and could handle the sport. Lauren again heard the coach's same remarks as during the first tryout:

"Come on, are you going to let yourself get beat by a girl?"

"Come on, don't let a girl beat you down!"

Then something happened . . . something instantly changed . . . . . Lauren "pancaked" an offensive player. The player was on the ground, visibly hurt. Coach had to come onto the field to attend to the hurt player. After the coach ensured the player was okay, the coach helped the player walk off the field. As the coach was walking, he stopped, turned around to Lauren and said quietly enough so no one else could hear, "Nice job. Good, forceful effort." Finally, Lauren felt validated; she felt like the coach had finally recognized her effort and skill.

***

After tryouts, Lauren's mom picked her up and, on the drive home, inquired about tryouts. This time, Lauren couldn't wait to tell her mom what happened.

Lauren blurts out, "Mom, you will never believe what happened? I pancaked somebody!"

"What does 'pancaked somebody' mean, Lauren?"

"It is where you completely take someone down on the field; you know, you flatten 'em like a pancake," Lauren boasted proudly.

"Oh, Lauren, good job," Mom simply replied.

Although Lauren's mom knew Lauren was athletically skilled, she couldn't help but question if this situation occurred because the "pancake" boy underestimated her ability—that he got blindsided, so to speak. Of course, Lauren's mom would not want to put that doubt in Lauren's mind, out of concern that it would diminish how proud Lauren was of her accomplishment.

FINAL TRYOUT

As Lauren began the final tryout, she felt like things were looking pretty good for her. And again, she heard that all the players might make the team. Regardless, she was still determined to prove herself. The tryout went well; nothing unusual happened. Lauren felt good about her performance.

THE CUT

After the tryout, the coach said he would post the roster the next day at school. That night, the coach called Lauren's house. Lauren's dad answered the phone.

"Hello?"

"Hello, this is Coach Krueger, Lauren's football coach. Is this Lauren's dad? Mr. Smith?"

"Yes, this is he," replied Lauren's dad.

"Mr. Smith, I just want to talk to you about Lauren's performance. I have to admit, I was a little uneasy and uncertain about Lauren trying out for the football team. But I want you to know that Lauren has impressed me. She certainly has athletic skill. She can sure run fast and does a helluva job tackling," Coach asserted.

"Well, good to hear. She certainly seems to have been enjoying it all. I appreciate you letting her try out for the team," Lauren's dad remarked.

"But, Mr. Smith, I need to tell you. Although Lauren shows athletic skill, I am afraid I can't allow her to play on the team. Some boys have complained to me that they just don't feel comfortable tackling her. You see in football, players will reach under the pads as they tackle. Some players just don't feel comfortable reaching under the pads to tackle her. And Mr. Smith, you know, in football, so much is 'fair game' so to speak to get the job done," asserted the coach.

Coach continued, "Mr. Smith, some boys are threatening not to play. I just cannot risk multiple boys not playing at the expense of one girl playing. I hope you can see my predicament," pleaded the coach.

Lauren's dad simply replied, "Well, I am disappointed in this and not sure what I will tell Lauren or what we might do, but I may be in touch."

Lauren's dad hung up the phone and thought to himself, *I just don't know what to do. What do I tell Lauren? What should I not tell Lauren? Should I talk to the other players' parents? Should I talk to the school board? What is the right thing to do?*

He contemplated all these questions as he walked downstairs for movie night with the family. *What irony*, he thought. *We are watching the movie Friday Night Lights.*

DISCUSSION QUESTIONS

1. If you were Lauren's dad, what, if anything, would you specifically say to the coach at this point?

2. What would you tell Lauren? What would you NOT tell Lauren?

3. If you were Lauren's dad, what are some available options? Talk to the school board? Talk to a lawyer? Talk to some football players' parents? Do nothing?

KEY TERMS

Gender diversity in sport, Family relations and sport, Coach-athlete relations, Gender and sport identity

CASE 34: FETUAO'S DILEMMA

Negotiating Gender and Sexuality in the Hypermasculine World of Rugby

Gust A. Yep
San Francisco State University and Ohlone College

Nicholas T. Chivers
San Francisco State University and Ohlone College

ABSTRACT

Collegiate athletics is a rich site for the negotiation of identity and difference, rife with potentially difficult interactions in myriad relationships between athletes and other athletes, coaches, administrators, and many others, all in a pervasive social environment of hegemonic masculinity. This case study follows the story of Fetuao Tafolo, a transgender Tongan rugby player, as he contemplates transitioning from male to female. More specifically, it highlights the challenges and complexities of his decision and its potential consequences on his relational network, including the relationships to his girlfriend, family, teammates, coach, and the university, and his own personal and professional future.

***

"Yaaaah ha ha ha!!!" Fetuao Tafolo burst out of the locker room amidst a deafening chorus of raucous laughter and guttural screams. It was another great match for the Grand Lakes University men's rugby team; another week leaving it all on the pitch, another step closer to the Collegiate Rugby Championship. Fetuao's body felt bruised and battered, but, for now, he was floating.

"Fetuao, drink a beer with us!" his teammates cheered.

"Yeah, on me, man. After what you did today, it's the least I can do, huh?"

"C'mon! Your lady will still be there in the mornin'. She can wait. Let's rage, man!"

"Alright, alright," Fetuao conceded. "I don't know about raging, but I'll let you buy me a pint . . . or a pitcher," he laughed. "I can sure use one to take the edge off. That shit was brutal out there today."

"At least you can remember what a beer is!" His teammates joked. "Can't say the same for that full-back that kept trying to stop you!"

"I kept telling him to stay out of my way. He did look pretty fucked up at the end though, right? Maybe I should send him a bottle of aspirin or something. I feel like I owe him that."

His teammates laughed hysterically at Fetuao's joke as they headed down to the bar.

The next morning, Fetuao sent the injured young full-back a bottle of aspirin and get-well note.

Fetuao Tafolo is a star winger for Grand Lakes University's varsity rugby team. At five feet, eleven inches tall and 210 pounds, believe it or not, he is one of the smallest and fastest members of the team, and he is a natural. He grew up in the United States with his parents, but he began playing rugby, as a child, with his father, uncles, and cousins when he spent his summers in his native Tonga. He moved to College Park when he was offered a scholarship to play rugby at GLU, and couldn't pass up the opportunity to play the game he loves at a high level and get a top-notch education in return. He led the Green Dragons to the finals of the Collegiate Rugby Championship during his sophomore year. Now a junior, Fetuao is on track to earn his bachelor's degree in turfgrass science next year, and is hoping to bring home both a degree and a national championship before his years in Wisconsin are up.

In spite of his popularity, Fetuao is also different. With his shiny black hair, Asiatic features, and smooth dark skin, he seems exotic to most people on campus. Pacific Islanders consist of less than 1% of the student body of GLU, which combined with the moderate popularity of the rugby team, make him pretty well known on campus. He extends his presence in the rugby community by never missing an opportunity to see the women's rugby team play. The women's team is even better than the men's, bringing home multiple consecutive national championships, including every year that Fetuao has been on campus. The College of Agricultural Sciences is also a fairly small community, and turfgrass science is even smaller, and again, Fetuao is well liked among his peers and professors in the department.

Like most college juniors, Fetuao's life has hit a high gear lately, and decisions are looming. He is being actively scouted by both the US National Team and the Tongan National Team to go to the Summer Olympics in Rio de Janeiro in 2016, the first reemergence of the sport in the Olympic Games since 1924. Simultaneously, scouts from Tonga and New Zealand are looking at Fetuao to play for their growing professional leagues. His future in rugby looks bright and promising and his family expects to see him on their television screens.

Fetuao awoke, still in his street clothes, with his head still swimming with dreams of Olympic rugby, although the details were in a bit of a fog. Dreaming about rugby was not unusual for him, but he was having recurring dreams about women's rugby, either playing or coaching or watching. He was still trying to shake the cobwebs from his mind when he felt a sharp pain in his hip and let out a forced groan. The kitten named Chicken had decided that now was the time to play with Fetuao, and although the small cat only weighed a couple of pounds, he apparently found just the right spot to remind Fetuao how much rugby could hurt.

"What perfect timing," said a sweet familiar voice. Fetuao focused his consciousness just enough to see his girlfriend, Kari, come into the room, still in her pajamas with her hair pulled up. "God, this girl's amazing," Fetuao thought, even before he realized what she was holding. Kari sat down next to Fetuao on the bed, and offered him a plate of breakfast; the centerpiece an omelette that looked like it was made from a half a dozen eggs.

"Veggie omelette, bacon, orange juice, and some aspirin," Kari said with a smile and a kiss on the forehead. "Morning, stud. Thanks for the text last night. How was the match?" Fetuao started simultaneously devouring the delicious breakfast while relaying all the details of the night before while Kari gently rubbed his aching legs.

Fetuao's girlfriend is Kari Thomason, a sophomore majoring in nursing at GLU. Smart, beautiful, playful, and a cat lover, Kari is a Wisconsin native and only daughter to her parents, Charles and Janice. Kari's father Charles passed away when she was young, and afterwards her distraught mother found religion and became very involved in her faith. Fetuao and Kari met in a communication class when they did a group project together during Kari's first year at GLU. They quickly fell in love and have been together ever since. Although Kari was initially concerned about her mother's reaction to the interracial relationship, Fetuao and Kari decided to move in together after more than a year as boyfriend and girlfriend. It felt right. In their new apartment with two adopted kittens, they are slowly and steadily making plans for a future together. Fetuao and Kari are happy, optimistic, and secure about their love for each other like never before, which made their friends and Fetuao's teammates a bit envious.

Recently, Kari had been noticing that Fetuao seemed to be feeling an uncharacteristic level of anxiety and depression. Over the previous weeks Kari had seen it come and go in Fetuao, but he assured her that everything was fine. But even today, the day after a big win, Kari noticed the change, and repeatedly asked him what was bothering him. After hours of dodging the questions, and Kari's persistence, Fetuao felt that he owed it to her to talk about it. They found a quiet bench in a corner of campus to stop, sit, and chat, and finally Fetuao said what was on his mind. It had been on his mind for years, but he had never told anyone but his counselor. With a weight in his voice and a serious yet apologetic tone, he said, "I'm transgender."

Kari's immediate response was not the one that Fetuao was expecting. She asked, "Does this mean you're leaving me?" Fetuao was so overwhelmed with joy and love at her response that he simply pulled her close in a tight embrace, engulfing her small frame in his athletic chest and arms. "Not now," he said. "Not ever."

Following that initial reaction, the questions came hard and way too fast for Kari to even ask them. With their arms around each other and concerned about Fetuao's privacy, they decided to walk home together.

Interrupting the silence and the growing and confusing fissure between them, Kari asked, "How long have you known?"

Fetuao was pensive when he said, "Since I was a little boy."

"You knew that you were transgender since you were a boy?" Surprised that she almost whispered the word "transgender" while her volume was increasing, Kari added, "And you never told me?"

"Well, I wanted to . . . I really wanted to but I couldn't even say those words to myself. I wanted you to like me because I liked you since I first saw you in class." With tears in his eyes, Fetuao emphasized, "No, I didn't just like you. I really liked you!"

"So you lied to me. You deceived me into liking you back." Feeling immediately guilty after saying these words, Kari was utterly confused—she was experiencing shock, anger, betrayal, concern, love, and attraction all at the same time. Watching her boyfriend's vulnerable face, she wanted to kiss him, hug him, and make love to him. Above all, she wanted all of this to just go away and she took a deep breath. "I guess I'm not being fair. Maybe I don't fully get it. But I feel betrayed." She was feeling her anger rise up again.

"You have the right to feel angry and betrayed. I'm really sorry I never told you. I didn't know what to do! I felt I had so much to lose," tears running down his face. "You know that I never wanted to hurt you. I love you, Kari."

She wiped off his tears with a tissue from her purse. She wanted to hug him but held back. She wanted to run, but held back. *I'm going mad*, she thought. *This is crazy.* They walked the rest of the way home in silence hoping that neither one ran into someone they knew.

Upon opening the door to their little apartment, Chicken and Waffles, their two little kittens, greeted them. Kari immediately went to feed them before locking herself in the bathroom to cry. Her tears kept flowing and she was afraid that they would never stop. She wanted Fetuao to hold her and she wanted him to leave her alone. "If I stay with him, would it make me a lesbian?" she wondered. "We've had sex . . . am I already a lesbian?" She shook that one off, it sounded ridiculous. "What would I tell my mom and my friends? My mom will probably disown me, my friends will surely tease me," and felt ashamed for thinking it. She finally stopped crying and realized that she had been in the bathroom for a very long time. Looking at her reflection in the bathroom mirror, she saw a little girl who just wanted to be understood and loved. She imagined Fetuao as a little boy next to her, holding hands and smiling at each other. She knew then that they would get through it, somehow. Slowly, she opened the bathroom door and saw Fetuao standing there, concerned and waiting for her. Kari took his hand.

"I need to say two things," she started, moving the conversation to the kitchen. "First, I feel betrayed, hurt, shocked, confused, scared, and many other things. There may be times when I feel like I need to protect myself before it all gets to be a burden too heavy for me to bear. There is a part of me that just wants to run." Fetuao poured her a glass of water, handed it to her with trepidation as she continued. "But secondly, and perhaps more importantly, that feels selfish. For all of the mixture of awful things I'm feeling, it must be three times worse for you. So, I want to give you my best and be here for you." She paused, mustered up her courage, and looked into his tired eyes. "What do you need? What do we do?"

"That's really the million dollar question, isn't it?" Fetuao responded. "Fact of the matter is, I'm not really sure. The one thing I know for certain is I cannot go on much longer like this. I mean, I see women like Tyra, Beyoncé . . . I remember as a kid watching the Williams sisters play tennis and thinking that *that* is what I want to be like. And then I look at my own body and feel disgusted. The anxiety, fear, depression, pain . . . it's all, just, torturous and I can't go on forever like this. I've even considered killing myself just to make it stop. The really awful thing is that the very things that have stopped me from doing it are the things that make we want to do it. I mean, the only things that keep me going right now are my family, rugby, and you. Those are the things that make me live. But at the same time, if they are slashed when I transition, if I were to lose all those things . . . what would I live for then?"

Kari took a deep breath. "Well, you don't have to worry about me. Not now. Not yet. So that just leaves your family and rugby . . ."

Fetuao just stared at the ground.

"I'm sorry," Kari said. "I didn't mean to brush off your feelings. The pain you feel has got to be just awful and when you mentioned suicide, my heart sank . . . but being kind of 'real life' about it I think is helping my process . . ."

"No, no, no, you're right," Fetuao assured her. "I've been thinking about it and I just keep going around and around in circles and I just want to sit and cry. I don't know how my family would react. I'm sure they love me, at least my parents do, but so much of their joy in me is tied to rugby. At least I think it is. They have such high expectations for me. I know they want me to play for Tonga in the Olympics. But if I transition I may not be eligible for the 2016 games. And if I miss those, I may be off the radar completely before 2020. Would US women's rugby even have me? Would Tonga? And who knows if I can even stay in good enough shape throughout the transition to compete? And my family has such high expectations for me . . . would playing women's rugby be enough for them? It's all, like, tied up in knots . . . I can't see a way out."

"Not to pile on, but we may be getting ahead of ourselves," Kari chimed in. "What about this season? Will you be able to finish it? What would your team think? And coach? How will the athletic director respond? She might take this on as a public relations hassle . . ."

"And that's exactly what I don't want to be!" Fetuao exclaimed, getting frustrated. "Either a task for public relations, a headache for the AD, or both." He was now thinking of the recent scandal with the football team. GLU had probably seen enough.

"Hey, it's alright. Who knows, maybe everybody will be supportive. Your team, your coach, they all love you. I'm sure they'll support you if this gets to the athletic director. Times are changing, Fetuao. Look at Michael Sam. I'm sure they'll understand . . ."

"This feels very different," he replied calmly. "First, Michael Sam is gay, not trans. There's a pretty big difference. Second, he hasn't really had an easy time at all. Third . . . we're in Wisconsin."

"OK, sure, it's different, but maybe it's a sign that the sporting world is ready for a trans athlete."

"But am I ready to be *that* athlete?"

***

Several weeks have passed and life for Fetuao and Kari was returning to normal—well, almost. Lying together in bed on a lazy Sunday morning with Chicken draped across their bodies and Waffles sleeping by Kari's feet, they looked deeply into each other's eyes and smiled. Suddenly noticing that Kari had drifted off to a very private world, Fetuao asked, "What are you thinking right now?"

Kari hesitated before responding, "What kind of woman do you see yourself as?"

"A beautiful and athletic one," he said playfully.

"Really?" Kari said with a chuckle. "But you are a pretty muscular guy . . ." and immediately regretted saying it.

Fetuao's tone changed. "You mean big women can't be beautiful? Don't people come in all shapes and sizes? Didn't you say that you learned in that women and gender studies class you took that keeping women small and skinny is a product of patriarchy?"

"Yeah, but that's not what I meant. I mean . . . what's the word?" Kari searched around her mind for the term she learned recently. "Can you *pass* as a woman?"

"Well, Dr. Nickel said that it's possible. It'll be a while . . . I start with hormone treatment first before any surgeries . . ." Suddenly remembering, Fetuao added, "But I have to be diagnosed with GID—you know, gender identity disorder—first."

"I know. I've been reading and thinking a lot about it. It seems ridiculous that you have to be diagnosed with a psychological disorder before you can be yourself. You're already perfectly healthy! What's wrong with you now?" She said it with a groan. With some trepidation in her voice, Kari added, "Will you still be attracted to women?"

"I'm totally attracted to you." With a mischievous grin, Fetuao sat up, nudged the kittens off the bed, and added, "I'm going to show you how much right now."

***

The next several weeks were hectic for the young couple—exams, papers, projects, Fetuao's practice, games, medical appointments, and meetings with various recruiters. Everything was moving so fast. Fetuao returned to the apartment to find Kari studying with Waffles purring on her lap.

After giving her a kiss, he couldn't wait to tell Kari, "Big news, honey! I spoke to the Tongan scout after practice today. The Tongan National Team wants me to start practicing with them this summer! They want me to play for them!" He quickly added, "My family will be so pumped! I should call my father."

"A recruiter came by the apartment today, too! He wants you to try out for Team U.S.A. He said it was urgent and you weren't answering your phone."

"Oh my god! I was in practice and left it in my bag. I still haven't even looked."

Wanting to get petted by Fetuao, Chicken had now moved to a pile of letters sitting on the hallway table. When Fetuao looked at the adorable kitten, Chicken immediately started purring loudly with anticipation. Picking up the cat on one hand and reaching for his mail with the other, Fetuao clumsily opened the first envelope. He turned to Kari and solemnly announced, "Well . . . I now officially have GID."

Feeling deeply ambivalent about the meaning of the letter, Kari uttered the obvious, "You could start to transition."

"This is happening way too fast" was what both were thinking. Fetuao flopped down on the couch and looked at his phone, and there were 13 messages: two from friends, three from the Tongan coach, five from the US National Team recruiter, one from the New Zealand professional league recruiter, and two from his parents. What should have been exciting and uplifting suddenly felt ominous.

***

Later that evening, Fetuao and Kari were sitting down for dinner. Fetuao had been moody and brooding, pacing around the apartment all afternoon. He even pushed the kittens away from him every time they nuzzled for affection. Finally they sat down, Kari poured a couple glasses of cheap wine, and Fetuao started speaking for seemingly the first time in hours.

"Maybe I can have a career in women's rugby—by the way, I found I would be technically eligible to compete two years after surgery and with documentation of hormone treatments. So that's assuming I can still compete at a high level after going through all that. Which I honestly have no freaking idea if I will," Fetuao wondered aloud.

Kari sat, attentive, eating, nodding, trying to listen carefully and be sympathetic. Sensing the emotional heaviness of the situation, Chicken and Waffles kept looking at both of them from the kitchen counter.

Fetuao continued, "Maybe I try out for team U.S.A. and hope to make it; the publicity would be better than in Tonga which could potentially increase my chances for work in the sport after 2016. But the brighter spotlight could be a double-edged sword. A Tongan Olympian coming out as trans would sound a lot different than a US Olympian coming out as trans."

"And reach a lot less people. I don't think anybody in the US cares much about Tongan sports." Kari added.

"Well, yeah, that's annoying, but exactly. But is that a good thing or a bad thing? I don't know . . ."

"And perhaps," Kari hesitantly chimed in, "if you were an Olympian first, and then came out to your family as trans, they might be a little more accepting of the idea . . .?"

"Damn, I don't know. I feel like that it can go either way . . . either more accepting, or even more upset."

Kari didn't know what to say. She started wondering again about how her mother, family, and friends would react.

Suddenly feeling his inner sense of urgency, Fetuao said emphatically, "I want to begin transitioning immediately. Or, well, the sooner the better. The sooner I start transitioning, the sooner I can start seeing results and living a "normal"-ish life—whatever that means—and hopefully end all this daily torture."

"I don't mean to be a rain cloud here . . . but what about school? If you go through the transitioning process so close to graduation, do you think you'll be able to finish?" Kari added.

"I am pretty confident I can. I mean, I'm one of the only Islanders on campus and I've been dealing with that. So I don't see why I can't be one of the only trans people on campus and deal with that."

"Well, the social pressure you might be able to handle, although you said yourself the stress and anxiety led you to consider suicide . . . That scares the shit out of me, Fetuao, and I don't want us to think that it's going to be easy. We have to be prepared. And as hard as that might be, we still don't know what the physical changes are going to be like. I mean, we're talking messing with your hormones and body chemistry here. That is never simple. I should know. I'm going to be a nurse." Kari added with a little smile.

"Shit, I didn't really think of that. I've always been so confident with the way my body works I never considered it wouldn't. And that brings me to another complication of transitioning immediately: the team. I mean, it's going to be crazy both socially and physically. Let's take the unsafe assumption that I am still physically able to play through the transition: will they have me on the team? It's all about chemistry and I know I'm going to upset the balance. And I mean . . . they're not bad guys—not at all. But they already give me a hard time about not being a man just 'cause I don't rage at parties or brag about getting chicks. I really don't know what they would do . . . but the thought alone scares me."

There was a long pause as both just sat, staring at their empty glasses.

"This might sound crazy," Kari started, refilling their wine glasses. "What if you went straight to the New Zealand pro league? You're clearly a strong enough player. And if we postponed transitioning, like five years or so, maybe the social climate will change enough where your transition will not only be more generally accepted, but celebrated? I mean, you could be the Laverne Cox of the sporting world!"

"Oh god," Fetuao groaned as he let the idea sink in. "I mean I get it. Making money on rugby sounds real good. That's always been the plan, if I can make it happen. And maybe now is the time. But the idea of, like, 'cashing in' on being trans . . . I don't know. The idea kind of makes me sick."

"Well," Kari continued, "maybe it's not so much 'cashing in' as it is leading the charge."

"And that brings me back to the question, 'Am I ready to be *that* athlete?' It just seems like so much pressure and so much work. Doing that work here at GLU is one thing. Doing it on a huge scale—national, international even—seems like way too much." After a deep breath and finishing his glass of wine, Fetuao sighed, "We need to decide . . . What should I do?"

"To be honest," Kari said, "I am not sure. I feel really confused right now."

Fetuao agreed.

DISCUSSION QUESTIONS

1. If you were Fetauo, what would you do? If you were Kari, what would you tell Fetauo? Consider the consequences for all the different agents in their lives.

2. What is Fetauo's sexuality? What about Kari's? Why?

3. If Fetauo decides to go ahead with the transition, how might people—teammates, fans, coach, friends—define Fetauo's identity before, during, and after the process? How would mainstream media characterize Fetauo's situation?

4. What does this case study say about the intersection of gender, sexuality, and race in the world of sports?

KEY TERMS

Gender, Hegemonic masculinity, Race/ethnicity, Sexual orientation

Julie L. Taylor
SUNY New Paltz

ABSTRACT

Highly sought after recruits are invited to a fun-filled recruitment weekend at the University of Big State. Events such as exotic dancers, alcohol, and selected girls are lined up to satisfy these athletes. This case study explores the consequences of such weekends with potentially problematic outcomes in relation to organizational values, perspectives, and language in common practices. (Please note: content is explicit in order to be as representative of the respective populations as possible.)

***

"Hello, Bobby?" confirmed Coach Jones as he called upon his latest recruit.

"Yeah, Coach, it's me. Listen, I am so excited about this weekend. My boys and I are coming to the University of Big State, it's going to be off the hook" Bobby replied with complete enthusiasm.

"Well, Bobby, we are really pleased to have you and the guys out for the weekend. We are going to show you what the school is about and how we treat our athletes. Also, I am going to put you in touch with one of our players, Cooper. He will be your tour guide for the weekend. You have a piece of paper to write down his number?" As Coach Jones gave Bobby Cooper's number, plans were confirmed and recruitment weekend at the University of Big State was on a roll.

Coach Jones and the rest of the coaching staff knew that it was important not only to get the award-winning recruits to campus early, but also to show them a good time. Athletes on campus were prized like rare animals, men wanted to be them and women wanted to be with them. The athletic scene played out like every teenage movie about athletics and fandom (e.g., *Varsity Blues* and *Friday Night Lights*). However, he also knew that the NCAA had rules against certain practices, but what he didn't know couldn't hurt him. Coach Jones knew that Cooper would know just how to show the guys a "good time." *As an official employee of Big*

State, I could never do what these boys could. But, they know what the guys want, Cooper will know how to show them what our girls will do for the top athlete. Heck, I remember being "the guy" on campus, I knew what I wanted and what I got . . . things don't change that much. Oh, if only to be young again . . .

RECRUITMENT WEEKEND

"Holy shit! This campus is off the chain," Bobby proclaimed to his fellow recruits.

"Yeah, I hear that you don't even have to go to class to get a degree," Gavin laughed.

"Ooooooh snap, I bet the girls will be dropping their panties when they see us coming in the room," Murphy remarked.

The recruits fantasized about all of the possibilities that came with being a college athlete at one of the largest campuses in the country. They stood on a campus that was known for its athletic superiority, party culture, and most of all the hot chicks. The general female populace at this school walked around being hot, strutting in their short skirts, appropriately paired heels or boots, and an insatiable desire to "jersey chase." (Jersey chasing is a commonly used term for girls who want to hook up with athletes as a prize. As a result male athletes rarely, if ever, hear "no" from their female counterparts; these girls wanted a part of the glory as well). The recruits talked about the trophies they would "bang"; the prospects were endless. For just a moment, conversation subsided and almost in unison the guys thought: *hot pussy for days.* In a metaphorical popping of their thought bubble, their tour guide had arrived.

"Hey guys, I am Cooper and I will be your party guide this weekend. Let's get your bags to the hotel and then we will show you how we do it up on a Friday night."

The guys loaded into Cooper's rented, fully loaded SUV for an action-packed weekend. Cooper couldn't wait for the weekend to begin. He loved recruitment weekends because they consisted of three important elements: booze, hot chicks, and more hot chicks. As they were driving to the hotel, Cooper was pumping the guys up, talking about all of the women who would be at the parties, the kegs they had lined up, and the special surprise. "Dudes, something you need to know about Big State is that other schools rate their women on *our* standards. Yo, yo, check this out; a chick could be a 5 here but a 9 at Mountain University. You see what I am saying? Our chicks are hot and they want a piece of the glory, a piece of the action, a piece of you gentlemen." *I need to call and confirm that the strippers will be showing up*, Cooper thought. *Oh I should be setting the mood and playing some jams.*

Cooper selected the song on his iPhone, and through the speakers James Brown's "It's a man's world" started playing over the speakers. *Yes it is,* thought Cooper, *it's all about the men this weekend.*

Murphy started singing and thrusting his hips in a slow motion sort of R&B style . . . "This is a man's, man', man's world, but it wouldn't be nothing, nothing without a woman or a girl . . ." He breaks from the lyrics to question "where are the girls? I am ready to show them about this man's world."

***

Friday nights at the University of Big State bring lots of memories. Weekends are considered "epic" and reminiscent of slogans such as: "Nights I can't remember with friends I will never forget." However, this Friday night was going to include something even more explosive, something that most guys dreamed of—girls, girls, and more girls. *Man these guys are in for a treat. They have no idea that their worlds are about to be rocked—happy endings anyone?* Cooper smirked, as he knew who was about to arrive at the house party.

The recruits looked around the house as if confused about where they were. *I thought we were promised hot chicks?* Gavin questioned to himself. *This is clearly just a sausage fest.* As he continued to look around he notice that the curtains, while ill-fitting, were drawn, the paint on the walls had lots of scuffs but were painfully white. This house was clearly not a place with a "woman's touch"; this was a place where men came to sleep, drink, and repeat. The guys were positioned in a room that had one stained couch that look like it came from the 1970's, and a stack of red solo cups.

"Ding Dong" sounded the doorbell.

As Cooper jaunted toward the door, his teammates handed each of the recruits a pre-rubber-banded stack of dollar bills. There was a magical smell and feeling that came from this money, or was it the connection to what was about to happen—they knew what was coming. Already showing signs of excitement, the guys were positioned in the center of the room, assuming the correct position for the upcoming lap dancing in mediocre folding chairs and with wads of cash in their hands.

"Gentlemen, get your ones ready!" Cooper yelled as he ushered the hired exotic dancers toward the living room.

As cliché as it sounds, in walked a cop asking, "Are there bad boys in the house?" The recruits and current players started hollering, each ready for the show to begin.

Gavin sat in his chair trying to play it cool but thinking, *holy shit, 36-24-36 does exist. These women are fine and all mine.* The recruits enjoyed every minute of the strippers rubbing up and down on their manhood, encouraging undivided attention, and even pulling them into private rooms.

The private rooms were physically a downgrade from the appearance of the main room, but during this time the men were not concerned with paint and pictures. *Big boy? Did Trixxxy just call me a big boy?* Murphy sat up a little taller at this thought and decided to take matters into his own hands. *She said anything goes, so I hope she is ready to ride the pleasure train to Murphy town.*

The women were paid to pleasure the men as much as they wanted. Legality was not of concern during recruitment weekend. The current athletes had only one goal: to show the recruits a good time and to get them to commit to the University of Big State. Plus, the faces and comments from these exotic dancers suggested that they too, were having a good time. At one point in the evening Bobby yelled from the back room, "Oh you like that, don't you . . ." Event number one was a huge success, climactic if you will.

"I smell like stripper," Gavin proudly proclaimed, "I bet other bitches will want me more. Chicks love to smell other chick smell on you; lets them know other chicks will fuck me. Get in or get out, that's what I say."

As the strippers were dismissed from the house, the guys sat around drinking and boasting about what they had just accomplished. "Oh yeah, she brought toys, some I had never seen." Bobby expressed in shock. "I cannot wait for tomorrow night, meet those dime pieces you have been telling us about." And with that the guys passed out in various locations around the house.

***

Saturday was spent drinking Gatorade, hydrating, and getting ready for round two. "Dudes, you had better stop being little bitches if you are going to go here, this is every weekend. And imagine when there's a game in there, no sleep – just party. Partying is like your civic duty on this campus." The other guys laughed at this proclamation, puffed their chests and prepared for another night of drunken debauchery.

Hopping in the SUV the guys were ready to experience a party that until this point they had only seen on TV. The next stop was more than likely going to be their final destination, full of college women and booze, there would be enough to keep the guys busy and happy through the rest of the evening. As the guys stepped up to the house it was reminiscent of fraternity parties pictured in *Animal House* and *He Got Game*. In other words, the girls were sporting "barely-there" clothing choices, keg stands were happening in the entryway, and college students were just having a good time. The only thing that seemed to be missing was the whipped cream bikini à la *Varsity Blues*.

As the guys entered the house Cooper screamed, "LAAAAAADDDDIESSSS . . . We are here . . . show these guys a Big State good time . . ." And with that, previously selected chicks that were rated "10's" and rated "whore-y" enough by the teammates grabbed the recruits to show them to the keg.

The event progressed with free flowing libations, dancing, sexual suggestions, and laughter. This college party represented every college guy's fantasy: hot chicks prime for the picking, the taking, and the conquering. These girls weren't just jersey chasers, they were jersey pleasers. "I will keep you ready for every game, we need you focused on the games, not on sexual tension," Sarah seductively grinned to Bobby. With that statement, the two slipped off into a room to consummate their agreement.

However, the girl whom Murphy was talking to was clearly not as into a rapid sexual encounter as the other girls appeared to be. Murphy excused himself and walked up to Cooper and questioned, "Dude, is she down? I thought you said these girls were down to show us a good time?"

Cooper proclaimed, "Dude, stop being such a pussy, get some pussy. You can tell she wants you so bad, you are an athlete, they all want a piece of you."

Murphy looked at Lacy and she smiled back at him. *Had she heard Cooper?* He thought. *Well maybe I need to switch up the scene, perhaps Lacy doesn't give it up in public.* "Hey beautiful, do you want to go for a walk . . ."

Lacy nodded in agreement, she wanted to get away from all of the people yelling, screaming, and throwing up around her.

However, off in the corner was another team member who was witness to these party charades week in and week out. Lance knew that he had to keep up his image by going to the parties, but he didn't appreciate the way that the women were treated. *My momma raised me better than this,* Lance reflected. *Each weekend these women are lured into a lion's den. These guys don't want them for anything more than a night.* It was the same tired routine, every weekend. Often Lance would maintain a presence around the couples just to make sure that no one got into too much trouble. This evening was no exception. He thought, *I don't know this Murphy guy, but I do know Lacy, she is in my stats class. I am going to keep an eye on her just in case he tries to drive off with her.* With that, he slowly followed Lacy and Murphy as they left the party.

***

As Lacy and Murphy exited the party, Murphy winked at Cooper as to suggest that the relationship between the two was about to progress. Cooper performed congratulatory air-pelvic thrusts and the obligatory smacking of ass as if to say, "Yeah, go get it in."

"How about we go sit in the park?" Suggested Lacy. *What a romantic evening, I love the park and I get to be accompanied by a handsome future Big State athlete. Maybe dreams do come true. I know the guys wanted me to sleep with Murphy, but I want to do this differently. I want him to like me, not just leave me like the other guys. He seems nice enough, I am sure he will understand.* Lacy smiled as she led Murphy to the grassy knoll that overlooked the city lights.

The two were talking for about ten minutes and then Cooper's statement echoed in Murphy's head *"don't be a pussy, get some pussy."* Murphy promptly leaned into Lacy and kissed her. To his excitement she leaned into him, kissing back, and even adding tongue. *She does like me,* Murphy confirmed in his mind as the physical encounter continued.

As the two were getting more intimate Lacy started to push back a little, but Murphy remembered a moment like this. In fact, Louis CK had a skit about a similar situation with a girl who "didn't want it." He remembered the skit went something like "We were making out, and I put my hand up her shirt and she stops me . . . I put my hand on her ass, and she stops me . . . the next morning she asked, *why didn't we have sex last night?* Uh, why did you keep stopping me? *I wanted you to keep going for it . . .*"

In remembering this skit, Murphy *knew* that girls were turned on by power, by men taking what they wanted. Murphy heard Lacy's pleas to stop, but he assumed they were playful and that she wanted him to keep going.

Lacy had read about moments like this, in fact she had even talked about them in her college classes, but it had never happened to her. *This can't be my fate, this can't be happening to me tonight.* In order to block out the actions Lacy drifted off into a land of enchantment remembering her family vacation to the beach, sand between her toes, the sun on her face . . .

Lance had been keeping enough distance during this time to not be seen. However, when he realized that things had gone from friendly to "no means yes," Lance ran into the scene and took Lacy away. *I don't know if she is going to hate me or not, but who is this guy? This is exactly what I worry about every weekend. I have to get her home.*

"Come on man, we were just messing around" Murphy yelled as Lacy was being pulled away from the situation. "Cooper said she wanted me . . ." *Cooper lied, what a jerk. I thought all of the girls were down . . .*

NO MEANS YES AT UNIVERSITY OF BIG STATE

Recruitment weekend ended, just as they always did. The boys had put on a great show and the recruits had verbally committed to join the team; they were excited to become a part of the athletic tradition. Life per usual went on for everyone, well, everyone but Lacy.

Lacy was conflicted, as she knew that she had initially agreed to be one of the trophies of the weekend, but she actually really liked Murphy. She knew the drill with these weekends, "pump and dump" as the guys would chant after the weekends were over. *I wanted Murphy to be different. I want to be wife-material.* Lacy cried as she recapped the events of the evening in her mind. *Should I even tell anyone? Would anyone even believe me? I did go to the park with him. Would Lance stand up for me, or would he back his new teammate?* Lacy felt blame about the situation, and she decided to confide in a close friend, Megan—a fellow jersey chaser.

Upon explaining what had happened on that Saturday evening, Megan replied, "Come on, Lacy, you know this is what happens every time they bring recruits in. Your job as a hot chick on campus is to help get good athletes. This wasn't rape. This was helping out your school. You are lucky to have been chosen."

Lacy put her head down and attempted to accept the situation. She felt invalidated by the comments, but also knew that she had initially agreed to participate. However, something just didn't feel right. *Lucky? Really, I am lucky to have been raped by a future star, oh so lucky. I wonder how many other girls have been so lucky? Does the university support recruiting like this? If these have been practices for a long time, does the president know?* As Lacy began the painful yet necessary process of critical reflection she knew that she had to tell someone. Lacy didn't like saying the word "rape" or even being identified as the "chick who was raped," but she knew that she needed to stand up for herself. Bravely, Lacy decided to meet with the president of the university to explain what had happened.

***

"Hi President Smith, my name is Lacy and I appreciate you meeting with me," Lacy shyly introduced herself.

"Hello Lacy, what can I do for you?" questioned President Smith as he closed the door to his office, ensuring privacy during the meeting.

Lacy went on to describe the events of the evening of the recruitment weekend. She explained her connection with one of the recruits and how they had gone to the park together for what she assumed would be a romantic evening. As she was recapping the details, President Smith furrowed his brow and thought: *There was alcohol involved, I wonder if Lacy was drunk? Yes, perhaps she drank too much and thought that the young man came onto her. Oh, if this gets out this will be bad for business. We are set to win the championship this year, and we don't need this kind of publicity. We are also going to have to talk with Lance to confirm that this doesn't get out.*

As Lacy concluded her story to the president she was thanked for her time and information and told that they would "be in touch." The response was one chosen out of respect for professional communication and an attempt to mitigate any potential litigation against the school. *This could be a nightmare if word gets out,* President Smith thought as he placed his head in his hands in worry.

President Smith knew that he was going to have to confirm the details of the story with Coach Jones. However, President Smith also knew that the organizing of weekends such as this one operated off a "don't ask, don't tell" strategy. As President Smith remained at his desk he thought *well, boys will be boys, won't they?*

DISCUSSION QUESTIONS

1. If you were President Smith, what would you do? For example, what would his first step be in handling Lacy's revelation? Do you think that President Smith should contact Lance? Would Lance go against his teammate, because he was at the party?

2. If President Smith decides to hide the truths of the event what does this say about the university's organizational values? Conversely, if President Smith decides to emerge with details about the situation, what does this say about the university's organizational values?

3. How does the language that was used by the players (re)enforce hegemonic masculinity at the standard organizing construct? What material consequences ensue? For example, think about the use of chicks or girls versus women.

4. What does the standard of hiring females for males assume about the sexual orientation of all of the players? In what ways is this potentially problematic?

5. What are potential larger implications about an organization that preferences hegemonic masculinity and (re)enforces women as sexual objects? For example, consider athletic culture and the prevalence of sex for sale around these events, or even the notion of engaging in prostitution (exchanging sex with the players for money). Or, think about the initial submission from the women to participate in "jersey chasing" and then a desire by one woman to change her mind, does she have the agency to do this (or is yes always yes)?

KEY TERMS

Collegiate sports, Gender, Hegemonic masculinity

CASE 36: WHOSE BALL IS IT ANYWAY?

Mary C. Toale
SUNY Oswego and SUNY New Paltz

Katherine S. Thweatt
SUNY Oswego and SUNY New Paltz

ABSTRACT

A couple, Virginia and Jack, are superfans of the Jackson Jaybirds and meet as a result of their fandom. The Jaybirds' star player, Bo Jordan, is a hometown boy who is heralded as the next hometown hero. Bo is set to break the homerun record and lead his team to a national championship. Along the way, the couple and Bo encounter a situation that leads to an international media flurry.

***

FAN CHAT ROOM

Virginia: "Hello, my name is Virginia and I saw your posts on Monday after the Jayhawks beat the Indiana Indians. I loved your insight into the will demonstrated by Bo Jordan as he approaches beating the all-time homerun record of Barry Bonds in his next season."

Jack: "Hi Virginia, thanks for the compliment! I hope Bo can keep up this incredible run. Do you go to the games????"

Virginia: "Hey Jack! I go to every game I can get to . . . you?"

Jack: "Hey, VA. I'm there all of the time when I'm not waiting tables."

Virginia: "Ha, ha—VA! I love it. I wait tables too!"

Jack: "That's awesome—big fans of the same team and the same job! I'm going to be at next Tuesday's game. Wanna meet up?"

Virginia: "Hey Jack, the Jackson fan, that would be great!"

Jack and Virginia are Jackson Jaybird superfans. They met online in a chat room for their team's fans. They go to all the home games, and try to make it to as many away games as they

308

can afford on their waiterstaff salaries. They make their work schedules around the game times. When they are not going to games, they are talking strategy for their fantasy sports leagues. They also spend time online in team chat rooms and forums. Their romantic relationship revolves around their love of their team, the Jackson Jaybirds.

After dating for the entire 2015 season, Jack and Virginia were excited about the upcoming 2016 season. As the season began, Jack and Virginia were becoming increasingly excited about Bo Jordan's continued demonstration of will as he worked toward beating Barry Bonds' record. Unbeknownst to Virginia, Jack was planning a little something special for Virginia during the game in which Jordan was expected to break the record.

PLAYER'S WILL

Bo Jordan was Jackson's hometown boy. Jordan began playing for the Jaybirds straight out of high school. He attended a high school in Acorn just about 70 miles from Jackson. He was watched from the time he was in junior high school as a promising young athlete. Hordes of people, including scouts, showed up to watch Jordan play. Jordan was groomed to be the next star of the Jaybirds. He was the hero who would turn around the Jaybirds' slump and finally bring the World Series Championship to Jackson. After signing with his hometown team and playing for several seasons, it became clear that Jordan was a stellar player. He was also a stellar role model.

On the field, he allowed for very few errors at shortstop, but his batting is what set him apart. His at-bat record was .397. He was amazing. Despite hitting homers on a regular basis and regularly having tremendous percentages, his teammates weren't up to par. Bo's efforts weren't enough. After two more seasons of making it to the playoffs and not winning, Bo needed to consider his options. Bo began talking to his confidante, Ron, about what to do.

Bo: "Ron, I'm giving it everything I've got and it's just not enough."

Ron: "No one could ask for any more from you. You have the will to win, but there are eight other players on the field who have to have the same will."

Bo: "They are good guys. They support me, but I'm frustrated. I think I need to talk with the GM and owner about how I'm feeling."

Ron: "Yep, you need to be straight with them and ask them to make a few trades for some guys who can bring home the World Series. Our city WANTS it."

Bo reached out to the GM and owner and a meeting was set.

GM: "Hey Bo, it's nice to sit down with you off the field."

Owner: "How's the backbone of our team doing?"

Bo: "I'm great and I'm hoping we can bring home the series win."

Owner: "We know you are doing everything you can. What do you think it's going to take?"

Bo: "I'm hoping you might have some suggestions."

Owner: "Well, the GM and I have been talking and we think we need to make a few changes to our roster. We're already negotiating a few trades."

THE PANIC

The meeting went as Bo had hoped and new players began arriving. Before changes to the team were obvious, news of the meeting leaked to the media. Jackson was in an uproar thinking their hometown boy might pick up and leave. Panic set in among the very loyal fan base. Some fans began to question Bo's loyalty. Some began to say that he didn't have "enough will." They began comparing his "will" to that of basketball great, Kobe Bryant, saying Bo's didn't compare to Kobe's.

Jack: "Virginia! Did you see that Bo met with the owner and GM to discuss his disappointment and frustration with not bringing home the series? If he leaves, he'll beat that homerun record wearing another team's jersey. I'm sick."

Virginia: "Me too! I will die if he leaves, but he has to do what's right for him. Walking through the restaurant today, the only word I could hear was "Bo." "Bo, Bo, Bo . . ." People are upset."

Fan Chat room Guy 1: "Bo is good, but he's not good enough. Kobe Bryant wasn't always surrounded by the best, but his will got the team through. I know I'm comparing baseball to basketball, but still!"

Fan Chat room Guy 2: "He's whining when he should be rallying his team."

Jack: "We don't know the whole story. We don't know why he met with the GM and Owner."

Virginia: "Bo is awesome. As much as I want him to stay, he needs to think about himself sometimes."

Fan Chat room Guy 2: "He needs to get it together."

After the news story leaked, fans began showing up at "The Jack" a.k.a. Jackson Field. Thousands of fans showed up to show their support for Bo. The owner was getting death threats and his office was inundated with hate mail. Social media blew up.

2016 SEASON

As the 2016 season opened, the panic settled down. New players were on the team and their stats were amazing. Several of the players were probably past their prime, but had been on teams that had won the series. They knew what it was like to win and they were hungry for another win.

Press Release from New Player: "I'm happy to be a member of the Jaybird team that already feels like family. My goal is to win the series here for the Jaybirds' incredible fan base. I know what that win feels like and I want you, Bo, and the rest of the team to now share in that experience. You've already been great and I'm looking forward to my first season with you. Let's get that series win!"

Preseason was going beautifully. The team seemed to gel in a way they hadn't before. The team sailed through the first few games of the season with easy wins. The fan base was hyped.

DAY OF "THE GAME"

On a humid August day, Jack and Virginia headed out to their favorite baseball team's game. This was not just any game; it was "THE game." Bo was expected to break the homerun record that day, propelling his team one step further toward that coveted series win. They splurged and purchased tickets in the right field bleachers where Bo hits 75% of his homerun balls. They read an article, "How to Catch a Souvenir Ball" on The Art of Manliness website. http://www. artofmanliness.com/2008/04/15/how-to-snag-a-souvenir-baseball/. They read "Snagging Balls" by Zack Hample who caught over 3000 balls. They knew the rules of ethical fan behavior like the back of their hands. On the day of "the game," Jack and Virginia carried their gloves with them and sat in the prime homerun seats which cost them over $500, or nearly a week in tips.

Crowd: *"Take me out to the ballgame . . . take me out with the crowd . . ."*

Virginia: "Tied game, and Bo has had only one hit. This is torture! I'm heading to the bathroom, want anything?"

Jack: "Grab me a couple of beers!"

Virginia: "Anything else?"

Jack: "No."

Virginia: "Be right back."

Crowd: *". . . root, root, root, for the home team . . ."*

Jack: "That was quick, thanks!"

Virginia: "Got lucky, short lines."

Jack: "Alright, Bo is up first. Are you ready? Where's your glove?"

Virginia: "Yes, got it! This is going to be it!"

Jack: "Since we say it every time, maybe this time it will be true."

Jack: "Alright, looks like Lefty McMillan is pitching this inning. Bo doesn't always do well with lefties. Not sure this will be it, hon."

Virginia: "Have faith, Jack!"

Umpire: *"BALL ONE!"*

Virginia: "Geez, this is tense!"

Jack: "I know it, but I have to ask you something. Hold out your glove."

Virginia stuck out her glove and Jack got down on one knee.

Jack: "Virginia, I want us to remember this day forever and not just because Bo will break the homerun record. I want you to remember that even in the midst of baseball and our love of the game that my love for you is stronger. You are my priority. You are my love. Will you marry me?"

Virginia: "I love you! Of course, I will marry you."

CRACK!

Jack: "Holy crap! It's coming our way."

THUD!

Jack: "I can't believe it!! You caught it!!!!"

Virginia: "WOW! I can't believe this!"

Security Guard: "Ma'am, are you okay?"

Virginia: "YES! I'm fantastic!"

Security Guard: "What is your name?"

Virginia: "Virginia Coker. Did you drop your beer too?!"

Jack: "Yea, don't worry about it!"

Security Guard: "Ma'am, can we get your signature on this sheet? It just says that you weren't injured."

Virginia: "Sure."

Security Guard: "Enjoy the rest of the game."

Virginia: "Jack, can you believe I caught it!?! I caught the freakin' ball! Holy crap!"

Jack: "So cool! You caught the ball, but I caught YOU!"

At the end of the eighth inning the head of security, Jim McCann, approached Virginia.

Jim: " Ms. Coker, can you please come with me?"

Virginia: "Okay, but where are we going? My fiancé Jack needs to come with me. Can't we wait until the game's over?"

Jim: "He can come. The owner would like to speak with you before the game ends."

Jack: "Let's go. It'll be alright."

Virginia: "Okay."

Jack and Virginia exchanged glances as they walked behind Jim. They saw on the television monitors that the Jackson Jaybirds were now up 7–2. They were pretty certain their team would win.

Jim took them to the elevators for the private suites. They proceeded to the owner's box. As they entered the room, they noticed the owner and a couple of other people.

Jim: "This is Virginia Coker, the woman who caught Bo's homerun ball."

Owner: "Nice to meet you, Virginia. And this is..?"

They shook hands.

Virginia: "This is my fiancé, Jack."

Owner: "Nice to meet you, Jack. You're one lucky guy to have caught Virginia here."

They shook hands.

Jack: "Yes, and she is one hell of a catch and catcher!"

Owner: "Right. Have a seat. This is Patrick, our Chief Executive Officer and Heather, our Media Relations Manager. So let's get straight to it. Congratulations on catching Bo's homerun ball."

Jack: "Bo's RECORD BREAKING homerun ball."

Owner: "Yes. Record Breaking. We'd like the ball so we can display it here at the stadium. How would you like a couple of jerseys, hats, and tickets behind home plate in exchange for the ball?"

Virginia and Jack looked at one another, but didn't know what to say. Finally, Virginia broke the silence.

Virginia: "I am a die hard fan of the Jaybirds, Bo, and baseball. I am not sure what you are offering in exchange for this ball is enough."

Patrick: "As a fan, you know the significance of that ball and what it means to the team and to baseball."

Jack: "Yes, we both do."

Patrick: "Then what we can we do to get it on display for the rest of the fans?"

Virginia: "Perhaps Jack and I can have some time to talk about it?"

Owner: "How much time do you need? We'd like to have this on display as soon as possible."

Virginia: "I don't know."

Heather: "Let's get a picture of you holding the ball."

Virginia: "Okay. Come on Jack, get in the picture with me."

Heather: "How about we set up a meeting to discuss this within the week? You will be our guests for tomorrow's game."

Virginia: "Okay, Great!"

Jim escorted Virginia and Jack to the parking lot. Jim congratulated them and told them to ask for him when they arrived the next morning.

Jack and Virginia saw the ball as the ultimate fan memorabilia they could pass on to their children. However, they also saw it as a way to secure their financial future. Maybe they could get their wedding and reception paid for and a lifetime of family tickets and money to buy a house and college money for future kids. There were so many possibilities!

WHAT HAPPENED NEXT . . .

Jack and Virginia's proposal was caught on camera and the Jaybirds' media relations team sensationalized the proposal and the catch with taglines such as "she caught the ball and he caught the girl!" Jackson went wild that night pronouncing their hometown boy as their hometown hero. Bo didn't sleep that night and the entire city stayed up to celebrate. That night, the question of the ball never came up in the hometown media, but a flurry was brewing across the world. The homerun record was the focus in Jackson, though.

The next day, when some of the excitement wore off, the fan chat room blew up with questions over the ball. Whose ball was it?

Fan 1: I wonder if Jack and Virginia will keep the ball . . .

Fan 2: She caught the ball right after he proposed . . . that's a tough one.

Fan 3: I don't care if she gave birth in the stadium and then caught the ball. She needs to give it to Bo.

Fan 4: No way. Bo should give it to the couple as an early wedding present.

The city became divided over whose ball it was. Both sides of the issue were discussed on every social media site, radio show hosts couldn't quit talking about it and the fans kept calling in with differing opinions for different reasons. On the Big Jon and Little Joe show, Big Jon thought she should keep the ball and Little Joe said it should go back to the player.

The most prestigious law firm in town contacted Virginia and Jack. The firm represented them pro bono. Their lawyer released the following statement:

"Virginia and Jack have not made any decisions at this time. The newly engaged couple wishes for the incredibly loyal fan base, as well as Bo and the Jaybirds, to know that the gravity of this situation warrants careful thought and matters of this level of importance cannot be settled quickly. Virginia and Jack are weighing their options as they consider their own as well as the best interest of others."

Reactions on social media intensified.

Virginia and Jack were tortured over this decision. They were such huge fans that having the ball was almost more important than the money they could earn selling the ball. Also weighing on them was the fact that the ball was "the ball." It was the ball with which Bo broke the record. Maybe it should go back to Bo. Being such huge fans, they almost felt like they were betraying the team and Bo if they kept the ball.

There was so much buzz around this topic throughout the world that it became a media nightmare for Virginia and Jack. Part of their city called them traitors for not giving the ball back immediately. They got death threats. Other diehard fans thought they should keep the ball for a souvenir. Still another camp thought they should sell the ball to the highest bidder which may or may not be Bo Jordan. Some argued that the young couple could be set for life if they sold the ball. After all, they made their living waiting tables. Until they could make a decision, the media buzz made it necessary to lay low for a while.

Bo's life following his record-breaking hit was full of celebration and praise, but the question of the ball, and who it belonged to, began to overshadow his accomplishment. The media was asking him directly whom the ball belonged to in this situation. Bo was torn. The implications of any decision he could make affected different groups of people, but Bo still felt like that excited little boy on the inside who had just hit a homer. He wanted his ball. Virginia and Jack also felt like little kids who caught the ball. They wanted it, too.

DISCUSSION QUESTIONS

1. How should Virginia and Jack's media relations experts handle the media flurry surrounding their situation on social media? To manage this situation, what actions should the media relations experts recommend to their clients, Jack and Virginia?

2. Should Virginia and Jack's lawyer have released the statement? Was the content acceptable?

3. What strategies should be used to combat the negative messages being generated about Virginia and Jack and Bo? How should messages about the couple and Bo differ? Why do these messages need to be different? To manage this situation, what actions should the media relations experts recommend to their client, Bo?

4. How should Bo's media relations experts handle the following message on social media: "Bo has a responsibility to his team to let this record breaking hit become the focus so he should just give the ball to the couple to end this media flurry. His indecision is detracting from this city's and his team's proud moment."

5. How should Virginia and Jack's media relations experts handle the following message found on social media? "If Virginia and Jack were truly loyal to Bo and our team then they would give the ball back."

KEY TERMS

Social media and sport, Fan culture, Team and fan relations

CASE 37: "JUNK IN THE TRUNK"

Body Shaming in Women's Soccer

Diana L. Tucker
Walden University

ABSTRACT

The Los Angeles Raptors, a team with the American Women's Indoor Soccer League (AWISL), have a new coach. When he says some inappropriate things about the bodies of the Latinas on the team, the women band together to try to right the wrong. But no one seems willing to take the problem seriously.

***

"He said what?!?" Yasmin Costa said incredulously.

"Let me play it for you," Gabriella Hernandez said as she fumbled with her iPhone. "It is on the radio station's website. Here it is."

Radio DJ: "So, Coach Nazarov, what needs to happen to make the Los Angeles Raptors ready to make a play for the American Women's Indoor Soccer League's championship series this year?"

Coach Stepan Nazarov: "We, we need to get faster. We got some ladies with, what do they say here? 'Junk in the trunk'? Yes, so we need to lose some of that junk. Mostly it is the Hispanic players, because they really like their tortillas I guess. So, I'm going to start with some strict diet and toning regimens."

Radio DJ: "Well, that will surely please the guys who might want to come to the games!"

"Oh my God! I just can't believe this. He was body shaming us!" Yasmin growled.

"Body shaming, what's that?" asked Gabriella.

"I read an article about it. It was mostly about how kids are using Facebook and stuff to call girls fat and stuff. It is a type of bullying," Yasmin explained.

"Why was he on the radio anyway?" exclaimed Eva Toledo.

"I guess they were trying to generate interest in the league, get more people to come to the games. I hear he was making the rounds of some of the radio stations and morning TV shows in Southern California," explained Gabriella.

"Why are they just having him do it? Shouldn't the women on the team be doing that? I mean we are the players in THE WOMEN'S INDOOR SOCCER LEAGUE!" Eva bellowed with exasperation.

"I know, I think because he is our new coach and he was well known as a coach in the European Men's League, they thought he might generate more interest? I don't know," said Gabriella. "But let's get back to the point about WHAT he said. We can't let this stand, what should we do?" Gabriella directed this to Silvia Gonzales, the oldest member of the team, one of the team captains, and someone they all looked up to.

"I am just livid, we need to talk to the rest of the team, make sure they will back us on whatever we do. I'll call a team meeting." Silvia looked at her younger sister, Maria Elena. "Maria Elena, you are very quiet, what are you thinking?"

"I don't know. I'm just sad. I thought this was going to be our year and that Coach Nazarov was going to help us win a championship. He seemed cool when we all met him last week." Maria Elena wouldn't even look up from her lap as she said this, she seemed defeated.

"What did we expect? He is Russian!" Eva asserted. "They don't live with a lot other cultures and stuff over there and I hear everyone is racist and shit. And we gotta make sure he learns that we are Latinas, not 'Hispanic.' Racist asshole."

"Let's not start saying stuff like that, Eva, that would be considered by many people to be just as bad as what he said about us," Silvia reasoned. "But yes, we will address the 'Hispanic' label too."

"Yeah, well I'm mad and he's racist," Eva mumbled.

"I know, I know. Thanks for bringing this to our attention, Gabriella," Silvia said. "I'm gonna text the other girls and ask them to come a little early to tomorrow's practice so we can have a team meeting and fill them in."

THE TEAM MEETING

"I can understand why you'd all be upset," said Lindsey Hart once Gabriella was done playing the interview. "That just isn't right."

"I knew you'd all understand and have our backs on this," Silvia said with a smile.

"Well, yes, I understand, but I don't think you all should do anything," Tasha Smalley, the other team captain, said.

"What do you mean we shouldn't do anything? This guy is a racist asshole!" yelled Yasmin.

"Yes, but if you guys say anything, that is going to ruin the team dynamic and he might hold a grudge against some of you, our best players. Or management might fire him and then we won't have a coach and no chance at a run for the championship," explained Tasha. A number of the other non-Latina players nodded their heads in agreement.

"Well, I can't believe management wouldn't already know he has said this stuff. They are the ones who sent him on this publicity tour and surely they then listened to what he said!" exclaimed Gabriella.

"Yes, and so if they don't do anything without you complaining, what is the likelihood they'll do anything if you do complain?" reasoned Tasha.

"Maybe you all could just have a heart-to-heart-like talk with Coach? Explain that he hurt your feelings and you hope he won't say things like that in the future," Dana Ripley suggested.

"But you all won't have that talk with him with us, you don't got our backs?" Silvia asked.

The other players all looked at their hands, their feet, the ceiling, anywhere but at their Latina teammates' eyes. "Well, I guess that answers that. I'm really disappointed," Silvia said and walked out of the locker room. Maria Elena rushed after her.

"You all should be ashamed of yourselves. Come on Gabi, Eva," Yasmin exclaimed and they marched out after Silvia.

Outside, Silvia, Maria Elena, Yasmin, Eva, and Gabriella stood in a circle.

"So, what do we do?" asked Gabriella.

"I can't believe this! First he says that shit, then our teammates don't want to stand up to him? This is crazy. We can't let his time coaching us start like this with him getting away with that," Eva's exasperation was palpable.

"I agree. But, I do sort of like Dana's idea of just trying to have a heart-to-heart with Coach," Maria Elena suggested.

"Yeah, I suppose that's a start," agreed Silvia. "But we can't go in there all yelling and stuff, that won't get us anywhere and will make him feel like we are ganging up on him."

"Then you don't want me in there, cause I'm gonna yell and tell him what I think!" Yasmin huffed.

"Why don't just Silvia and I just go talk to him right now and see if he is apologetic at all?" Gabriella suggested.

"Yeah, okay, I'm good with that," Eva answered.

"Yeah, that's good," Yasmin agreed.

"Yes, good idea," Maria Elena said.

COACH NAZAROV AND THE LA RAPTORS

Coach Stepan Nazarov was hired in the off season as the LA Raptors' new coach. He had been assistant coaching in the European Men's Football League (EMFL) for ten years after playing professionally for eight years before that. He had been let go from the Luxembourg Lyons when a new head coach had been hired, but that was more because the head coach wanted to bring in his own people, not because Stepan Nazarov was a bad coach. While he had never been a head coach before, he had been on the coaching staff for two league champion teams in 2007 and 2010. As a player he had won MVP three times with the Rome Real. Unfortunately a torn ACL took him out of play in 2005, which is when he started coaching as an assistant in the EMFL.

Starting his head coaching career with a women's indoor soccer league was not really what he had planned, but his wife, an American he met while vacationing in Hawaii in 2006, really wanted to live back in the States. There had been no job openings in the American Men's Soccer League (AMSL) when he was looking, so he started to look at the women's outdoor and indoor leagues. The American Women's Indoor Soccer League (AWISL) had begun just two years ago and had a decent following. The LA Raptors especially were doing well with ticket sales given the large soccer enthusiastic Latino culture in the Southern California area. Stepan had been surprised when the Raptors' President, Raul Lanzino, said they sold out most home games and that the community was really supportive. Stepan started to believe that with one or two years of success in the women's indoor professional league, it would get him an "in" with the AMSL. Raul told Stepan that he felt fortunate that his team was getting such a high-caliber coach, that this was their year to take it all, and hiring Stepan was the key to winning. Stepan was feeling very good about his future.

As he was contemplating how best to start his first practice with the LA Raptors team, he heard a knock on his office door.

"Come in," he called.

The door opened to reveal Silvia Gonzales, one of the team captains who played forward, and Gabriella Hernandez, a goalkeeper.

"Ladies, please come in. What can I do for you?" Stepan said without getting up.

"We wanted to talk to you about something, Coach," Silvia said.

"Yes, go ahead," Stepan said.

"Coach, we heard what you said during the interview with KBIZ radio on Monday," Gabriella stated.

Coach Nazarov looked at the two women blankly.

"You know, where you said that the 'Hispanics' on the team had 'junk in the trunk' because we liked to eat too many tortillas?" Silvia reminded him.

Coach started to laugh. "Yes, of course, you know I was trying to use the American jargon. It got some laughs."

Silvia and Gabriella looked at each other incredulously. "Well, we did not find it funny, Coach," Gabriella retorted.

"Well, you have to admit you'd move faster if you lost some of the weight back there," Coach Nazarov came back with a chuckle.

"That is how we are made, Coach." Silvia rolled her eyes. "We run our asses all over the field and work out every day. No amount of diet and more exercise is going to change how my ass looks. It is pure muscle. The same for any other Latina ass on this team you might think has too much 'junk in the trunk.' And that's another thing, why are you calling out the Latinas? Many women of all races and ethnicities who work out regularly have bodies like ours. And it is 'Latina' or 'Latino'; we also thought you should know that the term 'Hispanic' is not what people should use any more."

Coach Nazarov rolled his eyes right back at Silvia. "You girls need to lighten up. It was a joke. To get laughs. Even President Lanzino thought it was funny, he said so himself. Yeah, okay, so you don't need to lose more weight, or CAN'T do it. We'll still see if we can make you faster."

"So, that's it? You're not going to apologize or make amends in any way?" asked Gabriella.

"I don't see a need to apologize. IT. WAS. A. JOKE. I'm SORRY you can't see it that way," Stepan replied. "Now go get ready to practice," he said dismissively and looked back at the playbook he was working on.

Silvia and Gabriella left the office.

Twenty minutes later when he went to the indoor field they used as a practice arena, the five "Latinas" were nowhere to be found. *Typical women,* thought Stepan, *blowing everything out of proportion and creating drama. This is why I did not really want to coach in the women's league. Well, let's just do this practice and, if they don't plan on participating, then they won't be a part of this team.*

"Ladies, move your asses, let's get going!" Coach Nazarov blew his whistle and motioned for everyone to come gather around him.

***

"I'm so upset," Eva said to the others as they sat around a table at their favorite bar, Los Guachos. "I can't believe he didn't acknowledge that what he said was even slightly offensive."

"I know," agreed Maria Elena. "What is going to happen now that we didn't show up for practice?"

"I don't know, but I just couldn't go," replied Silvia.

"Me either," everyone chorused.

"Well, I know what I'm gonna do, I'm getting on Twitter and I am going to call this gringo asshole out! He needs some shaming now!" Yasmin was obviously fuming.

"Wait, Yaz, please, don't do that. Not yet," Silvia pleaded. "We need to be more rational and calculated about our next move. Let's not stoop to his level."

"Fine," Yasmin huffed. "But I know we will get the Latino community together by taking to social media. THEY will have our backs!"

"I know, that's an idea," agreed Silvia. "But I want to go talk to management first. Maybe they will come through for us and make some amends."

"I think we should all go this time, show a united front," Eva stated emphatically.

"Okay, but we can't go off," Silvia reasoned. "We need to be calm and collected or we will look like the crazy ones and they won't listen to a word we say. Can you all remain calm?"

"I'll try," said Yasmin. "But it will be hard."

"Just remember, we were wronged and the better we present ourselves, the more stupid he looks. Besides, President Lanzino is Latino! I know Coach said Lanzino thought it was funny, but that is hearsay. Hopefully he will be open to hear our side of this story. Let's have a little faith in our Latino brother, eh?" Silvia implored.

"Yeah, you are right," chimed Gabriella.

"Good, I'll get us a meeting with Lanzino as soon as possible," Silvia declared.

MEETING WITH THE PRESIDENT

"Ladies, please come in, have a seat. I am anxious to talk with you all about your concerns," Raul Lanzino smiled and shook each woman's hand as he led them into his office and motioned for them to take seats.

"So, your administrative assistant explained why we were here, Mr. Lanzino?" asked Silvia.

"Yes, yes, I understand you were offended by Coach Nazarov's comments about you eating too many tortillas," Lanzino said with a grin.

"Yeah, but he was calling the Latinas out specifically and that's racist!" Yasmin exclaimed.

Silvia gave Yasmin a warning look and continued, "Sir, yes, we are upset that he did that publicly. But we went to him to express privately that what he said was not acceptable and we wanted an apology. He refused to apologize and does not seem to see anything wrong with what he said."

"Ladies, ladies," Lanzino crooned. "I understand your feelings. I myself love my Latinas with a little 'junk in the trunk,' as he put it. But I'm hoping you all can be the bigger people here and will let this go for the good of the team and the season. We have great expectations for you all. I see a championship in the future and then some pay raises for you all if that were to happen."

"How can we play for a guy like that when he is allowed to get away with that kind of behavior? I just don't think I can do it," Eva stated adamantly.

"Well, that would be your choice then, Ms. Toledo. I am sure we can find other players who would love your position," Lanzino answered.

"Well, if you don't have any Latina players, you really think all your Latino fans are going to keep coming to the games?" Yasmin countered.

"I do not take kindly to such threats, Ms. Costa. I feel confident we could even get some new Latina players in here who would not let some petty comment from the coach get in the way of a successful career," Lanzino sat back with a smirk on his face.

Silvia stood up, "Well, I understand your point of view Mr. Lanzino. We thank you for your time, we have some things to think about." With that the five women left the office.

As she led her troop down the hall and out of the building, Silvia's mind was reeling. *What should they do now? Do they suck it up and go back to practices like nothing ever happened? She didn't think Yaz would be willing to let it go. What about Yaz's idea to take it to social media? Would that help them, or make things worse? There were many options to consider.*

"Let's go back to Los Guachos and talk about what to do," Silvia threw over her shoulder and kept walking.

DISCUSSION QUESTIONS

1. Have the Latina players done a good job communicating with others in this case about their concerns? What, if anything, might they have done differently?

2. Is President Lanzino being negligent? Or a good businessman?

3. Body shaming as a bullying tactic has been an issue discussed a lot in the media lately. How might the team take this instance and use it to further add to the discussion on body shaming in the media?

4. What is the best next step for this group? Will they be able to get the kind of restitution they are looking for? If so, how? If no, why not?

KEY TERMS

Body shaming, Race relations, Administration negligence

AUTHOR BIOGRAPHIES

Carlee Tressel Alson (M.F.A., Hamline University) has served as an adjunct instructor at the college level, specializing in first-year composition and sports literature, and has led numerous creative writing workshops for students and writers of all ages. As a practitioner in the communications field, Ms. Alson has worked in advertising and public relations agencies developing and creating both print and interactive media for educational institutions, privately owned companies, and start-ups. Currently, she provides communications strategy and writing services to clients as an independent contractor. She is based in northwest Indiana.

Taylor Anguiano (M.A.L., Boise State University) is Head Athletic Trainer at Mountain View High School in Boise, Idaho. She is a recent graduate of the Master of Athletic Leadership program at Boise State University and served as the athletic trainer for Boise State's women's volleyball and sand volleyball. Throughout her graduate assistantship, she served as a preceptor to undergraduate sports medicine students. When Taylor isn't working, she enjoys baking, outdoor activities, and spending time with her dogs.

Jordan Atkinson (M.A., Morehead State University) is a Ph.D. student at West Virginia University. His areas of research include family communication and instructional communication. His recent research involves the intersections of family and instructional communication involving first-generation college student identity formation and the tensions that form in family relationships. He also uses family communication theories to investigate parent-child relationships. Jordan has taught numerous courses at WVU and also serves as a co-advisor for Lambda Pi Eta and the Undergraduate Communication Association.

Hannah Ball (M.A., West Virginia University) is a doctoral student in the Department of Communication Studies at West Virginia University, where she teaches undergraduate health communication and research methods courses. Hannah's main research interest is developing evidence-based social influence messages that promote pro-social health behavior and she has worked on projects related to organ donor consent, testicular cancer awareness, and obesity/diabetes prevention and management. Additionally she is interested in how family communication affects individual member health. Her research has been published in *Communication Education*, *Communication Quarterly*, and *Qualitative Research Reports in Communication*.

Shaniece B. Bickham (Ph.D., University of Southern Mississippi) is a contributing faculty member in the College of Undergraduate Studies at Walden University. Dr. Bickham is also a strategic communications consultant for Bickham Communication, LLC. She has years of experience teaching communications courses in the areas of public relations and journalism. Dr. Bickham has also worked in the news industry, as well as in media relations and community affairs. Her research interests focus on influences on media content, censorship, and the student press.

John F. Borland (Ph.D., University of Connecticut) is an associate professor of sport management in the School of Health, Physical Education and Recreation at Springfield College in Massachusetts. His teaching specialization is in sport communication and sport sociology. In addition, he teaches courses in sport facilities and budgeting. His research interests include sport leadership, gender and race in sport, and media and sport. He is the lead editor of *Sport Leadership in the 21st Century*.

Dana Borzea (M.A., Western Michigan University) is a full-time first-year doctoral student and graduate teaching assistant in the Department of Communication Studies at West Virginia University. Her teaching experience involves a variety of introductory communication courses, including interpersonal communication and communication within the public context. Research interests include family communication and interpersonal communication.

Maria Brann (Ph.D., University of Kentucky; M.P.H., West Virginia University) is an associate professor in the Department of Communication Studies at Indiana University-Purdue University Indianapolis and affiliate faculty with the Injury Control Research Center at West Virginia University. Dr. Brann explores the integration of health, interpersonal, and gendered communication. Her primary research interests focus on the study of ethical issues in health communication contexts and promotion of healthy lifestyle behaviors. Specifically, Dr. Brann seeks to understand the many facets of health communication, including the promotion of preventive screenings and physical activity, safety education, communicative negotiations in gender constructions, and family relationships. She is the editor of *Contemporary Case Studies in Health Communication: Theoretical & Applied Approaches*. Additionally, her work has been published in numerous refereed journals and several scholarly books, including *Gender in Applied Communication Contexts* and *Casing Persuasive Communication*.

Shannon M. Brogan (Ph.D., Ohio University) is an Associate Professor in Speech Communication at Kentucky State University. Dr. Brogan teaches Interpersonal Communication, Public Speaking, Group Discussion and Debate, Persuasive Speaking, Interracial/Intercultural Communication, Institutional Communication, Voice and Diction, and Oral Interpretation. She also serves as the advisor for Speech Communication minors. Dr. Brogan's research interests include instructional communication, interpersonal communication, and service learning.

Patrick Carey (B.S., Economics Clemson University) is currently a financial analyst for a marketing firm in New York City. He plans to build a career in financial services and eventually return to school for his M.B.A. He has always enjoyed competing in athletics, playing multiple sports in high school and college, and continues to participate in adult leagues today.

Nick Chivers (M.A., San Francisco State University) is a lecturer at San Francisco State University and Ohlone College in Fremont, California. Nick's work focuses on bringing social justice issues and critical theory into the community college classroom. He is a popular presenter in the Ohlone College Speech Colloquium series with his lectures on the social construction of identities and their relationships to power and privilege. He is also a lover of ska music and distance running.

Mary Collins (B.A., Communication Studies, Clemson University) is currently working in the staffing industry as a commercial recruiter. While at Clemson, she was a Communication Studies major with an emphasis in Sport Communication and hopes to work in the sport industry in the future.

Gregory A. Cranmer (M.A., West Virginia University) is a Ph.D. candidate in sport communication in the Department of Communication Studies at West Virginia University. Gregory explores various aspects of sport communication, such as athlete-coach communication and the portrayals of athlete gender, sex, and race within sport media. His research aims to improve athlete experience, athlete-coach relationships, and the scholarly understanding of how sport media shapes the way in which athletes are viewed by audience members. He has served as a guest reviewer for *Communication & Sport*, and his scholarly works within the realm of sport communication have been published in *The Routledge Handbook of Sport & New Media, Communication & Sport, The International Journal of Sport Communication, Western Journal of Communication, Communication Research Reports,* and *The Howard Journal of Communications*.

Nancy Curtin (Ph.D., Southern Illinois University Carbondale) is an Associate Professor and Chair of Communication at Millikin University in Decatur, IL. Dr. Curtin's teaching areas include gender, interpersonal and organizational communication. Research interests center on gender issues in interpersonal and organizational contexts and same-sex grief of bereaving partners.

Jeffrey Eisenberg (M.A., Villa Nova University) is Coordinator for New Media, Communications and Events at the Neumann University Institute for Sport, Spirituality and Character Development. His work at the Institute centers on developing valuable resources for athletic stakeholders, like student-athletes and coaches, and includes content aimed specifically at guiding those in the athletic world towards responsible social media practices. He holds a M.A. in Strategic Communication from Villanova University, where his research centered on media ecology theories, new and emerging media, and communication and social causes.

J.D. Elliott (B.A., Sports Communication and B.A. Political Science, Clemson University) is currently writing freelance and working as a paralegal in Columbia, SC. He plans to become a sports attorney. In his free time he enjoys competing in athletics and rooting for his hapless Atlanta Braves and Carolina Panthers.

Erin E. Gilles (Ph.D., University of Kentucky) is an assistant professor of public relations and advertising in the communications department at the University of Southern Indiana in Evansville, Indiana. Dr. Gilles teaches advertising campaigns, media planning, communication research methods, digital media, and health communication courses at the undergraduate and graduate levels. Dr. Gilles' research interests include gender studies, the mass media, and critical communication studies.

Erin Gilliam (Doctoral Candidate University of Kentucky, MA University of Kentucky) is a full-time professor in the history department and the school of education at Kentucky State University. Professor Gilliam prepares future social studies and elementary students to be quality teachers in educational settings. She currently teaches a wide variety of history and education courses. Her research interests include race and education and the history of gender leadership and communication in the early African American Church.

Karen L. Hartman (Ph.D., Louisiana State University) is an assistant professor in the Department of Communication, Media & Persuasion at Idaho State University. Dr. Hartman has taught courses in sport communication, sport public relations, the rhetoric of sport, and sport reporting. Her research interests include sport, rhetorical criticism, myth, morality, apologia, heroes, and race. Her research has been published in the *Journal of Communication Studies, International Journal of Sport Communication, Academic Exchange Quarterly*, and the edited volumes *Myth in the Modern World* and *The ESPN Effect*.

Angela S. Jacobs (Ph.D., Southern Illinois University, Carbondale) is an assistant professor in the Department of Communication Studies at Eastern Illinois University. Dr. Jacobs teaches courses in interpersonal, intercultural, and family communication. She has also taught special topics courses related to gender and sports communication. Her research interests include family and relational communication, with particular interest in the narrative construction of identity, family socialization into organized youth sports, and bereavement and coping in the family. Dr. Jacobs stays active in her community through her work with a local widow support group and by regularly speaking in community forums about issues of suicide awareness and prevention.

Joanna Jenkins (Strategic communicator, Sr. Creative and Professor.) As a professor Joanna is experienced in strategic and visual communication as well as advertising and psychology. Among courses taught are Advertising, Copy Writing and Design, Research and Marketing, Media Planning and Buying, and Design History. Joanna is currently an assistant professor at Howard University. She has previously taught at American University and Bowie State University. Within industry, Joanna has led creative initiatives and worked with notable clients and agencies. Joanna has produced IMC creative campaigns in diverse media ranging from television and print to radio, interactive and digital. Joanna is skilled as a strategist, creative director, senior creative, art director, and designer. Joanna is dedicated to service, mentorship and collaboration. She is involved in professional and service organizations. Joanna's primary research interests include convergence, advertising, and mass communications. – www.joannajenkins.com

Thomas C. Johnson (Ph.D., University of Minnesota) is an Assistant Professor of Communication Studies at Luther College. Dr. Johnson teaches courses in critical media studies and media production. His research interests include pedagogy, sport media, television studies, gender studies, and documentary film.

Michael W. Kramer (Ph.D., University of Texas) is professor and chair of the Department of Communication at the University of Oklahoma. He has been teaching organizational and group communication to undergraduate and graduate students for over 25 years at three institutions. His organizational research primarily focuses on employee transitions as part of the assimilation/socialization process such as newcomer entry, transfers, exit, and corporate mergers. His group research focuses on decision making, membership, and leadership. In addition to over 50 journal articles, he has written books on uncertainty management and socialization, and recently has coedited three books on volunteers and nonprofit organizations.

Allison Levin (JD, Washington University in St. Louis) is an independent scholar and President of Social Network Advisors. She examines the intersection of economics, technology and sport. Her research focuses on the relationship between media and sports, with a focus on social media. Ms. Levin has presented her work all over the world, including at the SABR Analytics Conference, SABR National Conference, the International Association of Sports Communication, the International Association of Communication Research, and the Celebrity Project. She is also a frequent reviewer for SABR as well as the National Communication Association.

Corey Jay Liberman (Ph.D., Rutgers University) is an associate professor in the Department of Communication and Media Arts at Marymount Manhattan College. His research spans the interpersonal communication, group communication, and organizational communication worlds and he recently coauthored a textbook dealing with organizational communication (*Organizational Communication: Strategies For Success*, which was published in 2013) and edited a case study book dealing with persuasion (*Casing Persuasive Communication*, which was published in 2014). He is currently working on his next two book projects, both of which deal with risk and crisis communication. Currently, he is most interested in the social practices of dissent within organizations, specifically the antecedents, processes, and effects associated with effective employee dissent communication.

Stephanie Poole Martinez (Ph.D., Southern Illinois University Carbondale) is an associate professor of communication and basic course director at St. Edward's University in Austin, Texas. Recent studies focus on heath communication during the Ebola crisis in Dallas, Texas and occupational identity in higher education. She also conducts and is interested in service learning. In her free time, she enjoys the company of her partner, Chris, and her daughter, Anya.

John G. McClellan (Ph.D., University of Colorado at Boulder) is an associate professor of communication at Boise State University where he teaches a variety of courses focused on organizational communication, group communication, critical theories, and gender in the workplace. He also teaches the introductory athletic organizational communication course for the master in athletic leadership at Boise State University. His research explores the discursive qualities of organizing with attention to issues of knowledge, identity, and collaborative organizational change. His recent work exploring organizational communication pedagogy appears in *Management Communication Quarterly* and *The Review of Communication*.

Jason R. Moyer (Ph.D., University of Iowa) is an assistant professor of communication arts at Malone University. Dr. Moyer teaches a variety of courses, including persuasion, organizational communication, and American God talk. Research interests include the relationships between presidential rhetoric and denominational theology.

Scott A. Myers (Ph.D., Kent State University) is a professor and Ph.D. graduate studies coordinator in the Department of Communication Studies at West Virginia University. Dr. Myers teaches small group communication and communication research methods courses at the undergraduate level and communication pedagogy, instructional communication, and organizational communication courses at the graduate level. He is the Director of the Educational Policies Board of the National Communication Association. His research interests include instructor-student communication, student communication motives, and adult sibling relationships.

Gwendolyn Nisbet (Ph.D., University of Oklahoma) is an assistant professor of strategic communication in the Mayborn School of Journalism at the University of North Texas. Dr. Nisbet's research examines the intersection of mediated social influence, political communication, and popular culture. Her research incorporates a multi-methods approach to understanding the influence of fandom and celebrity in political and civic engagement.

Chuka Onwumechili (Ph.D., Howard University) is professor and chair of the Department of Strategic, Legal, and Management Communication at Howard University. He also serves as Editor-in-Chief of *The Howard Journal of Communications*. Dr. Onwumechili's research interests cover a wide range of fields including sports, Africa, telecommunications, conflict, and culture. He has published widely in both books and peer-reviewed journals. Additionally, he has written several cases for teaching intercultural communication, conflict, and negotiation. Dr. Onwumechili also contributes articles to the web-based newspaper *The Conversation,* which combines "academic rigor and journalistic flair." His articles in *The Conversation* widen understanding of African sports and larger issues of politics, culture, and economy during major sporting tournaments. His most recent co-edited book on sports is titled *Identity and Nation in African Football.* He also hosts a sports blog and keeps the largest database on Nigerian national team football.

Raul Feliciano Ortiz (Ph.D., University of Western Ontario) is currently a lecturer in the Department of Communication Arts of the State University of New York at Oneonta. His professional interests include media literacy and the socio political, cultural, and economic analysis of sports media. He writes a monthly column on these matters in *Revista Cruce* (www.revistacruce .com), a publication of the School of Social Sciences, Humanities, and Communications at the Metropolitan University in Puerto Rico. He is also the director of social media and web master at *Revista Miradero* (www.miradero.org), an online journal of Puerto Rican and Latin American folklore studies.

Regina Pappalardo (M.F.A., Emerson College) is assistant professor of journalism in the Division of Arts and Letters at Mount Saint Mary College (Newburgh, NY). She has also taught at William Paterson University of New Jersey (Wayne, NJ). Ms. Pappalardo specializes in journalism, media writing, and integrated communication.

Joshua Daniel Phillips (Ph.D., Southern Illinois University Carbondale) is a lecturer in the Department of Communication Studies at Southern Illinois University. His academic specialization is at the intersection of rhetoric and intercultural communication with particular interests in sport, media narrative, pop culture, sexual violence, and poverty. His recent publications include "LeBron James as Cybercolonized Spectacle: A Critical Race Reading of Whiteness in Sport," "Black Women and Gender Violence: Lil' Wayne's 'How to Love' as Progressive Hip-Hop," and "Crystal Mangum as Hypervisible Object and Invisible Subject: Black Feminist Thought, Sexual Violence, and the Pedagogical Repercussions of the Duke Lacrosse Rape Case."

Theo Plothe is a doctoral candidate in the School of Communication at American University. His research focuses on the intersection of video games and remix culture, and his current projects include an investigation of gaming culture through participatory remix video. Other academic interests include social media, mimetics, and sports communication. He has presented at the International Association of Communication and Sport's annual conference on such issues as NFL players and their use of Twitter, NBA and NFL player tweets during their respective drafts, and a critical analysis of Samoan identity in professional wrestling.

Stephen Puckette (B.A., Communication Studies, Clemson University) is a Master's student at Clemson University in the Communications, Technology, and Society program. His research interest primarily examines the ways in which teams and organizations communicate with fans.

Deleasa Randall-Griffiths (Ph.D. Southern Illinois University Cardondale) is an associate professor in the Department of Communication Studies at Ashland University. She teaches the basic communication course, along with courses in interpersonal communication, health communication, and performance studies. Her research interests include medical humanities, health narratives, and historical performance. She engages in community service by chairing the Ashland Chautauqua Planning Committee which brings history alive through performance. She is the winner of the 2012 Ohio Communication Association's Innovative Teacher Award.

Elizabeth Ravaioli (B.A., Communication Studies, Clemson University) is currently a Communications Director in Charlotte, NC. She has enjoyed competing in athletics throughout her life, including club sports throughout college.

Dariela Rodriguez (Ph.D., University of Oklahoma) is an Assistant Professor of Communication, and Coordinator of Sport Communication at Ashland University in Ashland, Ohio. Dr. Rodriguez' expertise is in interpersonal communication with a specialization in sport communication. She has published journal articles in publications such as *Communication Education*, *Qualitative Health Research*, and *Communication Research Reports*. Her current research includes work in concussions in sport and leadership preferences of Millennial generation athletes.

Julio A. Rodriguez-Rentas teaches at the State University of New York (SUNY)–Westchester Community College (Valhalla, NY) and at Iona College (New Rochelle, NY), and has taught at Pace University (Pleasantville, NY) and Western Connecticut State University (Danbury, CT). Mr. Rodriguez holds a B.B.A. from Pace University—New York City, and an M.A. in Media Communication from Pace University—Westchester.

Kimberly A. Sipes (M.S. Accounting, University of Kentucky) is an assistant professor of accounting in the School of Business at Kentucky State University in Frankfort, Kentucky. Professor Sipes is also a Certified Public Accountant (CPA). Professor Sipes teaches financial accounting at the principles and intermediate level, federal income tax, auditing, introduction to business, and leadership and development courses at the undergraduate level. Professor Sipes' research interests include corporate social responsibility, business ethics, and business communication.

Stacy Smulowitz (Ph.D., Rutgers The State University of New Jersey) is an assistant professor in the Department of Communication at the University of Scranton. Dr. Smulowitz's teaching specialization is advertising. Research interests include organizational change, leadership, and assessment.

John Spinda (Ph.D., Communication Studies, Kent State University) is currently an Assistant Professor in the Department of Communication Studies at Clemson University. He is also the Acting Director of the Sports Communication major at Clemson. His teaching and research interests are focused broadly on sports communication, technology-mediated communication, social media, fantasy sports, and mass communication effects.

Margaret Stewart (Ph.D. Indiana University of Pennsylvania) is an Assistant Professor of Communication Studies in the Department of Communication at University of North Florida in Jacksonville. She has a Ph.D. in Communications Media and Instructional Technology from Indiana University of Pennsylvania (IUP). Her research expertise is in the area of social media and emerging communication technologies, particularly among military-affiliated and sports-athlete populations. To date, she has published in *Communication Reports, The Journal of Technologies in Society*, and *The Journal of Communications Media*. Dr. Stewart is also a certified social media strategist and trainer for the National Institute of Social Media (NISM).

Julie L. Taylor (Ph.D., University of Utah) is an assistant professor at the State University of New York at New Paltz. Her teaching style invites students to engage in critical thinking, and to complicate the reality between theory and praxis. Her research interests are in organizational communication, gender studies, and interdisciplinary studies. Past research questions have explored the communication in the disciplines framework in connection to teaching ethics in STEM classrooms and creating more critically engaged students in the STEM fields. Current research questions investigate the organizing of the sex industry. More specifically, asking questions that concern the role of gender in policy construction and implementation, and the consequence of silence as an organizing element of discourse.

Katherine S. Thweatt (Ed.D., West Virginia University) is an Assistant Professor of Communication Studies, at State University of New York, New Paltz. Her focus is on interpersonal communication with her most recent work exploring the influence of health care provider communication on patient perceptions. She has multiple publications in the field of communication as well as healthcare. Her career experiences include overseeing large, grant funded research programs in cardiology and diabetes. She also conducted the assessment of the Veterans Affairs National Quality Improvement Initiative which included assessing over 600 projects in over 130 facilities across the U.S. and Puerto Rico. After working for the Veterans Affairs Medical center for a number of years, she transitioned into the private sector and was employed as Sr. Manager of Clinical Quality at the third largest Medicare Part D sponsor in 2007. Her work in this arena led to National Best Practice Awards related to medication adherence in HIV beneficiaries and the addition of ace inhibitors in diabetic beneficiaries. She returned to academia, full-time, in 2010. She has upcoming publications in the areas of instructional communication, sports communication and servers on the editorial board of *Communication Research Reports* and *Communication Teacher* as well as serving as a reviewer for *Communication Education*.

Mary C. Toale (Ed.D., West Virginia University) is the Department Chair and Graduate Coordinator in the Department of Communication Studies at SUNY Oswego. She is currently working on the National Communication Association's Lumina Grant team investigating Learning

Outcomes in Communication. She is serving on the National Faculty Advisory Board for Lambda Pi Eta, the editorial review board for *Communication Teacher*, and as the ECA Representative to the NCA Nominating Committee. She has served on the editorial review boards of *Communication Quarterly*, *Journal of Intercultural Communication*, and the *Ohio Communication Journal*. She has also been a communication consultant for individual clients and the media, as well as a private mathematics and statistics tutor. She is the recipient of the 2007 Strosacker Award for Excellence in Teaching at Baldwin Wallace University and a life member of the Eastern Communication Association.

Taylor Wilson (B.A., Communication Studies, Clemson University) is a Master's student in Communication, Technology and Society at Clemson University. Her research interest areas include mass media communication and how it intersects with various sports publics. She is a sports writer, and has written for a number of sites based in South Carolina and Georgia.

Gust A. Yep (Ph.D., University of Southern California) is professor of communication studies, core graduate faculty of sexuality studies, and faculty in the Ed.D. program in educational leadership at San Francisco State University. His research focuses on communication at the intersections of culture, gender, sexuality, and health. In addition to three books, he has published over seventy articles in (inter)disciplinary journals and anthologies. He is the recipient of the 2006 NCA Randy Majors Memorial Award for outstanding LGBT scholarship in communication, the 2011 San Francisco State University Distinguished Faculty Award for Professional Achievement ("Researcher of the Year"), and the 2015 AEJMC LeRoy F. Aarons Award for significant contributions to LGBTQ media education and research. He lives with Yogi Enzo and Pierre Lucas, his affectionate and vivacious Pomeranian companions.

Alaina C. Zanin (Ph.D., University of Oklahoma) is an assistant professor at the University of Central Missouri within the Department of Management. She researches leadership communication and organizational communication in unique organizational contexts. She specializes in structuration, sensemaking, and framing theories as well as issues surrounding power, control, resistance, gender, and body work. She recently completed her dissertation where she builds upon unobtrusive control theory by exploring the structuring processes of resistance and control within an NCAA Division I athletic program.

Paul Ziek (Ph.D., Rutgers University) is an assistant professor in the Department of Media, Communications, and Visual Arts at Pace University. He holds a B.A. from Rutgers, the State University of New Jersey, and an M.A. from New York University. He can be reached at pziek@pace.edu.

APPENDIX: CASE ANALYSIS WORKSHEET

This worksheet is designed to help you think through the decision-making process in a decision-based case study. The worksheet is designed to be worked through step-by-step.

Initial Analysis of the Case

Important Decision Makers: Who are the key decision makers in this case study? List them by name and identify their role in the case (add others if necessary).	
Name	Role

Problem Statement: State the communication problem of the case. Try to state it in a single sentence and then expand to a few more sentences (if they are necessary). Then summarize your diagnosis: the primary cases of the problem.

Remember, you cannot attempt to recommend possible alternatives until you are clear on what the communication problem is within a case. Often cases have multiple communication problems; select the one that you think is either the most encompassing or the one that is the most urgent.

Communication Problem:

Causes: Once you have clearly articulated the communication problem discussed within the case, you need to look for any and all causes of the communication problem. When creating your list of causes, make sure you do not add too many causes to your list because you may end up bogging yourself down in causes that cloud the overall problem.

Cause:	Evidence/Example from Case
Cause:	Evidence/Example from Case
Cause:	Evidence/Example from Case
Cause:	Evidence/Example from Case

Applicable Research/Theory

Research and Theory: No alternative should be developed until you thoroughly understand the relevant sport communication research/theory related to the general decision being made. As such, after reading the textbook and other relevant research, what research or theories are you using to help you understand this case? How does this literature apply? What types of alternatives does the literature suggest for this case?

Source #1:

How does this research/theory help you understand the case?

How are you applying this research/theory to the current case?

What possible alternatives does this research/theory suggest for the current case?

Source #2:

How does this research/theory help you understand the case?

How are you applying this research/theory to the current case?

What possible alternatives does this research/theory suggest for the current case?

Source #3:

How does this research/theory help you understand the case?

How are you applying this research/theory to the current case?

What possible alternatives does this research/theory suggest for the current case?

Decision Criteria

> **Decision Criteria:** Select the three most important qualitative and/or quantitative decision criteria you believe are necessary for selecting an alternative in this case.

Criterion Number 1:

Definition/application in this case:

Argument for including this criterion:

How you will measure it?

Criterion Number 2:

Definition/application in this case:

Argument for including this criterion:

How you will measure it?

Criterion Number 3:

Definition/application in this case:

Argument for including this criterion:

How you will measure it?

Decision Criteria Ranking: Rate your decision criteria on a scale from 1 (not overly important) to 10 (very important).

Criterion 1:	Not Overly Important	1	2	3	4	5	6	7	8	9	10	Very Important
Criterion 2:	Not Overly Important	1	2	3	4	5	6	7	8	9	10	Very Important
Criterion 3:	Not Overly Important	1	2	3	4	5	6	7	8	9	10	Very Important

Now rank your criteria in the order of their importance. (1) most important criterion to (3) least important criterion:

1) Most Important Criterion:

2) Middle Important Criterion:

3) Least Important Criterion:

Justification: Please provide a justification for how you ranked the criteria in this section.

Decision Alternatives

Decision Alternatives: List a minimum of three possible alternatives the main character in the case should take. Decision alternatives should be clear and concise.

Remember, all alternatives should be realistic and implementable given the confines of the case.

Alternative One:

Alternative Two:

Alternative Three:

Decision Alternative Analysis

Recommended Alternative: State the decision you are recommending and summarize the reasons for it. Also, provide evidence from the textbook or other course readings to help support your recommended decision. Be brief!

Decision:

Justification from Research/Theories: Apply any relevant sport communication research or sport communication theories you have used to help you make your decision.

Application of the Criteria: In this section, demonstrate how you see the three criteria clearly applying to this decision alternative. Please remember that all three of the criteria should clearly point to this decision alternative.

Justification using Criterion #1:

Justification using Criterion #2:

Justification using Criterion #3:

Risks Associated with the Recommended Alternative: What do you think are the major risks associated with the alternative you have chosen? How will you mitigate the likelihood of these risks turning into crises?

Risk	Mitigation

Decision Alternatives Not Selected Analysis

Non-Selected Alternatives: In this section, you are going to clearly explain why you opted not to choose the other two alternatives. First, you need to make your arguments using relevant communication research and/or theories. Second, you need to make your argument using the three criteria that you have selected.

Decision Alternative Not Chosen #1:

Justification from Research/Theories: Apply any relevant sport communication research or sport communication theories you have used to help you make your decision.

Application of the Criteria: In this section, demonstrate how you see the three criteria clearly applying to this decision alternative. Please remember that all three of the criteria should clearly point to this decision alternative.

Justification using Criterion #1:

Justification using Criterion #2:

Justification using Criterion #3:

Justification from Research/Theories: Apply any relevant sport communication research or sport communication theories you have used to help you make your decision.